ERICH EYCK was born in Berlin in 1878, and received his education at the Universities of Berlin and Freiburg. Although he held the degree of Doctor of Philosophy, the law was his career, and he served in the Court of Appeals from 1906 to 1937. He was also the legal correspondent for *Vossische Zeitung* from 1915 to 1933. He was a City Councillor in Charlottenberg and Berlin from 1928 to 1933.

In 1937 Dr. Eyck emigrated to England, where he lectured at the Universities of London and Oxford and turned to the writing of history. *Gladstone* was published in 1938 (in both English and German); *Pitt versus Fox: Father and Son* was published in English in 1950; *Bismarck and the German Empire* (1950) is based on a series of lectures delivered at Oxford and also on Dr. Eyck's monumental three-volume study *Bismarck.*

Dr. Eyck was a Fellow of the Royal Historical Society, and a member of the Mont Pélerin Society. He died in 1964.

BISMARCK AND THE GERMAN EMPIRE

BY ERICH EYCK
PH.D.

W · W · NORTON & COMPANY

New York · London

FIRST PUBLISHED IN THE NORTON LIBRARY IN 1964 BY ARRANGEMENT
WITH THE MACMILLAN COMPANY

W. W. Norton & Company, Inc., 500 Fifth Avenue, New York, NY 10110
W. W. Norton & Company Ltd., 10 Coptic Street, London WC1A 1PU

ISBN 0-393-00235-7

PRINTED IN THE UNITED STATES OF AMERICA

3 4 5 6 7 8 9 0

PREFACE TO THE FIRST EDITION

THIS volume is based on a course of lectures which I had the honour of holding, at the invitation of the History Faculty of Oxford University, in the Hall of Balliol College. I have attempted a summary of the salient points of my larger work, the three-volume *Bismarck*, published in German by Eugen Rentsch Verlag, Erlenbach-Zürich, during the war. The scholar who wishes to scrutinize my methods and arguments will, of course, have to refer to the full edition. He will there, too, find in the appendix to each volume a detailed documentation.

I want to thank my son Frank Eyck for assisting me with getting ready the English version and also for seeing this book through the press during my absence overseas.

HAMPSTEAD, 1949   ERICH EYCK

FOREWORD

BY FRANK EYCK

WITH sadness and yet with joy I accepted the invitation of the publisher to write a foreword to a new edition of this book by my father, who died in London in June 1964. The loss of his companionship is felt once more with especial keenness when writing these lines, coupled with thankfulness for the continuing interest in his life's work.

Even after completing his Bismarck biography, my father continued to follow new publications on the period with intense curiosity. What fascinated him above all was the opening of the archives on the Hohenzollern candidature for the Spanish throne and the origins of the war of 1870. 1957 saw the publication of hitherto secret documents from the German Diplomatic Archives in *Bismarck and the Hohenzollern Candidature for the Spanish Throne*, edited with an introduction by Georges Bonnin and translated by Isabella M. Massey, with a foreword by G. P. Gooch (London: Chatto & Windus). While the official German version of Bismarck's passive role in this affair had been steadily undermined over the years, Bonnin was able to give irrefutable evidence of the chan-

i

cellor's involvement. Without Bismarck's support, Leopold of Hohenzollern-Sigmaringen would have never accepted the candidature and the King of Prussia would not have given the necessary approval as head of the dynasty. A brief footnote composed by my father is to be found on Page 186 in the later editions of the present book.[1] Fundamentally my father believed that his account written before the Bonnin edition was if anything strengthened by the latter. Bismarck's motive in supporting a candidature liable to lead to friction with France remained puzzling. In a review of Bonnin's book, my father came to the conclusion that Bismarck must have welcomed a collision (*Zusammenstoss*) with France over the candidature, as he regarded a Franco-German war as inevitable in the near future.[2] Whereas Bonnin had based his publication mainly on the captured German Foreign Ministry documents, a pupil of Gerhard Ritter, Jochen Dittrich, relied in his book *Bismarck, Frankreich und die spanische Thronkandidatur der Hohenzollern* (Munich: Oldenbourg, 1962) primarily on the Sigmaringen house archives. My father rejected Dittrich's inference that Bismarck did not want war (p. 81).[3]

The other revelations from the archives which greatly interested my father were *The Holstein Papers* edited by Norman Rich and M. H. Fisher which were published by the Cambridge University Press from 1955. He devoted two chapters in the collection of his essays *Auf Deutschlands politischem Forum. Deutsche Parlamentarier und Studien zur Neuesten Deutschen Geschichte* (Zürich: Eugen Rentsch, 1963) to a reconsideration of the important Foreign Ministry official Friedrich von Holstein in the light of the new sources. He largely found himself unable to accept the more favourable interpretation of Holstein's personality at which the editors arrived as a result of their researches. In particular, my father adhered to his belief that Holstein had behaved dishonourably towards his chief in the Paris embassy, Harry von Arnim (as described on page 212 of the present book). In the chapter "Holstein

---

[1] See also my father's Historical Association pamphlet on Bismarck, published with some additions in *From Metternich to Hitler*, edited by W. N. Medlicott (London: Routledge and Kegan Paul, 1963), p. 165–182, particularly p. 166, footnote 2.

[2] *Deutsche Rundschau* 84, 8 (August 1958), p. 732. Reprinted in Erich Eyck, *Auf Deutschlands politischem Forum* (Zürich: Eugen Rentsch, 1963), p. 91–112.

[3] See his review in *Deutsche Literaturzeitung*, Jahrgang 84, Heft 7/8 (July/August 1963), col. 619.

and Bismarck" in *Auf Deutschlands politischem Forum* (p. 115) my father recalled how one of Arnim's defence counsel in the trial of 1874 told him of the very poor impression Holstein made as a prosecution witness. Most of a further chapter on Holstein has been published in *Studies in Diplomatic History and Historiography in honour of G. P. Gooch*, edited by A. O. Sarkissian (London: Longmans, 1961) under the title "Holstein as Bismarck's Critic" (pages 251–265). He regarded very highly the contribution volume II of the Papers, the Diaries, made to an understanding of the Bismarck circle (p. 252). Referring to the period after the Chancellor's dismissal, my father concluded: "That Holstein was already before this era a critic of Bismarck, his diary bears irrefutable witness" (p. 265).

My father recognized the tremendous work in the archives which went into Otto Becker's *Bismarcks Ringen um Deutschlands Gestaltung*, edited and supplemented posthumously by Alexander Scharff (Heidelberg: Quelle & Meyer, 1958). But he regarded this detailed account of developments in the German question between 1862 and 1871 as too favourable to Bismarck.[4] He welcomed the publication of the diary of the Baroness Spitzemberg, an affectionate, but not uncritical admirer of Bismarck.[5]

The German 3-volume biography *Bismarck, Leben und Werk*, (3 vol., Zürich: Eugen Rentsch, 1941–1944) and the present book (first published in 1950) have thus stood up well to the pressure of new material. Even critics have admitted his mastery of the sources.[6] What challenge there has been to my father's work on Bismarck has been mainly in the field of interpretation. My father admired Bismarck's gifts, his grasp of European diplomacy, the quickness of his perception, his ability to size up friends and opponents, and to influence them when he so wished. But he condemned what he regarded as the chancellor's lack of certain moral principles, such as his frequent untruthfulness, and the ruthless exploitation of his superiority over his opponents at home. He certainly did not rejoice in his criticism of one of Germany's leading statesmen. In

---

[4] See his review in *Deutsche Literaturzeitung*, Jahrgang 82, Heft 6 (June 1961), col. 545 to 550.
[5] *Das Tagebuch der Baronin Spitzemberg*, edited by Rudolf Vierhaus (Göttingen: Vandenhoeck & Ruprecht, 1960), reviewed in *Contemporary Review*, 201 (June 1962), p. 322–324.
[6] See "Erich Eyck" by William H. Maehl in *Essays on eminent Europeans, Some 20th Century Historians*, edited by S. William Halperin (The University of Chicago Press, 1961), p. 227–253.

personal life, my father was kindly and warm-hearted, tolerant and very careful in his judgments on people. This was partly due to his training as a lawyer. The effect of his experience in the courts has sometimes been misinterpreted. The long years he spent as an advocate did not incline him to harsher judgment of individuals and he found the lawyer's discipline in weighing evidence a help and certainly not a hindrance as a historian. Similarly the source of his critical attitude must not be sought in any anti-German feelings. Ever since his visit to England in 1906 in the heyday of Liberalism, British political institutions had excited his admiration. He was full of gratitude to this country for giving asylum to him and to his family after the Nazis came into power, and he was proud of his naturalization after the war. But these sentiments were quite compatible with a strong, continuing and basically sympathetic interest in the fate of his native country. Even as a lawyer in Berlin he had found time for intensive historical reading. He had come increasingly to the conclusion that German academic historians had failed to present an objective account of Bismarck. As a practising liberal politician, he resented what he regarded as the unfair treatment meted out to the Chancellor's liberal opponents. When the Nazi régime destroyed the Germany in which he believed, he set about trying to find the historical causes of Germany's political calamities. Thus a critical and fearless examination of Bismarck's career appeared to him of the greatest historical and political importance. The historian had the—often unpleasant—duty to be objective even about a nation's most highly treasured achievements. He had a vital part to play in the necessarily painful national healing process. Political cure had to be preceded by a realistic examination of the country's past. The historian's work could not be regarded as merely "academic", for his findings were bound to have some influence on future events. My father, for all these reasons, never wrote simply for the specialist, but also for the wide non-specialist reading public. There can be little doubt that there was a considerable popular response in Germany to his new interpretation of the Iron Chancellor in the years after 1945. The 3-volume biography filled a real psychological need. The reception from academic historians in Germany was more mixed, some of it favourable, but in the main reserved or hostile. This is not surprising. For the very reasons which led my father to re-examine the Bismarck problem—to have a fresh look at Germany's past—made his theories unacceptable to most nineteenth century historians there. Also the Life and Times of a great statesman, executed on a considerable scale, had become unfashionable among German historians, who for various causes preferred to concentrate on narrower aspects.

My father made some assumptions when writing on Bismarck which are no more susceptible to proof or to disproof than those of his critics. One of these was that a synthesis between moderate liberalism and democracy was feasible in the Germany of the 1860's, as happened gradually in Great Britain. The theme of liberal democracy was developed in a paper entitled "Freiheit und Demokratie 1848–1948" which my father read to the historical centenary congress on 1848 at Rome in 1948.[7] A reasonably permanent and mutually satisfactory amalgamation of moderate liberals and radicals *might* have happened in Germany, as in Britain, but the obstacles in the way of co-operation were far greater on the European continent. Unlike England, Germany had experienced a revolution in 1848. Thus members of the Progress Party (*Fortschrittspartei*) of the Bismarck period had only a few years earlier faced each other across the barricades.

My father regarded parliamentary government as a more efficient method of administration than personal rule and he was confident that conditions in Germany during the 1860's and 1870's were ripe for the transition. Few German historians would to-day wish to assert the reverse of the first part of this proposition. Generally the value of effective parliamentary criticism would be readily granted for the period of William II's rule, if not so much for that of Bismarck.

The main argument has centred round the assumption made by my father that the German liberals would have proved capable of uniting Germany and without the use of many of the unpleasant methods employed by Bismarck which were such a heavy mortgage on Germany's future. By his discipline, the historian is handicapped in dealing with might-have-beens. Bismarck delivered the goods, in whatever form, which the German liberals had failed to do. My

[7] *Convegno di Scienze Morali Storiche e Filologiche*, Oct. 1948 (Rome: Accademia Nazionale dei Lincei, 1949), p. 23–97.

father believed that German unification in the third quarter of the nineteenth century was a natural and desirable development. Otto Pflanze in *Bismarck and the Development of Germany*, vol. I: The Period of Unification 1815–1871 (Princeton University Press, 1963) argues differently:

'The common view of German nationalism as an irresistible current sweeping down the decades to fulfilment in 1870 is a fiction of nationalistic historians, derived from the hopes and aspirations of those *kleindeutsch* leaders, like Sybel and Treitschke, who were their intellectual forebears. Only under the stimulation provided by Bismarck for his own political ends did German nationalism begin to move the masses' (p. 13).

The extent to which the German Empire of 1871 could in fact be regarded as a national state has also been carefully scruntinized, for instance by Theodor Schieder in *Das deutsche Kaiserreich von 1871 als Nationalstaat* (Cologne: Westdeutscher Verlag, 1961).

The interaction of men and events on each other has always engaged the attention of the historian, not least to determine the extent of Bismarck's achievement. Two diplomatic historians have examined this question. W. E. Mosse in *The European Powers and the German Question 1848–71* (Cambridge University Press, 1958) concluded that Bismarck's task of unifying Germany "was made easier by circumstances. If he played his hand with great skill, it was a good one in the first place" (p. 372). In *Bismarck and Modern Germany* (London: English Universities Press, 1965), W. N. Medlicott sums up: "to preserve a sense of proportion we must remember that his (Bismarck's) admirers often exaggerate the extent of the obstacles in his path" (p. 188).

A detailed constitutional history for the period is now available in Ernst Rudolf Huber, *Deutsche Verfassungsgeschichte seit 1789*, vol. III: Bismarck und das Reich (Stuttgart: Kohlhammer, 1963).

The debate on Bismarck will continue. In its very nature, my father's work could not end the controversy, but only create a new beginning. The questions raised by him are likely to occupy historians for many years to come.

SEPTEMBER 1967   FRANK EYCK

CONTENTS

INTRODUCTION

THE subject of these chapters is the most important personality in the history and development not only of Germany, but of the whole of Europe, in the second half of the 19th century. The results of his actions are more far-reaching than those of any other statesman of his time. The unification of the German nation in the centre and heart of the European continent, the expulsion of Austria from Germany as well as from Italy, the fall of the Second Empire, the defeat of France, and in consequence of it the lasting antagonism between France and Germany, the alliance of the German Empire with the Habsburg Monarchy, the dismemberment of the Kingdom of Denmark—all these developments are landmarks in the history of Europe up to the first World War, and all of them are the achievements of Bismarck. Everybody sees that; what is not so apparent, but not less important and far-reaching, is the transformation of the spirit and mentality of the German people, for which he is also responsible.

For most people Bismarck is the man of "blood and iron". There is a good reason for that. He himself coined this phrase, and we shall see that he lived up to it. But he was much more. He had an intellectual ascendancy over all the politicians of his time, and his superiority was acknowledged not only by his own people, but by foreign statesmen all over Europe. Jules Favre, the Foreign Minister of the French Republic after the fall of Napoleon, had the difficult task of negotiating the armistice after the defeat of 1870. He had certainly no reason to love Bismarck. But he calls him "a statesman who surpasses everything that he can imagine". Lord Salisbury, the British Prime Minister, a sharp critic of Bismarck's methods, writes after his fall: "The Achitophel of the Germans is gone—but one misses the extraordinary penetration of the old man".

About Bismarck's reminiscences, *Reflections and Recollections* (*Gedanken und Erinnerungen*), an English historian so widely read as George Gooch says that "its value as a manual of statecraft is unsurpassed" and that it "must always remain the chosen companion of the statesmen, teachers and students of history". Be that as it may,

it is undoubtedly a literary masterpiece. Some of its scenes are unforgettable. Let me add that he is a letter-writer of the first order.
Thus some of his letters to Johanna, his betrothed and later his wife,
are among the most wonderful letters ever written in German.

All this merely means that Bismarck is a man well worth studying.
But it is quite another question whether his eminent gifts were
applied in the service of true ideals, whether his deeds and achievements helped the genuine progress of Germany and Europe,
whether he belongs to the forces of Good or of Evil. The following
pages will attempt to answer this question.

Bismarck was born in 1815, the year of Waterloo. He was eleven
years younger than Disraeli, and six years younger than Gladstone.
He became Prussian Prime Minister in 1862, when Palmerston was
Prime Minister of Great Britain and Abraham Lincoln President of
the United States, and he ruled over Prussia and the German Empire
for twenty-eight years, until he was dismissed by William II in 1890,
in the fifty-third year of Queen Victoria's reign. He died in 1898, in
the same year as Gladstone, at the age of eighty-three. The zenith
of his life is the 18th January 1871, when he proclaimed the foundation of the German Empire and the elevation of the King of Prussia
to the dignity of German Emperor in the same hall of the Palace of
Versailles, in which, forty-eight years later, the peace treaty of 1919
was signed.

CHAPTER I

THE YEARS OF PREPARATION

1. *Parents and Youth*

BISMARCK's father was a Prussian Junker. There is no English translation of the term "Junker", because there is no English equivalent of this social and political category. A Junker was a nobleman, and as a rule a great landowner. His status as a nobleman was expressed by the preposition "von" before his name. The Junkers were a kind of aristocracy. But they could not be compared to the English aristocracy. They were aristocrats of a less important type both in material wealth and in political influence. Hardly any of the Prussian Junkers of the 18th or 19th century would have been able to live in the style of an English lord. Many of them belonged to the small nobility and depended on their salary as officers or civil servants. The line of division between the Junker and the commoner was more rigorous than in England, because *all* descendants of the nobility preserved the adherence to it, which was outwardly visible in the preposition "von". In England, on the other hand, only the eldest son of a baron succeeds to the title, while the younger sons become commoners. Winston Churchill, the grandson of a duke, is simply Mr. Churchill because his father was the younger son. Bismarck too was a younger son, but he was Otto *von* Bismarck. So the name separated all the members of the nobility from the commoner, the simple citizen, the "bourgeois", the "Bürgerlichen". These usages were not only of social but of legal importance, especially from the reign of Frederick the Great onwards. King Frederick's declared policy was to keep the landed estates, significantly called *Rittergüter* (estates of Knights), in the hands of the Junkers, and to recruit army officers exclusively from their ranks "because", as he wrote, "the sons of the nobility defend the country and their race is so good, that they should be preserved in every way". By the time of Bismarck's birth these privileges had been abolished in law, but not in practice. In point of fact, no commissions in the Prussian army, especially in the crack regiments of the guards or the cavalry, went to any other man than a nobleman. The legal position of the noble landowner had undergone a very important change owing to the reforms of the Freiherr von Stein and Graf Hardenberg after Prussia's defeat by Napoleon at Jena in 1806. Till then the peasants were hereditary serfs (*erbuntertan*) of the noble landowner. Stein emancipated them and made them *free* peasants. But that was only in the year 1807, not more than eight years before Bismarck's birth. Legal reforms of this kind do not, of course, change social and mental habits in a few years. Besides, the nobleman continued to be the administrative head of the municipal rural community and exercised the jurisdiction over its inhabitants. Thus the young Bismarck grew up at his father's country estate among people who were accustomed to accept the rule, even the dictatorship, of the nobleman, and who regarded every member of his family as a born master.

But the most important difference between the Junkers and the British aristocracy was that there was never among the former a Whig party. There were, of course, some liberally minded men among the Prussian Junkers (the Reichs-Freiherr von Stein, the great reformer, does not belong to them; he was not a born Prussian but a son of Western Germany). For instance, the parliamentary leader of the radical Progressive Party during the 'sixties was a nobleman from Eastern Prussia, Freiherr von Hoverbeck. But as a class the Junkers were politically always of one mind. They were strictly conservative, fervent enemies of reforms, strict upholders of their own legal, material, or social privileges. They had opposed ruthlessly, and unfortunately with considerable success, the reforms of Stein and Hardenberg, and they had stopped them altogether after Prussia's hours of danger had passed with the downfall of Napoleon. One of their leaders accused the reformers of wanting to turn "good old Prussia into a new-fangled Jewish state", and another cried: "Our country places will become hell to us, if free peasants are our neighbours". The Junkers were ardent Royalists, but on the understanding that the King would maintain their old privileges and prerogatives, especially the preferential promotion in the army and the administration.

Bismarck considered himself as a member of this class; in 1848 he said to a Liberal member of parliament with whom he was on friendly terms: "I am a Junker and want to profit from it". But he belonged to the nobility only on his paternal side. His mother was not of noble descent, but came from middle-class stock. She was simply Wilhelmine Mencken, the daughter of a high official, trusted by King Frederick William III. No doubt the mother was by far the more intelligent, and mentally the more important, of Bismarck's parents. His father lacked any qualities which might have raised him above mediocrity. The mother had a well-defined outlook on many questions such as the purpose of human existence, the moral obligations it involved and on education to this end. But Bismarck never had a good word for his mother, because she lacked unselfish motherly love and because she interfered too much with his wishes. Nevertheless, he inherited from his mother not only his very sensitive nerves, but his vitality and superior intelligence.

As a younger son of a noble family Bismarck had the choice of two careers, that of an officer in the army or that of an official in the higher grades of administration or in the diplomatic service. He had no liking for military service and its strict discipline. To obtain a post in the Prussian administration it was first necessary to study Law and then to pass some years as an unpaid *Referendar* or *Auskultator* in the judicial and administrative service. Bismarck began his studies outside Prussia at Göttingen in Hanover, at a date when its King was at the same time King of Great Britain. He did not take his studies very seriously and very seldom attended any lectures. He lived the irresponsible life of a "corps-student", drank very much, had not less than twenty-five duels, and contracted considerable debts. Similarly, he avoided contact with the university and its eminent professors in Berlin, where he spent his later terms. Nevertheless, he passed his examinations without difficulty, and became an *Auskultator* in Aachen (Aix-la-Chapelle), in the Rhein province, near the Belgian frontier. Aachen was then a famous international health resort, and Bismarck mixed much with the international society. Here he met a beautiful English girl, with whom he fell in love. It seems that the object of his love was a Miss Russell, a niece of the Duke of Cleveland. He became engaged to her, and followed her and her family to other places, deserting his official duties. He even wrote to a friend about his prospective wedding, which was going to take place in March 1838, at Scarsdale in Leicestershire. We do not know what exactly happened. In a letter to a friend at a later date there is a reference to a fifty-year-old colonel with one arm and five thousand a year income who "captured the ship". Defeated Bismarck returned to his duties, only to send in his resignation some months later. In a very remarkable letter some years later Bismarck gave his reasons for this decision. One sentence in it contains the essence of his personality: "The Prussian official is like a member of an orchestra, but *I* want to play only the music which I myself like, or no music at all". This was the authentic Bismarck. Even as a young man he wanted to be the leader, the first wherever he might be, never the member of an orchestra who has to play what another leader prefers.

He now turned to agriculture and managed some of the paternal estates. But again it was a disappointment. He felt extremely bored. He tried many methods to overcome boredom. His extravagances in those days earned him the nickname *Der tolle Bismarck* (the wild Bismarck). He visited Britain, which he liked, although he detested the British Sunday. In later days he used to relate that, when one Sunday he whistled while walking in the street in Leith, someone told him bluntly, "Don't whistle, sir". Fortunately he read much, some philosophy, poems like those of Heine and Lenau, and a good deal of history. Nevertheless, when he was approaching the thirties his life seemed to be a failure.

The turning-point of his life was his friendship with a woman, Marie von Thadden. She was the daughter of a Pomeranian nobleman, Adolf von Thadden in Trieglaff. This Herr von Thadden was the centre of a strange circle of very pious gentlemen of very definite and somewhat peculiar Christian beliefs. They were Pietists, and firmly believed in the inspired character of every word of the Bible. A deep gulf separated Bismarck from this outlook. He was then a free-thinker, an agnostic who looked to Spinoza and the radical followers of Hegel for guidance. He met Marie von Thadden, who was engaged to a friend of his, Moritz von Blanckenburg. Marie and Bismarck had many religious conversations. They felt a strong mutual attraction, but Marie married Blanckenburg. Then came the tragic end. Marie died in the first year of her married life. When she was seriously ill Bismarck, in his deep anxiety for her, prayed to God for the first time for sixteen years. He felt that a phase of his life was over.

Marie had introduced him to a young friend, Johanna von Putt-kamer, a member of the same pious circle. He knew it was Marie's wish that he should marry Johanna. He learned to love her and proposed to her. She loved him too, but made it clear that she would marry only a believer in Christianity and that he had to get the approval of her pious father. The letter which Bismarck wrote to her father in December 1846 is one of the most important documents of his inner life. It is a wonderful letter, open-hearted, virile, and extremely clever. He tells, in a fascinating way, the story of his religious development, and makes his first prayer for Marie its centre and turning-point. He was successful, and a few weeks later he became engaged to Johanna.

The important question arises whether this famous letter is the genuine expression of his real religious convictions, or whether it is only a diplomatic expedient to gain his end—the hand of Johanna. It is probably both. There *was* a genuine conversion from agnosti-cism to Christianity, but, nevertheless, the letter contained a strong element of diplomatic adroitness. Bismarck was a past-master in the art of understanding men and of dealing with them. He knew how to bring to the front always those arguments and sentiments which were best calculated to win over the other man. This quality is constantly manifested in his letters. He had some-thing irresistible. He may in this respect be compared with Disraeli, who manifested the same skill in his letters to Queen Victoria.

As a matter of fact he called himself a Christian from this day on. His letters to his wife are for some years full of expressions of religious feeling. He attended Divine Service, at any rate for some years. But whoever thinks that the real test is the application of religious precepts to practical life will wish to enquire whether Bis-marck was at any time of his life influenced in his private or political actions by Christian teaching or, indeed, by any religious prin-ciples. In the opinion of this writer no proof of that can be found. That is small matter for surprise if one recalls some of the words with which Bismarck applied his religious belief to questions of warfare during the French campaign of 1870. Comparing the martial virtues of German and French soldiers he said: "The French-man lacks the sense of duty of the German, who rigidly stands alone in the darkness at his post, in peril of his life. That comes from what is left of religious belief in our people; they know there is somebody who sees when the Lieutenant does not see." This attitude is illustrated by the sarcastic remark of another diplomatist, who said: "If Bismarck believes in his God, God himself must be a Prussian". There is a still more striking example. After the Battle of Sedan he told the English diplomatist Edward Malet that he had decided to hang all persons who were found with arms without wearing uniform; that is to say, all *francs-tireurs*. "I attach little value to human life *because I believe in another world*." When Queen Victoria read this report, she exclaimed: "This conversation gives a most horrid idea of Bismarck's character". Indeed, a Roman Catholic Grand Inquisitor would have used the same argument for burning heretics.

Politically his conversion was of great value for Bismarck. It brought him into harmony of outlook with the Junkers who were to be his political comrades in the struggle of the next years. It was particularly important that some persons of great influence with the King Frederick William IV belonged to this circle of decidedly Christian noblemen. The two outstanding men among them were the brothers von Gerlach—General Leopold von Gerlach, the General Adjutant, *i.e.* personal aide-de-camp to the King, and Ludwig von Gerlach, President of a High Court of Appeal. These brothers were the leaders of the High Tories in Berlin and in court society. It was to them that Bismarck looked for advice and information when he came to Berlin in spring 1847, as a member of the first Prussian parliament, the "United Diet" (Vereinigter Landtag).

2. *The United Diet of 1847*

What was this United Diet, what was its origin, and why did it bear this particular name? In 1847 Prussia was still an absolute monarchy. The King had exclusive control not only of the executive but also of the legislative power. The word of the King made and unmade laws. No representation of the people existed in any form whatsoever. But in the days of his greatest danger, in the days of Napoleon's triumph, King Frederick William III had promised to give his people "a representation of the nation for the provinces, as well as for the whole state". This promise was repeated in 1815, when Napoleon returned from Elba. But this the King almost forgot when the danger was over and the war of liberation had been won with the help of a patriotic and loyal nation. All that remained was a royal order of January 1820, declaring that the King would in future raise a public loan only with the consent of the Estates of the Realm (*Reichs-Stände*).

Who were the Estates of the Realm? That remained to be seen when the order was to be put into practice.

This case did not arise during the reign of King Frederick William III. He died in 1840 and was succeeded by his eldest son. Frederick William IV was a man of many gifts. He had spirit, eloquence, wit, and a fine understanding of art and literature. But he was destitute of all those qualities which are necessary to a king and ruler, especially in troubled times. He completely lacked any fixed purpose, and had an invincible aversion from doing the simple and logical. His confidant and friend, General von Gerlach, wrote in his diary: "The King thinks his ministers are asses [*Rindvieh*, block-head], because they have to discuss current state business with him". He hated what was the best in the Prussia of that time, the bureaucracy, the civil service, which did its work loyally, incor-ruptibly, and without much prejudice. He found ringing words for his absurd ideas, but that only made it worse. Bismarck said about him in later years: "If you tried to come to grips with him, you would only find a slimy substance".

The King's hour of trial came when the question of the national representation could no longer be eluded. The era of railways had begun. The Prussian state was obliged to build railways. From the military point of view the most important of them was a line which was to connect Berlin, the capital, with the most remote part of the monarchy, the province of Eastern Prussia. It was a necessity also for economic reasons. But the state was unable to construct this railway without a public loan. Thus the moment for consulting the Estates of the Realm had arrived, and all the points had now to be settled about the exact form these Estates were to assume. What was to be their structure and composition? The Prussian people, or at least the educated middle class, had interpreted the term Estates of the Realm in the light of the former royal promises. They hoped for a national representation, for a Prussian constitution. But national representation and a constitution were liberal demands and the King hated liberalism which he identified with revolution. A national representation was in his eyes connected with the dreadful principle of popular sovereignty, and therefore incompatible with his Divine Right (*Gottesgnadentum*). On the other hand, he considered the separation of the people in different estates (*Stände*) as the "natural" and Christian order. Everyone remembered that the French *États Généraux* of 1789 began as three *États*, namely the nobility, the clergy, and the *tiers état*. The first revolutionary act was to destroy this division and to amalgamate them into a single assembly. Frederick William wanted to return to the pre-revolutionary position and to convoke an assembly of the estate of the nobility (*Ritterschaft*), the estate of the urban middle class (*Bürgerschaft*), and the estate of the peasants (*Bauernschaft*). Each of the Prussian provinces had a provincial diet (Provinzial-Landtag), constructed on these lines. Therefore, the King convoked, by order of 3rd February 1847, a united assembly of all these Provincial Diets as United Diet.

The royal order was received very badly by the public, which felt deceived, and with good reason. The United Diet was not the promised national representation, but the artificial invention of a faint-hearted and nervous romanticist. But with all its drawbacks it was an immense step forward to constitutionalism for one reason: the King allowed the verbatim reports of the debates of the Diet to be published by the newspapers, which had hitherto been forbidden by the censor to deal in any way with German or Prussian political affairs. Through the publication of these debates the newspaper readers in Berlin or Magdeburg, Königsberg or Cologne, were for the first time able to read something about their own affairs. For a country without a free press it was an immense advance. In this way the Prussian people became acquainted with the men who defended popular rights and liberties fearlessly in impressive speeches. These men at once became popular. On the other hand, the few men who opposed all liberal demands acquired an unpopularity bordering on hatred.

One man, however, was not only indifferent to the stigma of unpopularity, but apparently eager to court it. That was the deputy of the Saxon Knighthood (*Sächsische Ritterschaft*), Herr von

Bismarck-Schönhausen. He not only had the most conservative and reactionary views, but expressed them in a most offensive manner. He was in close touch with the brothers von Gerlach, and at times brought to the tribune of the House the ideas and arguments he had discussed with them. But he expressed these arguments in a way which was entirely his own, with a concentration of force and sarcasm of which no other Junker was capable. Here already, as a young man, he showed his skill in interpreting the words of his adversaries in such a way that he could destroy them with their own weapons. His opinions and his provocative manner of expression could not fail to infuriate public opinion. It saw in Bismarck the very incarnation of the medieval spirit, to put it in the words of one of the Liberal leaders. On the other hand, the court party and the Junkers very soon came to regard him as the most effective champion of their ideas and interests.

The session of the United Diet came to a premature end when it rejected the loan for the East Prussian railway. This rejection is especially significant because it throws a characteristic light on the mentality of the Prussian people in this period. The usefulness, nay, the necessity of the railway was never in doubt. If the majority of the deputies, with the most directly interested deputies of East Prussia foremost among them, nevertheless threw out the loan, it was for purely constitutional reasons. They denied the constitutional validity of the United Diet, that is to say, they challenged its conformity to the law of 1820, which had never been abrogated and which they therefore still regarded as binding. Thus these deputies put the law higher than their own interests. They regarded the Prussian Monarchy as a *Rechtsstaat*, that is, a state in which the Rule of Law was supreme, binding even the King, and they were of the opinion that an infringement of this principle would do more harm to the future of their country than the delay in the construction of an unquestionably important and useful railway. It is noteworthy that this Prussian parliament was by no means radical. The liberalism of the majority of the members of the Opposition was so moderate that in England it would hardly have been considered as liberal at all.

After the closing of the Diet Bismarck married Johanna von Puttkamer in July 1847. The marriage was ended only by the death of Johanna in November 1894, after forty-seven happy years. It brought with it for Bismarck all the happiness he wished from it. She was the wife he wanted, although her mental gifts were in no way comparable to his own, or even more than mediocre. He did not want a wife who was able to be his helpmate or to share in his ideas. Johanna never understood or even cared about them. She did not even read his speeches when the whole world was discussing them. But Bismarck did not look on this as a shortcoming in his wife; in his opinion a wife belonged exclusively to the domestic sphere, and in this sphere she was all he wanted. She was a loving, careful wife and mother, who looked after his comfort, admired and followed him in every way. She took a purely personal view of Bismarck's political conflicts. She was a friend to his friends and followers, and she disliked heartily and even hated his opponents.

On their honeymoon Bismarck met King Frederick William in Venice and had a long personal conversation with him, which showed that the monarch appreciated and highly approved of his speeches and actions in the Diet. Bismarck might thus hope for advancement from his King. But great events happened before such expectations could materialize.

3. The Revolution of 1848

In February 1848 the French King, Louis-Philippe, was dethroned and France became a republic for the second time. A few weeks later the all-powerful Austrian Minister, Prince Metternich, the foremost representative of the ancient order, was compelled to resign. The revolutionary wave passed over Germany and reached Prussia. On the 18th March street fighting broke out in Berlin. The next day, the 19th, the King withdrew his soldiers from the capital and conceded the principal popular demands: a constitution with elected parliament, freedom of speech, freedom of the press, etc.

The German revolution has two aspects. On the one hand, the German people in the different German states wanted to put an end to the absolute government and to obtain their share in the government. This aim was achieved to some extent. With the exception of the two petty dukedoms of Mecklenburg absolutism definitely came to an end. Prussia became a constitutional monarchy, although the

Prussian parliament fell far short of the ideal for which the German Liberals had hoped and the people had fought. The Austrian Monarchy had a relapse into absolutism after the breakdown of the revolution, but after its defeat at Solferino in 1859 it had to return to constitutionalism.

The other aim of the revolution was national unity. In this respect it may be considered as an upheaval against the work of the Congress of Vienna in 1815. The statesmen who assembled in the Austrian capital after the downfall of Napoleon had bitterly disappointed the hope for national unity of two peoples: the Italian and the German. In Italy the position was still worse than in Germany, in so far as a considerable part of the country was subject to foreign rulers. Milan and Venice became provinces of the Habsburg Monarchy. Metternich flatly denied the national homogeneity of the Italian people, and called Italy merely a "geographical conception".

In Germany only the most northern part, Sleswig-Holstein, belonged to a foreign state, the Kingdom of Denmark. But the German people continued to belong to thirty-eight different states, beginning with two Great Powers, Austria and Prussia, four other kingdoms, Bavaria, Wurtemberg, Hanover, and Saxony, and so forth, down to states which were so small that they could hardly be found on the map. True, all these states were combined in the Deutscher Bund (the German Confederation). But this Confederation was constituted in such a way that the German people were left without a voice in their affairs, and that a unified policy based on German interests and designed to achieve German ends was practically impossible. The Confederation was only a *Staaten-Bund* (a federation of states). What the German Liberals wanted was a *Bundes-Staat* (a federated state). The Confederation only had one common organ, the Bundestag (Federal Diet) in Frankfurt-am-Main, composed of the delegates of the governments of the individual states and presided over by the representative of the Austrian Emperor. The Bundes-Staat, on the other hand, would have its own government, its own parliament and legislature, and its own administration and civil service, perhaps even its own army. The member states like Prussia, Bavaria, etc., would not cease to exist, but would merely be subordinate parts and members of the Bundes-Staat, which alone would have the right to make a foreign policy.

Federated states of this type existed already in the United States of North America and in Switzerland. But the German form still had to be found.

The abolition of the German Confederation had apparently been achieved when its representatives, the Bundestag (the German Diet), dissolved themselves under the pressure of the revolution. The task of finding the form for the German state was attempted by a German national assembly, a parliament elected by the whole German people, that assembled in the old Free City of Frankfurt-am-Main in the Paulskirche, the church of St. Paul. It was to this Paulskirche and the very eminent men assembled there, that the hopes of all the best minds of Germany turned.

In Berlin the Prussian King, feeling that the ground was being cut away from under his feet, with his usual impulsiveness embraced the national cause for a moment, and tried to lead it. A few days after the withdrawal of his troops the King of Prussia, on horseback, the black, red, and gold flag of Germany flying over his head, led a solemn procession through the streets of Berlin and made enthusiastic speeches. "I want German freedom and German unity." In a proclamation he said: "Prussia will henceforth be merged in Germany".

Qn the day of this proclamation, Bismarck, who had been in the country, arrived in· Berlin. He was not only full of indignation about the revolution, he simply did not understand it. He imagined it was no more than a street revolt, which could be put down by a counter-revolution of the rural population. This he hoped to organize, but everybody to whom he spoke made it clear to him that there was not even the smallest chance of success for a movement of this kind and that nobody wished to take part in it. The most important event in this episode was a conversation Bismarck had with the wife of Prince William, Princess Augusta. Prince William, the King's eldest brother, as presumptive successor to the throne, had the title "Prince of Prussia". He was considered by the people an ardent absolutist and a strict opponent of the new order. He was, therefore, after the victory of the revolution, compelled to flee furtively from Berlin. He went to London, then the rendezvous of many exiled potentates and statesmen. The Prince was well received by Queen Victoria and her consort, Prince Albert, who never ceased to be interested in a modern and liberal development of his old country, Germany. The weeks which the fugitive prince spent in London were all to his good; his conversations with Albert taught him to understand many things which had been hidden from him as a general of the Prussian army.

Augusta, who had aided the flight of her husband, stayed in Potsdam, and it was here that Bismarck went to meet her. Of his conversation with Augusta Bismarck often gave very distorted versions, particularly in his *Recollections*. In actual fact he apparently came as an emissary of Prince Charles, a younger brother of the King. Charles was not only a reactionary who was strongly in favour of a counter-revolution, he was also well known in the royal family as an arch-intriguer. His plan was to get into his hands the young son of William and Augusta, Prince Frederick William, the later Emperor Frederick. Bismarck seems to have proposed to Augusta that the Prince of Prussia should abdicate in favour of this son, and that Prince Charles should unfold the banner of the counter-revolution in this infant prince's name. Augusta, who had a liberal outlook and hated Prince Charles, indignantly declined this offer.

The whole plan collapsed immediately. But Augusta never forgave Bismarck for lending himself to such a sordid intrigue. When Bismarck became Prussian Prime Minister in 1862, the young Prince Frederick William, now Crown Prince, wrote in his diary that his mother Augusta regarded Bismarck as her "mortal enemy". Indeed, Bismarck always looked upon the Queen as his bitter enemy and considered her responsible for everything that went wrong. All his writings and conversations are full of the most embittered attacks upon her. Some years after the revolution he had a duel with the leader of the moderate Liberal Party in the Prussian Chamber, Georg von Vincke; the ostensible motive was a parliamentary encounter, but the real reason was Bismarck's knowledge that Vincke was Augusta's confident in the days of his Potsdam interview with her. He hated Vincke because Vincke was aware of his unpleasant mission and his moral defeat.

A few weeks after this fateful interview Bismarck was again in Berlin as member of the United Diet, which met only in order to prepare the transition to the new constitutional state and to dissolve itself for ever. Almost all the deputies, even those who some weeks before had been ardent absolutists, welcomed the new development. Not so Bismarck. In a speech to the House, he said: "The past is buried, and I regret it much more deeply than many of you, that no human power will be able to resuscitate it, after the crown itself has thrown the earth on its coffin". Thus Bismarck put the blame for the defeat very distinctly on the King himself. He did so, even more directly, some weeks later, when the King gave him an audience. He reproached the King to his face for his weak-heartedness, and when the Queen intervened and tried to excuse the King on the grounds that he had not been able to sleep a minute during the critical days of March, Bismarck retaliated sharply: "A King *must* be able to sleep".

Bismarck's parliamentary career was now over for the time being. The new Prussian National Assembly was elected by universal suffrage and no constituency had the smallest wish to be represented by a medieval Junker like Herr von Bismarck. But his political activities did not stop. He helped with all his energy to build up the party of the Junkers and to prepare the counter-revolution. He was in close touch with the brothers von Gerlach, who now became a decisive factor in court and around the King. They, and some court-generals, formed the notorious *camarilla* or the *ministère occulte*, which worked in secret to undo everything that the official ministry did. Frederick William's conversion to constitutionalism and German unification was, of course, only feigned and superficial. He was ashamed of the rôle he was compelled to play, and wished nothing more heartily than to wipe out the dreadful March days and to return, as quickly as possible, to the old splendour of *Gottesgnadentum*. He heard eagerly what Gerlach and the other members of the *camarilla* whispered into his ears. The very day when the first constitutional ministry of Prussia was formed, Gerlach was able to write into his diary, "formation of the *ministère occulte*".

Two important things were significant in this resurrection of the Junker party. They founded a daily paper, the *Kreuz-Zeitung* (*Journal of the Cross*), which took up the cudgels in a most aggressive spirit. Bismarck was one of its chief contributors, writing very arrogant and sarcastic articles. The other thing was the formation of a political doctrine which Friedrich Julius Stahl gave to the reactionary party. The *Geheimer Rat* Stahl was professor of juris-prudence at Berlin University and one of the eminent lights of the German learned world. He was the son of Jewish parents, and had been converted to Protestantism in his student days. He was a highly gifted man, an excellent speaker and writer. People used to say that when Stahl rose in the Upper Chamber (Herrenhaus), the Prussian Junkers crowded around him and listened to his words as if the Holy Ghost Himself was dispensing His wisdom. Bismarck, in a letter to his wife, compared him with Disraeli, and Stahl would certainly have been able to say what Disraeli said, that he had "educated his party". He was much too intelligent to overlook the fact that the days of absolutism were over, and that a repre-sentation of the people was inevitable. But in this inevitable con-stitutional state he wanted to preserve as much of the royal power as possible. He invented what was later called "German constitu-tionalism" as distinguished from parliamentary government. This doctrine taught that the government of Prussia should not be dependent on the confidence of the parliamentary majority, but on that of the King. In Great Britain, or the other countries governed according to the parliamentary system, the government is com-pelled to resign whenever a parliamentary vote of want of confidence is passed against it. Stahl fought this doctrine tooth and nail, and, indeed, with the greatest success. Throughout the existence of the Prussian Monarchy no Minister could be compelled to resign as long as he had the confidence of the King, even if a huge majority of the parliament opposed him with the utmost vigour and passion. We shall have to see that it was Bismarck's achievement to carry through this principle against the strongest popular opposition in Prussia and even to transfer it to the new German Empire.

Even during the year 1848 the revolution began to lose its strength. In June 1848 the insurrection of the French Socialists and Radicals was defeated by General Cavaignac in ferocious street fights in Paris. Louis Napoleon Bonaparte was elected President of the French Republic by an enormous majority in December 1848. In October the soldiers of the new Austrian Emperor, Francis Joseph, led by the Croat General Jellachich, defeated the revolu-tionary Hungarians, and his General von Windischgraetz conquered revolutionary Vienna. By December 1848 complete success had rewarded the efforts of the *camarilla* in Berlin. General von Wrangel occupied Berlin. Another General, Graf Brandenburg, an illegitimate descendant of the Royal House of Hohenzollern, became Prime Minister and dissolved the Prussian National Assembly. On the 5th December King Frederick William proclaimed a constitution without any consultation with a parliament. He dictated it, and it was called the *octroyierte Verfassung* owing to the fact that it had been imposed dictatorially. It did not, however, differ very much from the constitution upon which the committee of the National Assembly had agreed and which was called by the Junkers the *Charte Waldeck*, because the radical deputy Waldeck, a member of the highest Prussian court, was the president and the moving force of this committee. The dictated constitution retained even the universal suffrage. A new Chamber had to be elected, and this time Herr von Bismarck managed to obtain a seat with a very narrow majority in a constituency in Brandenburg. He naturally became one of the leading men of the extreme Right of the Chamber.

One of the reasons which had prevented the King and his ministry from giving the new Prussian constitution a much more reactionary form was that the question of German unity had not yet been solved. The Frankfurt parliament in the Paulskirche was still deliberating the constitution of Germany. It had to solve now the great question whether Austria or Prussia should be the leading power in Germany. Two schools of political thought fought for supremacy, the *gross-deutsche* and the *klein-deutsche*. The *gross-deutsche* (Greater German) Party demanded that the German part of the Habsburg Monarchy, Deutsch-Österreich, should remain part of the new German Empire. The *klein-deutsche* (Smaller German) Party considered the total exclusion of Austria inevitable. It felt that only one Great Power should be a member, and thereby the leading member of the new Germany; that meant that Germany should henceforth be led by Prussia. After a long and ardent struggle the *klein-deutsche* Party carried the day. The Assembly decided that an Emperor (*ein Kaiser*) should be head of the German state, that he should be elected by the Assembly, and that the Imperial crown should thenceforth be hereditary. Thus, on the 28th March 1849 the King of Prussia was elected Emperor of Germany, and the great task of giving a constitution to the new Germany seemed to have been achieved. A deputation of the Assembly was sent to Berlin to offer the Imperial crown to Frederick William. The leader and speaker of the deputation was the excellent president of the Assembly, Eduard Simson, Professor in Königsberg, a highly respected man of Jewish origin.

It was now up to Frederick William to fulfil the ardent desire of the German nation for unity by accepting the Imperial crown. Frederick William was not the man whom the historic hour demanded. He detested election by a parliament, a crown offered by the representatives of the people. That was revolution, and he hated the revolution all the more as he remembered his own humiliation before it. So he declined the crown on the grounds that he would accept it only if offered unanimously by the German princes.

In the Prussian Second Chamber, of which Bismarck was a member, the question was discussed in April 1849. The speech Bismarck made in this debate is significant for the immense gulf which separated him from the feeling of the nation. It is a bitter and sarcastic criticism of the Frankfurt constitution, which he stigmatized as "organized anarchy" because it gave universal suffrage to the German people. Who could foresee that seventeen years later he himself would demand a German parliament constituted on the basis of universal suffrage? He confessed that everybody wanted German unity, but, with such a constitution he did not want it, and he preferred that Prussia remained Prussia. It was an unambiguous pronouncement of Prussian particularism and diehard Toryism.

With the refusal of the Imperial crown by Frederick William the German revolution of 1848 had failed in practice. Nevertheless, it had not been in vain. It was a step forward which could never be undone completely. For the first time the Frankfurt parliament had clearly stated the issue, the solution of which was to be decisive for Germany's future, the alternatives of Prussia and Austria, of *klein-deutsch* and *gross-deutsch*. Although the first parliament of the whole German people had failed, the organization of Germany without a German parliament was henceforth out of the question. This first parliament had been so full of political ideas, of high idealism, of oratorical excellence, that it could never be forgotten. It was a middle-class parliament, as the whole revolution had been a middle-class revolution. This German middle class (*Bürgertum*) was very young. In the whole of the period which began with the Thirty Years' War in the middle of the seventeenth century and ended with the appearance of Lessing in the middle of the eighteenth century, there is—except in the musical world—hardly an independent middle-class German whose name is worth remembering. Leibniz, who could be quoted as an exception, is rather more an international than a German personality. Nevertheless, the parliaments in Frankfurt and in Berlin had shown how well endowed with political talent the German middle class was.

In the Paulskirche in Frankfurt one of the most famous Germans of his time, the poet Ludwig Uhland, said some poetic and prophetic words: "Never will a head shine forth over Germany that is not anointed with a full drop of democratic oil". It was the achievement of Bismarck to unify the German people, but to give it a head which had not been touched by even a small drop of democratic oil.

After the refusal of the Imperial crown, the reaction in Prussia, as in the whole of Germany, was soon in full swing. The Prussian Chamber was dissolved by the King a few days after Bismarck's speech against the German constitution. This speech had made him so unpopular that he would not have been elected if the universal suffrage had not been abolished by an order of the King. It was replaced by the three-classes suffrage (*Drei-Klassen-Wahlrecht*), in which the voters were divided into three classes according to the amount of taxes they paid. The richest men, who paid a third of the taxes, came in the first class. The second class contained the men of moderate means, who paid the second third. All the rest, the overwhelming majority of the voters, belonged to the third class. Every class had to vote indirectly for *Wahlmänner* (electors) who had to elect the deputy. In this way the two first classes always outvoted the third class, which was practically without any representation. No doubt that was what the government, headed by the archreactionary Otto von Manteuffel, wanted. The democratic party considered this order as illegal and unconstitutional, which it certainly was, and decided to abstain from voting as long as the order was not cancelled. But that never happened.

Under these circumstances Bismarck did not have any difficulty in getting a seat in the new Chamber, where he continued to speak and vote in the most reactionary way. Only one of his speeches need be mentioned, because it is of great biographical as well as historical interest.

After the downfall of the Frankfurt parliament the Prussian King made, under the influence of his friend, General von Radowitz, a half-hearted attempt to bring about a unification of a part of Germany. But Austria, whose leader was then a strong and arrogant statesman, Prince Schwarzenberg, would have nothing of it, and the Russian Czar, Nicholas I, the brother-in-law of Frederick William, took Austria's part. The Prussian King, not at all a courageous man, climbed down and renounced all his ambitions in the Treaty of Olmütz (28th November 1850). This Treaty of Olmütz is considered the deepest humiliation in Prussia's history since the Battle of Jena and the Peace of Tilsit. It aroused a whirlwind of indignation. William, the Prince of Prussia, was particularly irritated and angry. He became more and more opposed to the reactionary government and his pusillanimous brother. Even in the Chamber, which as a rule was dominated by the government, strong opposition arose. One speaker, however, not only approved the treaty but praised it highly. Bismarck, the man who fifteen years later defeated Austria and drove it out of Germany, now pronounced a eulogy on Austria and called it a "German power which was lucky enough to rule over foreign peoples". In short, this speech was a perfect contradiction of everything that Bismarck in his great days said and did. But it contains one sentence which was in complete accordance with the Bismarck of 1866 and 1870: "The only sound basis of a great state is egoism, not romanticism. It is unworthy of a great state to fight for anything that does not form part of its own interests."

This spirited defence of the government's policy was some months later rewarded by Bismarck's appointment as Prussian Minister and plenipotentiary at the German Diet (Deutscher Bundestag) in Frankfurt. It was the work of his protector, General von Gerlach, who recommended him to the King. Bismarck was thus given what was then the most important post in the Prussian diplomatic service. He was no doubt very happy about this appointment, but he had some difficulty in persuading his wife that his entering on an official career was for the good of both of them. In a letter he wrote to Johanna the day after his appointment was announced officially he said: "I went to see General Gerlach to-day; while he was holding forth upon the subject of treaties and monarchs, I saw how in the garden beneath the window the wind tossed the blossoms of chestnut and lilac hither and thither, and I heard the nightingales and thought, if only I could stand with you in the window-bay of the panelled room and look out on to the terrace—and I did not follow what Gerlach was saying".

Is this a genuine expression of his real feeling? Did he really long for a quiet, peaceful, contemplative life in rural seclusion, just at this very moment when his ambition had reached the first stage in that long journey which would be full of struggle and victory? Truly, this longing for the idyll, for the quiet rural existence, *procul negotiis*, accompanied this man of ambition and iron will through all the years of his great political career. It was almost forty years before he could retire, free from the burden of office, to the trees of the Sachsenwald. And then he pined away with grief that he was out of office, that another man stood in his place, and the Sachsenwald was to him no more than a place of exile.

4. *Bismarck in Frankfurt*

The 11th May 1851, when Bismarck arrived in Frankfurt as Prussian envoy at the German Diet, marks an epoch not only in his life but in the history of the German Confederation. With him the germ of destruction was planted in its very heart. The Diet had been dissolved by the Revolution of 1848. Its resurrection was the work of the reaction, especially that of Austria. The latter had the permanent presidency of the Diet, according to the constitution of the Confederation. The resurrection of the Confederation and Diet was one of the points Austria had carried through in the struggle which had ended at Olmütz. The Diet was the governing body of the Confederation. The members of the Confederation were sovereign states, and the Diet was composed of the envoys of these sovereign states. The members of the Diet thus voted, not according to their own opinion but according to the instructions they received from their governments. It goes without saying that a body of this type could move only very slowly, if at all.

Its voting procedure was regulated in a very complicated and artificial way. In some matters every state, be it large or small, had one vote, in others the larger states had more votes than the smaller ones. The two Great Powers, Austria and Prussia, each had four votes, but the other four kingdoms—Bavaria, Wurtemberg, Hanover, and Saxony—also had the same number of votes. If the two Great Powers took the same line, they were practically certain to have their way. But if they disagreed the majority depended on the votes of the middle states. Now, in the whole period from the foundation of the Confederation to the Revolution, Prussia had, as a rule, voted with Austria. For Austria was not only the presiding Power, but the superior statesmanship of the Austrian Minister, Prince Metternich, had swayed successive weak Prussian governments. Therefore, in this period the German Diet and the German Confederation carried out the policy of Metternich.

A return to this Austro-Prussian collaboration was impossible after 1850, because in the short time between the dissolution and the resurrection of the Bundestag (Diet) the Frankfurt parliament had proclaimed Prussia as the leader of the future Germany. The Prussian King had, indeed, refused the Imperial crown, but the fact remained that a majority of the representatives of the German people looked to Prussia for leadership. The antagonism of the two Great Powers and its importance for the future of Germany had thus been made manifest. This factor could not henceforth be ignored.

The Prussian King and the Prussian government did not wish to oppose Austria in Germany after their defeat at Olmütz. Bismarck was sent to Frankfurt because he had, in his speech about Olmütz, not only advocated an understanding between Austria and Prussia, he had even defended Austria herself. Besides, he was fully as reactionary and anti-revolutionary as any of those Austrian politicians who were sent to Frankfurt as representatives of the Emperor and presidents of the Diet. It was therefore to be expected that complete harmony would prevail in the Diet between them. Quite the reverse happened. Bismarck became the most determined and dangerous opponent of Austria; the meetings of the Diet were stormy as never before, and the Imperial envoy's most heartfelt prayer was to be delivered from this "terrible" Bismarck.

The curious thing is that Bismarck wrote only a fortnight after his arrival in Frankfurt that the Austrian statesmen would never take justice as the basis of their policy, that they had the attitude of impŭdent gamblers. What a contrast to his high praise of Austria in his Olmütz speech! But whatever may have been the motive of this sudden change, there can be no doubt that it became a great political conception of Bismarck and was decisive for the development of Germany. We are especially well informed about Bismarck's political ideas during his embassy in Frankfurt by his reports and letters to his chief, the Prussian Prime Minister, Otto von Manteuffel. These reports and letters were published under the auspices of Bismarck himself by Herr von Poschinger in the four volumes, *Preussen im Bundestag* (1882). They are to be found in a more exact and complete form in the first volumes of Bismarck's *Gesammelte Werke*. Another source for Bismarck's activity and development in this period are his letters to the General Leopold von Gerlach, the patron to whom he owed the post. The aim of this correspondence was to secure inside information about the intimate incidents at court and to influence the King through his aide-de-camp and friend in the direction of Bismarck's own policy. Some of the letters to Gerlach were written with the intention that they should be shown to the King. There were always intrigues and discussions at the court of Berlin. Gerlach and the *camarilla* frequently disagreed with the Minister von Manteuffel. In this situation Bismarck was careful to remain in contact with both groups. All these letters and documents are very well worth reading. Some of his dispatches are political essays of the highest order, documents of real statesmanship written in an excellent and impressive style and sometimes even in a picturesque language. The more private letters are full of humour, wit, and sarcasm. But they are, of course, extremely one-sided. Thus Bismarck's remarks about his colleagues, and the Austrians in particular, are very often quite misleading. One of them, the Freiherr von Prokesch-Osten, appears in Bismarck's letters as a pertinacious liar, a man without culture; he calls him "Tartar", "Armenian", "mouse-trap dealer". In reality, this Prokesch-Osten was a man of astonishing culture and universality, general and diplomatist, poet and scholar, historian and explorer, archaeologist and numismatist. But Bismarck lacked an eye for all these qualities in a man whom Goethe had embraced.

The climax of Bismarck's struggle against Austria came in the Crimean War (1854–1856). The Habsburg Empire was, owing to its geographical situation, intimately concerned in the Eastern Question. Its interests there coincided with those of the Western Powers, France and Great Britain, against Russia. This position was all the more difficult as Czar Nicholas had helped the Austrian Emperor in his hour of danger with his intervention in Hungary in 1849. The Czar was therefore bound to consider Austria's policy the height of ingratitude when she allied herself with the Western Powers. But the Austrian government which was in power after Schwarzenberg's death (5th April 1852) was too weak and vacillating to follow a definite line. It could not bring itself to take the final decisive step: to declare war on the side of the Western Powers as little Sardinia, guided by a real statesman, Cavour, did.

Vacillating as the Austrian policy was, it was surpassed in this respect by Prussian policy. There is hardly a more deplorable spectacle than the policy of Frederick William during the Crimean War. Czar Nicholas characterized it strikingly in the words: "My dear brother-in-law goes to bed every night as a Russian and gets up every morning as an Englishman". Probably the mental disease which overwhelmed the King some years later had already begun to develop. As a matter of fact he was perfectly unable to rule the different parties fighting at the court of Berlin. The Junkers, who considered the Czar as the leader of the European reactionary party and dreamed of a resurrection of the "Holy Alliance", were all for Russia. There was, however, a small but distinguished group of moderate Conservatives, who inclined to the Western Powers. They congregated round the Professor Bethmann Hollweg, the grandfather of the later *Reichskanzler*, and called themselves the "party Bethmann Hollweg". Popularly they were known as the *Wochenblatt-Partei*, because their leaders edited a weekly journal, *Das preussische Wochenblatt*, in which they polemized incessantly against the *Kreuz-Zeitung*. This party considered the Treaty of Olmütz, which Czar Nicholas had helped to bring about, as a shameful event and the nadir of Prussian history. The Prince of Prussia, who took the same view of Olmütz, favoured them. Among their number were some younger diplomatists, as for instance Graf Goltz, later Prussian Ambassador in Paris, and the very wealthy and intelligent Graf Pourtalès, a native of the Swiss canton Neuenburg, then a possession of the King of Prussia. In the crisis of the Crimean War these men thought that Prussia's place was on the side of the Western Powers, especially of England. They certainly hoped that Prussia would, through an alliance with England, be brought into a more liberal orbit, and that such a policy would help Prussia to fulfil its vital German task, *i.e.* the unification of Germany under Prussian leadership. This policy was favoured by the Prussian Minister in London, Baron Josias von Bunsen, who was highly esteemed by Queen Victoria and by the Prince Consort. The party seemed in the ascendancy when Graf Pourtalès was given an influential post in the Prussian Foreign Office.

Bismarck was firmly opposed to any participation of Prussia in the war at the side of the Allied Powers. His approach differed from that of Gerlach and the Junkers. He was not primarily concerned with party politics and the Czar as the leader of European reaction. He had long ceased to wish for a resurrection of the "Holy Alliance". But he saw quite clearly how hated Austria made herself in Russia by her policy, and he considered this juncture an excellent opportunity for securing the Czar's help to Prussia in that inevitable hour in the future when accounts with Austria would be settled.

"It would distress me", he wrote to Minister von Manteuffel, "if we should seek protection from a possible storm by tying our trim and seaworthy frigate to the worm-eaten and old-fashioned Austrian man-of-war. . . . Great crises are the very weather which stimulates Prussia's growth, if we turn them to our account fearlessly and, maybe, very recklessly." It is in words such as these that the quintessence of his political feeling comes to light. The same may be said of the following sentence in a letter to Gerlach: "Beware of sentimental alliances where the consciousness of good deeds is the only compensation for noble sacrifices".

Besides, there was no love lost between Bismarck and Pourtalès. The latter called Bismarck a Judas, and Bismarck called Pourtalès a *Hohlkopf* (an empty-headed ass).

It was Bismarck whom General von Gerlach called to Berlin when he feared that the influence of Pourtalès would bring the King into the alliance of the Western Powers. The intervention of Bismarck and other Junkers was effective. From one day to the next

Pourtalès found the door of the royal cabinet closed, and he was compelled to resign. Bunsen, too, who had worked out a rather fantastic "new order" for Europe, was dismissed, and so was the Minister of War, who, in the Committee of the Chamber, had said some words which were considered offensive in Russia. The Prince of Prussia, irritated by the sudden change of his royal brother, left the court and retired to Coblenz in the Rhein-Provinz. He uttered in his anger that the Russian rouble rolled even in the ante-chamber of the King. During the crisis Bismarck had an interview with the Prince. But William was by no means satisfied with his arguments. In a letter to Manteuffel he called them "the policy of a schoolboy" (*Politik eines Gymnasiasten*). Queen Victoria sent the Prussian King a very strong-worded letter, in which she wrote: "I have, hitherto, looked upon Prussia as one of the great Powers which . . . have been guarantors of treaties, guardians of civilisation, defenders of the right, the real arbiters of the Nations. . . . If you, dear Sir and Brother, abdicate these obligations, you have also abdicated that position for Prussia. And should such an example find imitators, then the civilisation of Europe would be delivered up to the play of winds; right will then no longer find a champion, the oppressed will find no longer an umpire." It was the Prince Consort who had drafted these sentences, stating the indissoluble connexion between politics and justice. Bismarck would have called that "sentimentalism".

The conflict over the policy of the German Powers during the Crimean War was largely fought out at the Diet in Frankfurt, where Austria tried to bring the Confederation into line with her own policy. Here it was Bismarck's aim to frustrate all her efforts. Even after the Prussian government had committed itself by a treaty with Austria, Bismarck tried to influence his government against an execution of the treaty. He constantly denied that anything which Austria wanted could be in the interest of all Germany. One of the most important points in Austrian policy was to obtain the withdrawal of the Russian troops from the principalities of the Danube, the present Roumania, which they had occupied. In a proposal to the Diet, which the Prussian government was obliged by treaty to support, the Austrian government had developed the idea that the whole of Germany was strongly interested in the countries on the lower Danube, where German industry and commerce could find a fertile field for their enterprise. That was by no means wrong, and in those times, when nationalism was still slumbering in the Balkan peninsula, there was perhaps a chance of its realization. But Bismarck denied outright that any German interests were involved in the Danube principalities, and he reproached the Austrian government with having as its only ambition "the obtaining by trickery of a few stinking Wallachians". His policy was thus exclusively Prussian, not in the least German. He used every possible means to embarrass Austria and her envoy, Prokesch-Osten. The efforts of the middle states to make a policy of their own were, as a rule, treated by Bismarck with the utmost contempt. But at this stage, when they tried to withdraw from Austrian leadership, he was full of praise. He went so far as to show confidentially to the Russian representative in Frankfurt a secret memorial against Austria that he had written for his chief, the Prussian Prime Minister. Although the King was bound by a solemn treaty of alliance to the Austrian Emperor, Bismarck was reckless and indisciplined enough to suggest to the Russian diplomatist an alliance of Prussia, Russia, and France. When the Russian asked whether it would be possible to win over the Prussian King to this change of policy, Bismarck answered: "If you entrust me with the task of prevailing upon the King, I guarantee its success". He advised the Russian government to act quickly, so that the prospective alliance would be in a position to attack the Austrians before they had time to concentrate their troops. That was the same Bismarck who later, when he was *Reichskanzler* and the Chief of the Foreign Office, said: "My ambassadors must wheel into line like soldiers".

Another time Bismarck made contact with the same Russian diplomatist and drew his attention to Article 36 of the constitution of the German Confederation. This article allowed a foreign Power which considered itself to have been offended by a member of the Confederation to enter at the Diet a complaint against this member. There was no article in the constitution of the Confederation which insulted the national feeling of the Germans as much as this Article 36. But Bismarck did not mind about that so long as a useful weapon was available for his anti-Austrian policy.

Prokesch was perfectly right when he called Bismarck "the most energetic but by no means the only representative of that Prussian policy whose aim it was to rob Austria of all success for her enormous efforts, to ruin her finances and her prestige, and to acquire for Prussia the *de facto*, and soon the *de jure*, hegemony over Germany".

Proof that Prokesch read correctly the thoughts of his great adversary is available in a most important memorandum written by Bismarck shortly after the Peace Treaty of Paris, which ended the Crimean War (30th March 1856). In ideas and in style it was one of the greatest state papers of that age. Here Bismarck developed the thesis which sprang from his experience in Frankfurt: that the German Confederation was bound to fall, that its constitution was rotten and inadequate, and that a co-existençe of Austria and Prussia within one political organism was impossible. "Germany", he writes, "is too small for both of us. Both plough the same contested field. Austria is and remains the only state to which we can lose for good and from which we can gain for good." Neither has he any doubt that there is only one way to solve this antagonism—war. "The German dualism has, since Charles V, regulated its mutual relations once in every century by a radical civil war. In our century, too, only a war will put right the clock of Germany's development."

Really, there is not the slightest trace of sentiment in this view. Hardly any of Bismarck's contemporaries would have envisaged a war between Germans and Germans, still less would they have proclaimed it as a legitimate political aim. But that is the method which some Germans call *Realpolitik*. Another side of Bismarck's *Realpolitik* comes to light in his correspondence with General von Gerlach about Napoleon III (1857). Bismarck himself considered this correspondence so important in his old age that he reprinted it in the eighth chapter of his *Reflections and Recollections*. He had met the French Emperor in the summer of 1855, when he visited Paris. He wanted to study this personality which was a very important factor in European politics and would presumably still play this part at a later date when he himself would be called upon to play his own part on the European stage. Napoleon was attracted by the personality of the Prussian diplomat, whom he called the only statesman in Frankfurt. Bismarck, for his part, pronounced a rather shrewd opinion on the French Emperor: "He is an intelligent and amiable man, but not nearly as clever as people think. His intelligence is overrated at the expense of his heart."

It became known at the court of Berlin that Bismarck considered a form of collaboration with Napoleon an admissible expedient for his political projects. But General von Gerlach opposed this on principle. The principle of legitimism was at stake here. Gerlach, who had fought in the Napoleonic War and remembered the time of Napoleon's rule over Germany, saw in "Bonapartism" the heir of the Revolution and therefore the very antithesis of legitimate government. Bismarck, on the other hand, had by this time freed himself from allegiance to any doctrine, excepting that of power politics. Thus, he exposes his new political conception to Gerlach: "I subordinate legitimism in France completely to my specifically Prussian patriotism. Without any regard to the person at the head for the time being, France counts for me merely as a piece, but as an unavoidable one, in the game of political chess, a game in which I am called upon to serve only my own king and my own country. I cannot regard as justified either in myself or in others that sympathies or antipathies with regard to foreign Powers and persons should take preference over my sense of duty in the foreign service of my own country. Such an idea contains the embryo of disloyalty to the ruler or the country which we serve. . . . In my opinion not even the king has the right to subordinate the interests of the country to his own feeling of love or hate towards foreigners.

"I acknowledge the principle of the fight against the Revolution to be mine also, but I do not consider it right to set up Louis Napoleon as the only or as the principal, κατ' ἐξοχήν, representative of the Revolution, nor do I believe it possible to carry out a principle in politics as something whose remotest consequences override every other consideration."

All this is very forcibly and convincingly put. But can the conclusion be drawn from these words that Bismarck thought no account should be taken, in the determination of foreign policy, of the principles on which the internal régime of other countries was based? That would not be in accordance with his acts and words in other situations. It is always dangerous to generalize from Bismarck's utterances, which apply to special occasions and are worded for particular practical purposes. In the case of Napoleon III it should be taken into consideration that he had no antipathy against the home policy of the French Emperor, who had overthrown the French Revolution and whose system contained much that Bismarck was eager to adopt. Furthermore, the following sentence in one of his letters to Gerlach should not be forgotten: "Bonapartism is distinguished from the Republic by the fact that it has no necessity to *propagate its principles of government.* . . . To threaten foreign states with the aid of the Revolution has now been, for some years past, the stock-in-trade of England." Here he apparently thought of Palmerston. In this connexion his words on his feelings about England are interesting: "As far as foreign countries are concerned, I have, throughout my life, had sympathy for England and her inhabitants, and I am, at certain times, not yet free from it. But the people there will not let us love them." This last sentence, however, does not express his real motive. He was afraid of the propagandist effect of English institutions upon the Prussian people. He knew that the latter was not likely to be tempted by the Napoleonic example—for Napoleon III was extremely unpopular in Germany— but that English institutions were popular particularly among the better-educated classes. He expressed himself quite clearly when the heir to the Prussian throne, the son of the Prince of Prussia, became engaged to the Princess Royal of Great Britain, Victoria. When Gerlach asked him what he thought of the English marriage, he answered with a stream of taunts about "the stupid admiration of the German Michel for Lords and gentlemen" and about "the Anglomania of parliaments, newspapers, sportsmen, landowners and presidents of tribunals". When the Princess Royal entered the Prussian capital in state, the old poet Arndt, the author of the famous poem, "What is the German's Fatherland?", jubilated: "Victoria in Berlin! May the English spirit inspire us!" Thus thought thousands of citizens of Berlin who crowded the streets to greet her entrance. But Bismarck returned from the wedding festivities in a depressed mood. He did not by any means relish a strengthening of the English spirit in Berlin. He feared that it might bring about a diminution of the royal power and an increase of parliamentary power, and he believed the young English princess, whose intelligence and political interest were well known, to be capable of working, by her influence on the future King, in this direction. This feeling of the man who was to become the real ruler of Prussia and Germany was decisive for the whole life and fate of the English Princess.

5. The "New Era" and Bismarck's Recall from Frankfurt

Bismarck's activity in Frankfurt came to an end when William, the Prince of Prussia, became Regent instead of his brother, and dismissed the Minister von Manteuffel. In the autumn of 1857, the insanity of Frederick William IV became manifest, and in November 1858 he was compelled to surrender his royal powers to his brother, who became "Prince Regent".

William was less gifted than his brother. He was a man of simple mind and not more than mediocre ability. But he was a much stronger character, firm of purpose. He was modest enough to take good counsel, he supported consistently those Ministers and officials whom he had found reliable, and he had some sense of justice. However, he lacked great political ideas. He was first and foremost a soldier, and his interest belonged to the army, which he considered his own exclusive affair. His highest ambition was to become the permanent Commander-in-Chief of the German Confederation. If he could obtain this concession, he did not care much about the other aspects of the German question. In home politics, he was a Conservative of the old type, but he hated the party of the *Kreuz-Zeitung* and its intrigues, which offended his moral sense, and he could not forget that Manteuffel was the man of Olmütz, Prussia's deepest humiliation. His antagonism to Manteuffel and the *Kreuz-Zeitung* Party was more of a moral than of a political character. But circumstances compelled him to look to the Moderate Liberals when he dismissed Manteuffel and had to form a new government.

He appointed as Prime Minister Prince Charles Anton of Hohenzollern, who had been sovereign ruler of the diminutive principality of Hohenzollern, but had resigned his sovereignty to become a member of the royal house of Prussia. He was the father of Prince Charles, the first Prince and later the first King, of Roumania, and of the hereditary Prince Leopold, the famous pretender to the Spanish crown and pretext of the Franco-German War. Prince Charles Anton was a personal friend of the Prince Regent and a man of slightly Liberal views. Most of the members of his cabinet were Moderate Liberals. The new cabinet was immensely popular in Prussia, and people spoke of the "New Era" which had begun with the Regency. The general election resulted in a Chamber of Deputies whose overwhelming majority was ministerial and moderately Liberal and in which the Conservative Party, only recently so powerful, had dwindled to an insignificant minority. One consequence of this change of policy was the recall of Bismarck from Frankfurt. The Prince Regent did not like Bismarck's policy, but he thought too highly of his capacities to dismiss him altogether. He gave him instead the most distinguished post in Prussian diplomacy, the Embassy at the Russian court of St. Petersburg. William valued this post all the more highly because the Czar, Alexander II, was his nephew and had the highest respect for his Prussian uncle. Nevertheless, Bismarck was almost furious about his recall from Frankfurt. He regarded it as a loss of prestige and a disavowal of his German policy, which he rightly considered as his personal contribution. His anger was increased by the fact that a member of the *Wochenblatt* Party, von Usedom, became his successor. He looked down upon Usedom and hated his eccentric wife, who was of Scottish origin. Bismarck and his wife parted with a heavy heart from Frankfurt, where they had lived a very comfortable and agreeable life. But that did not help Frankfurt in the least when it became, in the year 1866, the victim of his policy.

On his journey from Frankfurt to St. Petersburg Bismarck stayed a few days in Berlin. Here a former Liberal member of the Prussian Chamber of 1849, who was on friendly terms with Bismarck, von Unruh, paid him a visit. In his open-hearted way Bismarck gave Unruh his opinion about Prussian policy. Prussia, he said, could not find a reliable ally among the Great Powers, their interests being too divergent. *The sole reliable, lasting ally* whom Prussia could secure, if it set about it the right way, was—*the German people*. As Unruh looked rather bewildered, as well he might, at this staggering confession of the one-time anti-revolutionist, Bismarck continued: "I am the same Junker that I was ten years ago when we became acquainted in the Chamber. But I would have to be without eyes and brains not to see how things really are."

6. St. Petersburg

Bismarck stayed in St. Petersburg from April 1859 to April 1862. These three years were important for his policy because he became acquainted with one of the Great Powers which was to play a part in his future policy, and with its governors. These persons were the Czar, Alexander II, a well-meaning but not very strong man, and his Chancellor, Prince Gortchakoff. The latter was a very able man, very well versed in European politics, and an excellent conversationalist. But he was extraordinarily vain, and Bismarck hated vanity. He used to say: "Vanity is a mortgage that must be deducted from the value of a man".   Although they treated each other with the utmost politeness and courtesy, in their heart of hearts they disliked each other. Gortchakoff later became jealous of Bismarck's world-wide fame and authority, but he was clever enough to hide this feeling under one of his witty bon-mots: "Prince Bismarck likes to call himself my pupil", he said to the German Ambassador. "That is just as correct as the great painter Raphael being called pupil of the much smaller Perugino."

Gortchakoff's policy aimed at revenge against Austria and a friendly understanding with Napoleon, only recently Russia's enemy in the Crimean War. A few days before Bismarck's arrival in St. Petersburg in March 1859 a highly secret treaty had been concluded between Russia and France. It secured for Napoleon the benevolent neutrality of Russia in the imminent war against Austria, which he was about to fight as an ally of the Kingdom of Sardinia, in consequence of the secret agreement concluded with the great Sardinian Minister, Cavour, at Plombières (July 1858).

The Franco-Sardinian war against Austria raised a very important and difficult problem for Germany, and especially for Prussia. Should they help Austria, or should they allow Napoleon to overthrow the Austrian Emperor and to deprive him of his two Italian provinces? On the one hand, Austria was the presiding power of the German Confederation and a victory of Napoleon in Italy could be the prelude to French aggression on the Rhine. Moltke, the great strategist, for instance, told the Prussian Prince Regent in a memorandum: "If we leave Austria in the lurch, she would suffer a deep wound through the loss of Lombardy. As the war of 1806 (that is, the battle of Jena) followed the war of 1805 (that is, Austerlitz) France's next step would be to attack Prussia."

On the other hand, Napoleon and Cavour fought against the same settlement as the friends of Germany's unification: the Treaty of Vienna. The Italian people and the German people had the same ideal: national unification. Public opinion in Germany was being stirred up by a violent controversy in the newspapers and in many pamphlets. Ferdinand Lassalle, for instance, the founder of the German Social-Democratic Party, urged the Prussian government " to proclaim a national war, in which the German Democracy itself would bear the Prussian standard ".

The Prussian government was in doubt as to which side to take. It was willing to help Austria, but only under certain conditions, the foremost of which was that the Prince of Prussia should be made commander-in-chief of all the troops of the German Confederation. Bismarck, however, had no doubts. For him there was only one enemy: Austria. He wrote a letter to the aide-de-camp of the Prince Regent which no doubt he hoped would be read by the Regent himself, in whom he wanted "to fan the flame of royal ambition". The letter contained the following characteristic sentence: "The present situation has once again put the great prize in the lottery-box for us, if we only allow Austria's war against France to eat quite deeply into her substance. Then let us march southwards with our whole army, with the boundary-posts in the soldiers' knapsacks, and drive them into the ground either at the Lake of Constance, or there where the protestant confession ceases to prevail."

That was, indeed, wonderfully and thrillingly put. But at the same time it is a striking illustration of Bismarck's phrase that Prussia had to turn the great crises to her account not only fearlessly but very recklessly. He showed himself absolutely regardless not only of moral but also of legal obligations. Prussia was still a member of the German Confederation, which forbade its members all acts of foreign policy directed against other members, which pledged the German princes in the very first article of its constitu-

.tion "to preserve the external and internal security of Germany and the independence and integrity of the individual German States". Bismarck's advice to the Regent was nothing less than an invitation to break recklessly the solemn obligation which the Prussian state had accepted towards the German Confederation.

But Bismarck told his Chief, the Foreign Minister von Schleinitz: "I consider that the present Federal institutions are fettering Prussia in such a way as to endanger her life in critical times. I look upon our membership in the Confederation as a disease for Prussia of which we have to be cured, sooner or later, *ferro ignique*." These words, *ferro ignique* (by iron and by fire), already show the Bismarck who three years later startled the world with his famous formula, "by blood and iron".

This letter to Schleinitz contained another sentence which was an excellent description of his favourite method: "We have to seize every lawful opportunity which our confederates give us *to assume the rôle of the injured*". Bismarck's real meaning becomes clearest if the adjective "lawful" is omitted from this sentence. "To assume the rôle of the injured" was the method he always applied with skill and success in moments of decision.

Neither the Regent nor Schleinitz were the men to follow Bismarck's reckless advice. They played a waiting game and they came too late. Beaten at Magenta and Solferino, Francis Joseph suddenly concluded with Napoleon the armistice of Villafranca, purchasing peace with the surrender of Lombardy. Prussia, who had mobilized her army, though neither stating, nor indeed knowing, against whom, suddenly found herself in the position of the man who has drawn his sword but has to put it back into the scabbard because there is nobody to fight against. Prussian opinion was all the more embittered as the Austrian Emperor had solemnly declared that he had been left in the lurch by his natural ally. The Prussians reproached him with having preferred to treat with Napoleon rather than to make any concessions to his ally. But this reproach was not justified, as Francis Joseph knew that the Prussians were by no means willing to help him to reconquer Lombardy. The peace which Napoleon was willing to give him was, indeed, no worse than the terms he would have secured after prolonged fighting with the assistance of Prussia.

7. *The Consequences of Villafranca and the Army Reorganization in Prussia*

The Treaty of Villafranca made an enormous impression in Germany. It clearly manifested that she had no voice in decisions which affected the future of Europe, even when they concerned vitally one of her members. The general feeling was that the constitution of the German Confederation incapacitated her from taking part in the shaping of European policy and from coming to swift decisions. But what could be done to change this constitution? In which direction should it be changed? Here the opinions varied as widely as they had done in the years 1848 and 1849. Again the parties split under the slogans, *Gross-deutsch* and *Klein-deutsch*, Austrian or Prussian hegemony. But at last the time of slumber, enforced by the reaction, was ended by the "New Era" in Prussia. Vigorous organizations sprang up in which the citizens expressed and propagated their own opinions. The most important was the Deutscher National-Verein (German National Union). It was the organization of the Liberals in Prussia and outside of Prussia who wanted a reorganization of Germany under the leadership of Prussia, but with a national representation; in other words, the continuation of the policy which the Frankfurt National Assembly had attempted during the years of revolution. Its president was the leader of the Liberal Opposition in the Chamber of the Kingdom of Hanover, Rudolf von Bennigsen, who after 1866 became the leader of the German National Liberal Party. He was the representative of moderate Liberalism, in whom particularly the educated upper middle classes placed their confidence. By his side stood a leader of Prussian democracy, Herman Schulze from Delitzsch, the founder of the German free Co-operative Associations, and another Hanoverian, Johannes Miquel, who, after Bismarck's overthrow, became in 1890 the ablest Minister of Finance Prussia had in half a century.

If the Prussian government of the "New Era" had possessed the energy to put forward a thorough programme of German reform, they would have had excellent assistance from the National-Verein. Possibly some of the Liberal Ministers were inclined in this direction. But they were too weak to carry through a policy which was not in accordance with the legitimist principles of the Prince Regent. In his proclamation of November 1858 William had proclaimed: "In Germany Prussia has to make moral conquests". But Prussia could make such moral conquests only with the help of the German people in the teeth of the opposition of the German princes, who were unwilling to sacrifice even part of their precious sovereignty. However, it would have been against William's legitimist principles to rely upon the people in order to compel the resisting princes.

Moreover, William's harmony with his Liberal Ministers was soon disturbed by disagreement on other questions, in which his conservative, almost absolutist, disposition came to light. Here, too, it was another consequence of Villafranca which had the most far-reaching results.

The mobilization of the Prussian army during the Italo-Austrian War had disclosed some shortcomings of its organization. The Regent was first and foremost a soldier. He had, in his youth, been educated for the army, not for government. Military affairs were the only ones about which he had confidence in his own judgment. He now wanted a complete reorganization of the army. To help him in this work he appointed General von Roon as Minister of War. Roon was an excellent organizer and—although not a genius —a first-class military expert. But he was also an unscrupulous intriguer. The first duty of a member of a government would seem to be to work harmoniously with his colleagues. Roon did the very opposite. He was a strong Conservative and he considered it his duty to overthrow his Liberal colleagues. Although he was a religious and pious man and although, as a soldier, he knew very well the duty of comradeship, he did his best to undermine the confidence William had in his other Ministers. When these Ministers advised him in favour of some Liberal measures, Roon wrote to William: "I cannot bear it in my heart of a Prussian soldier that my King and master should submit his own will to any other man's". He warned him against the increasing power of parliament, dangerous for his own "strong active kingship".

His plan was, by getting rid of his Liberal colleagues, to make room for his friend Otto von Bismarck. An example of Roon's methods was the affair of William's coronation. The mad King, Frederick William IV, had at last died in January 1861, and the

Prince Regent became King under the name of William I. There had to be a solemn coronation. Now William wanted to hold this coronation in the form which had been usual *before* the constitution, as if Prussia were still an absolutist monarchy as in the days of his father. He wanted solemn homage by the Estates of the Realm, although there were no such estates in the constitutional monarchy. The Ministers felt it their duty to oppose the King's whim, but their colleague Roon wrote to Bismarck: "The homage question is almost ripe for an explosion. The King cannot give way without ruining himself and the Crown for ever. Nor can the majority of the Ministers yield; if they did, they would slit open their immoral bellies and commit political suicide. They cannot help being and remaining disobedient. . . . If you agree with me and think that the attitude of the Ministers is mere doctrinaire humbug . . . you will have no objection to entering the King's Council." But Bismarck did not care to come into the forefront as the champion of a medieval caprice on the part of the King, and he answered that he did not understand why the homage quarrel had become so important for both sides. The question was, indeed, settled by a compromise, although there remained enough in the King's behaviour at the coronation to arouse a widespread opposition, because it showed to the people that he was still deeply imbued with the antiquated notion of divine kingship. The Prussian people of this time were a very loyal people who wanted nothing more than to be in agreement with their king. They were easily satisfied with a few liberal and progressive acts. But by withholding such measures and by proclaiming old-fashioned absolutist doctrines, William repulsed the goodwill of his people.

On the other hand, the King felt irritated against his Liberal Ministers because they had compelled him to give way, if only partially.

But what really brought about their downfall and the end of the "New Era" was the question of the reorganization of the army. That was the wedge that Roon drove successfully between the Ministers and the King, and between the Ministers and the Chamber of Deputies.

One part of the reorganization was undoubtedly sound. The principle of universal conscription had been law in Prussia since the War of Liberation. Every healthy young man had to serve in the army. But in later years this principle was only partially carried out. Only a section of every age-group was, in fact, called to the colours. It was possible and politically sound to conscript a greater proportion and thus to increase the strength of the army. This part of the project did not meet any serious opposition. On this point the King could have easily had his way. But there were two questions which were hotly disputed. One thing was the length of time for which the men should be called to the colours. The old law laid down a period of three years. But in practice the soldiers were sent on permanent leave after two years. Now the King wanted to keep the conscripts with the colours for the full three years. His reasons were of a political as much as of a military nature. He considered three years of uninterrupted military service necessary not so much to train them as soldiers, but still more in order to destroy their civilian outlook.

The problem of the Landwehr (militia) was intimately connected with that of the length of time of conscription. Once more the background was as much political as military. The Prussian Landwehr was a creation of the War of Liberation, and it had done glorious service in that war. The people were proud of it, and considered it much more their own than the standing army. The *Landwehr-Mann* (militiaman) was the citizen in arms. The Landwehr had its own officers, whose majority were not "Junkers" like the officers of the standing army. It is for this reason that the arch-conservative General von Gerlach called the Landwehr the one really liberal institution in the country. But what endeared the Landwehr to the people made it suspicious to the King and to Roon. They disliked the *Landwehr-Mann* as too intimately connected with civil life. The Landwehr man of to-day was the voter of yesterday and of to-morrow. When in the year 1849 Prussian troops were sent against the South Germans who had risen to fight for the German constitution of the Frankfurt Assembly, some Landwehr men had clearly shown their discontent. The King wanted to avoid a repetition of similar signs of political independence. His plan of reorganization aimed at a weakening of the Landwehr.

These two points, the length of service with the colours and the "playing-down" of the Landwehr, were the real reasons of the widespread popular opposition still more than the heavy financial burden, which the reorganization implied. Even in the thoroughly governmental Chamber this discontent was very clearly expressed. Unable to overcome this resistance, the government withdrew the reorganization bill and only asked for a sum of nine million thalers for military expenditure in the next year. The Ministers emphasized that this expenditure would only be of a provisional, a temporary character. The majority cf the Chamber, anxious to help and to sustain the Liberal Ministers, granted the supply on the express condition of its provisional character. But no sooner had the supply been granted than the King formed new regiments which were, of course, there to stay. It was a clear breach of faith.

The King acted on the advice of his military advisers. Among them General Edwin von Manteuffel, the Chief of the Military Cabinet of the King, a cousin of the former Prime Minister Otto von Manteuffel, was the most influential, with the exception of the Minister von Roon. The "Military Cabinet" was a strange, specifically Prussian institution. It was not to be found in the constitution, which, on the contrary, provided that all the King's acts of government (*Regierungsakte*) were valid only if countersigned by a responsible Minister. The Military Cabinet was developed as a means to enable the King to act in army affairs without a ministerial countersignature and thus to avoid accountability to the Chamber. This point was emphasized by an anonymous pamphlet entitled *Was uns noch retten kann* (Our only way of deliverance). Its author was a young judge in Berlin, Karl Twesten, an ardent patriot and a convinced Liberal of real political understanding. He had the courage to point to Edwin Manteuffel and to call him "a disastrous man in a disastrous place". Manteuffel's answer was to challenge Twesten—who did not hesitate to confess his authorship—to a duel. To avoid the blame of cowardice Twesten accepted the challenge and was wounded by the General. He understood perfectly well the idea of this procedure: every criticism of military affairs was to be made impossible. Whoever could read aright the signs of the time saw that militarism was in the ascendancy and firmly resolved to fight for its privileged position with every means. Nevertheless, the majority of the Chamber granted once more the supply for the military expenditure for the year 1861, although the government had not kept its promise to bring in a bill to settle permanently the question in dispute.

But now the feeling grew that the ministerial party was too ob-
sequious to the government. Some younger members of the Chamber
seceded and formed a new party which at once gained popular
support. It was called the *Deutsche Fortschrittspartei* (German Progressive Party). The word "German" was just as important as the
word "Progressive". The programme of the party asked for "a solid
unification of Germany with a central power led by Prussia and
with a common German parliament". At the same time the Conservative Party proclaimed: "Prussia shall not be submerged in the
filth of a German Republic. We abhor the robbing of crowns and
the humbug of nationality." It is clear on which side the Prussian
government would have found support if it had been courageous
enough to carry on a resolute German policy. The King, however,
was not concerned with this aspect of the new Progressive Party,
but only with its home policy programme: development of the
constitution, maintenance of the *Landwehr*, and two years' service
with the colours. He was very annoyed when the Progressive Party
won a very considerable success in the elections of November 1861,
having offered candidates for the first time. It won so many seats that
it became a decisive factor in the Chamber of Deputies. The party
of the Liberal Ministers lost heavily, and the Conservative Party
was completely routed. Even Roon lost his seat in the Chamber.

From St. Petersburg, Bismarck followed these developments in
home and party politics with the greatest interest, all the more as he
now aspired quite openly to a seat in the government. His friend Roon
did his best to persuade the King to send for him. Bismarck himself
came to Berlin to promote his candidature. But the King could not
bring himself to include into his government this self-willed person
whose policy aroused his suspicion no less than it had done some
years previously, when he had called it the "policy of a schoolboy".

Bismarck now indeed had a policy quite of his own. It cannot be
identified with the programme of the Conservative Party. When
he read those words about "humbug of nationality" in the Conservative proclamation, he criticized them with the utmost vigour
and mocked at the "completely unhistoric, *godless and lawless,
sovereignty-humbug of the German Princes*". Moreover, he alarmed
his Conservative friends by advocating a representation of the
people at the German Diet. To be sure, he did not yet wish this

representation to be elected by the people, but only appointed by the Chambers of the individual states.

Bismarck knew quite well that these views differed widely from William's. He wrote openly to Roon in the letter previously quoted, about "the legitimist direction which the personal will of the King gave to our foreign policy", and he added very shrewdly: "My belief is that nothing but a change in our 'foreign' attitude can liberate the position of the Crown in domestic matters. . . . *We are almost as vain as the French*; if we can make ourselves believe that we are respected by Foreign countries we are ready to put up with a good deal at home." And then comes one of his most characteristic sentences: "To my Sovereign I am faithful like a Vendean [*bis in die Vendée*—the most royalist part of France], *but for all the others I do not in one single drop of my blood feel the smallest obligation* to raise even a finger on their behalf. I am afraid that this way of thinking is so far removed from that of our most gracious sovereign that he will scarcely consider me a suitable adviser of the Crown."

But the King was even more suspicious of Bismarck's aims in foreign policy than of his attitude in questions of principle. He considered Bismarck a partisan of an alliance between Prussia and Napoleon. He was not the only one who suspected the Ambassador in St. Petersburg. Some journals wrote that Bismarck was in favour of the cession of the left bank of the Rhine to Napoleon in return for help to Prussia in annexing Hanover, Saxony, and the electorate of Hesse-Cassel. This rumour does not seem to have been entirely devoid of any foundation. It was repeated by men who were connected with the Prussian Foreign Office. That does not mean that Bismarck was actually willing to give these parts of Germany to Napoleon, but that he wished to tempt the Emperor with a promise of this kind and then to find a way of not delivering the goods.

Be that as it may. Certainly Bismarck considered it a grave mistake to shun Napoleon on principle. He illustrated his view with one of his striking analogies in the last letter he ever wrote to General von Gerlach: "I cannot play chess if you bar, from the outset, sixteen squares out of the sixty-four". What he wanted was a completely free chessboard, without being hampered by any considerations of principle or tradition. Some years previously, during his last days in Frankfurt, when war was clearly imminent between the Franco-Sardinian alliance and Austria, Bismarck had said to an Austrian diplomatist after a good dinner: "*Il y en a des arrangements avec Dieu, et il y en a avec le diable, et si on n'en fait pas, le diable s'en mêle*" ("There are arrangements with God, and there are arrangements with the devil, and if one avoids them, the devil interferes"). In other words: Bismarck did not care whether Napoleon III was a devil or not; but he was not, under any circumstances, prepared to spoil his own position by shunning Napoleon.

8. *Ambassador in Paris*

In March 1862 the King recalled Bismarck from St. Petersburg, but without indicating his new post. Bismarck expected to be called into the cabinet and went to Berlin. Here the internal situation was again grave. The King had, under a pretext, dissolved the Chamber and dismissed his Liberal Ministers. Roon and some other more Conservative Ministers, among them Count Bernstorff, Minister for Foreign Affairs, and von der Heydt, Minister of Finance, had retained their posts. But the election had ended with a further defeat of the government and another splendid victory for the Progressive Party. Nevertheless, the King could not yet bring himself to entrust to Bismarck a post in the ministry. He always had difficulty in making up his mind. On the other hand, Bismarck was quite willing to bide his time until the situation had been so much aggravated that the King definitely had no other way out. He only wanted to become Minister at that stage when the King would be absolutely compelled to follow him through thick and thin, as he himself put it quite bluntly some years later. Thus he first went as Prussian Ambassador to Paris.

On his way to Paris, Bismarck met, in Frankfurt, his former colleague Sir Alexander Malet, British Minister to the Diet, and talked to him quite openly about his plans. Malet wrote to London: "Bismarck is in the first place Prussian, in the second out-and-out Prussian, and in the third place German by Prussia. . . . I believe no scruples will hamper him, if the territorial aggrandisement of Prussia is at stake, which is the goal of his life and the object of his political ambition."

Bismarck remained Ambassador in Paris only a few months, most of which he actually spent away from the French capital. He paid a visit to London, where the Industrial Exhibition was then being held. One event during this visit was remarkable. He met Disraeli and made a deep impression on him. "Take care of that man," Disraeli said, "he means what he says."

Bismarck had one important conversation with Napoleon III. He gathered the impression from the Emperor's words and attitude that he would be able to rely on Napoleon's co-operation at that future time when he would be in charge of Prussian foreign policy. Napoleon, of course, believed that he himself would then direct the policy of both countries, while Bismarck was planning to use the Emperor for his purposes. He wrote to his Chief, Count Bernstorff, that the Emperor had the "most unchaste proposals of alliance on the tip of his tongue" and that he, Bismarck, had to play the rôle of Joseph to the wife of Potiphar. He could not do anything else, knowing his King's strong aversion to Napoleon, whom William considered the national enemy of Germany and Prussia.

In August Bismarck went to Biarritz, the famous French bathing place on the Atlantic coast. Here he met the Russian Princess Katherine Orloff, the young wife of the Russian Minister in Brussels. In her company he spent some of the most delightful weeks of his life. The letters he wrote from Biarritz to his wife and to his sister are most wonderful and poetical. They are full of the charms of the landscape and of this intelligent, witty, musical young woman. They remind the reader of a scene in the *Midsummer Night's Dream* and of Oberon's enchanted forest. Nobody who knows only the man of "blood and iron" would think that he was capable of writing such poetical and charming letters.

During the whole of this time Bismarck was on tenter-hooks. He was waiting for a letter or a telegram from Roon which would call him to Berlin. But the call did not come. He received letters from Roon and Bernstorff, but they were disappointing. The King was still hesitating. At last, after his return to Paris, Bismarck received, on the 18th September, a telegram from Roon: "*Periculum in mora. Dépêchez-vous*" (Delay dangerous. Make haste!). It was the pre-arranged signal. The next day Bismarck hastened to Berlin.

9. *The Appointment as Minister-President*

In Berlin, a crisis of the first order had in the meantime broken out. The government found that it could not carry the military proposals through the Chamber of Deputies without considerable concessions to the popular demands. Some Radical members of the Chamber wanted to throw out the whole new organization. But a considerable portion of the Progressives preferred a compromise. Twesten, now member for Berlin, proposed a compromise of this kind in an excellent speech in the Chamber. Its principal point was the two years' service. If the government was ready to concede this point, the greatest part of the military reorganization could be saved and a crisis of the whole state and of the constitution would be avoided.

In a constitutional state, parliament is in a position to influence the policy of the government by holding the purse-strings. Stahl, the theorist of Prussian Conservatism, always bore in mind the danger that even a Prussian parliament might be able to dislodge the monarchy from its preponderant position by this power to withhold revenue. He had, therefore, smuggled into the constitution Article 109, which laid down that existing taxes and duties should continue to be collected until they were changed by a new law. According to the then current interpretation of this article citizens had to pay taxes and duties even when the budget had not been passed by parliament. But, on the other hand, the constitution (Article 99) provided in so many words that both revenue and expenditure should be annually assessed in advance and embodied in the budget and that the budget should be fixed annually by law. A law presupposed the consent of both Houses of Parliament and the King. Any lawyer who wished to interpret this clause objectively would necessarily be driven to the conclusion that a government which spent a single penny without the consent of parliament was acting unconstitutionally. Whenever a budget had thus not been approved by parliament, the government would not be able to spend any money, although taxes would continue to flow into the coffers of the exchequer in accordance with Article 109.

Thus far the constitution seemed quite clear. But from the Greek sophists on there have always been some people who have had the talent of seeing black what everybody else sees white. The Prussian sophists said: "A budget becomes law if (1) the second chamber, the Chamber of Deputies, (2) the upper house (the Herrenhaus), (3) the King agree. If one of these three bodies does not agree there is no budget." A normal mind would draw the conclusion that in that case no money could be spent. But the Prussian sophists negatived this statement and claimed that there was "a gap" (*eine Lücke*) in the constitution; the state, however, had to live; therefore the government could spend what it thought justified in the interests of the state. That was the notorious *Lückentheorie* (the theory of the constitutional gap). As the Upper House consisted of an overwhelming majority of the most reactionary Junkers, it was always possible to bring this gap into being if the Chamber of Deputies voted a budget which the government did not like.

This theory was not only a sophism. The Ministers themselves, who propagated it in their press, knew quite well that it was a sophism which could not hold water. That is evident from a memorandum they put before the King in those critical days. Here they said quite openly and distinctly that a rejection of the budget by the Chamber of Deputies would deprive the government of the constitutional basis of administration; they would act unconstitutionally if they tried to spend revenue against the explicit vote of the Chamber. This memorandum was signed by every member of the cabinet, including Roon.

The King was extremely angry about this memorandum and tried to argue with his Ministers. But at first they stuck to their guns.

The precariousness of the governmental position became apparent during the first divisions in the Chamber of Deputies. One defeat of the government followed the other. Then suddenly, on the morning of 17th September, Roon rose in the Chamber to declare in the name of the whole cabinet that the government did not by any means want a conflict and that Twesten's motion could be taken as the basis of a possible compromise, provided that the Chamber was ready to give some "compensations".

That was not much. But it was enough to change the feeling of the House in a moment. Without any further ado the House adjourned to give the government the opportunity to come to an understanding with the Chamber in a secret session of the budget committee. So eager for a compromise was this Progressive Party, which the King considered revolutionary, and against which his military advisers were secretly preparing violent measures!

But all hopes were at once destroyed by the King. He did not listen to his Ministers, who advised him to concede biennial service; he only heard the voices of his military advisers, whose feelings were described by a very moderate man in these words: "The military party thirsts for a conflict as the hart thirsteth for water". The King held a Council in the evening of that 17th September on the morning of which Roon had proclaimed the readiness of the government for a compromise. The Minister for Foreign Affairs, Bernstorff, and the Finance Minister, von der Heydt, advised the King on the lines of the common memorandum of the cabinet. They were furious when Roon suddenly changed front and declared to the King that he was ready to carry on the government without a budget. It was this quite unexpected statement on the part of Roon which made the conflict between King and parliament inevitable. And Roon cannot have been in any doubt that by doing so he broke his oath of allegiance to the constitution. But he did not allow that to trouble him. He knew there was a man who was equal to the task of governing Prussia without any constitutional scruples. The moment the Council had come to an end Roon sent Bismarck the telegram quoted, urging his immediate appearance on the scene of the crisis.

Of course the deputies were very angry when Roon told them not merely that the government was not prepared to make any concessions but that he had never offered any. The inevitable consequence was the throwing out of the military budget by the Chamber. Now the conflict had broken out openly.

Before Bismarck arrived in Berlin a last effort to bring the King to a compromise was made by the Crown Prince. The Prince was liberal, like his whole generation, and he was anxious to guard the young constitutional life of his future kingdom against a convulsion, the consequences of which could not be foreseen. Furthermore, he had no doubt that a military service of two years was quite sufficient. The King was not able to refute his arguments. But he laid before him a document in which he abdicated in the Prince's favour and asked him to signify his assent by signing it. The Prince firmly declined. In spite of all differences of opinion he loved his father and was by no means prepared to place the crown on his own head during his father's lifetime, as Shakespeare's Prince Hal had done with the crown of Henry IV.

Was the way now open to Bismarck? The Crown Prince could not possibly have thought so. For the King told him he would not call Bismarck, whatever might happen. No doubt he acted under the influence of the Queen, who considered Bismarck her mortal enemy. But three days later the Queen was defeated and Bismarck was Minister.

The historic audience of the 22nd September 1862 is told in his inimitable way by Bismarck himself in the eleventh chapter of his *Reflections and Recollections.* The tale is well worth reading, although it is not accurate. The essential point was that the King now had no other way open than to entrust the government to the only man who was willing, as well as able, to defy parliament, and who did not care whether the constitution was being broken or not. Bismarck impressed the King deeply with his absolute fearlessness, his stern energy, and his unconditional willingness to serve him as a liege man serves his feudal lord. When the audience was over it was not only certain that Bismarck would become Prime Minister and Minister for Foreign Affairs, but also that he would be unhampered by any programme such as the King had at first wished to propose.

There is no need to question Bismarck's genuine wish to be a faithful servant of his King. But he knew William too accurately, with all his limitations and weaknesses, not to be certain that he would lead the King and not be led by him. And he knew in his heart of hearts that he was destined to lead the King to a goal of which William did not even dream. While promising William to follow him, Bismarck was convinced that the King would be compelled to follow him through thick and thin, and that thus his conditions for taking office would be fulfilled.

Twenty-four years before, in September 1838, Bismarck, then a youth of twenty-three years, had written: "I want to make only that music which I myself like, or no music at all". Now, in September 1862, he was in a position to lead the orchestra and to make that music which *he* liked. That music was heard through twenty-eight years by Prussia, by Germany, nay, by the whole of Europe.

CHAPTER II

THE STRUGGLE AGAINST PARLIAMENT AND AUSTRIA

A. TO THE GASTEIN CONVENTION

1. *The Minister-President's First Steps*

BISMARCK'S appointment made a great but on the whole a very unfavourable impression. The London *Spectator* called him the most outspoken Junker who had ever ruled in Prussia, and a man of strong but limited understanding. The German, and particularly the Prussian, Liberals felt that a great struggle was ahead. One of the leaders of the Progressive Party wrote: "Bismarck, that is to say: government without budget, rule by the sword in home affairs, and war in foreign affairs. I consider him the most dangerous Minister for Prussia's liberty and happiness." This expressed the popular feeling rather accurately. In the theatres, every malicious allusion to the King was received with a storm of applause.

Bismarck's first task was to form his cabinet. The Foreign Minister, Count Bernstorff, and the Minister of Finance, von der Heydt, again declined to govern unconstitutionally without a budget and retired from the government. At first Bismarck tried to make contact with moderate Liberals. For instance, he asked Twesten, the mover of the compromise amendment, to see him. Bismarck did not have strong views about the length of military service. For his own person he would have accepted the two years' period; but as the King was opposed to it there was nothing he was able to offer to Twesten. So the interview came to nothing. It is remarkable, anyhow, for the rather startling and indiscreet way in which Bismarck talked to this member of the Opposition about the King who just had appointed him. He compared the King with a horse that shied at every new object and became restive and unmanageable if one tried force, but would get accustomed to it little by little.

Bismarck never had the serious intention of taking a Liberal into his cabinet. As a matter of fact, he composed it of reactionary officials who had no other merit than their conservative opinions and their noble birth. In later years Bismarck spoke of most of them in the most depreciating and disdainful way. The Finance Minister, von Bodelschwingh, he calls "a liar", and the Agricultural Minister, von Selchow, an ass (*Rindvieh*). Only the Minister of the Interior, Graf Eulenburg, was a man of gifts, though idle and frivolous. However insignificant these Junkers were, they met the two requirements for which Bismarck wanted Ministers: they were all ready to help him to crush the Opposition and to let him make his foreign policy without putting any obstacles in his way.

In parliament, Bismarck began his activities by withdrawing the budget for the next year. Asked in the committee of the House what he proposed to do next, he made a speech which caused the greatest sensation. He took from his pocket-book an olive-branch—it was the olive-branch Katherine Orloff had given him when they parted in Avignon—showed it to the members of the committee with the words that it had been his intention to offer it to the House as a token of peace, but that he had now reluctantly come to the conclusion that it was still too early. He then spoke about Prussia's present situation and future task. Germany did not look, he said, to the liberalism of Prussia but to her power. Unfortunately, her frontiers were unfavourable to a healthy state. The great questions of the time could not be solved by speeches and majority votes—that was the great mistake of 1848 and 1849—but by *blood and iron*.

The sensation these startling sentences made was the very reverse of favourable. Even Roon grew angry about these "racy excursions", which did not help in any way. The historian Heinrich von Treitschke, later the most outspoken herald of Bismarck, raged about the ridiculous vulgarity of this shallow Junker boasting of the blood and iron with which he wanted to subjugate Germany. The King was not gratified either. He was in Baden at the time in the company of the Queen, their daughter, the Grand Duchess of Baden, and their son-in-law, the Grand Duke. Bismarck knew that none of them was his friend, and he was afraid that they would turn his words against him. To win back the King, he met him in

the train at the last station before Berlin, Jüterbog. Of this episode
Bismarck has given a masterly description in his *Recollections*
(chapter 12).

Whatever the King may have thought about Bismarck's utterances, he knew that he was indispensable for dealing with the
Chamber. In the great debate which arose there, and in which
moderate and radical members alike refuted Bismarck's constitutional arguments, one of the moderate speakers, the famous
lawyer, Professor Gneist, emphasized the point of principle. He
warned the Minister to respect an elementary quality of the German
people: its belief in a firm moral and legal order as the last and
decisive factor in the history of states. Gneist was right. Such was
then, indeed, the feeling of the most important section of the
Prussian people. The great question was whether this belief in the
decisive power of the legal and moral order would be justified by
events.

At first, developments took quite the opposite turn. The budget
voted by the Chamber of Deputies was thrown out by the feudal
Chamber of Seigneurs (Herrenhaus) and the government ruled
without a budget. It continued to collect taxes and duties and to
spend the collected money for military purposes quite arbitrarily.
As it was a period of flourishing economic life, the yield of the
taxes increased, so that the government was not embarrassed owing
to want of money. The Chamber was unable to stop this process.
It lacked the legal means either to stop the collection of the taxes
or to impeach the government. The constitution declared that the
Ministers were responsible, but it did not open a way for their
impeachment if they broke the constitution. Therefore, the power
of the Chamber of Deputies was weak. Foreign critics failed to
understand this position. English journals, for instance, often ascribed
to lack of firmness in the Opposition what was, in fact, a weakness
in its constitutional power.

How deeply Bismarck's methods offended the sense of justice of
the German people came to light in the debate of the Chamber of
Deputies on the address in January 1863. The official speaker of the
committee of the House was the famous historian, Heinrich von
Sybel, the same historian who under the auspices of Bismarck afterwards wrote his *History of the Foundation of the German Empire by*

William I. He was not at all a Radical, but a warm admirer of Prussia and her history. Sybel said: "The Ministers and the majority of this House speak a different language; their thoughts are ruled by a different logic and their actions by different moral laws". But the climax of the debate came when Bismarck bluntly told the House: "If a compromise cannot be arrived at and a conflict arises, then the conflict becomes a question of power. Whoever has the power, then acts according to his opinion." It was not a Radical but the moderate Count Schwerin, a former Minister of King William during the "New Era", who answered with these words: "The sentence in which the speech of the Prime Minister culminated: that 'Might before Right', that 'you may talk as you like, we have the power and will therefore force through our theory'—this is not a sentence which can support the dynasty of Prussia in the long run. The sentence on which the greatness of our dynasty and of our country rests, and the reverence which Prussia's sovereigns have enjoyed and will enjoy for ever and ever, is quite the reverse: 'Right before Might'." These words made a deep impression, and Count Schwerin was hailed as the defender of the good old Prussian tradition.

Bismarck defied the Chamber, as the young William Pitt, in 1783, defied Charles Fox and the majority of the House of Commons. Both relied on their King. But there was a very important difference. Pitt knew that the voters, or those who directed the voters, were on his side, that he only had to bide his time to dissolve parliament in order to get a favourable majority. Bismarck knew that the people was even more passionately against him than the Chamber. Time and again he dissolved the Chamber: the voters always elected the same majority. All the vehement and often illegal pressure of the government did not succeed in making them vote for govermental candidates. The Prussian Opposition in the years 1862–1866 is, indeed, the only one in the whole history of constitutional Germany which could effectively depend upon their voters. In later years, 1878, 1887, 1893, 1907, a dissolution always gave the government the majority it wanted, because enough voters deserted the oppositional deputies. Only in the time of the Prussian constitutional conflict did they stick invariably to their guns. True, they voted according to the three-classes-suffrage, and the middle-class voters of the two first classes decided the election. But there can be no doubt that the majority of the workers in the third class sympathized fully with them.

2. The Order against the Press, and the Opposition of the Crown Prince

A government that encroaches on the constitution at one point, cannot stop there. It is forced by circumstances and by its own action from one illegality to another. The next point of attack was the freedom of the press, guaranteed by the constitution. The great majority of the newspapers was Liberal and supported the Opposition energetically. Bismarck tried to suppress them by an order of the King in June 1863, which empowered the police to suppress oppositional papers. By dissolving the Chamber he managed to silence the press during the election. Nevertheless, the Opposition was again victorious at the polls and the Order had to be cancelled after having been in force for five months.

This royal order against the press had a startling effect in an unexpected quarter. The heir to the throne, the Crown Prince, openly declared his opposition to it. The Crown Prince and his wife, Victoria, did not by any means approve of Bismarck's methods. They objected to his encroachments on the constitution and were afraid that they would open an insuperable gulf between the Prussian people and the dynasty. The Prince warned the King against a breach of the constitution. The King had ordered him to attend the councils when he himself presided (*Kronrat*). But the decision to make the royal order against the press had been made when the Prince was absent. He was on a tour of military inspection in the eastern provinces of the monarchy, when he suddenly learnt of the order for the first time by its publication in the press. On the advice of Princess Victoria, who accompanied him, and of the Liberal Chief Burgomaster of Danzig, Winter, he declared, answering a speech by Winter in the Danzig Town Hall: "I did not know anything of this Order beforehand. I was absent. I am not one of those who advised it."

These words inevitably caused a tremendous sensation. The Prussian people was deeply moved by the open opposition of the heir to the throne; the King, on the other hand, was extremely angry and wrote his son a furious letter treating him, as Victoria wrote to her mother, like a little child. Victoria's letters, published by Sir Frederick Ponsonby in the *Letters of the Empress Frederick* and partly in the Second Series of the *Letters of Queen Victoria*, show the immensely difficult position in which the Crown Prince and his wife then found themselves. The Danzig episode became a decisive event in their lives. Bismarck never either forgot or forgave this opposition. Thus began the isolation of the princely couple, which from that time onwards cast a shadow over their lives. Bismarck's own point of view is given in his correspondence with the King, published in chapter 16 of *Reflections and Recollections*. His marginal notes on the memorandum of the Prince state his case in a masterly manner. He based his arguments on the thesis that a crown prince did not have any official "status" and was therefore not entitled to play a political rôle and to make opposition to his father. But what would Bismarck himself have done if he had had a king whose policy he disliked, and a crown prince who supported him—in other words, if Frederick III had come to the throne, not struck down by his terrible and mortal malady but in full strength, and if his reign had lasted longer than merely ninety-nine short days? Fate has spared Bismarck this test. But whoever knows the story of those tragic ninety-nine days of 1888 will doubt whether Bismarck would have acted according to his doctrine of 1863.

3. *Conflicts with Austria*

While the constitutional struggle was in progress Bismarck's thoughts were primarily concerned with the problems of the foreign, especially the German, policy, where his adversary, Austria, was at this very time rather active.

After the defeat in Italy the Habsburg Monarchy tried to return to constitutionalism. In February 1861 a new constitution was promulgated, giving a central parliament to the whole monarchy. In this parliament the German Liberals were in the ascendancy. The constitution was the work of the Minister Anton von Schmerling, who in the year 1848 had been a leading member of the Austrian

Party at the Frankfurt Assembly and a Minister of the Reich. He looked upon Austria's return to constitutionalism as a means of preserving Austria's hegemony in Germany. Unfortunately, German affairs did not belong to his department but to that of the Foreign Minister, Baron von Rechberg. While Schmerling was considered a Liberal, Rechberg called himself a Conservative statesman and a pupil of Metternich. These two Ministers were not likely to establish a harmonious collaboration. Rechberg had been Bismarck's colleague in Frankfurt, where he had presided over the Diet; he had come to know Bismarck intimately and had been greatly impressed by his ability, his energy, and his absolute ruthlessness. More than that, he was afraid of him. Before Bismarck became Minister, Rechberg talked of this "terrible" Bismarck, who was capable of taking off his coat and himself ascending the barricade. He shuddered when Bismarck's mere name was mentioned. Now this "terrible" man was the leading Minister of Prussia. What could Rechberg do to avoid his antagonism?

But antagonism between Prussia and Austria was, in fact, unavoidable. The German people had been convinced, ever since Villafranca, that a reform of the German Confederation was bound to come. The first statesman to propose a project of reform was the Minister of the King of Saxony, Baron Beust, a highly clever although very vain man. He advised the Imperial court in Vienna to bring about a conservative reform of the Confederation as quickly as possible while Prussia was handicapped by the weakness of its government. Beust himself worked out a detailed proposal. But it failed. A few months later, shortly before Bismarck's rise to power, Vienna proposed another project, supported by the middle states. To satisfy the demands of the population, the laws covering certain important matters, for instance, the course of procedure in civil cases, were to be unified for the whole of Germany. The most important point of this proposal was that delegates of the Chambers of the individual states were to be called together to deliberate on these laws. This would have been the beginning of a representation of the German people inside the Confederation, although only an indirect one. Bismarck, who just at that moment became Prussian Prime Minister, had suggested the same form of representation to the Prince Regent some years ago. But now he would have nothing of it, for he was afraid that this reform would prolong the existence of the Confederation and strengthen the influence of Austria. He would allow neither the one nor the other, for he aimed at the overthrow of the Confederation. He was therefore determined to defeat this reform by all the means at his disposal, and he succeeded.

In the course of the negotiations on this Austrian project, Bismarck had two interviews which should have shown the Austrians what they had to expect from the new Prussian Prime Minister. In his conversation with the Austrian Minister in Berlin, Count Karolyi, Bismarck did not mince his words in the least. Although he found no difficulty in evading the truth, if that served his purpose, he was not on principle averse to telling the truth, as the diplomatists of the old school were. He knew that in certain situations bluntness was the best method. Thus, he told the Austrian envoy candidly that the relations between Austria and Prussia were of such a nature that they would in the end lead to war, if they were not improved soon. What could be done to avoid this armed conflict? The Habsburg Monarchy should *move the centre of its gravity eastwards*, to Hungary. This would have meant the surrender of Austria's position in Germany, particularly in the northern part of Germany, which Prussia considered her natural sphere of influence. If the Habsburg Monarchy followed this advice, Prussia would become its faithful ally. But if not—catastrophe would lie ahead.

It was impossible to speak more openly and more threateningly. Had a true statesman directed Austria's foreign policy he would either have followed Bismarck's advice or prepared for war. But Rechberg did neither the one nor the other.

The other interview of Bismarck's was with Count Thun, who had once been his Austrian colleague at Frankfurt and was now Austrian Ambassador to Russia. He came to Berlin to talk things over with his former colleague and to try and reach a compromise. Bismarck was again quite frank and revealed to the Austrian diplomatist what he thought about the sanctity of international treaties. *Pacta sunt servanda* (Treaties are to be kept) is the foundation of International Law. Bismarck, however, told Thun: "Austria and Prussia are states which are too great to be bound by the text of a treaty. They can be guided only by their interests and their convenience. If any treaty should be in the way of these interests and convenience, that treaty must be broken."

Are not here the germs of that doctrine which in a later period was summed up in the words "a scrap of paper"?

Rechberg who, as a pupil of Metternich, was brought up to respect international treaties deeply, made two big exclamation marks on the margin of Thun's report when he read this Macchiavellian profession of Bismarck. But that was all he did.

The rupture between the two German Powers was avoided because the Frankfurt Diet outvoted the Austrian proposal by a small majority. When the votes were taken, the Prussian envoy read a very strong declaration by Bismarck, which contained an astonishing sentence. To outbid the Austrian proposal of delegations from the Chambers of the individual states, Bismarck declared bluntly: "To give the German people its due influence in their common affairs it must have a representation directly elected by the whole people". This was a truly revolutionary proposal. Here Bismarck adopted the fundamental idea of the Revolution of 1848, expressed by the Frankfurt parliament, and the programme of the National-Verein. Made by any other statesman it would have had a tremendous effect. But nobody believed that Bismarck meant it in earnest. How could the dictatorial Junker who deprived the Prussian parliament of its constitutional rights be the champion of a popular German parliament?

The sanctity of treaties was also at stake in the other dispute with Austria with which Bismarck had to deal when he came to power. It concerned a question of the greatest economic importance.

European commercial policy had, in 1860, entered a new phase with the commercial treaty between France and Great Britain, the common work of Napoleon III, Cobden, and the British Chancellor of the Exchequer, Gladstone. It was the greatest triumph of the policy of Free Trade. Following the same idea, Napoleon concluded in 1862 a commercial treaty with France's eastern neighbour, Prussia. But in matters of tariffs and commerce Prussia was not an entirely independent unit. She was a member, and furthermore the leading member, of the German Zollverein (Customs Union), which enforced on its members a common tariff policy. The Franco-Prussian Commercial Treaty could take effect only after it had been adopted by the Zollverein, and many of its members were by no means willing to do so.

Austria was not a member of the Zollverein, which was founded by Prussia in the 'thirties against Austrian wishes and interests. But in the years after the Revolution of 1848, a far-seeing Austrian statesman, Bruck, the Minister of Commerce, had propagated the great idea of a Central-European Customs Union, comprising all the countries from the North Sea to the Adriatic Sea, from Hamburg to Trieste. This great plan was frustrated by Prussian resistance. The only concession Austria had obtained was a clause in the Austro-Prussian Commercial Treaty of 1853, by which Prussia promised Austria that she would enter into negotiations about a commercial union before the Prussian treaty with the other members of the Zollverein expired, that was to say, before the end of the year 1865.

Austria considered Prussia's treaty with France a breach of this obligation, because it made its fulfilment impossible. This view was correct. The curious thing was that the leader of Prussia's commercial policy, Rudolf Delbrück, later Bismarck's most important assistant as President of the Imperial Chancery, in his heart agreed with the Austrian point of view. He confessed in a secret memorandum that the treaty with France made a union with Austria impossible and was therefore a breach of the clause under discussion. Nevertheless, he supported the treaty with the interesting argument that no state could sacrifice its vital interests to a promise wrung from it by pressure some years previously. This argument is very similar to that of Bismarck against the sanctity of treaties. But Delbrück, who had been brought up in the good old tradition of the Prussian Civil Service, still had some scruples about the new doctrine of *Staats-Raison* (*raison d'état*) overriding all other obligations. Bismarck, of course, lacked all such scruples. He was firmly bent on carrying through the treaty with France by all the means at his disposal, and compelled the other members of the Customs Union to accept it. In this endeavour he had the firm support of the majority of the Chamber of Deputies for economic as well as for national reasons. The Prussian Liberals were Free Traders, and they considered the Customs Union as a pillar of Prussian influence in Germany.

4. *The Polish Insurrection of 1863*

One motive for Bismarck's decision to maintain the commercial treaty with France was his desire to be on good terms with the Emperor Napoleon. But in the spring of the year 1863 another question of foreign policy brought him into sharp antagonism with him. This was the Polish question. It arose as a result of the Polish insurrection against Czarist rule.

Poland then belonged to the three Powers, Russia, Austria, and Prussia, which had seized it by the three partitions of the eighteenth century. Western Europe looked upon these partitions as a terrible blot on modern history. The three Eastern Powers, however, considered partition justified on the grounds that the Poles were incapable of maintaining a strong, orderly government. Nevertheless there was, even among the German people, a feeling of sympathy with the unfortunate, subjugated Poles. But none of these sentiments had the slightest influence on Bismarck. He considered the whole Polish question exclusively from the point of view of the power of the Prussian state. It cannot be doubted that this power would have been weakened considerably by a secession of its Polish provinces. But he went further. He considered the Poles the enemies of Prussia, against whom any method of suppression was justified in the interest of the state. In a letter to his sister, written from Petersburg in 1861, Bismarck exclaimed: "Strike the Poles in such a way that they will despair of their lives; I have every sympathy with their situation, but if we want to exist we cannot do anything else than *exterminate* them. The wolf, too, is not responsible for being what God has made it, but we kill it, nevertheless, if we can." In the same year he rejected in a letter to his Minister the criticism the Prussian Consul in Warsaw had made of the brutality of the Cossacks against the Poles. "Brutality and despotism is here equivalent to severity. As things stand at Warsaw, every blow which fails to come home is a pity. Every success of the Polish national movement is a defeat for Prussia. We cannot conduct the fight against this element according to the rules of civil justice but only according to the rules of war."

When Bismarck wrote these lines, which amounted to an outspoken declaration of war against the Poles, there had not been any

Polish resistance against the Prussian government. The insurrection of 1863, too, was confined to Russian territory, as it was solely caused by acts of the Czarist régime. It never touched Prussian territory. Nevertheless, immediately after the outbreak of the insurrection Bismarck mobilized the Prussian regiments in the Eastern provinces and sent one of the aide-de-camps of the King, General von Alvensleben, a diehard reactionary of the *Kreuz-Zeitung* type, to Petersburg to tell the Russian court that the court of Berlin considered itself its ally against a common enemy. Following his instructions, Alvensleben concluded a convention in Petersburg by which both governments promised each other assistance for crushing the insurrection, and each government allowed the troops of the other to cross the common frontier in pursuit of fugitive Polish insurgents. As everything was quiet in Prussia there was no reason why Prussian troops should have to cross the Russian frontier. The convention thus meant only that Russian troops would have the right to ignore the Prussian frontier in order to pursue fugitive Polish subjects of the Czar.

The convention was secret, but Bismarck spoke about it quite frankly to a Prussian deputy, the member for Danzig, and even exaggerated its scope, insinuating that the convention entitled Prussian troops to march as far as Warsaw. Of course these indiscretions spread quickly. There was a general irritation about the convention in Western Europe, where sympathy with the Poles was strong. The English Ambassador in Berlin, Sir Andrew Buchanan, told Bismarck that Europe would not tolerate a Prussian occupation of Poland. Bismarck gave the characteristic reply: "Who is Europe?" "Several great nations", answered Buchanan. The *Spectator* thundered against the new "Unholy Alliance" and compared Bismarck, not with Strafford, whom it considered a better man, but with Lord Tyrconnel, the instigator of James II's evil deeds. In France, public opinion had been deeply stirred, and Napoleon told the Prussian Ambassador that he regretted the convention. "*Il la regrette* is always unpleasant", wrote King William, perplexed by this general opposition.

The opposition in the Chamber of Deputies was very outspoken, and Bismarck did his best to stir it up even further. He declined point blank to answer an interpellation of the House asking for information about the substance of the convention. " There is a convention which may lead our children into war", cried old Waldeck, one of the leaders of the Opposition, "and the Minister says, 'I refuse to lay it before you'." The Opposition certainly did not want Prussia to give up her Polish provinces, or demand that the Prussian government should be partial to the insurgents. But it was strongly opposed to the government's partiality for the Czarist government and demanded strict neutrality. It believed that the principles of humanity should not be neglected even in international affairs. This conception was the focal point of German Liberal opinion and the reason for its opposition to Bismarck and his doctrine of power politics. How completely Bismarck defeated this humanitarian conception became apparent about twenty years later. In the year 1885 he expelled from Prussian territory 30,000 Polish inhabitants who happened to be Russian or Austrian subjects, the great majority of whom were quite peaceful men and women who had been living for many years, even decades, in Prussia. It was a measure of unheard-of cruelty. But the Prussian Chamber of Deputies approved it explicitly by a great majority and the National Liberals were among this majority. Only the Progressive Radicals remained true to the old Liberal tradition.

The Alvensleben Convention has for a long time been praised as a master-stroke of Bismarck's policy, through which he gained Russian assistance in the critical years 1886–1871. Bismarck himself did all he could in his speeches and writings to further this view. Now, after the opening of the archives, it is clear that it was nothing of the kind. The American historian, Professor Lord, has given a much more realistic version. The convention involved Bismarck in many troubles, not only with the Western Powers but also with Gortchakoff, who never liked it.

Nevertheless, it is true that the Polish insurrection caused a re-grouping of the European Powers, which facilitated Bismarck's task considerably. France, Great Britain, and Austria presented a joint note to the Russian government asking for some concessions to the Polish population. Bismarck refused the invitation to take part in this diplomatic pressure. He was not in the least interested in reforms of this kind and merely considered the question from the point of view of Prussian interests. It was to Prussia's advantage only to show the Czar that Prussia was his friend, while other Powers joined hands against him. The consequence was a diplomatic defeat of the three Powers and a ruthless suppression of the Polish insurrection.

Two events of this diplomatic campaign are particularly important. Throughout his reign Napoleon III endeavoured in his foreign policy always to have at least one ally. He had tried to arrive at an understanding with Russia, but this necessarily came to an end when he entered into the Polish controversy. Of the two German Powers, Prussia was nearer to his heart. He considered it the more progressive Power. As the champion of the principle of nationality he disliked Austria, whose very existence was incompatible with this idea. But now, when Bismarck led Prussia into the Russian camp, Napoleon turned to Austria and offered her an alliance. He wrote to Francis Joseph that this alliance would put an end to present uncertainties and future dangers. But Austria declined the offer. Rechberg stated that with an alliance of this kind the risk would be certain but the advantage problematic. But which other policy was less risky for Austria? Rechberg did not know. He only hoped still to come to an understanding with Prussia, although Bismarck had warned him clearly enough. But Rechberg was a Conservative and considered Bismarck a fellow-Conservative. He was simple-minded enough to write to Bismarck "that all the Conservatives of Europe must join together to fight revolution and to defend the legitimate structure of Europe as a whole". How grimly Bismarck may have smiled in reading these naïve utterances of his former colleague in Frankfurt! The "legitimate structure of Europe" was the situation created by the treaties of Vienna in 1815. But it was exactly this settlement which Bismarck was determined to destroy.

The other proposal of alliance was made to Prussia by Czar Alexander II in June 1863. Bismarck himself first revealed this proposal twenty-five years later in a speech to the Prussian Chamber in which he defended his Polish policy. But he then gave quite a misleading version, which he repeated and amplified in his *Reminiscences*. He told the world that the Czar had offered his assistance to Prussia against Austria to set up a new régime in Germany, but that he and King William had declined it, as they were activated by national German motives, because they abhorred the idea of a foreign Power interfering in German affairs. This version is an example of Bismarck's tendency in later years to present the work of his whole life from a national German point of view. But the documents, which have been published in the meantime, show this incident in quite a different light. What the Czar offered to Prussia was not an alliance against Austria but an alliance against Napoleon III, to be composed by Russia, Prussia, and Austria; in other words, a revival of the old Holy Alliance. Bismarck was certainly right in declining this offer and very clever in the way in which he disguised his refusal under a cloak of sham counter-proposals. But there was no trace of any national and German motives. His outlook was governed exclusively by a very shrewd and accurate calculation of the advantages and disadvantages for Prussia from the point of view of power politics. Against the interference of foreign Powers in German affairs he had not the least scruples, provided it was directed and regulated by himself. Later developments make this evident.

But both these proposals and their rejection show up the difference between Rechberg's and Bismarck's statesmanship. Rechberg rejected the French offer from bias and from lack of decision. He did not know what to do, and therefore he did not do anything. Bismarck knew exactly what he wanted to do, and for this reason he avoided all entanglements which would restrict his freedom of action.

5. The Congress of the German Princes in Frankfurt

Short-sighted as the Austrian politicians were, they could not fail to see that the constitution of the German Confederation was utterly inadequate and that a solution of the German problem was urgent. Something had to be done to satisfy the desire of the German people for a stronger and more efficient central power and for its participation in the general direction of affairs. Things could not possibly remain as they were, and if the presiding Power, Austria, did not take the initiative, it would come either from the Prussian government or from the people itself, neither course appealing very much to the court of Vienna. Therefore the Emperor and his advisers, Schmerling and Rechberg, resolved to take the initiative.

A great deal of work was done during these months in the German

Chancery of the Austrian government and by various politicians who helped voluntarily in the effort to solve this most difficult problem. Most of them were Roman Catholics who feared the ascendancy of the Protestant Prussian Monarchy. They were not Austrians by birth but came from the middle states of the south-west. Thus, the head of the German Chancery in Vienna, Baron von Biegeleben, was born in Hesse-Darmstadt. He was easily the best expert of the Austrian government for German affairs and accordingly carried great weight. He is the author of most of the dispatches which the Hofburg sent to Berlin; most of them were very well written. He was deeply suspicious of Prussian ambition and hoped to frustrate it by establishing a co-operation of the Austrian court with the courts of the middle states.

All these men were agreed on a conservative reform of the Con-federation, *i.e.* a reform which did not go the whole length of popular demands, either with regard to representation of the people or to unification. They wanted to conserve as much as possible of the sovereign powers of the individual confederated states. Their aim was not a unified German state, but a reformed Confederation.

This conservative reform failed. For this reason historians have treated it disdainfully. The unification which was achieved in the end went so much further that a reform of the Confederation which stopped half - way appeared pusillanimous and still - born. But success is not the only criterion for judgment. In spite of their failure the German patriotism of these men who planned a con-servative reform cannot be doubted. There was one theorist who never ceased teaching that federalism and not unification was the natural way of life for the German people—Constantin Frantz. During his lifetime he was one who cried in the wilderness. Long after his death, when Bismarck's Empire had been defeated, attention was drawn to this solitary and forgotten writer who was full of ideas, though no less full of oddities.

The two principal innovations which Austria wanted to propose were a Directorate invested with the executive power, and an Assembly of Delegates. The directorate was to be composed of six members, among them the Emperor and the Kings of Prussia and Bavaria. The Assembly of Delegates should be the representa-tion of the German people. But they were to be elected indirectly by the Chambers of the individual states, *e.g.* seventy-five by the Austrian Reichsrat and seventy-five by the Prussian parliament. The method proposed for putting this Austrian project into practice was a congress of all the German princes (Deutscher Fürstentag), to be held at Frankfurt-am-Main. The Emperor invited each prince personally, and he himself wanted to preside over it. There was no doubt that the great majority of the princes would be happy to accept this invitation of the Emperor. There was, however, one vital hurdle to be overcome. It was still uncertain whether the Prussian King would participate. King William, at this time, was taking the waters at Gastein, on Austrian territory. On the advice of his Ministers, Francis Joseph decided to pay the King a personal visit and to present his invitation personally. This seemed to be the most polite way and the one which promised the best chance of success.

But the King was not alone at Gastein. Bismarck was in his company. He wanted to be near the King as much as possible in order to prevent the monarch from being subjected to influences opposed to his policy. Indeed, there can be no doubt that William would have accepted the invitation if he had been alone and left to his own counsel. After having talked at first between themselves, Francis Joseph wired to Vienna: "King not yet decided, but seems favourable. I think he will come to Frankfurt." William did not yet like "blood and iron" and did not object to a peaceful reform. But then Bismarck saw his King. He was, from the first moment, firmly resolved not to allow him to go to Frankfurt. He was afraid that William, surrounded by a galaxy of princes, would be willing to collaborate and to help. But the success of the "Princes' Conference" would not only strengthen Austria's prestige but infuse new life into the Confederation. Perhaps the German people would be willing to accept this reform, at least as an instalment, and then the initiative in future development would pass to the new organs of the Confederation, particularly to the proposed Assembly of Delegates. Whatever might be the outcome of this development, it would certainly not be the exclusion of Austria and the indisputable ascendancy of Prussia. The only way to make a development of this kind impossible was to stop it at the beginning, that is to say, to wreck the Congress of Princes by preventing the attendance of the King of Prussia. He had no doubt that the congress would collapse if William were not present. His difficulty was that he could not tell the King his real arguments. William would have repudiated them with indignation. So Bismarck turned to his favourite method: to assume the rôle of the injured. He tried to persuade the King that the Emperor had insulted him by inviting him, without any preparation, a few days before the date fixed for the opening of the congress. This was not easy. Bismarck had to strain all his powers to persuade the King to decline the invitation. But Bismarck was afraid that the King might change his mind on his return to Baden, when he would be under the influence of the Queen. He therefore accompanied him to Baden so as to maintain his personal ascendancy over his sovereign. This proved to be a very necessary precaution. For as soon as the Congress of Princes had assembled at Frankfurt, it sent one of the crowned heads to Baden in order to repeat the invitation in the name of all of them. This was King Johann of Saxony, a much-respected man of the highest culture, famous as the translator of Dante's *Divine Comedy* into German verse.

King William, who called Johann his friend, felt unable to reject an invitation of thirty princes conveyed by a king as messenger and postillion. But again Bismarck brought all his energy to bear on him. It was a hard and exciting struggle. Finally, William was seized by a crying-fit; and when Bismarck returned to his room after having carried his point, his nerves were so much on edge that he snatched a large bowl and dashed it to the ground, and then he cried that the victory was his and the invitation definitely declined.

Victory had indeed been won. The absence of the King of Prussia made the Congress of Princes a hopeless affair. Although the Emperor Francis Joseph himself presided over the congress with surprising skill and the princes did their best to come to an agreement, and although an agreement was reached which found favour with a strong section of the German people—no reform was, of course, possible if Prussia abstained. Rechberg had neither the capacity nor the will to carry through the policy of the princes' congress against Prussian opposition, although Beust and Biegeleben did their best to persuade him to take some energetic action. He did not like Austria's position in the company of middle and small states and opposed to the Great Power, Prussia. Thus nothing was done, and things were, after the congress, left very much as they had been before.

Bismarck did, of course, have to justify his wrecking of the congress by a declaration of Prussian policy. This was done in a report of the Prussian government to the King, of 15th September. Its most important point, which created an enormous sensation, was the demand for a *true national representation elected directly by the whole German people*. After Austria had put forward the idea of a German parliament elected indirectly by the Chambers of the individual Federate States, Bismarck now felt compelled to propose a more democratic institution. It was, of course, easy to expose the contrast between this democratic demand for Germany and his autocratic governmental practice in Prussia. The Prussian voters, indeed, showed in the next election a few weeks later that they had not been led astray by the apparent change of front of their Prime Minister. But many observers, even among his strongest opponents, now realized how reckless and unfettered by any doctrine this Herr von Bismarck could be in choosing the means for his ends. The *Frankfurter Zeitung*, a vehement opponent of Bismarck, could not help paying tribute to something like genius in the adroitness with which he used the dominant ideas of the time for his own purposes.

Bismarck certainly was not guilty of overstatement when he told the Austrian Ambassador that the reform of the Confederation now had one foot in its grave. Only a few years more and not only the reform but the Confederation itself were dead and buried.

A few weeks after the Congress of Princes another congress was the topic of conversation and negotiation. On the 5th November 1863 the Emperor Napoleon III invited the European sovereigns to a European congress in Paris. This congress had even worse luck than that of Frankfurt. It never met, thanks, firstly, to the insuperable mistrust of Lord Russell—the British Foreign Secretary—of Napoleon. Bismarck did not like the idea of this congress either, but he was clever enough to leave it to others to frustrate it. Failures always invite criticism, and thus Napoleon's idea has often been ridiculed. Many historians have scoffed at the idea of solving by a congress problems which could only be settled by war, and they have contrasted Bismarck's realism and Napoleon's dream. The man of the 2nd December, of the *coup d'état*, was not popular in his own day, and people were inclined to take his fine words as sheer hypocrisy. But more recent events may enable the present generation to appreciate the meaning of words such as these, which he addressed to the French parliament (Corps législatif). Referring to the troubles caused by the Polish insurrection, Napoleon asked: "What is there left for us to do? Do we have to choose merely between silence and war?" It was with the following words that he invited the European sovereigns: " Let us not wait till irresistible events suddenly disturb our judgment and drive us, against our will, in opposite directions. . . . Called to the throne by Providence and by the will of the French people, but brought up in the school of adversity, I am less than anybody else allowed to ignore either the rights of the rulers or the rightful aspirations of the nations. He who has passed through so many vicissitudes of life is, as a rule, governed by the spirit of moderation and justice, and it is this spirit which I want to bring to the congress. It is not from vaingloriousness that I take the initiative. But because I am the sovereign to whom, more than to any other, ambitious projects are attributed, it is my heart's desire to prove that my only aim is to achieve a pacification of Europe without a conflagration."

Europe was indeed on the threshold of "irresistible events", of three wars, of the era of blood and iron. Whoever knows the cost of this era, not only to the generation of 1863 but to its children and grandchildren, may see in this strange proclamation the death-warrant of an era which has gone for ever.

Only one week after Napoleon's manifesto King Frederick VII of Denmark died, and with his death Bismarck's great opportunity had arrived.

6. *The Sleswig-Holstein Question*

The death of King Frederick of Denmark on the 15th November 1863 brought the Sleswig-Holstein question to an acute stage at a most critical moment, after having been the terror of the European Chanceries for more than a decade. Lord Palmerston's jest about this highly complicated problem is well known: "Only three men have ever understood it. One was Prince Albert, who is dead. The second was a German professor who became mad. I am the third and I have forgotten all about it."

The elements of this question, stated as simply as possible, can be summarized in the following manner. After the Treaty of Vienna of 1815, Denmark was much larger than it is now. It extended to the outskirts of Hamburg; Altona, now almost a suburb of Hamburg, was a Danish city. The King of Denmark ruled over three distinct parts, which were united only by a personal union: (1) The Kingdom of Denmark proper, the islands in the Baltic Sea, and the northernmost part of the Jutland peninsula; its population was of Danish stock; (2) The southernmost part of Jutland, from the Elbe to the little river Eider, was the Duchy of Holstein; its population was of German stock; the very important Baltic port of Kiel formed part of this territory; (3) Between Denmark proper and Holstein lay the Duchy of Sleswig; its population was mixed, predominantly German in the south, but mainly Danish in the north. The Duchies Holstein and Sleswig used to be called the Elbe-Duchies.

The population of Denmark proper was about twice as large as the combined population of the two Elbe-Duchies.

Of the two Duchies, one, Holstein, was part of the German Confederation. The King of Denmark was, as Duke of Holstein, a member of the Confederation and his plenipotentiary sat in the Diet in Frankfurt. Sleswig, however, was outside the German Confederation, which had absolutely no authority over it. In spite of this important difference the two Duchies considered themselves indissolubly bound together, referring to an old proclamation of the Danish King in the 15th century that they should remain undivided for ever and ever. *Up ewig ungedeelt* was the catchword of every German inhabitant of the two Duchies.

To complicate the question still further, different laws for the succession to the throne applied to the Kingdom of Denmark on the one hand, and the two Duchies on the other. In the Duchies the "Salic" Law of succession was valid, which excluded females from the succession. It was this same law which separated Hanover from the English crown in the year 1837, when Victoria became Queen of England. According to Danish law, however, the crown was hereditary also in the feminine line. King Frederick VII of Denmark did not have any children. The question who should become his successor in the Kingdom on the one hand, and in the Duchies on the other, had been hotly disputed for many years. The Germans in the Duchies, hoping that the succession would bring about the separation of the Duchies from the Kingdom, were in favour of the succession of the Duke of Augustenburg to the throne of the Duchies, and many learned pens were busy proving his right to the succession.

For many years Danes and Germans had lived together peacefully. In the 18th century the leading Ministers of Denmark were Germans like the Counts Bernstorff and the famous Dr. Struensee, who had been a physician in Altona. The King of Denmark had, as a rule, been benevolent to his German subjects. The great German historian, Theodore Mommsen, the author of the world-famous *Roman History*, a son of the Duchy of Holstein, owed it to a grant made by the Danish King that he could follow a learned career. But the growing spirit of nationalism destroyed these easy-going conditions. German nationalism broke out in open violence in the year of revolution, 1848. The Germans in Sleswig and Holstein rose against the "foreign Danish yoke", assisted by many volunteers from Germany and, for a while, by the King of Prussia. The Duke of Augustenburg became the head of a provisional government. But the Prussian King left the Sleswig-Holsteiners in the lurch, and the insurrection collapsed. The Duke of Augustenburg was compelled to fly.

At this stage the Great Powers intervened. They were, for different reasons, interested in the maintenance of the integrity of Denmark. England was specially interested, because Denmark controlled the Baltic Straits, then of paramount importance for British trade and navigation. A conference was convened in London. Its outcome was the Treaty and Protocol of London (May 1852), which laid down the integrity of Denmark, including both Duchies, and settled the question of succession by declaring Prince Christian of Glücksburg heir to the throne of Denmark as well as to that of the Duchies. This treaty was signed by the two German Great Powers, Austria and Prussia, but not by the German Confederation. The Duke of Augustenburg was induced to conclude a treaty with the King of Denmark, which was negotiated by the Prussian plenipotentiary to the German Diet, Otto von Bismarck. In this treaty the Duke promised upon his princely honour, for himself and for his family, not to do anything "by which peace in the territories of the Danish King might be disturbed or endangered, and not to oppose the settling of the succession and the constitution". The treaty did not include an explicit resignation by the Duke of his pretended right to the succession, because the Danish government claimed that this right to the succession had never existed and could therefore not be resigned. This was a heavy blunder on the part of the Danish government, for which Denmark had to pay dearly. The Duke resigned into the hands of the Danish King his extensive landed property in the Duchies. In return he received a payment of some million thalers, equivalent to £400,000.

This treaty caused endless controversy. But even more disputes arose from the declaration with which the Austrian and the Prussian governments had accompanied their signatures to the London Treaty. On the one hand, the Powers, Prussia and Austria not excluded, had agreed that a common constitution should be created by which Denmark and the two Duchies should be united into "one well-ordered whole". On the other hand, Austria and Prussia demanded that both Duchies should keep their special representation (or Stände) and that the Duchy of Sleswig should not be incorporated into the Kingdom and that no steps should be taken which aimed at this incorporation.

The Danish government was thus confronted with a problem which was wellnigh insoluble. It was quite impossible to discover a constitution, so long as it had to be accepted not only by the Danish parliament (Rigsraad) but also by the Stände of the two Duchies. For these Stände would find any constitution unacceptable which was convenient to the Danish Rigsraad. The insuperable difficulty was the proportion of the German to the Danish population. The Germans were less than a third of the whole population and would therefore be a perpetual minority in a common parliament, if both peoples were represented on the same scale. Only a doubling of the German representation would have prevented this danger, and that was a concession which the Danes were not ready to grant. It was, indeed, nothing less than putting the round peg into the square hole, as Bismarck himself called it.

Even before he became Prussian Prime Minister, Bismarck had

come into contact with the affairs of Sleswig-Holstein. It was peculiar and characteristic that he never viewed them from a German point of view. He did not care whether the Germans in Sleswig were maltreated by their Danish rulers. Speaking to a British diplomat, he even mocked at the German enthusiasts who could work up patriotic excitement when a drunken German was handled roughly by a Danish official. He saw all problems exclusively in the light of the extension of Prussian power. Prussia did not have, either in law or in history, the smallest title to the Duchies. Nevertheless, Bismarck's aim from the beginning was their annexation by Prussia, and he considered everything which happened to them only from the point of view as to whether it would forward or hamper this aim. As early as 1857 he wrote to Manteuffel from Frankfurt: "I do not see what *we* [*i.e.* Prussia] would gain, if the conflict is settled quickly and to the complete satisfaction of both parties. It is certainly right to manage our action in such a way that people do not get the impression that we are evading the clear and definite demands of our mission, to stand for Germany against foreign countries; but as soon as the Holsteiners are living very happily under their Duke, they will no longer be interested in Prussia. This interest may still become useful to us, if not at the present time, yet in possible future exigencies."

Thus, in his eyes, the welfare of the Germans of Holstein was opposed to Prussian interest. What the majority of patriotic Germans ardently desired, the independence of the Duchies under their own hereditary prince, he abominated most, because it would be the end of any Prussian hope to annex them. That Prussia did not have any claim at all to annexation did not disturb his mind. There was always one title overpowering every title of law or history: the title of conquest. True, this title could be had only at the cost of a war. He saw this quite clearly, but he was not afraid of war. Only a few months after having taken charge of Prussian affairs he wrote: "I have not the smallest doubt that the whole Danish business can be settled in a way desirable for us only by war. The occasion for such a war can be found at any moment we consider favourable for waging it."

This favourable moment came with the sudden death of the Danish King. It occurred at a moment of high tension, because the Danish Rigsraad had just, a few days previously, passed a new constitution, which was considered in Germany—rightly or wrongly —as an incorporation of Sleswig into the Danish Kingdom and therefore as a breach of the promise the Danish King had given to Austria and Prussia in 1852. The constitution had not yet received the royal signature when Frederick VII died. His successor according to the London Treaty, Prince Christian of Glücksburg, ascended the throne as King of Denmark and Duke of Holstein and Sleswig. Under pressure from his government and the population of the capital, Copenhagen, he signed the constitution.

But at the same time there appeared a proclamation of Prince Frederick, the eldest son of the Duke of Augustenburg, claiming that he had assumed the government of the Duchies. His father, the Duke, had resigned in his favour his own claims to the succession of the throne. Thus the very situation had arisen for the prevention of which the London Treaty had been concluded.

The legality of this curious procedure by the Augustenburgs was, and is still, hotly disputed. It was rightly pointed out that the so-called resignation of the Duke in favour of his son was incompatible with his solemn promise not to do anything by which peace in the territories of the Danish King would be disturbed and endangered. On the other hand, the Germans pointed out that he had never resigned his right of succession and that the payment he had received was, at most, an equivalent for the landed property he had ceded to the Danish King. They claimed that the treaty could not under any circumstances be binding on his son, who was of age at the time of its conclusion and had never signed it. The most important aspect of the case, however, was that the population of Sleswig-Holstein argued that the succession to the throne of the Duchies could not be resigned without their consent and that their representatives, the *Stände*, had never done so. For them, the Augustenburger was their Duke, treaty or no treaty.

Be that as it may from the strictly legal point of view, these arguments were sufficient to convince the Germans that they fought for a just cause in assisting the Prince of Augustenburg and in striving for the independence of the Duchies. Not only the National-Verein and hundreds of other popular organizations declared for the Prince, even King William was inclined to favour him and the cause of the Duchies. He did not dream at this time of annexing Sleswig and Holstein; and Bismarck knew quite well that he could not under any circumstances tell him a single word of his real plans. It was one of his numerous and enormous difficulties that he had to conceal his plans from everybody, from the King, from the Crown Prince, who was a friend of the Augustenburger, from his Ministers, from the Chambers, and, of course, from all foreign Powers. In this he succeeded almost completely. The only foreign diplomatist who occasionally became suspicious was the British Ambassador, Sir Andrew Buchanan, a shrewd Scot, who wrote in a report of 12th December 1863: "May not the war assume a character by which Prussia as the principal belligerent may lay claim for the territories which she will have conquered. . . . I shall be surprised if Bismarck does not endeavour to obtain more solid advantages for Prussia . . . than the honour of having placed a Prince of Augustenburg on the ducal throne of a Sleswig-Holstein state." Buchanan, indeed, read Bismarck's mind quite correctly.

Looking at Bismarck's difficulties at the time of the death of the Danish King, one must consider it almost a miracle that he managed to overcome them all and to be victorious and triumphant in the end. His virtuosity and his cunning, his energy, his courage, and his tenacity of purpose, his resourcefulness and his suppleness, his unscrupulousness and his self-assurance were never greater. But it must never be forgotten that it was power politics and cabinet policy without the least admixture of national or moral motives. Bismarck himself stressed this aspect of his policy, its pure power politics, in his *Recollections*. "I reminded the King", he wrote, "that every one of his immediate predecessors, even including his brother, had won an increment of territory for the state . . . and I encouraged him to do likewise." As to cabinet policy, another word by Bismarck may be quoted. In a letter to Rechberg he made the following suggestion to his Austrian colleague: "We should both take our stand on the practical basis of cabinet policy and not allow the fog which arises from the doctrines of German sentiment-politicians to blur the situation".

He was, indeed, absolutely free from what he calls "national sentiment" politics and what other people would call German national feeling. He did not even hesitate to incite a foreign Power against Germany. In the last days of December 1863, when the German people waited anxiously for the moment of liberation for their fellow-countrymen in the Duchies, Bismarck had an interview with the British Ambassador, Buchanan. The British Foreign Office proposed a note protesting against the policy of the German Confederation. This is what Buchanan had to communicate to Russell about Bismarck's utterances: "The only suggestion which Bismarck had to make on the nature of Your Lordship's proposed communication was that the language which Her Majesty's Government proposed to use is *not sufficiently decided* to attain their object, as an impression prevailed throughout Germany, which is daily increased by the Liberal press, that Great Britain will not seriously oppose an attempt of the Confederation to separate Sleswig and Holstein from the Danish Monarchy—Her Majesty's Government should use the *strongest language* compatible with diplomatic forms . . . a course which may expose their coasts to a *blockade by the British fleet*".

What an extraordinary spectacle! The great statesman whom the German people came to consider the very hero of German national feeling, inducing England to threaten the coasts of Germany with a blockade by the British fleet!

Two factors were in Bismarck's favour and he knew how to make the most of them: the complexity and confusion of the political and legal situation, and disagreements among the Great Powers. There was, in fact, only one Power which took its signature of the London Treaty seriously—Great Britain. Palmerston, the British Prime Minister, considered the integrity of Denmark important enough to fight for. But he was an old man of eighty who had long passed his zenith. He was now no match for Bismarck; besides, he was handicapped by the Queen, who tried to see every problem in the light in which she thought her dead Consort, her "Angel", would have seen it. At heart she was not pro-Prussian but pro-German, disliked the London Treaty, and put her hopes in the Prince of Augustenburg. Palmerston was rash enough to declare in the House of Commons in July 1863, without having previously consulted the cabinet: "We are convinced—I am convinced at least—that if any violent attempt were made to overthrow these rights [of Denmark] and interfere with that independence, those who made the attempt would find in the result that it would not be Denmark alone with which they would have to contend".

This threat could not frighten a man like Bismarck. What could England do without an army of any size? An army could have been provided by France, and there is reason to suppose that Palmerston was hoping for French assistance when he made this declaration. Collaboration on the part of France and Great Britain could have frustrated any attempt to solve the Sleswig-Holstein question by the sword. But this co-operation had been very much handicapped by the diplomatic events of 1863 and their handling by Lord Russell, the British Foreign Secretary. Napoleon felt that Russell had left him in the lurch in the action against Russia concerning the Polish insurrection and was deeply offended by his frustration of the European Congress. Another factor contributed to the failure of the two Powers to come to an understanding. The ideological basis of Napoleon's whole policy was the principle of nationality. The London Treaty, which subjected a population of German nationality to the rule of Danes, was incompatible with this principle. Napoleon's ideal was to divide the Duchies according to the nationalities of their inhabitants: the Danish population of Northern Sleswig thus should go to Denmark, the rest to Germany. Bismarck let him understand that he was quite willing to leave North Sleswig to Denmark.

Before King Frederick died, the German Diet was busy with a "Federal Execution" against the King of Denmark as Duke of Holstein. Holstein was undoubtedly a member of the Confederation. A member who offended against his federal obligations was liable to become the object of an "Execution" by the Confederation. The constitution contained detailed rules about the "Execution", which had to be complied with very punctiliously. It was therefore a very slow and lengthy process. The leaders of the Confederation in this question were the statesmen of the medium states, Beust of Saxony and the Bavarian plenipotentiary, von der Pfordten. They were strong adversaries of the London Treaty, which neither the Confederation nor their states had signed, and champions of the national German movement.

The same view prevailed in the Prussian Chamber, where Twesten interpellated the Prime Minister in April 1863. He asked the government to declare that they regarded the London Treaty as having been broken by the Danish government, and therefore null and void. But Bismarck declined to commit himself about the validity of the London Treaty. On the other hand, he offended the Chamber in the sharpest possible manner by declaring: "If we consider it necessary to wage war, we shall do so with or without your consent". The London Treaty was at that time the nightmare of the German people, the King of Prussia included.

After the death of King Frederick the Confederation considered that an "Execution" was no longer appropriate. An "Execution" was only possible against a member of the Confederation, and the King of Denmark had ceased to be a member of the Confederation if he was not Duke of Holstein. The prevailing view among the confederated governments and the German people was that he was not Duke of Holstein. Therefore not an "Execution" but an "Occupation" by the troops of the Confederation should take place, an "Occupation" on behalf and in the interest of the lawful owner. Who this owner was the Diet would have to decide.

That was exactly what Bismarck would not permit. If the Diet decided that the Prince of Augustenburg was the lawful Duke, any hope of a Prussian annexation was over. He therefore employed all the means at his disposal to prevent a decision of the Diet on the question of succession and to compel it to go forward with the "Execution". The only way to get a majority in the Diet was to induce the Austrian government to collaborate with Prussia.

At this moment the decision about the future was therefore in the hands of Francis Joseph and Rechberg. Bismarck's plans were bound to fail if they declined Bismarck's offer and joined the medium states. Prussia would have been in a hopeless minority in the Diet, and Austria would have been hailed by the overwhelming majority of the German nation as the leader of the national cause. But the Emperor and his Minister failed to grasp the importance of the moment. True, Austria had signed the London Treaty, and every respect is due to Rechberg's legal arguments that this treaty was still binding, notwithstanding all the Danish proceedings. But these legal arguments were not the decisive motives in Rechberg's case. His conservative mind did not like the popular movement. In his eyes the medium states did not form a bulwark against revolution in the way he considered the Prussian government was one, as it fought its own parliament so energetically. There was another argument which he put forward to the Emperor and the other Ministers. To adhere to the treaty was, he said, in the well-understood interest of Austria. For if the Prince of Augustenburg became Duke of Holstein, he would no doubt follow the Prussian flag, *i.e.* vote with Prussia in the Diet. The curious thing was that Bismarck employed the same argument in the opposite sense. He told his King that the Prince of Augustenburg would vote against Prussia in the Diet. Thus, it so happened that the unfortunate Prince was declined by both Great Powers on strictly opposite assumptions about his future attitude.

For all these reasons Rechberg induced his Emperor to accept Bismarck's offer of collaboration. Austria and Prussia together compelled the very unwilling Diet to resolve that the "Execution" had to begin before the 1st January 1864. This resolution provoked the greatest irritation in Germany, because it was thought to be the first step in a new subjection of the Duchies to Denmark. Five hundred deputies, members of the Chambers of the individual German Federated States, assembled in Frankfurt to protest against this resolution and to institute a committee of thirty-six deputies to defend the lawful rights of the Duchies and of the Prince of Augustenburg. Prussian deputies like Twesten, Sybel, Schulze-Delitzsch were members of this committee.

But not only the deputies and the newspapers condemned Bismarck's policy. Almost all the Prussian officials were against him, even his own diplomatic representatives. This is clear from Bismarck's letter to the Prussian Ambassador in Paris, Graf von der Goltz, which Bismarck himself reproduced in his *Recollections*. It should, however, be read in conjunction with Goltz's answer, which shows the other side of the picture. It is here sufficient to quote one passage from Bismarck's letter: "You do not trust Austria. Neither do I. But I consider it the correct policy at present to have Austria with us. Whether the moment of separation will come and on whose initiative, we shall see. . . . I am by no means fighting shy of war, quite the reverse. . . . Perhaps you will very soon convince yourself that war is also included in my programme." Goltz, on the other hand, wrote: "You are not the Minister of a majority,

your ministerial existence is based exclusively on the confidence of
the King, and the King must remain in a position to preserve this
confidence *en pleine connaissance de cause*" (in the full knowledge of
all sides of a question). He reproached Bismarck with preventing
the ambassadors "by a kind of terrorism" from reporting their
views to the King, who was thus no longer properly informed about
the various points of view. "That is", he writes, "certainly not
parliamentary government. But neither is it monarchical government; rather, it is the Dictatorship of the Minister of Foreign
Affairs." In later years, more than one German Ambassador would
have been inclined to repeat this statement.

But all these difficulties did not prevent Bismarck from going his
own way step by step, with the greatest caution but with absolute
fearlessness and astonishing recklessness. Knowing how important
Napoleon's attitude was, he employed every means to win him
over. In the last days of December, the French General Fleury,
whom the Emperor had sent to Copenhagen, came to Berlin and
saw Bismarck. The Prussian Minister referred to the abortive European Congress and told the General that he could not agree to
a general Congress because it would touch the Polish question.
That would be unbearable for Prussia. "Rather die than permit
discussion of our possessions in Poland", he continued. "I would
rather cede our Rhenish provinces."

Why did Bismarck talk of the Rhineland? Fleury had not said a
word about it. Bismarck's reason for this hint was due to his knowledge that Napoleon dreamed of acquiring the left bank of the
Rhine. It was perhaps no more than a dream, but what an entice-
ment it would be for the Emperor to help Bismarck if he could
hope, in return, to see this dream realized.

7. *The War against Denmark, and the London Conferences*

Once the troops of the Confederation had marched into Holstein
and the Danes had withdrawn without firing a shot, Bismarck's aim
was to move Prussian troops into Sleswig and to bring about a
war with Denmark. As this was only possible in concert with
Austria, an alliance with her had to be concluded. Bismarck succeeded not only in doing this, but also in eliminating from the

treaty any clause which might restrain his future liberty of action. Even Rechberg could not fail to see that the interests of the two partners would not always be identical in future. The Duchies were separated from Austrian territory by the whole breadth of Germany, but they were in the immediate neighbourhood of Prussia. While Austria, therefore, could not think of annexing the Duchies for herself, she was bound to suspect Prussia of this aim. It was, therefore, quite a necessary protection against unfavourable developments when the Austrian proposal of a Treaty of Alliance provided that Austria and Prussia bound themselves not to surrender the integrity of the Danish Monarchy and Christian VII's right of succession without mutual agreement. If this clause had stood as part of the treaty, Austria would have been able to play the rôle of the dog in the manger, preventing Prussia from devouring the morsel which Austria herself could not digest. But, by a really marvellous stroke of diplomacy, Bismarck induced the Austrians to drop the clause and to acquiesce in another formula proposed by Bismarck, which in the end proved worthless.

Karolyi, the Austrian Ambassador in Berlin, was now convinced that Bismarck was a true friend of Austria. If only he had heard a little dialogue which Bismarck had with the Italian Minister in Berlin, de Launay! Meeting him at a ball, Bismarck pointed to de Launay's sword and said with a smile: "The sword of Italy". De Launay answered: "It seems that you do not need the sword of Italy, as you have chosen another ally". "Oh," said Bismarck, "the other one, we have hired him." "Gratis?" asked de Launay. "*Il travaille pour le roi de Prusse.*" And he then turned to the French Ambassador, telling him with much gusto the excellent joke he had just made at the expense of his ally, on the very eve of the joint invasion of Sleswig by the Austrian and Prussian forces.

Rechberg went into this war blindfold, although he received warnings from many quarters. In the Austrian parliament the question was debated for four full days, and many Liberal speakers sharply criticized his policy. Their speeches showed evidence of much more political insight and a sounder judgment than the government displayed. A leading Liberal said, very shrewdly, that every Austrian mistake would increase Austria's unpopularity in Germany, while not even all the sins of the Prussian statesmen could destroy the hope which the German people had in Prussia. Another prophesied that Prussia would come out of this war very much strengthened, because as a result of it a unified leadership would fall into the hands of an energetic, self-willed and daring man. A third asked a very pertinent question: "Prussia has just digested Silesia, stolen by Frederick II, and now she turns her claws on the Duchies. But we let our troops play their nice regimental music and conduct the Prussians into the Duchies with the roll of the drum and the sounding of trumpets. But to what tune will we be conducting them out again?"

That question was to be repeated by Austrian patriots again and again during the following years.

On the 1st February 1864 Prussian and Austrian troops crossed the frontier of Sleswig. The Danes decided to fight, hoping that England would come to their aid. Bismarck did his best to strengthen this hope on the part of the Danes, for he had to have fighting Danes to win the title of conquest. A peaceful occupation would not do. But Russell did no more than ask the two German Powers to declare in binding form that they would not violate the integrity of the Danish Monarchy. Bismarck induced the reluctant King to give this declaration in a somewhat tortuous way. Of course, he never had the intention of keeping it. His motto was: *In verbis simus faciles*. He knew that possession was nine points of the law and that he would be able to speak another language once the Duchies had been occupied by Prussian troops. He told the King in the Council that his promise would not restrict his future freedom of action and that it would not commit Prussia definitely and perpetually to a maintenance of the integrity of Denmark.

It was at the session of the Council of the 3rd February, after the invasion of Sleswig, that William consented to the declaration. At this Council Bismarck revealed for the first time the real aim of his action, the annexation of the Duchies. Although the description Bismarck gives of his revelation in his *Recollections* is not trustworthy, so much is certainly true that the King was startled and did not agree with Bismarck's policy, as a marginal note in his hand to the protocol shows. But Bismarck overlooked that without scruples. So long as William let him have his own way, he was free to write into secret documents whatever he liked. Bismarck had not the slightest doubt that in the end William would take what he could get, true to the sacred Hohenzollern tradition.

The Danes were, naturally, much too weak to resist the Austrian and Prussian army in the long run. On the 18th April Prussian troops stormed the last Danish stronghold, the entrenchment of Düppel, and were thus in possession of the whole of Sleswig. It was only at this stage that Britain intervened and convoked a conference of the signatory Powers of the London Treaty in London. Bismarck could not help sending Prussian delegates to this conference, but he knew how to manage the situation in such a way that nothing would result from this conference which would handicap him in any way. He did not go to London himself, trusting that he would be able to pull the strings much better from Berlin. He also welcomed the invitation extended to the German Confederation to attend the conference, and its representation by Baron Beust. He knew that Beust and the Austrians did not see eye to eye, and that it was therefore the easier for him to evade a settlement and any binding obligations. He indeed made a settlement impossible by continually increasing his demands, whenever the Danes reluctantly and belatedly made any concessions.

Rechberg, who wished nothing more than to conclude this war which could not bring any advantage to Austria, was completely helpless. The British plenipotentiary, Lord Clarendon, said angrily: *"Bismarck est un homme sans foi et loi et Rechberg est son nègre"*. The climax of the conference came when the other Powers compelled Austria and Prussia to declare their war aims in a clear and unmistakable manner. To the meeting on the 28th May the Austrian delegate read, in the name of Austria and Prussia, a declaration demanding the complete separation of Sleswig and Holstein from Denmark and their union in a single state under the sovereignty of the Prince of Augustenburg, "who not only had the best right to the succession, so that his recognition by the Diet was assured, but who also possessed the undoubted consent of the overwhelming majority of the population". As Denmark could not accept this proposition, the conference broke down and the war continued.

The jubilation in Germany was unanimous. Thus, at last, the Prince of Augustenburg would come into his own. The solemn declaration of Prussia and Austria could not possibly be understood in any other way.

There was only one man who understood it differently. Not for one moment did Bismarck dream of being bound by this declaration. For a mere three days the Prince of Augustenburg could entertain the hope of becoming Duke of Holstein and Sleswig. Then it was all over. Three days after the solemn declaration to the London Conference, during the night of the 1st June, the Prince had a conversation with Bismarck, and when this conversation was concluded his doom was sealed—to remain a prince without territory for the rest of his life. Bismarck knew how to frighten and irritate the Prince so completely by extreme Prussian claims that he gave answers which could be represented to the King as showing the Prince's ingratitude. If Bismarck had wished to bring about a settlement it would have been quite easy. He did not, however, desire a settlement but a conflict, and, as he held all the trumps, the Prince was helpless.

It is no defamation if we interpret Bismarck's attitude thus. He himself had put it in a much franker and more cynical way. In the autumn of 1865 he met his old adversary Beust at Gastein. Their conversation was quite friendly and open, and Bismarck, whose policy had triumphed by now, did not hesitate to mock at the unfortunate Prince of Augustenburg. "At the London Conference", he said, "I hitched the Prince to the plough as an ox, to get it moving. Once the plough was in motion I unhitched the ox." "*Verba ipsissima*", wrote Beust, and nobody who knows Bismarck will challenge the authenticity of this truly Bismarckian comparison.

The inevitable military defeat of Denmark brought Great Britain face to face with the question whether it should intervene by force of arms. Palmerston and Russell were in favour of intervention, although it was now known that Napoleon was likely to keep aloof. The Queen was against it. In the cabinet Palmerston was defeated by a majority led by Gladstone, who asserted that England simply was not ready for war. In that argument he was, no doubt, right. England did not have an army with which it could oppose two mighty military Powers single-handed. But it was a bitter hour for Palmerston, the gravest defeat in his otherwise so successful career. The bitter feeling of a section of English public opinion was expressed by Lord Robert Cecil, later the Marquess of Salisbury and Prime Minister of Great Britain, in the *Quarterly Review* of April 1864. "The crisis has at last come. The concessions upon which England has insisted have proved futile. The independence which she professed to value so highly is at an end. The people whom she affected to befriend are in danger of being swept away. One of the most wanton and unblushing spoliations which history records is on the point of being consummated. But as far as effective aid goes, England stands aloof. . . . Her pledges and her threats are gone with last year's snow, and she is content to watch with cynical philosophy the destruction of those who trusted to the one, and the triumph of those who were wise enough to spurn the other."

Abandoned by all the signatories of the London Treaty, Denmark was compelled to sue for peace. Peace was concluded at Vienna in August 1864. The King of Denmark had to give up the Duchies and to cede all his rights to the Emperor of Austria and the King of Prussia. Bismarck himself went to Vienna for the negotiations. At Schönbrunn, the Imperial palace near Vienna, Francis Joseph and William talked in the presence of Rechberg and Bismarck about the question as to what the victors should do now with the booty. Austria was ready to cede the whole booty, that is to say, both Duchies, to Prussia, provided that Prussia bound herself not only to defend Austria's Italian province Venetia but also, under certain circumstances, to help her to regain Milan and Lombardy. Bismarck relates how William declined Francis Joseph's offer of the Duchies with the words that he had no right to them. But this was not the decisive argument. Nothing could be further from Bismarck's intentions than to help Austria in Italy against Napoleon and Vittorio Emanuele. As to the Duchies, he was in no hurry. He was quite certain that he would get them sooner or later, and much else besides.

To celebrate the peace, Rechberg invited his famous Prussian colleague to his country house, Kettenhof, for a dinner with all the foreign diplomats. Here Bismarck took the opportunity of talking to the French Ambassador, Duke of Gramont, in his particular indiscreet manner. He told him not Britain, but only Prussia, would be able to give Napoleon the left bank of the Rhine. "We can march with France better than anybody else, for as a start we can give her what other Powers could only promise. We do not desire a European conflagration. But if it comes we shall not be among the losers. This perspective does not frighten us." Is this not the same idea which he expressed years before to Otto von Manteuffel when he wrote: "Great crises are the very weather which stimulates Prussia's growth, if we turn them to our account fearlessly and, maybe, very recklessly" ?

No European statesman could by now have any doubt that Bismarck was not only fearless but absolutely reckless. And whoever heard about his indiscreet talk with Gramont might have an idea that his ally at that moment, Austria, was to become his enemy, to be fought by him fearlessly and recklessly.

8. *The Consequences of the Danish War*

By the Peace of Vienna the King of Denmark had ceded to the Emperor of Austria and the King of Prussia all his rights to the Duchies. But what were these rights? Most Germans answered: None at all! They referred to the declaration of 28th May 1864 at the London Conference, in which Austria and Prussia had emphasized that the Prince of Augustenburg had the best right of succession to the Duchies. Beust tried to strengthen this declaration by a decision of the German Diet in favour of Augustenburg. But by strong threats Bismarck prevented the Diet from coming to any decision. He did his best to put as many obstacles as possible in the way of the Duke, for instance, by inventing a new pretender in the person of the Grand-Duke of Oldenburg, who was related to the Czar and therefore supposed to be certain of his assistance. Bismarck opposed the Prince of Augustenburg not only as a rival to Prussian ambition but as an outspoken Liberal and a personal friend of the Prussian Crown Prince.

On the other hand, Austria and Prussia could not agree about a definitive disposition of the Duchies. So they agreed to administer them provisionally as a common possession. They installed what was called a "condominium". An Austrian and a Prussian authority had to administer the Duchies in conjunction with each other. That meant, in practice, that Prussia advanced to her goal step by step and that Austria was reluctantly compelled to give her assent.

An illustration of this situation was the treatment of the troops of the Confederation, which were still garrisoned in Holstein. Bismarck drove them out by threats of violence, without consulting his Austrian ally beforehand, although Austria was the presiding Power of the Confederation. It was a most unpleasant situation for the Austrian government. But being, above anything else, afraid to lose the alliance of Prussia, it tried a policy of appeasement by asking for some formal concessions and conceding the substance of the matter.

Austria was no longer represented by Rechberg. The failure of his policy was felt not only by the Austrian people but by the other Ministers. Thus Schmerling, who still had a strong parliamentary position, asked the Emperor to choose between himself and Rechberg. Francis Joseph dismissed Rechberg, but appointed another Conservative as his successor, with whom Schmerling was not likely to see eye to eye. Francis Joseph did not like uniformity of opinion among his Ministers. His own power was greater if he could set the one against the other. Rechberg's successor was a former general, Count Mensdorff, a mediocrity of noble birth and ample means, who happened to be related to Queen Victoria and other European sovereigns. As Mensdorff lacked the power of political leadership, Biegeleben, the head of the German Department of the Austrian Foreign Office, now became the more influential. He had gradually become a critic of Rechberg's policy. Rechberg himself had only begun to suspect Bismarck's true nature during the last days of his ministry when he sent one of the Prussian Minister's letters to his Emperor with the comment: "The language of this letter is worthy of a Cavour". Cavour was, for the Viennese court, the embodiment of evil. Rechberg's tragic responsibility lay in understanding the real nature of Bismarck and his policy only when it was too late.

Bismarck had considered the expulsion of the troops of the Confederation as a trial of strength, and now he knew he had won it. Wantonly he told the British Ambassador, Lord Napier, that the German peasants were accustomed to send all the cows to the pasture-ground at the beginning of spring and then let the bulls fight it out among themselves. "The strongest bull will win and for the rest of the summer there is peace. That is what I have done now. I have fought it out and hope to have no more difficulties."

Prussia's treatment of the German Confederation and Austria's acquiescence in it made it quite clear to Beust, the acute Saxon Minister, that the Confederation had become untenable in the form it then had. He told the Austrian envoy that a German parliament, elected directly by the people, was henceforth unavoidable and that Austria would do well not to leave this trump card to Bismarck. Bismarck would proceed from the annexation of the Duchies to the subjugation of the German states. As this policy could not be put into effect by violence alone, the courageous Bismarck would seek and obtain the sanction of a German parliament. Bismarck, he said, was such a formidable force because he was the prototype of the Prussian spirit. He warned the Austrians not to hope that the honesty of King William would preserve them from the worst. "I fear scrupulous Prussian kings more than unscrupulous ones. The dangerous Prussian policy remains the same under the one as under the other. There is only one difference: against the unscrupulous king everybody is on his guard. But the scrupulous king inspires by his character a confidence which his acts do not justify."

What an accurate prediction! But Beust's proposals were too daring for the Austrian statesmen, who still hoped to come to an understanding with Bismarck. At any rate, they could not fail to see that an endless prolongation of the provisional "condominium" was not in Austria's interest, and they tried to obtain Bismarck's consent to a definitive settlement. Austria did not want the Duchies or even part of them. She was in favour of the installation of the Prince of Augustenburg, whose right of succession she had acknowledged in the declaration to the London Conference and who alone could prevent an annexation of the Duchies by Prussia. Biegeleben did his best, by excellent dispatches, to induce Prussia to agree to this settlement. It was expressly stated in these notes that Prussia had a claim to certain privileges in the Duchies on account of her sacrifices and her geographical position. Bismarck, at first, did not answer. At last, in February 1865, he could delay his answer no longer. But it was an answer which surpassed the worst expectations on the part of both Vienna and the Pretender. Bismarck's conditions for installing the Prince of Augustenburg as Duke were so comprehensive that almost every important function would have been in the hands of the Prussian government and the Duke would have obtained no more than a nominal position. Bismarck was bold enough to say to the Crown Prince that he had formulated his conditions so that neither Vienna nor the Prince could possibly accept them. When Biegeleben read the note, he exclaimed: "Rather cultivate my potatoes as a simple farmer than be Duke under such conditions".

Negotiations between Vienna and Berlin were almost at an end. Bismarck aggravated the situation still further by converting the excellent port of Kiel in Holstein into a Prussian naval station, and Roon by declaring openly to the Chamber of Deputies that Prussia was firmly bent on keeping this port under any circumstances. At the same time Bismarck demanded the consent of Vienna to the expulsion of the Prince of Augustenburg from the Duchies, and, when the Austrians declined, he reproached them officially with having destroyed the basis of the alliance.

Thus Prussia was, in practice, well advanced on the road to annexation by this time. But annexation was not her official policy, as King William had not yet approved it. He had still some scruples about his own deficiency of title and the better rights of the Augustenburger Prince. Bismarck knew his King well enough to understand the two conflicting arguments which fought for supremacy in his mind. On the one hand, he was not willing to take anything which lawfully belonged to another prince; on the other hand, however, he was just as eager for the possession of the Duchies as King Ahab had been to acquire Naboth's vineyard. He therefore wanted nothing more than to be released from the scruples which prevented him from obtaining the Duchies. Bismarck had to destroy these scruples, and he certainly knew how to do it. He asked the Syndics of the Crown to give a legal opinion about the question of succession to the throne of the Duchies. Bismarck was sure that he could depend completely on the willingness of the Crown Syndics to give that opinion which was most favourable to the Prussian crown. The Crown Syndics were an invention of Frederick William IV in his most reactionary mood. When he constituted the Upper Chamber (*das Herrenhaus*), as an instrument of the arbitrary royal will and of the interest of the Junkers, he reserved for the crown the right to appoint, "by special Royal confidence", some lawyers as members of the Herrenhaus and Syndics of the Crown. Except for the few years of the "New Era", only the most reactionary lawyers were appointed to the leading posts in the High Courts or the State Attorneyship. From these the Crown Syndics were selected. They represented the spirit of Prussian reaction in its most extreme and uncompromising form. Their chairman was the ultra-reactionary Minister of Justice, Count von Lippe. Indeed the majority of the Syndics gave an opinion which was more than surprising: that the King of Denmark, Christian, was at the outset the only lawful Duke of Sleswig and Holstein. Therefore, as he had by the Peace of Vienna ceded all his rights to the monarchs of Prussia and Austria, these monarchs now possessed the lawful rights of the Duke. *Quod erat demonstrandum.*

This opinion of the Syndics did not impress either the independent legal experts, who criticized it and made havoc of it, or the German people, or, indeed, the population of the Duchies. The Holsteiners continued to adhere faithfully to the Augustenburger, and most Germans agreed with the opinion of the famous President of the Paulskirche of 1848, Gagern, who said: "Only in an ironical sense will it in future be possible to speak of the sense of justice of the Prussian kings and of the sense of duty of the Prussian judges". But that did not trouble Bismarck in the least. What only did matter was that William had been released from his scruples. Now the King was able to persuade himself that he merely wanted that to which he was entitled. Moreover, Bismarck knew how to arouse the King's personal feelings against the unfortunate Prince to such an extent that he felt free from all obligations to him.

9. *The Crown Council of 29th May 1865*

The opinion of the majority of the Syndics of the Crown was known to the Minister of Justice when the King assembled his Ministers and some of his leading generals, among them Moltke, the Chief of Staff of the army, for a solemn Council to deliberate on the great question as to the extent of Prussian demands: whether the Prussian government should ask for annexation or only insist on the conditions of February, even at the risk of war. This Council took place on 29th May 1865. It was one of the most important, as well as the most curious, Councils of this period. The official protocol and the notes which General von Moltke made are still available. Nevertheless, almost every historian has another opinion about the policy which Bismarck proposed to this Council.

After a masterly analysis of the possible policies, Bismarck pointed out that Prussia would make a good bargain even if it moderated the February conditions by eliminating the most offensive of them, as, for instance, the oath of military obedience to the Prussian King which was to be sworn by the soldiers and sailors of the Duchies. As to war, he described the international situation as favourable. "In spite of all this," he continued, it was his advice "to try merely to obtain the moderated February conditions, and *only if this attempt failed to fix our eyes upon a higher goal.*" And then followed the most critical sentence: "If His Majesty is not satisfied with these conditions but wants the complete annexation of the Duchies, this can only be the result of a *free decision on the part of the King*".

All the other speakers, particularly the generals, Manteuffel and, in a more cautious form, Moltke, were in favour of war. Only the Crown Prince advocated the rights of the Prince of Augustenburg and a just settlement. He warned against a war with Austria and the South German states and called it a "German civil war". Bismarck protested strongly against this name and added: "If war in alliance with France against Austria is banned then a Prussian policy is no longer possible. But if war is waged against Austria it has to bring about not only the annexation of the Duchies but a new arrangement in the relations of Prussia with the German medium and small States." Here Bismarck expressed for the first time in the presence of the King his idea that Germany had to be reorganized by "blood and iron".

These utterances of Bismarck have been interpreted in many different ways and are, indeed, rather enigmatic. But they cannot be interpreted in the sense that Bismarck wanted to yield and thus to avoid the war against Austria by Prussian concessions. What he wanted to avoid was only a war at that very moment, because he was not yet sure of the attitude of France and Italy. He wanted the annexation as much as ever, but he thought it would be advantageous to attain this end by a somewhat devious route which would, however, have the advantage of letting Prussia appear in a favourable light as willing to compromise and to make concessions. This would make it all the easier afterwards to "assume the rôle of the injured". But much as he wanted annexation, he knew that a war against the present ally could not be waged on the exclusive basis of a demand for annexation. The war must have an aim which could justify it in the eyes of contemporaries and posterity. This final end could only be the unification of Germany. For this greater aim he had to prepare the slow mind of his King. For this reason he put all the responsibility upon the King, and for this reason he wanted to postpone the outbreak of the war. In the meantime he did all he could to prepare for the war financially, diplomatically, and militarily—and to aggravate the conflict in Sleswig-Holstein.

10. *Continuation of the Constitutional Conflict*

Bismarck did not seek a conciliation with his parliament. At that juncture it would not have been so very difficult. It is never easy to oppose a government which has been victorious in a war. It was particularly difficult for the Prussian Liberals because they had, before the war, advocated a policy which had become obsolete to some extent through the war. They had, like all the other German Liberals, been in favour of an independent German Sleswig-Holstein under the Prince of Augustenburg. But now the idea of a Prussian annexation became more popular from month to month among the Prussian people. The *Vossische Zeitung*, for instance, a progressive paper and the favourite organ of the educated middle classes of Berlin, acclaimed Treitschke, when he propagated annexation in his own fervent way. Old Waldeck, the hero of 1848, the leader of the most radical wing of the Progressive Party, was against a new medium state and for incorporation of the Duchies into Prussia. Mommsen, himself a native of Holstein, wrote a pamphlet by which he tried to convince his fellow-countrymen that incorporation into Prussia was to their own benefit. Other deputies at any rate favoured a treaty of the Duchy with Prussia that would give the leading German state a permanent privileged position. Twesten advocated this solution in a speech in the Chamber in June 1865. He gave high praise to Bismarck's foreign policy and accepted many of his aims. But he clearly manifested the great difference of principle which separated the Liberals from Bismarckian power politics. "We are no legitimists," he said, "and we know that even princely legitimism, like every other vested interest, has to give way to the permanent fundamental interests of nations. But rights of this kind, be they the rights of a prince or the rights of a people, should not be treated as scraps of paper and ridiculed whenever such rights become inconvenient."

The differences of opinion among the deputies were so large that they could not agree on any firm course. The greater Bismarck's ascendancy, the less he was inclined to arrive at a compromise with the House in the great constitutional question about which it could make no concessions, the government without budget. True, this was a point on which the King was most unwilling to make even the smallest concession. Now that his army had been victorious, he considered it, like any absolutist, as his purely personal concern, with which parliament did not have to meddle. The sole duty of parliament in the eyes of the King was to vote the money which he considered necessary for the maintenance of the army. A compromise was thus impossible, and Bismarck became still more aggressive. For instance, he attacked the report of the Committee of the House on naval questions in unmeasured and offensive terms. The author of the report was the famous pathologist, Professor Virchow, one of the great masters of medical science in the 19th century. When he answered Bismarck in the same way, Bismarck challenged him because he had cast a doubt on his veracity. That was a point on which he was extremely touchy, although he privately ridiculed politicians who did not know that lies were a part of political business.

The conflict remained as sharp as ever. Bismarck not only did not do anything to mitigate it, he was prepared to go on to still more drastic and provocative measures. He told the King that it was impossible to govern in accordance with the constitution and that a far-reaching alteration, a "blow" against the deputies, would be necessary either in the coming winter or in the following one. The "blow" could hardly be anything else than a *coup d'état*.

11. *The International Situation*

In the meantime, quarrels between the Prussian and the Austrian administrations in the Duchies became more frequent and grave from month to month. The Austrians were almost always on the defensive. It looked as if the Prussians worked with the deliberate aim of making their position untenable. The dispatches, too, which Bismarck sent to Vienna became still sharper and more aggressive.

Bismarck never made the mistake of underrating the strength of an enemy. He knew that Austria was still, in spite of all her difficulties, a great military Power. He therefore had to scrutinize the international situation very carefully before he committed himself irrevocably. There was nothing to be feared from Russia, which was as ill-disposed as possible towards Austria. But much depended on the attitude to be expected from Napoleon and Italy.

Napoleon's influence in Italy was great. The Italian government and people had good reason to be grateful to the Emperor, who had helped them in the war against Austria. But one important problem stood between them: the Roman question. Napoleon had in 1848, as President of the Second French Republic, sent French troops to Rome to assist the Pope, Pius IX, against Garibaldi and the Roman Republic. After a glorious struggle, so superbly described by Professor Trevelyan, Garibaldi was defeated and the Pope returned to Rome. But Napoleon had not been able to withdraw his troops. After the foundation of the Italian Kingdom it was less possible than ever. Every Italian patriot considered Rome the natural capital of his country. It was almost certain that the Italians would march in as soon as the French garrison was withdrawn. That would have meant the end of the secular rule of the Pope. Napoleon, whose rule in France depended upon the clergy and the clerically minded portion of the population, felt that a situation of this kind would be a dangerous blow to the security of his throne and that it must not arise under any circumstances. On the other hand, he wanted to withdraw his troops as quickly as possible. He therefore concluded, in September 1864, a treaty with the Italian Kingdom, by which Italy promised never to attack the territory of the Papal State and to defend it against all aggression. Napoleon promised to withdraw his troops from Rome two years after the transfer of the capital of the Italian Kingdom from Turin to Florence. This change-over was duly effected some months later, but the Italian people, nevertheless, did not waive its claim to Rome. The Pope on his part showed by his encyclical *Quanta cura* and the *Syllabus errorum*, which he proclaimed in December 1864, that he was not willing to make any concessions to the modern world.

The court of Vienna looked at this development with distrust. Would Italy, prevented from entering Rome, turn again to Venice? If Austria could expect help from Prussia against a new Italian attack, it would have been willing to make important concessions in the Duchies. But it was clear now that Bismarck declined this help categorically. Therefore Vienna turned to Paris and tried to obtain good relations with Napoleon by emphasizing their common interest in the maintenance of the temporal power of the Pope. Bismarck did not like these negotiations. It was his policy to have the road to Paris open exclusively for himself. As he mistrusted the Prussian Ambassador in Paris, von der Goltz, he cultivated his relations with the French Ambassador in Berlin, Mr. Benedetti, all the more. It was the same Benedetti whose interview with King William at Ems came to be considered as the cause of the war of 1870. But in these years the contacts between Bismarck and Benedetti were very friendly; Bismarck saw the Ambassador even when he was on his sick-bed, and he spoke to him more unreservedly and indiscreetly, for instance about the King and the Crown Prince, than to anybody else, and that meant a good deal. Benedetti was, indeed, a friend of a Franco-Prussian understanding and therefore did his best to emphasize Bismarck's point of view to his Emperor.

Napoleon's policy was, on the other hand, sharply criticized in the French parliament, the Corps législatif. It was open to criticism especially on account of the ill-fated expedition to Mexico, the failure of which became manifest in 1865. One of the sharpest and weightiest critics was Adolphe Thiers, the former Minister of Louis-Philippe, later the first President of the Third Republic. Thiers attacked the central point of Napoleon's policy, the theory of nationality. He tried to demonstrate that it was absolutely against the interests of France to help Italy and Germany to unify themselves. There will be a time, he cried, when the forty millions of Germans and the twenty-six millions of Italians will make an alliance of which France will be the victim.

But this criticism did not cause Napoleon to change the direction of his foreign policy. On the contrary, shortly after Thiers' speech Benedetti was authorized to ask Bismarck to explain frankly what he wanted from the Emperor and what he was willing to offer him. It was a thinly veiled offer of alliance. But Bismarck did not enter into it. Benedetti's interpretation of this attitude was that Bismarck knew the King would not be willing to make the sacrifices which French assistance would impose upon him. The concession he had in mind was, of course, the left bank of the Rhine. Only part of it belonged to Prussia, other parts to Bavaria and other German states.

To win over Italy, Bismarck used Prussia's influence in the Zollverein to induce the medium States to conclude commercial treaties with Italy. This was considered in Austria as an unfriendly act, as Italy was there still looked upon as the enemy. The Habsburg Monarchy had not yet officially recognized the Italian Kingdom. But the monarchy then had difficulties not only in foreign but also in home affairs. Schmerling's constitution only functioned properly with a part of the population. The greatest difficulties were made by the Hungarians, who declined to enter the common parliament, the Reichsrat. The consequence was that the Emperor lost his confidence in Schmerling and dismissed him. He appointed as his successor a member of the old Conservative aristocracy, Count Belcredi, who was justly reputed to be an enemy of constitutionalism and certainly no friend of German ascendancy in the monarchy. This, too, was a blow to Austria's position in Germany.

In this situation Bismarck began, in the summer of 1865, a sharp diplomatic campaign against Austria and intensified his attacks against her position in the Duchies. He demanded of Austria the consent to the expulsion of the Prince of Augustenburg from the Duchies; he gave her to understand that he would not hesitate to arrest the Prince and to put him into a Prussian fortress as prisoner. To show the Austrians what he was capable of doing, he had arrested, without any understanding with the Austrian administration, the editor of a Holstein newspaper, who happened to be a Prussian subject; he was marched off to a Prussian prison by Prussian troops. There was an outcry in Germany against this brutal method of dealing with the freedom of the press. But Bismarck was not in any way moved by it or by the protest of the Austrian administration in the Duchies.

The climax of the diplomatic campaign came in July 1865. Bismarck was then in Karlsbad in Bohemia to take the waters. From there he sent four dispatches full of grievances to Vienna, in which he declared that if Austria declined to agree to his proposals he would take the necessary measures unilaterally and carry them through at any risk. The situation was now so serious that Minister Eulenburg considered it his duty to inform the Crown Prince that the rupture with Austria might be nearer than anybody thought. The Prince, who was in a bathing resort on the North Sea, urged his father to come to an understanding with the Emperor on the one hand, and the Prince of Augustenburg on the other. In the absence of the Crown Prince the King held a Council of Ministers at Regensburg. The Ambassador Graf Goltz, who was called from Paris to participate in the Council, relates how Bismarck said in the presence of Roon that war with Austria was only a question of time and that the present moment was the most favourable. The outcome of the Council was a brief and offensive dispatch to Austria declaring that Prussia would decline any further negotiation so long as Austria did not accept the Prussian demands.

Before this dispatch had arrived in Vienna, Count Mensdorff, the Austrian Foreign Minister, had asked Bismarck, through the Prussian Ambassador in Vienna, whether the King would be willing to receive an Austrian confidential envoy in order to make a final effort to arrive at a settlement by means of a personal interview. Bismarck had agreed. The Regensburg dispatch made Mensdorff doubt whether the time for interviews of this kind might not be over. But Bismarck let him know that he was, nevertheless, quite willing to see his envoy. Although he did not shrink from a complete rupture, he did not wish to "slam" the door so long as any other solution was possible. This is quite characteristic of his methods. As long as possible he held every door open.

12. *The Gastein Convention*

At that time Bismarck and the King were at Gastein taking the waters. Thither came the confidential envoy of the Court of Vienna. It was the Austrian Minister in Munich, Count Blome. No man more unfit for this work could have been found. Blome was a strong Conservative who rejoiced over the downfall of Schmerling, and a Roman Catholic convert who considered it the highest duty of all governments to put their entire resources in the service of the realization of the ideas of the Papal encyclical of 1864. He had no sympathy either with the German national movement or with the Prince of Augustenburg. He regarded Bismarck as a Conservative statesman, nay, as a champion of the common Conservative struggle against the revolution. He fell into the trap of Bismarck's slogans more easily than any other man with whom Bismarck ever had to deal. Bismarck always had the upper hand in any personal negotiation, thanks to his superior intelligence and skill, but nobody made things easier for him than Count Blome.

The outcome of these negotiations was the Convention of Gastein (14th August 1865). It ended the Austro-Prussian condominium of the Duchies by dividing them. The administration of the Southern Duchy, Holstein, was transferred to Austria, the administration of the Northern Duchy, Sleswig, to Prussia. The small Duchy of Lauenburg was sold to the King of Prussia, who paid in cash to the Emperor of Austria. The fortification of Kiel in Holstein was entrusted to Prussia. In this way Austria obtained a possession which was enclosed on two sides by territories either belonging to or administered by Prussia.

The Gastein Convention was received on all sides with an outcry of indignation. For the German people it was the unpardonable violation of the principle to which not only Germany but Austria and Prussia had appealed from the very time that the Sleswig-Holstein question first arose, namely, that the Duchies should be "one and indivisible for ever and ever" (*up ewig ungedeeld*). Lord Russell condemned the treaty outright in a dispatch: "All rights old or new . . . have been trodden under foot by the Gastein Convention, and the *authority of force* is the only power which had been consulted and recognized". No less outspoken was the criticism of the French Minister, Drouyn de Lhuys: "We regret to find no other foundation for the Convention than force, no other justification than the reciprocal convenience of the co-sharers. This is a mode of procedure to which the Europe of to-day has become unaccustomed, and precedents for it must be sought in the darkest ages of history." Queen Victoria was full of indignation. Lord Clarendon called the now inevitable annexation of the Duchies the most infamous act since the partition of Poland. But, he added, King Bismarck I is the only man among forty million Germans who has a purpose and the will to give effect to it.

Even the Prussian Ambassadors were horrified by the principles underlying the Gastein Convention. The Prussian Ambassador in Paris, Count Goltz, wrote to the Prussian Ambassador in London, Count Bernstorff: "The Gastein Convention puts us permanently on the path of trickery, force, and violation of law".

Both contracting Powers were equally open to such reproaches. But, from the political point of view, there was no doubt that Prussia was the winner and Austria the loser. People were at a loss to understand how Austria could have been brought to conclude a treaty of this nature. The Bavarian Minister-President cried: "Whenever I have to negotiate a treaty I shall be happy if Bismarck accepts my power of attorney". Prussia, avowedly bent on power politics, could afford to break principles and treaties. Austria could not; for her very existence depended on treaties, and her policy was, in the last resort, based on the conservative principle of maintenance of law. Prussia openly defied the German Confederation, but Austria not only was its presiding Power, its whole German position depended on the goodwill of the German governments, which were deeply offended by the treaty. If only Austria could be certain that the Sleswig-Holstein question had been closed and that her possession of Holstein had become definite! But, too timid to go to the full extent of breaking the treaties, the court of Vienna had made an unpardonable mistake in proposing that the partition of the Duchies should be only *provisional*. In this way it gave Bismarck every opportunity to open the question anew and to disturb the Austrian administration of Holstein. But what was to be expected from the Emperor Francis Joseph, who asked Bismarck *his* opinion whether *he* thought that the treaty would be advantageous to Austria? *Quem Deus perdere vult, prius dementat.*

B. TO THE PEACE OF PRAGUE

1. *Biarritz, 1865*

Bismarck lost no time in pursuing his plans. During his negotiations in Gastein he had worked hard to bring Italy into an alliance with Prussia against Austria and to induce Napoleon to favour it. Both attempts had failed. Napoleon and the Italian Minister, General la Marmora, played the same game as Bismarck. Each one wanted to wait till the other had taken a step which could not be retraced. The Italians particularly wanted to be sure, before exposing themselves, that Prussia was unable to come to an understanding with Austria at their expense. La Marmora was therefore highly irritated when Bismarck concluded the Gastein Convention immediately after having assured him that an understanding with Austria was out of the question.

Bismarck now decided to approach Italy indirectly, that is to say with the help of Napoleon. Drouyn de Lhuys' sharp note had offended him very much. But he soon came to know that the Emperor, although he had himself taken the initiative with this note, not only did not wish to draw any practical consequences from it, but was afraid that it would bring Austria and Prussia together in a common opposition to France. He was therefore quite willing to converse with Bismarck when the Prussian Minister appeared in Biarritz a few weeks after concluding the Gastein Convention (4th and 11th October 1865).

Bismarck had prepared the ground for his conversation with Napoleon by some broad hints he had given to Benedetti's deputy, the French chargé d'affaires in Berlin. This was Lefebvre de Béhain, later Ambassador of the Third Republic to the Holy See. He told the young diplomat not only that the Gastein Convention did not contain any secret clauses against France—that was true—but he emphasized its provisional character and its ambiguous text which would allow him to involve Austria in new quarrels. That was only the introduction to his tempting hints. He had no objection, he told Lefebvre, if France looked for an increment of territory and influence in a sphere indicated by the affinity of race and language. This meant, of course, *Belgium*, the acquisition of which Napoleon was reputed to want very ardently. But still more was to come. He gave him to understand that after a Prussian war against Austria and the Southern German states, even an acquisition of German territory by the Emperor would become possible. Lefebvre, taken aback by this unexpected hint, asked Bismarck whether he was allowed to report it to Paris. Bismarck's answer was decidedly in the affirmative. He wanted Napoleon to know his intentions.

Immediately before Bismarck's departure from Biarritz Lefebvre returned to the question, and Bismarck was this time even more explicit. He showed him on the map of Sleswig-Holstein the frontier with which Prussia would be satisfied; it left the northern part of Sleswig, inhabited by Danes, to Denmark, which was in accordance with Napoleon's wishes and his principle of nationalism. But, Bismarck added, this programme could only be executed with the help of the French Emperor, who would then be entitled to expand his rule *"everywhere where French is spoken"*. This meant again, Belgium. It was the bait which Bismarck held out to Napoleon.

But Napoleon did not rise to it. What Bismarck and Napoleon said in Biarritz is not known exactly. But it seems rather certain that Napoleon did not start talking about Belgium, and so Bismarck was prevented from doing so himself. The truth seems to be that Napoleon did not want to come to a decision. That was never his strong point, but this weakness grew worse after his illness in the spring of that year. The illness was caused by stone in the bladder, which finally brought about his death.

On his return journey Bismarck talked in Paris to the very influential Italian Ambassador, Nigra. He told him that war with Austria was inevitable, and urged him to see to it that Prussia and Italy would fight it as allies. In Berlin he at once began to harass Austria with new notes, new reproaches, and new demands. Furthermore, he induced General von Manteuffel, who was now Governor-General of Sleswig, to molest the Austrian Governor of Holstein, Gablenz, incessantly. Bismarck's programme is revealed in a declaration in November: "We have to *faire le mort* (pretend to be dead) and behave as if we were quite satisfied with the provisional settlement; at the same time to complain without pause in Vienna against the Austrian administration in Holstein and to keep open such complaints against Austria as might be capable of sharper development under certain circumstances" (*Unter Umständen schärferer Entwicklung fähig.*) Thus, only a few months after the conclusion of the Gastein Convention, he was planning *war against his ally*. By the end of January 1866 he had managed so to exasperate the long-suffering Austrian government that it sent a sharp note to

Bismarck, which allowed him to say to Benedetti that he would not answer any more and that he considered the intimacy of the courts of Vienna and Berlin as over.

It was, therefore, only a question of opportunity when Bismarck would proceed to an open rupture.

2. *Aggravation of the Constitutional Conflict*

At the same time, the constitutional conflict was again aggravated by a new attack which Bismarck made on the constitution. Freedom of parliamentary speech was one of the elementary rights which the Prussian constitution explicitly guaranteed. It forbade, in so many words, any indictment against a deputy on account of words spoken in parliament. The framers of the Prussian constitution had learnt from the history of the English parliament. Nevertheless, Bismarck and his Minister of Justice, the notorious Count von Lippe, ordered an act of indictment against the Progressive deputy Twesten for having slandered Prussian Courts of Law in a speech in the Chamber of Deputies. Twesten was certainly neither a demagogue nor a radical but a Prussian patriot of moderate but firm principles. He was a judge himself. Thus his criticism was all the more effective, one more reason for Bismarck and Lippe to get him out of the way.

The courts before which this indictment was brought declined it as unconstitutional. But the Highest Court of the Prussian Monarchy, the Ober-Tribunal, packed by Lippe, allowed the indictment by a decision of January 1866 which circumvented the constitution by a sophistry not worth repeating. It is one of the darkest pages in the history of Prussian jurisdiction. Twesten was perfectly right when he apostrophized the miserable Lippe in the Chamber: "You may decorate your judges with all the orders of the Prussian Monarchy. Your decoration will not hide the wounds which *these judges have inflicted upon their own honour and upon the honour of our country.*" Eduard Simson, whom in later years Bismarck made the first President of the Reichsgericht (a kind of Chief Justice of Germany), said: "The present Government cannot rule with a free press; they cannot govern without improperly influencing the judges; they cannot govern with a parliament in which speech is free. But how they can squander irreplaceable hundredweights of Prussia's future for one grain of the moment, only to keep things going for a short while,—that is incomprehensible for my poor brain."

The debate of the Chamber was a moral execution of the government, and public opinion was in full agreement with the deputies. Benedetti wrote that it was excited beyond expectation, and Karolyi said that Bismarck's government was, in home politics, at its wits' end. Both thought that Bismarck would look for a way out of these difficulties by means of his foreign policy.

3. *The Crown Council of the 28th February 1866*

This was the situation on 28th February 1866, when King William presided over the Council of his Ministers to decide Prussia's future policy. The importance of this Council was emphasized by the presence not only of the Crown Prince, but also of the Ambassador in Paris, Count Goltz, and of the Generals Moltke, Chief of Staff of the Army, Manteuffel, Governor-General of Sleswig, and Alvensleben, principal personal adviser of the King. The question which the Council would have to answer was, indeed, nothing less than whether there should be peace or war.

Bismarck called the war with Austria inevitable and asked for the authorization of the King to send a special envoy to Florence in order to conclude an *alliance with Italy* and to try to obtain certain guarantees from Napoleon, particularly in case the *object of the war* should be a *higher one than the possession of the Duchies*. He did not consider it opportune to talk more explicitly about this higher object; but no doubt it was the new position of Prussia in Germany. The King must have suspected something of the aims of his Prime Minister, for, he declared, the aims of Prussian policy must *never* be the *dethronement of German Princes*. Only the Crown Prince opposed Bismarck and spoke of fraternal war (*Bruderkrieg*). But again he aroused no response. Moltke warmly supported the alliance with Italy, which he called an indispensable condition for a military success. The King gave the authorization for which Bismarck had asked. Now his way was clear; now war was indeed inevitable.

In the course of the discussion in the Council the Minister of the Interior, Count Eulenburg, argued that war would be a way out of the constitutional difficulties. But Bismarck answered that that could never be a reason for waging war. This fitted in with a word he had spoken in the Chamber: "For me Foreign Policy is an end in itself". He declined to use it as a means to another end.

4. *The Alliance with Italy, 8th April 1866*

The King's authorization to negotiate an alliance with Italy was of the highest importance to Bismarck. He had worked incessantly to win the Italian government over. But the conclusion of the Gastein Convention at the very moment when the Prussian Ambassador in Florence, Usedom, had assured General la Marmora that Bismarck was ready to conclude an alliance with Italy, had been such a shock to la Marmora that he was most reluctant to have any further dealings with the cunning Prussian Minister. He rather wanted to come to an understanding with Italy's old enemy, Austria. An Italian nobleman with excellent Austrian connexions, Malaguzzi, went to Vienna and proposed a cession of Venetia for the payment of a couple of millions. But Francis Joseph considered the question not from the point of view of power politics but from that of prestige. As the representative of the oldest monarchy in Europe he was too proud for a bargain of this kind, and some of his clerical counsellors strongly advised against an agreement with the enemy of the Pope. Thus nothing came of it, and la Marmora had to return to Prussia.

Bismarck had urged Usedom again and again to influence la Marmora in favour of an agreement with Prussia. He considered this alliance so important that he allowed Usedom to hear more of his secret thoughts than other men, although he did not like him at all. In a note of January 1866 he disclosed to him his idea of bringing Prussian policy back to the more fundamental national basis and of allying Prussia with the forces of nationalism. It was the same idea which he had, seven years before, on his recall from Frankfurt, developed to a Liberal friend, Unruh, with the argument that the only reliable ally Prussia had was the German people (p. 41). Despite all his Conservative catchwords and his violent attacks on

Prussian Liberalism, he had not forgotten the lesson he had learnt at the Diet of Frankfurt.

When at the Crown Council of 28th February Bismarck asked for the King's authorization to treat with Italy, he already knew that la Marmora was ready. Usedom had telegraphed on the 24th that the Italian King, Victor Emanuel, and his Minister were expecting Prussian proposals for an alliance, to wage a common war against Austria. Bismarck's plan was to send General von Moltke to Florence. In his really masterly instructions for Moltke of 12th March, Bismarck laid down his intention of concluding an alliance by which Italy should be obliged to follow Prussia in a war, but which should *not oblige Prussia to wage a war*. The alliance should therefore have the character of a *unilateral obligation* on the part of Italy. To the last moment Bismarck wanted to have both ways open—war and peaceful settlement; of this the Italians should, of course, have no inkling. But Bismarck instructed Moltke expressly to tell them "the higher aims of Prussian ambition". "We aim," he writes, "at least in Northern Germany, at that position which the National Constitution of 1849 had intended for the Central Authority." The National Constitution of 1849 was the work of the revolutionary Frankfurt Assembly, the same constitution which Bismarck as deputy, in his speech in the Prussian Chamber (1849), had condemned root and branch as "organized anarchy" (p. 27). He now wrote in his instructions for Moltke: "We consider this Constitution in its military and political aspects as the *expression of the natural needs of the nation*, although its other parts are influenced by party tendencies". What a long distance he had travelled since his anti-revolutionary days!

Moltke's mission to Florence was dropped, because an Italian special envoy, General Govone, came to Berlin in March 1866. Govone's reports of his conversations with Bismarck are most interesting, because they show his methods very distinctly. It was not all plain sailing. Each party entirely distrusted the other. The Italians feared that Bismarck sought an agreement with them only in order to show it to the Court of Vienna and so obtain all the desired Austrian concessions. At the beginning of the negotiations Govone wrote to la Marmora about outwitting Bismarck: "*Et la vipère aura mordu le charlatan*" (the viper will have bitten the charlatan). His distrust was increased when, on various pretexts, King William avoided seeing him. As usual, the King could not make up his mind. That in spite of all these obstacles the negotiations succeeded and a treaty of alliance was concluded was only due to the help of Napoleon III.

Bismarck had told Govone time after time that everything depended on the French Emperor, that he could only proceed with his own plans *if France agreed*. King Victor Emanuel sent an Italian nobleman who was a personal friend of the Emperor, Count Arese, to Napoleon to ask him whether he should ally himself to Prussia. Napoleon received him, unknown by his Ministers, and advised in favour of the alliance, adding, however, that he gave this advice only as a private person *without taking any responsibility*. What an absurd kind of policy, to give a decision of the most far-reaching consequences, and to try to decline responsibility for it! There was, of course, no way of escaping the consequences and the responsibility for them. A considerable portion of Bismarck's enormous success is, indeed, due to the fact that his adversaries were such weak politicians. Francis Joseph was a mediocrity without any political instinct, and Napoleon, who was much more intelligent, was always scheming and dreaming, but unable to make up his mind and to see the consequences of his acts and his omissions.

As far as the decisive point was concerned, the treaty gave Bismarck what he wanted: no obligation for Prussia to wage war, but the obligation of Italy to follow suit if and when Prussia declared war. But the Italians had carried through the clause that the alliance automatically terminated if Prussia did not declare war in *three months'* time. It was clear that Bismarck had to act at once.

This treaty, in fact, *destroyed the German Confederation*. The constitution of the Confederation explicitly forbade any of its members to ally themselves with a foreign Power against any other member. An alliance of this kind was, indeed, incompatible with the very existence of the Confederation, the aim of which was the common protection of all its members. Prussia's alliance with Italy against Austria was as fundamental a breach of the constitution of Germany as the secession of South Carolina and the other Southern States in 1861 was a breach of the constitution of the United States. Never in the fifty years of the Confederation had any of its members done anything of this kind. No wonder that King William hesitated to sign this treaty and that he never allowed the veil of secrecy which surrounded it to be lifted during the whole of his life. It was even worse that, when, some months later, war was imminent, he gave his *word of honour* to the Austrian Emperor, Francis Joseph, that no treaty of this kind existed. Was not Beust quite right when he said that a scrupulous Prussian King inspired by his character a confidence which his acts did not justify?

Bismarck, naturally, knew exactly what he had done. He said to Benedetti: "I have induced a King of Prussia to break off the intimate relations of his House with the House of Habsburg, to conclude an alliance with revolutionary Italy, possibly to accept arrangements with Imperial France, and to propose in Frankfurt the reform of the Confederation and a popular parliament. That is a success of which I am proud." He indeed had every reason to be proud. It was the complete victory of his own policy.

5. *Universal Suffrage*

Bismarck did not allow even a single day to pass after the conclusion of the Italian alliance before commencing the political campaign which could only end in war. The 9th April, one day after the treaty was signed, the Prussian Minister in Frankfurt brought before the Diet the long-prepared proposal to summon a German parliament *elected by the whole German nation directly by universal suffrage*, which was to receive and to discuss the suggestions of the governments for a reform of the Federal Constitution. It was the most revolutionary proposal ever brought before the Diet.

Its most sensational point was universal suffrage. It meant that every adult German should have an equal franchise: one man, one vote. So democratic a franchise did not exist anywhere in any of the German states. It was the franchise of the Revolution of 1848 and of the National Constitution of 1849 which Bismarck had called "anarchy", particularly on account of this franchise. Why had he so completely changed his ideas?

Universal franchise had been advocated during the preceding years with the greatest energy and passion by one man: Ferdinand Lassalle, the founder of the German Social-Democratic Party. He was a democrat and a revolutionary, but he hoped to overthrow, by means of this suffrage, the German Progressive Party, which he considered as the incarnation of the *bourgeoisie*, the middle class. The Progressive Party was also Bismarck's enemy. This common enmity brought the two men together. Bismarck had many secret nocturnal conversations with this Jewish revolutionary genius who impressed Bismarck very much with his ideas and his excellent knowledge, his brilliant conversational talents, and his personal charm. When he had to speak about his relations with Lassalle in the Reichstag in the debate on the bill against the Socialists in 1878, Bismarck praised Lassalle's personality in the warmest terms and said that it had always been a matter for regret when their conversations had to end after continuing for some hours.

Lassalle's argument was that the political position of the Progressives depended entirely on the three-class suffrage and that it would vanish immediately if universal suffrage were introduced. He even advocated its initiation by an order of the King, that is, by a *coup d'état*. Bismarck considered this proposal seriously, but found it too risky and its success too uncertain. But Lassalle's arguments impressed him. Each of them, of course, expected quite different results from the defeat of the Liberals. Lassalle had his eyes on the urban proletariat and hoped for a Socialist victory as a result of their vote. Bismarck thought of the agricultural districts. He knew from his own experience how powerful the influence of the Junkers and squires on the labourers and poor people was in these places, and thus hoped for royalist elections. When the King resisted so revolutionary a proposal Bismarck told him that universal suffrage would raise the King high up on a *rock which the waters of revolution would never touch*. And to Goltz he wrote: "In moments of decision the masses will always stand by the King, no matter whether he rules in a more Liberal or more Conservative manner". He considered the opposition against his arbitrary methods as a superficial excitement of the upper middle classes. He did not understand properly either the feeling of the middle classes or of the working-class. His practical model was Napoleon III, whose government was sustained by the masses and opposed by a portion of the educated upper middle class; Napoleon had introduced universal suffrage to get rid of the Second Republic and had been successful in that. Bismarck was confident that he would be able to achieve the same success.

There is no longer any doubt that Bismarck's foresight was at fault and that his calculations were completely wrong. True, he succeeded by his cunning and energy in weakening and humiliating German Liberalism by means of universal suffrage. But the winner was certainly not the King. Bismarck's most fervent enemies, the Catholic Centre and Social Democracy, profited most; and when the revolution finally came in 1918, universal suffrage was certainly not the rock upon which the threatened monarchy could rely.

True, Bismarck at the same time had another idea by the realization of which he hoped to avoid the dangers of universal suffrage. The parliament he planned was to be so *devoid of real political power* that it had only the name and not the normal functions of a parliament. It is remarkable that his proposal to the Diet did not contain a word about the normal competence and function of the German parliament. He wished to keep his hands completely free. But he was destined to see that even a man of such immense authority as he possessed after his victory would be unable to take away from the nation with one hand what he had given with the other. The *idea* which he had propagated was *stronger* than even his powerful personality. Weak as the German Reichstag was, it was nevertheless always a political parliament which could not be set aside at the will of the King.

Bismarck says in his *Recollections* that he proposed universal suffrage because it was the most powerful implement known at that time to friends of liberty. He hoped that Prussia would show by this proposal that she had the real interests and wishes of the German nation at heart, and that the nation would rally round her when she drew the sword for universal suffrage and national parliament against their adversaries. But this hope, too, failed. Austria and the medium-size states did not play his game by throwing out the Prussian proposal point blank. They sent it to a committee of the Diet and asked Prussia to lay before it a full project of reform. Moreover, Bismarck's proposal failed to move public opinion deeply. Distrust of Birmarck was so great that most people considered his project as a mere tactical manœuvre. Even Treitschke called it an "adventurer's policy". On the other hand, the Conservatives were split. The majority of the Prussian Conservative Party were simply government-followers. Their leader, Wagener, now in an important position in the Prussian Ministry, advocated universal suffrage as an instrument against Liberalism and parliamentarianism and proposed to adapt it to a form useful to his party's interests. But Ludwig von Gerlach, the brother of the late general Leopold von Gerlach, one of the founders of the Conservative Party and a Conservative not only by name, was firmly opposed to it. In foreign countries criticism was stronger than praise. The *Spectator*, however, wrote of Bismarck: "The man's policy is detestable, but his objects are great, his plans adequate and his ability marvellous".

6. *Efforts to avert War*

It was now clear to everybody that war was imminent. The excitement in Germany was enormous. In Prussia the great majority of the people were against war; many towns sent addresses to the King, praying him to preserve peace. The Germans of that time were certainly a peace-loving people, not a nation of war-mongers. They had not yet been infected by the gospel of "blood and iron". The diplomats of the foreign countries were busy in the same direction. Bismarck strained every nerve to goad Austria into aggression. He knew the weakness of her military system: that she required, for her mobilization, three or four weeks more than Prussia. She was, indeed, confronted by the dilemma of every militarily unprepared state: either to make hasty preparations and therefore to be accused of aggressiveness, or to keep quiet and risk defeat at the very beginning. Under these circumstances it is no small achievement of the Austrian government that it managed to succeed, by a clever diplomatic move, in bringing about a declaration of the Prussian government promising to demobilize its troops, provided that Austria did the same. It was a difficult situation for Bismarck, but he regained his freedom of action with the help of la Marmora, who declared on 28th April that Italy was compelled to mobilize her forces in order to defend herself. Now Austria declared that she was unable to demobilize her troops in the south, and Bismarck stated that in consequence of this declaration a Prussian demobilization was impossible. But a new danger arose through a move on the part of Napoleon. On 5th May he told the Italian Ambassador, Nigra, that Austria was willing to cede Venetia to France, who would transfer it at once to Italy, on the condition that Italy would give Austria a free hand to obtain an equivalent territorial compensation in Germany. Napoleon, who, of course, knew about the secret Prussian-Italian alliance, asked Nigra whether Italy would be able to drop it. La Marmora saved Prussia by promptly rejecting this tempting offer. "For us it is a question of honour and of loyalty not to let Prussia down", he wired to Nigra.

In this situation a German nobleman, Anton von Gablenz, a member of the Prussian Diet, tried to save the peace. He acted in agreement with his brother, the Austrian General Ludwig von Gablenz, Governor-General of Holstein. Gablenz negotiated in Vienna as well as in Berlin, and he was deeply impressed by Bismarck's resolution and grasp of the situation, in contrast to the confusion in Vienna. The curious thing is that Bismarck favoured Gablenz's mission, not from any motives of German patriotism, as he liked later to say, but in order to calm the conscience of the King. He was almost certain beforehand that nothing would come out of it and that he would then be able to say that Austria rejected a just compromise. That would help him effectively to overcome what remained of the King's scruples. It is remarkable, however, that in the draft of a reform which Bismarck gave to Gablenz there is not a word about a German parliament and universal suffrage. All the more exact were his proposals about the military constitution of the reformed Confederation; that is to say, about the stipulation that the King of Prussia should be Commander-in-Chief of the troops in Northern Germany. This was the only point in which William I was really interested.

The whole episode is characteristic of Bismarck's double-barrelled policy. He knew how to explore, at the same time, two entirely different ways, to keep open each of them and to postpone his own decision until he knew with absolute certainty which way would enable him to attain his ends most quickly and efficiently.

7. *Attempt on Bismarck's Life. Question of Indemnity*

At this time of the highest excitement an attempt was made on Bismarck's life. On 7th May, when he was walking from the Royal Palace to his own office, a young man took a shot at him in the street called Unter den Linden. The assailant was a student, Ferdinand Cohen, the stepson of Karl Blind, a participant in the Revolution of 1849, who lived in exile in London and was a friend of the great Italian revolutionary Mazzini. The attempt failed and Cohen killed himself in prison in the first night. Thus only very little is known about his plans. But there can be no doubt that he wanted to save German liberty by killing its most dangerous enemy. The sympathy of the population was with the assailant, not with Bismarck, so unpopular was Bismarck in spite of his proposals for reform. One example may be quoted. A professor of Berlin University hurried into a bookseller's shop in Unter den Linden exclaiming indignantly: "How bad revolvers in this country are!" This professor was the famous physiologist, Dubois-Reymond. Four years later this same Dubois-Reymond said in a solemn speech in the hall of the University: "We Berlin Professors are the *spiritual life-guards of the House of Hohenzollern"—Tempora mutantur et nos mutamur in illis.*

But not only small men are changed by time and circumstances. The great men, too, who make history, are changed by their own ideas and plans and their consequences. The Bismarck who went forward to make Prussia the head of a new German state, with a common German parliament, could not remain the oppressor of his own parliament and the party leader of the Conservatives. The national unification of Germany was a Liberal idea, and the statesman who tried to make this idea his instrument was forced into Liberal ways, whether he liked it or not. Despite all his caustic remarks about the Liberals, Bismarck was much too level-headed not to know that they were indispensable for his work. No German parliament, whatever the suffrage might be, was likely to have a Conservative majority. There did not exist Conservatives of the Prussian type in any of the other German states who would be willing to co-operate in the unification of Germany. It was no coincidence that in these days Bismarck's old friendship with Ludwig von Gerlach, his protector in the time of the counter-revolution, was broken off. Gerlach had too much character to follow Bismarck in ways which were completely at variance with his principles.

The most important consequence of this new situation was, that the Prussian conflict had to be ended. A settlement had to be arrived at. It was impossible to continue indefinitely with a government without budget. Moreover, Bismarck did not forget that the Crown Prince was a bitter opponent of the conflict, and nobody could know when he would succeed to the throne. A special factor worked in the same direction. The Minister of Finance, a convinced Conservative of the Gerlach type, was unwilling to follow Bismarck into the war. A new Minister had to be found who would be willing and able to deal with the very difficult financial situation and to procure the money which was indispensable for the war. Bismarck turned to von der Heydt, the former Minister of Finance, who had retired in the year 1862 because he declined to break his oath to the constitution by taking part in a government without a budget. Von der Heydt was ready to accept the dangerous position, but only on condition that Bismarck would promise to ask the parliament for an indemnity. Indemnity is a term of English parliamentary usage. Governments there occasionally ask parliament for an indemnity, namely, in cases where their expenditure went beyond the sum voted by parliament. Bismarck promised to ask for an indemnity for all the money spent in the years of the conflict, if he returned victorious from the war. Von der Heydt became Minister and succeeded in procuring the money.

On the other hand, an important section of the Opposition Liberals felt now that the whole future of the Prussian state was at stake and that all internal differences had to recede into the background. One of the most radical deputies of the Progressive Party, old Ziegler, a friend of Lassalle, cried out to the citizens of Breslau: "The heart of Prussia's democracy is there where Prussia's banner flies". Other less sanguine men wanted unity of the people against the foreign enemy. Bismarck had various interviews with Liberal deputies. Among them was Twesten, whom Bismarck asked to propose the draft of an indemnity bill. He had no objections to the really very moderate draft which Twesten made. But the King rejected it vehemently with the characteristic remark: "But that says the same as the Constitution does. Then, they can again take away my regiments." He had forgotten that he was a constitutional king. We can understand Bismarck saying to a Liberal deputy: "No man can imagine the difficulties against which I have to fight".

Twesten told Bismarck distinctly how far he and his friends were willing to go. What they would never do was to contribute, by sacrificing the law, to the general *demoralization*. Did Bismarck appreciate their point of view? We may doubt it, if we hear what Treitschke, certainly the most passionate advocate of Prussian ascendancy, said after an interview with Bismarck in the last days before the war. He confessed that he was very much impressed by Bismarck's personality, but he added: "Of the *moral powers* in the world he has *not the slightest notion*!"

8. *Proposal for a European Conference*

The enigma of the international situation was the attitude of the French Emperor. Nobody knew what would be his policy in case of war. The reason was very simple: the Emperor himself did not know it. True, by his advice to Arese he had helped Bismarck to secure the Italian alliance. But soon he became doubtful whether a Prussian victory would be to his advantage. He was not even sure whether he should wish for war or the maintenance of peace. At last he returned to his old idea of a European congress. On 24th May the three neutral Powers, France, Great Britain, and Russia, sent out invitations to a European congress to settle the three questions of Sleswig-Holstein, Italy, and the German Confederation. Bismarck was extremely annoyed by this invitation, which endangered his whole policy. But he knew that its rejection would stigmatize him as the peace-breaker. Therefore he was the first to accept it. For he was really a statesman; Francis Joseph's Ministers were not. They accepted it only on impossible conditions, although they should have welcomed it at least in the interest of Austria's military preparations. Again Bismarck was rescued from a very difficult situation by the mistakes of his enemies. Benedetti was with him when the telegram announcing the cancellation of the congress arrived. He jumped to his feet and cried out: " Now it is war. Long live the King!"

The days before this result was reached were a time of the highest tension for Bismarck. In order to win Napoleon's favour he was willing to go to extremes. Govone, the Italian general who had negotiated the treaty of alliance, was in these days again in Berlin. He asked Bismarck whether there was any frontier which would satisfy France. Bismarck answered: "Oh yes, the Moselle. I personally am *much less German than Prussian*. I would have no objection to ceding to France the whole of the territory between Moselle and Rhine: the Palatinate and part of the Prussian Rheinprovinz. But the King is under the influence of the Queen; he would have the greatest scruples and agree to these cessions only at a moment when it is a question of either gaining all or losing all." Two days later he told Benedetti that under certain circumstances he would use his influence with the King to obtain a cession to France of the territory on the Upper Moselle which, together with Luxemburg, would give France a favourable frontier. He added that the King's advice to France was to annex the territories where French is spoken.

It was neither the first nor the last time that he dangled this bait before the eyes of Napoleon.

9. *Outbreak of the War*

Since the impossibility of a settlement of the Sleswig-Holstein question by an understanding between Austria and Prussia was manifest, Austria was compelled to try and draw the German medium states to her side. Therefore she brought the question before the Diet in the first days of June. Bismarck answered with the order to the Prussian troops in Sleswig to march into Holstein. He hoped that a clash between Austrian and Prussian troops would throw the fire into the powder barrel. But Manteuffel, the commander in Sleswig, moved by a sense of chivalry, allowed Gablenz to conduct the Austrian troops peacefully out of Holstein. Bismarck was deeply disappointed and wrote to Manteuffel a letter which is one of his most remarkable and characteristic efforts. He knew that Manteuffel was a fervent admirer of Schiller's drama *Wallenstein*, the lines of which he was wont to quote at every occasion. Therefore Bismarck cited *Wallenstein* too. "You say", he wrote, "that a violent act would embarrass the mind. I answer you with the words of Deveroux [the murderer of Wallenstein], '*Freund, jetzt ist's Zeit zu lärmen*'." (Friend, now it is time for alarm). He ends with the words: "Excuse the hasty style of this letter, but your telegram this morning paralysed my nerves, and this is now the reaction. In haste but in old friendship, Yours, Bismarck." But the signature is followed by another quotation from *Wallenstein*. While his pen flew over the paper he thought of some lines which expressed his feelings better still. He ordered a copy to be brought to him, and when the letter was finished the book was before him. He found the lines spoken by Wallenstein at the decisive moment when only open rebellion is left to him, and he wrote under his signature:

> *Ich tat's mit Widerstreben,*
> *Da es in meine Wahl noch war gegeben.*
> *Notwendigkeit ist da, der Zweifel flieht,*
> *Jetzt fecht ich für mein Haupt und für mein Leben.*
>
> (*Er geht ab, die andern folgen.*)

> (Ling'ring, irresolute, with fitful fears
> I drew the sword—'twas with an inward strife,
> While yet the choice was mine. The murderous knife
> Is lifted for my heart! Doubt disappears!
> I fight now for my head and for my life.
>
> (*Exit Wallenstein, the others follow him.*))

Even the most critical reader cannot help feeling overwhelmed by this letter. No other statesman would have been able to write a letter of this scope at so critical a moment.

Austria's answer to the Prussian occupation of Holstein was a motion in the Diet to mobilize the troops of all the member-states of the Confederation with the exception of the Prussian Corps. By adopting this motion the Diet would have taken up a clear stand against Prussia. As the medium states wanted to avoid this clear position as long as possible, the Bavarian Minister moved an amendment which excepted not only the Prussian but also the Austrian Corps from mobilization. In this way he hoped to preserve impartiality. Bismarck, on the other hand, brought his project of reform before the Diet. Its principal feature was the exclusion of Austria from the future Germany. In other words, he returned to the constitution adopted in 1849 by the National Assembly in

Frankfurt. This project could be deliberated at the earliest only at the meeting of the Diet in which the Austrian motion was to be put to the vote. Deliberation on it was therefore impossible, as Bismarck was resolved to blow up the Diet the moment when the vote upon the Austrian motion was taken. He ordered the Prussian representative to read, immediately after the taking of the vote, a Prussian declaration that the motion itself and its acceptance by part of the Confederate states implied a breach of the constitution of the Confederation, which was therefore declared to be broken, null, and void. Bismarck's order was to have this declaration read even if the Austrian motion failed to secure a majority. This shows quite clearly that the legal arguments put forward for this alleged breach of the constitution were only pretexts, and that he himself knew that perfectly well. Indeed, how could the man who himself had broken the constitution of the Confederation two months before, by his treaty with Italy, reproach other members with breaking it?

The vote was taken on 14th June 1866. Not the Austrian but the Bavarian motion was adopted by the majority. At once the Prussian plenipotentiary rose and read the declaration ordered by Bismarck, although it did not fit the vote actually taken by the majority.

But what did that matter? Prussia's declaration was a *declaration of war*. Every federal state which had voted—not against Prussia, but for the Bavarian motion—was in danger of being attacked by the Prussian army.

Bismarck had reached his goal: war had broken out before the three months provided by the Italian treaty were over. Austria was threatened on two fronts. The last word was now with the sword.

It is here pertinent to raise the question, much disputed in later years by historians, whether Bismarck's intention was from the beginning, that is to say, ever since the peace with Denmark in 1864, to make war against Austria. He certainly never had any scruples about a war of this kind, which he himself in later years called "fraternal". But it is another question whether he *wanted* the war. The answer is that he would have been willing to do without the war if he had been able to achieve his aims by normal diplomatic means. It would have been out of harmony with his usual method if he had committed himself to war, even one day before he had made quite sure that no other way was open to him. He could not know beforehand what concessions Austria was prepared to make in order to avoid war. After the war, some people said Austria's best policy would have been to make sufficient concessions to have averted the necessity of recourse to the sword. Rechberg, for instance, asserted to the end of his life that the catastrophe could have been avoided if his policy had been followed. Needless to say, this was a biased view.

It is permissible to ask to-day, after the experience of two generations, whether Austria would have been able to save her alliance with Prussia on the basis of a renunciation to her claims in the Duchies in favour of Prussia in return for compensatory concessions elsewhere. The weakness of a policy of this kind lay, however, in finding a *quid pro quo* for this strengthening of Prussian power. A territorial compensation in the form of a cession of even the smallest part of Prussia was rejected categorically by King William. A compensation in Austria's position in Germany was out of the question. On the contrary, Bismarck was determined to take away from Austria her privileges connected with the Presidency of the Confederation. Any Austrian statesman, ready to throw over the Confederation as obsolete, was bound to ask for a concession in the field of European policy to offset her loss of influence. That could only have meant the granting of Prussian support against Italy, and Bismarck was decidedly against giving this support. Thus it is hard to see where the Prussian alliance could have been of any value to Austria. But no alliance is, in the long run, tenable if only one partner has all the advantages while the other remains empty-handed. Bismarck only liked alliances where he was in the saddle and his ally the horse. It was the same with the alliance which he concluded in 1879 with the Habsburg Monarchy. So long as he was the leading Minister, he was, thanks to his personal superiority, able to keep the position of horseman. His successors were not. Thus the alliance of 1864 broke down because Austria could not obtain her share. The alliance of 1879 did not break down, but when Austria got "into the saddle" it involved both partners in a catastrophe.

Thus the conclusion may be reached that, although Bismarck was not from the beginning bent on war with Austria, he was engaged in a policy which made war unavoidable. The mistake of the Austrian statesmen was that they did not see in time that war was indeed inevitable, and that military and political preparations were necessary; but they cannot be reproached with having failed to avoid a war which was in no way avoidable.

10. *Prussia's Victory*

The day after the vote in Frankfurt, on 15th June, the Prussian Ministers in Hanover, Dresden, and Cassel laid before these governments an ultimatum. Bismarck had sent this ultimatum to his envoys some days before the vote, ordering them to deliver it on receipt of a telegraphic order. This order was given immediately the news of the vote reached Berlin. A reply was required before midnight the same day. The ultimatum asked for unconditional acceptance of the Prussian plan of reform and for demobilization of the troops.

Saxony was in a state of preparedness and at once withdrew her troops to Austria, to link up with the army of the Emperor. The King of Hanover, blind George V, was a very stubborn man who had made many stupid mistakes. He had hoped against hope not to be entangled in the conflict and had not done anything to prepare an effective resistance. Bismarck had for some months tried to win over to his side the leaders of the Liberal Opposition in Hanover, Bennigsen and Miquel. But Bennigsen, although the champion of Germany's unification under Prussian leadership, declined to take part in any conversations about his country. He did not wish to become a traitor to his King and country. King George was determined to be true to his obligations to the German Confederation, of which he was a member. He saw the immense peril in which he stood, but he did not hesitate to reject the ultimatum. "As a Christian, a monarch and a Guelph," he said, "I cannot act in any other way." He marched with his soldiers southwards in the hope of effecting a link-up with the troops of the South German states. At Langensalza his soldiers won a skirmish against the Prussians, but some days later, on 29th June, they were completely encircled and compelled to capitulate. King George left for England.

On the evening of the 15th June Bismarck was in the garden of his office with the British Ambassador, Lord Loftus. When the clock struck midnight, Bismarck said to Loftus: "At this moment our troops are marching into Hanover, Saxony, and the Electorate of Hesse-Cassel. It will be a serious struggle. *If we are beaten, I shall not return.* I can die only once, and it befits the vanquished to die." There can be no doubt that Bismarck would not have survived a defeat—as so many others have done.

But there was no defeat. Three weeks later, on 3rd July, the Prussians defeated the Austrians decisively at Königgrätz or Sadowa, as the battle is called in Western Europe. The fighting was hard and fierce. All depended on the arrival of the army of the Crown Prince at the right time. He did reach the battlefield before it was too late, and Prussia won a great victory. When the Austrians fled, a Prussian general said to Bismarck: "Excellency, you are now a great man. But if the Crown Prince had come too late you would now be the greatest villain." That was perfectly true, and Bismarck knew it. But nothing succeeds like success, and the evening after the Battle of Königgrätz Bismarck was the hero of Prussia and the great statesman who had prepared the war and won it. Everybody recognized and acknowledged his genius. The success was won on the battlefield, but his policy had made it possible. He had, quite alone, surmounted innumerable difficulties.

11. *Napoleon's Attempt at Interference*

The great Prussian victory at Königgrätz made a tremendous impression throughout the whole of Europe. Everybody felt that a new era was beginning, but not only for Germany, for the balance of power had been altered radically. All the Great European Powers felt this change, and no country more than France. Napoleon was suddenly in a most dreadful position. Unable to come in time to a resolute decision, he had treated with both antagonists. He had helped Prussia to obtain the alliance with Italy in April, and in June he had concluded a secret treaty with Austria. He had expected a prolonged war, wherein he would be able to intervene in due course. But as everything had been decided within a few weeks he was not yet ready.

The day after the defeat the Austrian Ambassador in Paris,

Prince Richard Metternich, effected the transfer of Venetia to Napoleon, who promised to help to arrange for Austria peace terms with both her enemies. The next day the Emperor proclaimed that he had undertaken the rôle of a peacemaker and mediator. For a few days the French were enthusiastic because they thought that the Emperor was the arbiter of Europe and the saviour of its peace. But they were quickly undeceived. The Minister for Foreign Affairs, Drouyn de Lhuys, advised the Emperor to mobilize at least a part of his troops and to send an observation corps to the Rhine. But the Emperor did not follow his advice. Not only did he listen to other advisers, who opposed Drouyn; the principal reason for his fatal inactivity was his illness. During these very days he had to endure the greatest pain. The Empress Eugénie told Metternich: "The Emperor can neither walk nor sleep and can hardly eat". She even advised him to abdicate. Beust, who after Königgrätz had hastened to Paris to ask for help, was deeply shocked by the mental and physical condition of the man who had, only a few years before, been considered the cleverest and most powerful monarch of Europe. "Like a child, he stammered all the time: *Je ne suis pas prêt à la guerre.*"

That, too, is an aspect of personal régime.

Under these conditions Napoleon's attempt to mediate never had a chance. He now had to deal with a man of quick and firm resolution whose strength had been enormously increased by victory and who was, on the other hand, a perfect master of all the great and small arts of diplomacy. Bismarck not only knew how to prevent any serious damage to his plans resulting from Napoleon's intervention, he described Napoleon's action to him as hostile, for which he would have to pay dearly at the appropriate time. As he himself said later, he swore a "Hannibal's oath of revenge" when Benedetti arrived at the Prussian headquarters with the Emperor's demand that Prussia should negotiate a peace treaty with Austria. However, this attempt on the part of Napoleon to prevent a complete reversal of the European balance of power was no more than his duty from the French point of view, and certainly something Bismarck had to expect after his own repeated declarations and offers to Napoleon. He had said to Govone that his own plans depended on the good-will of the Emperor, and he had, in fact, to thank him for the Italian alliance. He had not only held out to Napoleon the bait of a French acquisition of all the French-speaking territory, he repeated it once more during these negotiations. To Lefebvre de Béhaine, who accompanied Benedetti to the Prussian headquarters, he said: "Do you remember Prussia's and Austria's famous treaties with Denmark of the year 1852, which twelve years later were instrumental for obtaining Sleswig and Holstein? Well, you have to say to the King of Belgium that the inevitable territorial and political aggrandise-ment of Prussia worries you, and that there is only one way to pre-vent the dangers and to redress the balance: he must join Belgium's destiny to yours, that Belgium becomes the northern bulwark of France, who is thus only once more restored to her natural rights." That meant, of course, that later on France should do the same with Belgium as Prussia was just then doing with the Duchies—annex her.

On the other hand, Bismarck did his best to delay the negotia-tions in order to give the Prussian army time to draw closer to Vienna. With perfect recklessness he left no stone unturned to bring the Austrian court to its knees. An example of this was the Prussian proclamation in Prague, addressed to the "inhabitants of the glorious Kingdom of Bohemia", which promised the Bohemians and Moravians, that is to say, the Czechs, the fulfilment of their national aims. That was not only a blow to the Austrian govern-ment, but an even greater blow to the German population of Austria.

12. *The Hungarian Legion*

Similar tactics were applied in forming a "Hungarian Legion" against Austria. Bismarck later told the Reichstag that he had under-taken its formation only after the intervention of Napoleon, when the necessity of obtaining a quick submission of Austria was most urgent. This is entirely untrue. Bismarck had begun to organize a revolt in Hungary *before* the outbreak of the war. He had treated with General Klapka, a revolutionary of 1849, who became com-mander of the Hungarian Legion which was to be composed of Hungarian deserters from the Habsburg colours. This incitement of soldiers to revolt and desert was indeed extraordinary behaviour for a military monarchy such as the Prussian, which alleged, furthermore, that it was defending the monarchical principle. In connexion with this manœuvre a remarkable dispatch by the Prussian Ambassador in Florence, Usedom, should be quoted, which became famous under the name, "*Stoss ins Herz*" (Thrust to the Heart) dispatch. In this dispatch of 16th June, Usedom advised General la Marmora, the Italian Prime Minister who was to become Commander-in-Chief of the Italian army, not to waste his time with sieges of Austrian fortresses in Italy but to march straight to Vienna and to meet the Prussians in the very heart of the monarchy. The two allied governments would then stir up a revolt in Hungary and form a partisan corps which would march into that country through Silesia. If that were done, the thrusts at Austria would strike not at her extremities but at her heart.

La Marmora created an enormous sensation when he published this dispatch prematurely in 1868. Bismarck baldly declared that Usedom had written it on his own initiative and that he had nothing to do with it. That, too, was untrue. The essence of the Usedom dispatch comes from an order which Bismarck had sent him some days before.

The Hungarian Legion greatly disappointed Bismarck's expectations. The population of Hungary did not have the slightest wish to be freed by the Prussians from Habsburg rule. Not only did they fail to rise at the call of the Legion, but they turned against it and helped to drive it out. As a matter of fact, the Legion invaded Austrian territory only after an armistice between the belligerents had been concluded (26th July 1866). The Legion transgressed the demarcation line drawn by the armistice. The Prussian officers supervising the Legion did not attempt seriously to prevent this breach of the armistice. The invasion failed completely. When the Legion hastily withdrew, an aide-de-camp of the Commanding General Klapka, Count Seherr-Tosz, was taken prisoner by the Austrians. Count Seherr was court-martialled and sentenced to death. Although this decision was no doubt correct and according to the law, it was not surprising that Bismarck did his best to save Seherr-Tosz, to whom he had personally given instructions. But the method Bismarck applied was surprising. He threatened to shoot ten citizens of Trautenau, who happened to be in a Prussian prison, if the sentence of the court-martial were carried out.

Trautenau is a small town in the German part of Bohemia that was later called "Sudeten-Germany". A Prussian army corps, crossing the mountains in the first days of the campaign, had taken it, but was driven out by the Austrian General von Gablenz. The Prussian soldiers asserted that the citizens of Trautenau had fired at them from their houses, and they took the burgomaster and nine other citizens with them as prisoners. The charge was completely unfounded, but mistakes of this kind were liable to happen in the panic of street fighting and retreat. But what happened afterwards was quite inexcusable. The citizens, men of fairly advanced years, were maltreated and kept in a Prussian prison, in shackles, for seven weeks, without being examined by a judge, without even being told with what offences they were charged. It was manifestly quite impossible to accuse them of anything. These were the victims whom Bismarck threatened to shoot if the Hungarian rebel were not allowed to escape unpunished.

Happily for the memory of Bismarck, the peace treaty contained a mutual amnesty, so that Seherr-Tosz could be released and the citizens of Trautenau return to their homes.

13. *Nikolsburg*

But recklessly as Bismarck prosecuted the war against Austria, he was in one point, the decisive one, willing of his own accord to do what Napoleon wanted. He did not seek the annexation of any Austrian territory by Prussia. He was convinced that any such acquisition would prove not a gain, but a burden to the Prussian Monarchy. Even more important was his far-seeing argument that it was not in Prussia's interest to make the Habsburg Monarchy her enemy for ever. Only a few days after Königgrätz he said to General Stosch, a military adviser of the Crown Prince: "We shall need *Austria's strength in future for ourselves*".

But this outlook did not fit into the head of King William. His was the simple idea that a conqueror was entitled to take something from his conquered enemy. Bismarck wrote to his wife: "If we do not exaggerate our demands and do not believe that we have conquered the world, we shall get a peace worth the efforts we have made. But we—that means, of course, the King—are as easily intoxicated as we are depressed, and I have the thankless task of pouring water into his wine and bringing home the truth that we do not live alone in Europe but with three neighbours." These are the thoughts and the words of a real statesman. But he had the greatest difficulty in carrying out this policy. The King fought for his idea with his accustomed stubbornness. It was at Nikolsburg that this struggle between the King and his Minister was fought out with the utmost bitterness. "Bismarck yesterday wept in my presence about the hard things which the King said to him", wrote the Crown Prince in his diary. It was the Crown Prince who finally helped Bismarck to defeat the stubbornness of the King. Bismarck had made his peace with the Prince the day after the victory of Königgrätz. The Prince was now convinced that Bismarck was right and that he was the indispensable man for the near future. Therefore he joined his own efforts to those of the Minister. At last the King gave way, although very reluctantly, complaining that "the conqueror at the gate of Vienna had to swallow the bitter pill and leave the final judgment to posterity".

Posterity has given its judgment, clearly and emphatically. Admirers and critics of Bismarck alike consider the moderation he showed in the preliminary peace of Nikolsburg one of the surest and best foundations of his enduring fame. When in 1879 he concluded the Alliance of the German Empire with the Habsburg Monarchy, the Peace of Nikolsburg was considered to have prepared the ground.

14. The Annexations and the Maltreatment of Frankfurt

But the same moderation was not shown in other parts of the peace. Four states of the German Confederation were totally annexed: Hanover, Hesse-Cassel, Nassau, and the Free City of Frankfurt. It is easily understandable that Prussia used her victory to destroy the territorial barrier which separated her territory in Western Germany from the bulk of her possessions farther east. But that could have been accomplished without total annexation and the expulsion of three old dynasties. All this was more than a matter of political expediency; it was a matter of principle. The divine right of kings was the corner-stone of the monarchical principle, adherence to which the Prussian government and particularly the Prussian King professed. A few months before the war King William had, in the Crown Council of February, protested solemnly that he declined any "robbery of crowns" (p. 111) as Victor Emanuel had done in Italy to the horror of every good Conservative Prussian. But now the King was all for the dethronement of his unfortunate brother monarchs; more so, it seems, than his Ministers. Bismarck wrote, a few days after Königgrätz, in instructions to the Ambassador in Paris, Goltz: "I personally do not consider the difference between a favourable reform of the Confederation and the immediate acquisition of these countries to be of sufficient practical importance as to risk for it the fate of our Monarchy". That was quite correct; but he did not act accordingly; rather he insisted on complete annexation. Probably he had to do it in order to obtain the King's approval for a policy of moderation towards Austria. He urged Goltz to persuade Napoleon to consent to the annexation of three to four million inhabitants of Northern Germany. On 22nd July, Goltz was able to wire to Bismarck that Napoleon had consented. It was more than Bismarck had expected, and it is, indeed, difficult to understand why Napoleon went so far. Bismarck and Prussian public opinion wanted to include Saxony among the annexed countries; but Austria opposed this energetically, because she felt that Saxony was the only ally of hers who had fully done her duty. So Saxony only had to enter into the new Confederation which Prussia now formed.

That the Free City of Frankfurt was incorporated into Prussia was hardly surprising. But the way this city was treated by the Prussians was quite extraordinary. The representative of Frankfurt had voted in the Diet for the Bavarian motion. This was a sufficient pretext for Bismarck to treat her as an enemy, although the city had actually never participated in any military acts. Frankfurt was occupied without any resistance, but was treated like a hostile, conquered town. The Junkers who led the Prussian army rejoiced in putting as much pressure on her as possible by requisitioning and levying high contributions, and Bismarck supported them in this policy without scruple. After having forced her to pay a contribution of six million guilders, the commander of the Prussian army, Edwin von Manteuffel, demanded a further payment of twenty-five million guilders within twenty-four hours. He was not ashamed to talk of plundering the city. The admirer of Schiller added that he would perhaps be compared with Alba, the cruel Spanish oppressor of the Netherlands, but he did not care. The Burgomaster of Frankfurt, who utterly despaired of finding a way out, hanged himself.

Bismarck himself gave the order for the levying of twenty-five millions. Moreover, the same day on which he had his sharp encounter with King William in Nikolsburg, he sent a telegram to Manteuffel that he should increase the contribution by one million for every day's delay and that he should forbid all communications with the town by railway, nay, close the city gates to incoming and outgoing men and goods—in other words, starve the population into surrender.

Not only foreign countries were shocked by these brutalities. Bennigsen called it an "unspeakably miserable business". Queen Augusta pleaded earnestly with the King to treat leniently a city which was to become a part of his monarchy. When some years later Frankfurt gave a considerable sum for helping needy Eastern Prussia, she said that she was ashamed to remember the bad treatment Frankfurt had suffered at the hands of the Prussians.

15. The Line of the Main

The conditions of peace gave Prussia an absolute ascendancy in Northern Germany. Austria was not only excluded from Germany, it consented to Prussia organizing Northern Germany according to her own will. But this new organization was not to include Southern Germany. That was the condition on which Napoleon had consented to Prussia's annexations in Northern Germany. The line of the Main was the hope to which Napoleon clung in order still to preserve something of a balance of power. Accordingly, the definitive treaty between Prussia and Austria, which was concluded in Prague on 23rd August 1866, limited to Germany north of the Main the new German organization which was to be in the hands of Prussia. The German states south of the Main were left out of this organization and obtained the right to form a union which was to have an *independent international existence*. But *before* signing this

treaty Bismarck concluded with Bavaria, Wurtemberg, and Baden
secret treaties of alliance (*Schutz- und Trutz-Bündnisse*) which
rendered an international independent existence of this kind quite
impossible. For in this treaty the Kings of Bavaria and Wurtemberg
and the Grand Duke of Baden promised to put all their troops at
the disposal of the King of Prussia in case of war, and to place them
under his command. Bismarck had compelled these states to conclude
these treaties by threatening them with annexation of part of their
territory. This method is called by Beust, in his memoirs, the height
of Macchiavellianism. "It is not a rare event in history", he wrote,
"that treaties are broken. But that a treaty is broken *anticipando*,
[beforehand], that was an innovation reserved to the genius of
Bismarck."

Justified as this criticism is from the point of view of international
law, it must not, however, be forgotten that these treaties of alliance
were a weapon Bismarck used in his struggle against Napoleon. He
thus made sure that the states of Southern Germany would follow
him in case of war against France. He considered this war as poten-
tially imminent when the French Emperor tried to obtain something
for himself.

16. *The Diplomatic Struggle with Napoleon*

Napoleon had formed the theory that he could not ask for anything for himself so long as his mediation lasted. But when these
negotiations were concluded he considered himself free to promote
his own interests. Therefore, on 23rd July, he charged Benedetti
with asking Bismarck whether he was in favour of a secret convention giving France the frontiers of 1814 and Luxemburg.
Benedetti had his first conversation with Bismarck at the Prussian
headquarters on 26th July. Bismarck treated the unwelcome question
with perfect virtuosity. He gave the Ambassador the most promising
hints, but warned him of the bad impression these approaches
would make on his King. Benedetti retired and wrote to his
Minister: "Bismarck is the only man in the whole of Prussia who
understands the advantage to the Prussian Government of a close
and permanent French alliance, even at the cost of territorial concessions". This letter fell into Bismarck's hands during the war of

1870. When he read this sentence he was so astonished that he wrote on the margin: "He actually believed it, then!"

Encouraged by this report from Benedetti, the French Foreign Minister, Drouyn, induced the Ambassador to lay before Bismarck the draft of a secret treaty of alliance in which he asked for excessive cessions of German territory. It was easy for Bismarck to decline this proposal. That was in the first days of August, after he and Benedetti had returned to Berlin. But Bismarck did more than that: he saw to it that the gist of this proposal and his refusal got into the hands of a French Opposition paper. The sensation which this publication made was highly damaging to the French government, and Drouyn had to resign.

Now Rouher, *ministre d'état*, the most powerful man in France after the Emperor, took the negotiations in hand. He was a sincere supporter of a Prussian alliance and an adversary of Drouyn. He instructed Benedetti to negotiate in the most friendly form and to avoid any form of threat. He did not ask for German territory but for Belgium and Luxemburg, the countries where French was spoken, to use Bismarck's own expression. Benedetti had, in the middle of August, a personal and confidential conversation with Bismarck. The outcome of this conversation he put into a draft which he wrote twice in his own hand, as he had been instructed to ensure absolute secrecy. One copy he sent to Rouher, the other he gave Bismarck, who promised to lay it before the King. Benedetti then left Berlin for Karlsbad to take the waters, expecting a telegram from Bismarck recalling him for the signature of the treaty. But he never received the telegram nor was the copy of the draft returned to him. He saw it in *The Times* on 25th July 1870, one week after the French declaration of war on Prussia.

By the publication of this draft Bismarck then tried to convince public opinion in England that the actual aim of Napoleon was the acquisition of Belgium. He largely succeeded in that, especially because *The Times* created the impression that the offer had been made, or renewed, quite recently. Bismarck himself assisted this interpretation by an official declaration. Benedetti, who was, of course, in a very awkward position, tried in vain to put things right with a rather clumsy declaration. He too mixed true with untrue statements, as Bismarck had done. But in this game Bismarck was by far his superior. Nevertheless, Benedetti was quite right when he said that this draft belonged to a period which had nothing to do with the origin of the war of 1870. Furthermore, it should not be forgotten that Bismarck had whetted the French appetite for Belgium in every way. Gladstone was perfectly right when he doubted whether Benedetti would have made such a proposal if Bismarck had not previously given him reason to believe that he was ready to proceed on the lines laid down in the proposed treaty.

CHAPTER III

THE NORTH GERMAN CONFEDERATION AND THE FRENCH WAR

---

1. *The Indemnity Bill*

PEACE had to be concluded not only with the foreign enemy but with the Prussian parliament and people. Popular feeling had, indeed, undergone a considerable change. That was shown by the general election of 3rd July 1866. Bismarck had dissolved the Chamber of Deputies before embarking on the war. The elections happened to be on the same day as the Battle of Königgrätz. The electors were, of course, unaware of the great Prussian victory at the time of the poll. But they were undoubtedly influenced by the war atmosphere, the influence of which few people can evade. Thus a large part of the electorate turned from the Opposition to the Government party, the Conservatives. The latter were returned with three times their previous number of deputies. The Liberal majority was not completely destroyed, but seriously weakened. Nevertheless, a member of the Progressive Party, von Forckenbeck, later Chief Burgomaster of Berlin, was elected President. He was on good terms with the Crown Prince, who consulted him frequently, and Bismarck too got to know and to trust him.

The principal question with which the new Chamber was concerned was that of indemnity for the government's infringements of the constitution. Bismarck only succeeded in obtaining the King's approval for this step with great difficulty. Some reactionary Ministers, like Count Lippe, had opposed him. But Bismarck stuck to his guns. He was much too far-seeing not to realize that Liberalism remained a powerful force in spite of its recent defeat, and that without a conciliation he would be seriously handicapped in his future plans. Besides, it was never his way to stumble over words. "*In verbis simus faciles*", he wrote at the end of the paragraph of his *Recollections* which dealt with his attitude on the question of indemnity. And elsewhere in the same chapter he wrote, quite correctly: "I never doubted the possibility of giving to the Royal Power the strength necessary for setting our clock right at home".

The Indemnity Bill was indeed no more than an acknowledgment that a budget voted by both Houses of Parliament was the indispensable basis of expenditure, and that, therefore, the expenditure of recent years had to obtain this constitutional basis through a subsequent vote. But what security did this bill give against a repetition of the same procedure in the future? If one heard the words of the King, none at all. He was naïve and bold enough to tell the President of the Chamber, Forckenbeck, after the vote on the bill, that he would *repeat the same unconstitutional procedure* if similar conditions arose again. Bismarck and Forckenbeck had to agree to treat these words as unofficial, in order to avoid a new crisis.

The vote on the Indemnity Bill was a decisive moment in the history of Prussian and German Liberalism. It was impossible to reject the bill, in spite of all misgivings and objections. But there were grave objections. The struggle for the constitution had been a struggle for principles. The principle of the *Rechtsstaat*, of the state governed by law, was at stake. At the beginning of the struggle Gneist had asked Bismarck to respect the belief of the German people in a firm moral and legal order as the last and decisive factor in the history of states (p. 60). Now this belief had proved deceptive. The defenders of law were defeated, not because they were wrong, but because the government which had broken the constitution had conducted a foreign policy which was full of genius and had, furthermore, a success which was very welcome to the opposition deputies and their voters. They had always aimed at a unification of Germany under Prussia's leadership. They could not but be thankful that this result had been effected under Bismarck's leadership. Victory had been achieved by the army, the reorganization of which they had opposed in certain points. It was more than probable that future generations would come to the conclusion that their opposition was wrong, root and branch. How easy it would be to forget the principle at stake; it is always much more difficult to arouse the attention of voters for a principle than for interests. Was it not to be feared that some time hence nobody would care for principles?

Different answers were given to these questions by various Prussian Liberals, and as a result the Progressive Party broke asunder on account of the vote of the Indemnity Bill. The deputies who voted for it formed a separate party, which developed into the "National Liberal Party". Some of the leading men went this way: Forckenbeck, Twesten, Unruh, and Lasker, who came more and more to the forefront. The importance of this party increased with the accession to it of most of the Liberals of the provinces newly acquired by Prussia and of the smaller states incorporated in the North German Confederation. It was of particular importance that among them were the former leaders of the Liberal Opposition in Hanover, von Bennigsen and Miquel. They were men of outstanding political gifts, but less devoted to principles. The Prussian founders of the party were sincere when they declared they would combine support of the government in questions of foreign policy with the duties of a *vigilant and loyal Opposition* in questions of home policy. They knew the Prussian government well enough to realize how necessary an Opposition would often be. But the Hanoverians, who had not gone through the same experiences, always inclined to a compromise, often enough before it was proved that a compromise was unavoidable. Miquel exclaimed: "The time for ideals is past, and the duty of politicians is not to ask for what is desirable, but for what is attainable". No worse password could have been found for a party which had the great but difficult task of collaborating with Bismarck. For here, in the National Liberal Party, Bismarck sought his parliamentary support in the coming ten years. A party which has to deal with a man of iron will must itself possess a strong will, otherwise it is in danger of losing its independence.

The change in the feeling of the Chamber was shown when the government proposed a bill to give donations to the victorious generals. The Chamber of Deputies insisted that Bismarck should head the list. He got no less than 400,000 thalers, about £60,000. With this money he purchased a large estate in Pomerania, Varzin, for many years his favourite residence, to which he retired when his health was weak, or when the King or the Reichstag made any difficulties.

2. *The Annexations before the Landtag. Bismarck's Illness*

All parties of the Chamber supported the government bills by which Hanover, Hesse-Cassel, Nassau, Frankfurt, and Sleswig-

Holstein were annexed to Prussia. On the question of the Duchies Twesten said: "I was convinced that the Prince of Augustenburg was the legitimate ruler of the Duchies, and this is still my opinion to-day. Now he has been removed and can under no circumstances be restored, but we must not distort and slander what we deemed right yesterday." Prussia lacked any title to the Duchies, but she was now the German state *par excellence*. The annexation was therefore justified by the eternal right of the future of the German people. The population of the Duchies, however, felt for many years that this incorporation had violated their own rights.

Stronger still was the opposition in Hanover, where a large party continued to uphold the banner of the dethroned King. In Prussia, only the old President, von Gerlach, and a few Conservatives without political influence opposed the dethronement of a king as a flagrant violation of the monarchical principle. This was also the opinion of Czar Alexander of Russia. King William was not happy when he received from his Russian nephew a letter in which he wrote: "I maintain my opinion that the monarchical principle has undergone a severe shock, when whole dynasties were destroyed by a stroke of the pen. It does not diminish this shock that it is effected not by revolution, but by royal power." From the point of principle the Czar was unquestionably right. King William himself sympathized with this point of view in so far as he continued to be biased against those Hanoverians who had abandoned their old King to become Prussian patriots, like Bennigsen.

Although Bismarck was responsible for this violation of the monarchical principle, he knew how to increase the power and authority of his own monarch to an extent which would have seemed impossible when he began his administration. It is one of his most astonishing achievements.

In September 1866 Bismarck had to go on leave for some weeks. His health had completely broken down. The incessant work, excitement, and tension of the last years was too much even for his iron constitution. His nerves failed him. For some weeks he could not hear or speak one word of politics.

"When he sits still", wrote Johanna, "and looks at the blue sky and the green meadows or turns the pages of a picture book, he is tolerably well." Some weeks of complete rest restored his health. In

December he was able to return to Berlin and to begin his new task, the drafting of the constitution of the North German Confederation.

3. *The Constitution of the North German Confederation*

The parliament that had to discuss the constitution of the new "North German Confederation" (Norddeutscher Bund) was a Reichstag elected by universal suffrage. The law which arranged for these elections was passed by the Prussian Chambers in October 1866. Many Liberals were not in the least enthusiastic about this universal suffrage. They were afraid that it would be used in the manner of Napoleon III to manipulate elections and to create a majority favourable to the government. But they could not, of course, oppose a democratic suffrage when it was proposed by a Conservative government of the King.

As a matter of course, universal suffrage had to be the suffrage for the parliament which the new constitution had to institute: the North German parliament (Norddeutscher Reichstag). It therefore seemed as though this constitution would have a democratic character. But nothing was further from Bismarck's plans. If he was obliged to grant a democratic suffrage to the new parliament, he at the same time wanted to deprive it of all political power. His programme, as he told the Saxon Minister, von Friesen, was, to *kill parliamentarianism through parliament*. The draft of the constitution which he laid before the individual confederated governments shows his aims quite distinctly. The Reichstag would have no power of voting on the budget. For Bismarck had learned from the Prussian conflict that the budget was a weapon in the hands of an energetic parliament. Almost the whole expenditure of the North German Confederation would be for the army and the (so far) unimportant navy. Bismarck proposed fixing the military budget permanently. His draft of the constitution determined on a permanent basis the number of soldiers to be called annually to the colours (*Friedens-Präsenz-Stärke*) at the rate of 1 per cent of the population, and the amount to be granted per soldier at a fixed sum. If this proposal had become law the Reichstag would have been compelled to grant the annual Army Budget without being able to influence it in any way. The government would, in fact, have been quite independent of parliament, which would not have any power of enforcing its will. But even that did not satisfy Bismarck. He went further still. He wished to avoid the establishment of a responsible ministry, so that the Reichstag would not have anybody on whom it could place the responsibility for any political act.

The instrument he wanted to introduce for this purpose was the Bundesrat (the Federal Council). It was designed on the pattern of the Federal Diet (Bundestag) of the recently abolished German Confederation. It too consisted of the delegates of the governments of the federal states, who had not to vote according to their own convictions but according to the instructions of their governments. Even the scale according to which the votes of the governments were graded was taken from the old Bundestag, with one modification only: the votes which formerly belonged to the annexed states were now added to those which Prussia had originally commanded. This Bundesrat was supposed to represent the government of the new Bund, the Verbündete Regierungen. It was an anonymous body which deliberated in secret behind closed doors and would take anonymous decisions for which nobody could be held responsible by the Reichstag. True, this Bundesrat was to be presided over by a Bundeskanzler, but this Kanzler was neither a Minister nor responsible, rather something like a head of chancery, who would not have to appear before the Reichstag in order to defend, explain, or motivate the decisions of the Bundesrat. The Reichstag would have the power to legislate in certain important, particularly economic, matters. But to become law, each bill adopted by the Reichstag would have to be approved by the Bundesrat, which therefore had an absolute veto.

The aim of this draft is clear: to make the Prussian King all-powerful in all matters of real political importance, without making this too manifest. The Bundesrat was the façade behind which the Prussian King could shelter. And the Bundesrat would always have to do what the Prussian King or his powerful Minister, Bismarck, wanted.

If this first draft had become law, political life in Germany would have come to an end. The Reichstag would have become a debating club without any political power, where no independent man could have found his place. The old Radical, Waldeck, likened the position which the draft sought to create for the Prussian King to that held by the ancient Roman Emperors.

The composition of the Reichstag before which Bismarck's draft of the constitution was laid was such that the National Liberal Party had the casting vote. There was a considerable number of Conservative deputies, but only part of them had the outlook of the old Junker party. A large section formed a more modern party under the name of *Reichs-Partei* or "Free Conservatives". They often voted with the National Liberals if they had not to fear that by so doing they would draw Bismarck's anger on themselves.

Now the National Liberals would have betrayed the very foundations of Liberalism if they had accepted Bismarck's proposition unchanged. The ideal of German Liberalism had been parliamentary government, and if this was now impossible under the prevailing conditions, the National Liberals at least had the duty of obtaining for the German parliament enough power and efficiency so that it could exercise a certain amount of political influence. Only in this way could they show the German people that the new German state was more than simply a Prussian military institution. If there was ever to be a hope of extending beyond the line of the Main and linking up with the brethren of South Germany, North Germany would have to be able to offer them something other than Prussian militarism, which did not attract South Germany but repelled her. The National Liberals were by no means inclined to stop at the Main. They considered it, as Miquel expressed it in his great speech on the draft of the constitution, only as a preliminary stop where the engine had to refuel and rewater in order to continue the journey.

This was, of course, also Bismarck's idea. He could not fail to see the convincing power of this argument. Besides, he saw in his negotiations with the confederated governments that he needed the assistance of the Reichstag to put enough pressure on them to get his own way.

Both sides, Bismarck as well as the National Liberals, wished to meet each other half-way. Although the concessions the Liberals received fell short of what they wanted, Bismarck did yield on certain points. They succeeded in obtaining *one responsible Minister*. On a motion by Bennigsen they changed the position of the Bundeskanzler in such a way that every political act of the President of the Confederation, that is to say, of the Prussian King, depended on the counter-signature of the Bundeskanzler, who with this signature assumed the responsibility for it. It made the Bundeskanzler the responsible Minister of the Confederation and the political and administrative head of its government. The consequence of this motion was that Bismarck himself became Bundeskanzler, which had not been his purpose at the beginning. It was, of course, the only position which corresponded to his political power. Later, when the North German Confederation grew into the German Empire, the Bundeskanzler was called Reichskanzler (Imperial Chancellor), and it is as Reichskanzler that Bismarck has gone down in history.

There were still some other points on which the Reichstag succeeded in increasing the importance and influence of parliament; for instance, in laying down its annual convocation. Bismarck, however, declined all concessions on the question of the payment of members of parliament. He hated *Berufs-Parlamentarier* (men who made parliament their profession), because he feared their influence.

The most difficult point was the military budget. This question was only solved finally by a compromise after a long and heated struggle, in which the Crown Prince did his best to mediate. Finally, a motion by Forckenbeck was adopted, which reduced the permanent budget to the period ending December 1871. After 1st January 1872 the number of men to be called to the colours was to be fixed by law, which involved the agreement of the Reichstag. Thus the principle of the annual budget seemed to have been secured. But Bismarck interpreted this compromise differently. Again and again he compelled the Reichstag to fix the number of men to be called to the colours (*Friedens-Präsenz-Stärke*) for several years, at first for four, later for seven years. More than once this policy brought about a crisis, and at last, in 1887, a dissolution of parliament. But every time he carried his point.

On the whole, the Reichstag amendments had a progressive effect. The outcome was certainly not parliamentary government, but something better than the veiled absolutism which Bismarck had at first wished to impose. In his speech during the debate on the constitution he spoke the famous words: "Let us put Germany in the saddle, she will know how to ride". If Bismarck's first plans had been executed, Germany would not have been able to "ride". The Liberal amendments of the constitution made it workable and enabled Germany to "ride". But, of course, as long as Bismarck was Chancellor he held the reins and the horse had to obey his wishes.

Some years later, 1869, Bismarck wrote to Roon: "The form in which our King exercises his rule over Germany has never been of great importance in my eyes. To secure the fact *that* he exercises it, I have used all the strength God has given me." This describes exactly and distinctly his aim in proposing his draft of the German constitution. He had not obtained all he wanted, but enough to be fully satisfied.

In one of his speeches during the debate on the constitution, Bismarck spoke about universal suffrage. This speech is famous particularly on account of his outspoken criticism of the three-classes suffrage. He called it the most absurd and miserable suffrage ever devised in any country. But what did he do to remove or, at least, to reform this absurd and miserable suffrage in Prussia? Nothing! He never reformed the suffrage for the Prussian Chamber of Deputies in any way, let alone replaced it by universal suffrage. He found that the elections always gave him a Chamber well adapted to his wishes, in spite of the three-classes suffrage. That was the only thing that mattered to him, whether it was achieved in accordance with his own judgment on suffrage or not. If the elections to the German Reichstag by universal suffrage, and to the Prussian Landtag by three-classes suffrage, had quite different results, so much the better for him. For in that case he could rely on the one against the other.

When the National Liberals voted for the constitution of the North German Confederation, although they could not carry all their principal points, they hoped that in times to come they would have the opportunity of developing and reforming the constitution. There, however, they encountered Bismarck's obstinate resistance. One point in dispute was the institution of other responsible Ministers for the Bund besides the Reichskanzler. It was, of course, in the long run impossible for one man, even a Bismarck, to direct all the branches of German policy and administration: foreign and home policy, finance, economy, and so on. What the Liberals wanted particularly was a responsible Minister of Finance. But Bismarck was adamant in his opposition. In no case was he willing to agree to a Minister-Collegium, that is to say a board, consisting of co-ordinated Ministers presided over by a Minister-President, as it existed and continued to exist in Prussia. He told the Reichstag in blunt words what difficulties he had to get this Collegium moving. When the Liberal deputy Lasker replied that they desired for the Chancellor a position equivalent to that of the English Prime Minister—who directed the policy of his cabinet and could enforce the resignation of an opposing Minister, his resistance weakened somewhat—but he still maintained his opposition. On no account was he willing to give up even a particle of his power.

Even if one of his collaborators, in fact, assumed completely the direction of a department, that is, a certain part of govermental work, Bismarck saw to it that he himself kept the formal responsibility. He indeed found an excellent collaborator for economic affairs in the person of Rudolf Delbrück. Economic affairs and economic legislation then were of special importance, as a unified code of laws for the new Northern Germany had to be created to put an end to the individual laws of the different states, for instance, a common trade and factory law, common weights and measures, a common currency, and so on. For all these projects Delbrück was the best man possible. He knew all about them, he worked indefatigably, and he was in agreement with the principles and aims of the National Liberals. He was always unbiased and objective and knew how to deal with the subjective and irritable Chancellor. Bismarck left him with his hands almost free in all these matters, without much interference. He knew that he could trust him. Nevertheless, Delbrück did not become a Minister of the Confederation. He had to be satisfied with the post of "President of the Bundeskanzler-Amt", a subordinate of the Chancellor.

4. The "Welfen-Fonds"

What were the feelings of the German people about the achievement of 1866, the unification of Northern Germany, the annexations, and the line of the Main. In Northern Germany the overwhelming majority of the people considered them a great step forward. Even in the annexed territories, opposition was not the invariable rule. True, in Sleswig-Holstein the majority was still in favour of the Augustenburger and considered the annexation by Prussia a breach of the law. But the opposition was not vehement. It was different in Hanover. A section of the population joined the National Liberals, but the other was deeply grieved with the annexation and remained true to the Guelph dynasty. They were called the *Welfen-Partei*. Their opposition did not weaken in any way through the course of time. A considerable portion of the population never became reconciled to the Hohenzollern and the Prussian administration.

Their opposition was only strengthened by the way Bismarck dealt with their dethroned King. George V had possessed a great fortune, about which negotiations had to be initiated between his representatives and the Prussian government. George's representative was Ludwig Windthorst, a former Hanoverian Minister, a convinced Roman Catholic, now a member of the Reichstag and the Prussian Chamber of Deputies. An agreement was achieved which was rather advantageous to the former King. A considerable part of his fortune was acknowledged by the Prussian government as his property. He was to receive, though not the capital, yet the interest from it. This treaty was accepted despite strong opposition by the Prussian parliament. The law embodying the treaty was duly published on 3rd March 1868. But the same day a royal order was published which sequestrated the whole income of King George and put it at the disposal of the Prussian government, to be used "for the control and suppression of the subversive attempts of King George and his agents against Prussia". To justify this surprising measure, the Prussian ministry emphasized that George declined to acknowledge the annexation of his kingdom by Prussia and that he kept in being the *Welfen-Legion* as the nucleus of an army against Prussia. That was true; but it was already known to the Prussian government and parliament when they concluded and accepted the treaty. From the legal point of view these arguments were quite untenable, as Windthorst pointed out convincingly in a speech to the Chamber. The Progressive deputy, Professor Rudolf Virchow, uttered a serious warning against leaving to the Prussian government the free and uncontrolled disposal of such a large sum.

He prophesied enormous corruption as its result. This prophecy came true. Bismarck used the *Welfen-Fonds*, popularly called *Reptilien-Fonds* (reptile funds) to bribe the German press and for other political aims which had nothing to do with the alleged "subversive tendencies of King George". We shall see what part the *Welfen-Fonds* played in the foundation of the German Empire. But I want to instance here one example which throws a characteristic light on Bismarck's way of thinking and acting. After his downfall he was particularly furious with the Secretary of State for Home affairs, Herr von Boetticher, whom he suspected of having conspired with the Emperor, William II, to overthrow him. In order to ruin Boetticher's reputation in the opinion of the public, he had the story published that he, Bismarck, with a large sum from the *Welfen-Fonds*, had years ago helped him out of great financial difficulties originated by malpractices of his father-in-law. The fact was true, except that Bismarck had concealed from Boetticher that the money came from the *Welfen-Fonds*: he had told him that it was a personal gift from the old Emperor.

The most characteristic feature of this sordid story is Bismarck's opinion that a gift from the *Welfen-Fonds* put the recipient under obligation to him personally, not to the state, or even the King.

It was only Bismarck's successor, Caprivi, who ended the scandal by abolishing the *Reptilien-Fonds* and delivering the income to the heirs of King George.

5. *South Germany and Austria*

In South Germany two Kingdoms, Bavaria and Wurtemberg, and two Grand Duchies, Baden and Hesse, were left outside the North German Confederation. Of the Grand Duchy of Hesse, however, one part, situated north of the Main, was incorporated in the Confederation. In Hesse the greater part of the population inclined to the National Liberals as the friends of German unification, but the government was strongly against it. In Baden the population as well as the government and the Grand Duke, the son-in-law of King William, were enthusiastic supporters of German unity. They were even inclined to enter the Confederation alone, without the other South German states. But a motion which the

National Liberal deputy, E. Lasker, brought before the Reichstag along these lines in February 1870 was vigorously opposed by Bismarck in an angry speech. "I do not wish", he said, "to skim the jug of milk and to let the rest [that is, the rest of South Germany] curdle."

For in Bavaria and Wurtemberg the position was much less satisfactory. In Wurtemberg not only King and court but also the democratic part of the population were opposed to "Prussianization" and "militarization". Wurtemberg had a very strong and active Democratic Party, which considered the North German Confederation an enlarged Prussian military monarchy; they hated militarism more than anything. Their suspicion was not quite groundless, as a conversation shows which General Schweinitz, then German Ambassador in Vienna, later in Petersburg, had with Bismarck in the spring of 1870. Schweinitz, an honest Conservative of the old type, said: "The limit of our power is there where we no longer have Junkers to fill our commissions in the army". Bismarck answered: "I am not at liberty to say that; but *I have acted accordingly*". Nobody in Southern Germany wanted to be ordered about by Prussian Junkers.

In Bavaria there reigned King Louis II, a young dreamer, interested in art and music, but not in the least in politics and government. His only political concern was the splendour of his royal family, the House of Wittelsbach, and jealousy of all other houses, including that of Hohenzollern, the splendour of which was likely to outdo his own. He ended as a madman, and was probably never normal. After the defeat of 1866 he had dismissed the government responsible for it and had appointed as Minister-President a high nobleman of Liberal and unitarian opinions, Prince Chlovis of Hohenlohe-Schillingsfürst, who was to be Imperial Chancellor later, at the end of the century. But Hohenlohe had no firm support either from the capricious and wayward King or from the Bavarian population.

The Bavarians were mostly Roman Catholics and very much under the influence of the clergy. Roman Catholicism in Germany did not like the idea that the old Catholic dynasty of the Habsburgs should lose its influence to the Protestant dynasty of the Hohenzollerns. But there were other and deeper reasons still why devout

Catholics could not feel happy about the turn of events. August Reichensperger, a Catholic member of the Prussian Chamber, a man of high culture and sincere piety, wrote in his diary at the end of the year 1866: "It is very hard for me to submit to recent divine decisions without coming to the conclusion that right only exists in the small things of civil life but that the great things are the dominion of force, cunning, and trickery and that with them religious or moral principles have no influence, either on the ends or the means". Another Prussian Catholic parliamentarian, von Mallinckrodt, said in the Reichstag: "I adhere to the old principle, *iustitia fundamentum regnorum*; but I was unable to discover *iustitia* by the cradle of the North German Federation".

This feeling on the part of Roman Catholics in alliance with Bavarian particularism thus created a strong opposition to any approach to the North German Confederation or, as they called it, to any Prussianization. The Opposition party called themselves significantly the "Party of Bavarian Patriots" (*Bayrische Patrioten-Partei*). It did not lose but gain strength during the following years. In spring 1870 it was strong enough to turn out the Liberal Minister, Prince Hohenlohe.

The strength of the particularist opposition, especially in Bavaria and Wurtemberg, became manifest when the people of South Germany elected deputies for the Zoll-Parlament (Customs-Parliament). The Zollverein had survived the war of 1866. It was now reformed by Bismarck, to whom the southern states had to submit. The principal reform was the institution of a Zoll-Parlament, elected by universal suffrage, to decide various problems of customs regulations. The majority of the southern deputies was opposed to unification, and the debates of this parliament were, as a rule, disappointing to the National Liberals, the party of unification.

The Peace Treaty of Prague had provided for an organization of the states south of the Main, a South German Confederation. But this never had a chance of success on account of the jealousy of the other states against Bavaria. They were never ready to submit to Bavarian leadership. Besides, what could a confederation of this kind do after the individual states had put their troops at the disposal of the Prussian King in the secret treaties of alliance (*Schutz- und Trutz-Bündnisse*)?

Austria had regarded South Germany as her legitimate sphere of influence according to the Treaty of Prague. In Austria a very interesting development had taken place. The Emperor Francis Joseph had appointed Beust to be his Minister for Foreign Affairs. Beust had been compelled by Bismarck to leave the Saxon ministry, for Bismarck had declined to negotiate the Saxon peace treaty with him. But a fortnight after this dismissal, to which King John agreed only very reluctantly, he became Foreign Minister in Vienna. Of course, his appointment was considered in Germany as the proclamation of a programme of Austrian *revanche*. If the Austrian Emperor entrusted his foreign policy to a man who had always been Bismarck's antagonist in German politics, it was very probable that he did not regard the decision of 1866 as definite and would try to reverse it whenever the international situation became favourable for an attempt of this kind. The North German press showered vituperation and ridicule on the Saxon who suddenly rose to so important a position. Bismarck certainly was not happy about the appointment; nevertheless, he told the Austrian Ambassador: "Please tell Baron Beust that I have not the least objection to him. On the contrary, I am glad to see him as Minister in Austria. In Germany, in Saxony, he would have inconvenienced me. There is no room for both of us there. In saying that, I hope that Baron Beust will not accuse me of any discourtesy." A very graceful way of greeting the defeated. But, of course, it did not prevent Bismarck from setting all his press-hounds on Beust whenever he suspected him of crossing his path. And Beust, indeed, could hardly do anything without exciting Bismarck's suspicion.

But it was Napoleon with whom Bismarck first came into conflict.

6. *The Luxemburg Question*

The Grand Duchy of Luxemburg, situated between Prussia, Belgium, and France, had been a member of the German Confederation. The Grand Duke of Luxemburg was the King of Holland. The capital of the country, the city of Luxemburg, was a fortress of the Confederation (*Bundesfestung*), the garrison of which consisted of Prussian troops.

The connexion between Luxemburg and Germany was only

external. The population did not consider themselves German. In his proposal to the Diet of a new German constitution on 10th June 1866—that is to say, before the war—Bismarck had explicitly excluded Luxemburg (*königlich-niederländische Landesteile*) from the new Confederation. The Prussian garrison in Luxemburg had lost its justification through the dissolution of the Confederation. Nevertheless, Prussian troops continued to garrison the fortress.

Now the Emperor Napoleon wanted to acquire Luxemburg in order to show the French people that he had managed to obtain something tangible. He was willing to pay hard cash for it, and the King of Holland, who wanted cash, was willing to sell his Grand Duchy. The question was, what would be Bismarck's attitude? In all his conversations with Benedetti the acquisition of Luxemburg by Napoleon played a great part, and Bismarck expressed a very favourable view. Benedetti was convinced that Bismarck would not put the least obstacle in the Emperor's way. Napoleon considered Prussia's help in his acquisition of Luxemburg as a token of her friendship, the idea of which he had not yet given up. These ideas were not, indeed, far from Bismarck's mind. After his return from leave in December 1866 Bismarck wrote to von der Goltz, who was himself a warm friend of a Prussian-French alliance. "I have, since the beginning of my administration, considered this alliance as the natural expression of the lasting accord of the interests of both countries."

In spite of all these favourable auspices, the transaction not only miscarried, but brought the two countries to the verge of a war. Bismarck favoured the cession of Luxemburg to Napoleon, but he was not prepared to commit himself in writing in any way that could prove his connivance. He advised the Emperor to present him with a *fait accompli*. But the King of Holland, willing as he was to sell Luxemburg, did not want to arouse Bismarck's anger under any circumstances. The monarchs of weak states knew by now how dangerous Bismarck's enmity was. The King of the Netherlands felt caution to be all the more necessary in view of the fact that national feeling in Germany was becoming excited. Two incidents seemed particularly menacing.

In the middle of March 1867 Bismarck published his secret military conventions (*Schutz- und Trutz-Bündnisse*) with the southern states. This publication was understood as a warning to France that she would have to deal with a united Germany should war break out over the Luxemburg question. The other incident was an interpellation, which the leader of the National Liberal Party, von Bennigsen, made in the Reichstag on 1st April 1867. Bismarck had secretly arranged the text of the interpellation with Bennigsen. It proclaimed the united national opposition of the German people to any attempt to tear an old German country away from the Fatherland, and requested the government to secure Prussia's right of garrisoning Luxemburg for good "at all risks". Although Bismarck's answer to this interpellation was rather cautious, it is not surprising that the King of Holland was little inclined to undertake any steps without Bismarck's previous approval. Bismarck not only refused this approval but reproached the French government with having mismanaged the affair.

Napoleon felt deeply insulted. For him, one of his favourite ideas had come to an end. In a conversation with Goltz he likened Prussia and France to two good friends who had a quarrel in a coffee-house and were thereby compelled to fight a duel, although they loved each other at heart. National feeling on both sides of the Rhine ran very high. For some time war seemed imminent, absurd as the idea of a war between two great nations over so minute an object as this small state of Luxemburg, or even the Prussian right of garrison, must be to the sober judgment of posterity. Bismarck himself was for some days not averse to the idea of war. He treated the affair as a question of Germany's national honour, and in a circular note to the Prussian missions at the other German courts he proclaimed the excessive and dangerous doctrine, "If a nation *feels* that its honour has been violated, then this honour *has* in fact been violated, and action has to be taken accordingly". But Bismarck acted quite cautiously in spite of this wild language. He never took a step he could not retrace. In the end, war was avoided by a compromise, arranged at an International Conference in London: Napoleon abandoned the scheme of acquiring the Grand Duchy and Prussia renounced her right of maintaining a garrison in Luxemburg, the fortifications of which were destroyed. The Grand Duchy was neutralized under the collective guarantee of the signatory Powers. This guarantee was practically worthless. For the

British Prime Minister, Lord Derby, and his son Stanley, the Foreign Secretary, declared to the British parliament that no single guarantor Power was thereby obliged to military action unless all the others acted similarly. Bismarck blamed them sharply for this interpretation. But there is good reason to believe that he knew beforehand that Britain would undertake the guarantee only in this very limited sense, and that he accepted it in order to be able to close the affair. As a matter of fact, the case for which the guarantee was intended, an attack by France, never arose. But in spite of her guarantee Germany did not hesitate to occupy Luxemburg when was broke out in 1914.

The Luxemburg question was settled by concessions on both sides. In later years Bismarck often referred to his attitude as evidence of his aversion to a preventive war. He claimed that he had avoided war owing to this aversion, although its success would have been as certain as it was in 1870. But it seems that his option for a peaceful solution was no less motivated by the fact that the South German states were neither prepared for war nor eager to undertake it. Furthermore, Bismarck's attempt to bring together a European coalition against Napoleon had failed.

The whole affair is important and remarkable in two ways. It opened a new chapter both in Bismarck's policy and in the relations of France and Prussia. If it is assumed that Bismarck at the beginning honestly intended to satisfy Napoleon's wishes (and the evidence, on the whole, points that way), he had found in the meantime that this policy was impossible owing to the opposition of German national feeling. Until then he had been engaged in a cabinet policy, which did not take account of public opinion and which was merely dictated by the interests of Prussian power politics. Now he saw that public opinion could no longer be ignored. Indeed, Bismarck found that the national feeling of the German people was the strongest weapon in his hand. From now on, he brought his public utterances into line with this idea. He spoke and acted as the champion of the German national cause. The Luxemburg affair was the turning-point in Bismarck's development from a Prussian to a German statesman.

Similarly, it was the turning-point in the relations between Prussia and France. Napoleon now went through the same experience which Austria had in 1866. He was not prepared for war and was now faced with the same dilemma as Austria during her crisis: either by hasty preparations, to draw on himself the reproach of bringing about a war, or to wait till he was attacked and defeated. From this experience he drew the conclusion that he had to reform the organization of his army as quickly as possible in order to be able to mobilize it at the shortest possible notice. This reorganization was performed during the following years under the direction of the Minister of War, Marshal Niel, in the face of a strong opposition. Niel died shortly before the outbreak of the war of 1870. Thus began the period of *la paix armée* (the armed peace), in which the nations of the European continent prepared for war by ever-increasing armaments and in which every nation tried to outbid the other.

From now on a feeling of nervous anxiety began to prevail in Europe. There was no longer any confidence in the maintenance of peace. Every European statesman was more or less suspicious of all the others. Small incidents seemed to assume the most menacing dimensions.

As an instance of these feelings, the affair of the Belgian railways, which disturbed the peace of Europe in the spring of 1869, may be mentioned. Belgium was at this time the prototype of capitalistic free enterprise. The Manchester doctrine was the ruling gospel. Railways were in the hands of private companies and the state interfered as little as possible. One of the most important railways connecting the French frontier with Brussels found itself in great financial difficulties, and the concern to which it belonged offered the management to a big French company, the *Chemin de Fer de l'Est*, which gladly accepted it. The Belgian government felt that it could not allow a French company to have the management of a line which served the capital of the country. It therefore rushed through parliament an act which gave it the power to prevent arrangements of this type, not only in the future but also retroactively for arrangements already concluded. When the Belgian government took steps to apply this power to the new agreement between the Belgian railway and the French *Compagnie de l'Est*, the latter applied for the protection of its government. The French government considered this interference as an unfriendly act and protested in Brussels.

The result was a general excitement in Europe, because the French procedure was suspected to be the beginning of the annexation of Belgium by France. The centre of this excitement was England. Queen Victoria's relations with the Belgian Royal House were very close, and she considered herself in duty bound to protect it against the sinister ambitions of the Emperor Napoleon. The Foreign Secretary, Lord Clarendon, looked at this question less from a dynastic point of view. He had been appointed by Gladstone after his great victory over Disraeli in the general election of 1868. Clarendon, who knew the Continent very well, was an upholder of the old tradition of British Foreign Policy, that the Low Countries were a sphere of special British influence, in which no other European Great Power could be allowed to interfere. He was therefore full of suspicion of the French Emperor. On the other hand, Napoleon and his government believed that the Belgian government acted at the instigation of Bismarck.

It seems that both suspicions were equally groundless. True, it is now known that Napoleon wrote a letter to Marshal Niel in February 1869, in which he pondered the question whether the Belgian affair was an opportune occasion for making war. But this does not by any means prove that he was at any time resolved to make war. With Napoleon III the step from deliberation to action was always a very difficult one. On the other hand, it is known that he did not have anything to do with the beginning of the affair, the agreement between the two railway companies, and that he afterwards did his best for a peaceful settlement of the affair.

That Bismarck had nothing to do with the action of the Belgian government is almost certain. Clarendon was perfectly right when he gave the French Ambassador in London his word of honour that Bismarck had nothing to do with Belgium's stubbornness. The Prussian Ambassador in London, Count Bernstorff, who was hoping that the Belgian affair would develop into an Anglo-French conflict, asked Gladstone and Clarendon what steps they would take against France. Bismarck ordered him to abstain from these questions. He was afraid that Clarendon would answer by asking what help Britain could expect from the North German Confederation in the case of a conflict with France. Bismarck did not wish to be confronted with this question, for he looked at the Belgian affair in quite a different way from the British statesmen.

He was not in the least interested in Belgian independence. He considered Belgium, even after the Luxemburg affair, as a pawn in the game. This is quite clear from a conversation he had in March 1868 with Prince Napoleon, the cousin of the Emperor. The clever, although frivolous, Prince Napoleon was an ardent champion of the principle of nationality, and a friend of national unity in Italy and in Germany. He vehemently abhorred the idea of war between France and Germany, which he considered an enormous danger to European civilization. He went to Berlin not as an envoy of his Imperial cousin, but of his own accord, in order to acquaint himself with German problems and to talk with Bismarck.

He had an intimate conversation with the Chancellor, who talked quite frankly and indiscreetly. He recommended to France the annexation of Belgium as a compensation for the extension of the North German Confederation to South Germany. When the Prince objected that England would intervene, Bismarck replied disdainfully: "What is England to me? The importance of a state is measured by the number of soldiers it can put into the field of battle. What can England do, if we agree? *It is the destiny of the weak to be devoured by the strong.*"

He talked along the same lines to the British Ambassador in Berlin, Lord Loftus, during the affair of the Belgian railways. He said that he could resign himself to the French annexation of Belgium. He would know where to find compensation, mentioning Bavaria, Bohemia, and the Netherlands. Loftus was so taken aback that he spoke of a *politique de brigandage*. Then Bismarck told him that England should join him against France. "If you would only declare", he said, "that whatever Power should wilfully break the peace of Europe would be looked upon by you as a common enemy, we will readily adhere to, and join you in, that declaration." When Lord Clarendon sent this report of Loftus to the Prime Minister, he wrote: "Bismarck's ways are inexplorable, we can never rely on him". He felt that Bismarck's aim was to separate England from France. But Clarendon was determined to avoid this under any circumstances.

The controversy between France and Belgium was at last settled peacefully. After this settlement Bismarck wrote in a note to his Ambassador, Count Bernstorff, on 7th June 1869, that Napoleon had mismanaged the affair. The right way would have been "to march into Belgium and then to wait whether other Powers would come forward for Belgium and attack France for her violation of the treaties".

This is the prescription which Bismarck's smaller successors followed in August 1914, and it is well known that the outcome was a catastrophe.

7. *Attempt at a Triple Alliance of France, Austria, and Italy*

After the Luxemburg affair, Napoleon was compelled definitely to abandon his hope of an alliance with Prussia and to seek other allies. Bismarck, too, who only in December 1866 had called an alliance with France the natural expression of the lasting agreement of the interests of both countries, now called France the suspected neighbour whom he had to watch, "a revolver in his pocket, his finger on the trigger". From then onwards he spoke of the *inevitable war* against France.

When Napoleon looked around for an ally for the coming struggle with Prussia, his eyes naturally fell on Austria, just defeated by Prussia. Both Powers, France and Austria, had one interest in common: not to allow Prussia to extend her rule southwards across the Main into the states of Southern Germany. In other words, their common aim was the maintenance of the peace of Prague. Austria's leading statesman, Beust, could be supposed to favour a French alliance which had this policy as its object.

Negotiations between Napoleon and Beust began in July 1868 and went on till October 1869. In December 1868 a third partner joined the negotiations, the King of Italy, Victor Emanuel. The story of these negotiations is particularly interesting, but it will have to suffice to mention the final results, obtained after careful study of all available documents.

The most important question to arise in this connexion is whether the aim of these negotiations was an *offensive* alliance, that is, an alliance for a common attack on Prussia and the North German

Confederation, in order to redress the balance of power and to take revenge for Austria's defeat. This question is vital, because it is in the light of the answer that Bismarck's policy in 1870 must be judged. Was he compelled to make war on France in order to destroy an aggressive coalition which Napoleon was in the process of forming?

It is the opinion of the present writer that the purpose of the prospective alliance between France, Austria, and Italy was *not an offensive one*. It was Beust who at every stage of the negotiations declined all obligations which might have involved Austria in war as the ally of an aggressive France. He did not, under any circumstances, want to become a partner in an alliance which might entice France into war with Germany. He himself wrote: "The question is, does France want to accelerate or to retard [*précipiter ou retarder*] a war against Prussia. What our monarchy wants is the maintenance of peace." So seriously did he take this point of view that he was willing more than once to let the negotiations drop entirely rather than make any concessions upon this point.

The outcome of all these long and complicated transactions was not a formal treaty but only an exchange of personal letters between the Emperors Napoleon and Francis Joseph. The letter of the Austrian Emperor is not on record. In Napoleon's letter the decisive sentences are: "If Your Majesty's Empire should be attacked, I shall not hesitate a moment to come to your aid with all the might of France. Moreover I assure you that I shall not negotiate with any foreign Power without having beforehand come to an agreement with you." Francis Joseph's letter certainly did not go further, and, if Beust is to be believed, not even so far, in that it did not contain any promise to aid France in case of attack. Under no circumstances was such aid promised unconditionally, certainly not for a war in which France would be the aggressor. As a matter of fact, when war broke out in 1870, Napoleon got no help from Austria.

The Italian King did neither receive nor write a letter of this kind. France and Italy were kept apart by the insoluble question of Rome. Napoleon had withdrawn his troops in 1866 in accordance with the September Treaty of 1864. But in the autumn of 1867 Garibaldi had attacked the Papal State with his bands, and Napoleon was compelled to send back his troops. These defeated Garibaldi at

Mentana on 3rd November 1867. Since then, he had not discovered any method of terminating the French occupation of Rome. Victor Emanuel's Ministers declined to conclude any treaty with Napoleon which did not provide for his evacuation of Rome. This the Emperor found himself unable to do.

The Roman question was still unsolved when the Franco-Prussian war began, and even at this moment of the highest danger Napoleon could not bring himself to buy Italian military help by abandoning the Pope. Nevertheless, some weeks later he had to recall his troops, so urgently did he then need them in France, and the temporal power of the Pope ended only a few weeks after the downfall of the French Emperor.

Thus the outcome of all these long-drawn-out negotiations was very meagre. It was certainly not of such a character as to menace Prussia.

True, there remained the question of the maintenance of the Treaty of Prague, which was identical with the question of Germany's unification. If Bismarck wanted to achieve the latter he would have to reckon with the opposition of France and Austria. But two factors are to be taken into consideration here.

The crossing of the line of the Main could be effected in two ways: by agreement with the southern states or by their subjugation, against their own will. The second method was practically out of the question. A voluntary joining of the North German Confederation by the southern states was less likely in the spring of 1870 than it had been immediately after the war of 1866. The feeling of the population, especially in Bavaria and Wurtemberg, had taken a decidedly anti-Prussian turn. The most impressive sign of this was the overthrow of the Bavarian Minister-President, the unitarian Prince Hohenlohe, by the majority of the Second Bavarian Chamber. This majority consisted of the "Bavarian patriots", adherents of the integrity of Bavarian sovereignty and independence, and adversaries of Prussian militarism.

For these reasons the crossing of the line of the Main did not arise in the spring of 1870.

The other factor which has to be taken into consideration is that the danger of an armed opposition by France to a unification of Germany had receded owing to internal developments within

Napoleon's Empire. There had been a sensational turn from absolutism to Liberalism. The man who brought about this change was the deputy Émile Ollivier, whom the Emperor appointed as his leading Minister on 2nd January 1870. His idea was the reconciliation of the Napoleonic Empire with Liberalism, and the replacement of the personal régime of the Emperor by liberal and parliamentary institutions. That is what Ollivier called *L'Empire libéral*. Under this title he later told, in sixteen massive volumes, the story of the reign of Napoleon III. These new liberal institutions were approved by an overwhelming majority of the French people in the plebiscite of 8th May 1870.

Ollivier was not only a sincere friend of peace; he had consistently professed, since 1866, the opinion that no foreign Power had the right to put obstacles in the way of the German nation, if it decided on unification. He was a declared opponent of French intervention in internal German affairs. After taking office, Ollivier endeavoured to make clear that he had not given up this point of view. He gave the Paris correspondent of the *Kölnische Zeitung* an interview in which he put on record a declaration that he was strictly opposed to any French interference in the event of German unity coming about one day as the result of a great popular, *i.e.* not artificially arranged, movement. This declaration is to be borne in mind in view of the events which now unfolded themselves.

There is only space for a brief reference to the move of Lord Clarendon, in the spring of 1870, in favour of European disarmament. Clarendon acted at the instigation of the French government, which, however, wished to remain in the background. Clarendon addressed some private letters to Bismarck, urging the idea. But nothing came of it. Nothing was further from Bismarck's mind than disarmament, which he called a "confused humanitarian idea". Quite different ideas were maturing in his head, as the world was to learn only a few months later.

8. *The Hohenzollern Candidature for the Throne of Spain and the Origin of the Franco-German War of 1870*

Anyone who reads the twenty-second chapter of Bismarck's *Reflections and Recollections* will receive the impression that in the spring of 1870 Germany, Prussia, King William, and Bismarck were in the most peaceful mood, and that they were drawn into a war quite unexpectedly and reluctantly by French insolence and wantonness. A pure family affair of the House of Hohenzollern, with which Prussia or the North German Federation had nothing whatever to do, was turned by Napoleon and his Foreign Minister, the Duke of Gramont, into a political affair, and Germany was compelled to draw her sword in order to defend her national honour.

The truth is quite different, nearly the opposite of Bismarck's tale. Nobody knew this better than the man to whom Bismarck dictated his reminiscences. This was Lothar Bucher, who had been Bismarck's most intimate collaborator in the Foreign Office during two decades and who, having some years previously retired to private life, accompanied his much-admired master after his overthrow into the solitude of Varzin and Friedrichsruh to assist, with his quick shorthand and his wide and accurate knowledge, in the composition of the Bismarckian reminiscences. Bucher was an unusual character and had a very peculiar career. He began as a radical and revolutionary deputy in 1848 and had to go into exile after the defeat of the revolution. He lived in London as correspondent of a Liberal Berlin paper, but in this country had lost his belief in Liberal principles and parliamentary institutions. Returning to Berlin in the 'sixties, he left his party and joined Bismarck. A solitary and suspicious man and somewhat of a mystic, he surrendered his soul completely to the great statesman, who became his one ideal. He was one of the very few persons for whom Bismarck felt something like friendship. Bucher certainly knew more of Bismarck's most intimate secrets than any other man, and he knew the inside story of the Hohenzollern candidature, because he had played a not inconsiderable part in it. He knew better than anybody else how completely Bismarck distorted the truth, and in conversation with his friend Busch he called the Hohenzollern candidature frankly a "trap which Bismarck set for Napoleon", and he added that neither the King nor the Crown Prince had the least idea of this feature of Bismarck's manœuvre.

The publication of documents from the different archives has now made possible a reconstruction of the actual course of events. A particularly important contribution is Professor Robert H. Lord's book, *The Origins of the War of 1870* (Cambridge, Mass., 1924).

Lord publishes the whole correspondence of Bismarck in the critical days of July 1870, and comments on it in a masterly way. Other important documents are to be found in the last volumes of the French official publications, *Les Origines diplomatiques*.

The Spanish throne had become vacant by the revolution of 1868, which had driven the dissolute Queen Isabella out of the country. The National Assembly of Spain, the Cortes, led by General Prim, had made a democratic but monarchical constitution. But they lacked a monarch to fill the vacant throne, and Prim was thus looking for a Roman Catholic prince who would be able and willing to wear the rather thorny Spanish crown. There were either pretenders who were not favoured by Prim, or princes who declined the crown he offered them. A few Spaniards, among them a certain Salazar, were in favour of the hereditary Prince Leopold of Hohenzollern. Leopold was the son of Prince Charles Anton of Hohenzollern-Sigmaringen, whom we have met before as the Prussian Prime Minister in the "New Era". He had become a member of the royal family of Prussia when he had resigned the sovereignty of his diminutive princedom of Hohenzollern-Sigmaringen in favour of the King of Prussia. The King of Prussia had thus become the head of his family with all the rights and duties which belong to the head of the reigning family of a monarchy. The "Dynastic Laws" of the royal family had become binding for this branch of the family and all its members. The principal point was that no member could accept a throne without the express permission of the head of the family, the Prussian King. Besides, Prince Charles Anton was a Prussian general and his sons were officers in the Prussian army. One of these sons, Prince Charles, had already ascended a throne, becoming Prince and—many years later—King of Roumania.

The Sigmaringen branch of the Hohenzollerns was Roman Catholic, while the royal branch was Protestant. They were connected by marriage with many foreign reigning houses, but they regarded themselves as Germans, nay as Prussians, and made no secret of it.

At first the candidature of Leopold of Hohenzollern was not taken seriously, either in Spain or at the foreign courts. It had only a very limited number of adherents in Spain. Salazar, who was its foremost promoter, had first heard the name of the Prince from a Prussian diplomat, von Werthern, who had in the meantime become Prussian Envoy to the Bavarian Court in Munich. The Hohenzollern Princes themselves did not care at all for the Spanish crown.

But in May 1869 Theodor von Bernhardi appeared in Spain. Bernhardi was a learned man, a historian and economist, who had excellent connexions in Berlin society, at court and in the government. He is well known to historians through his diaries, which form a valuable source for Prussian history. He had often been employed for confidential tasks by Bismarck and Moltke. Before and during the war of 1866 he was Military Attaché to the Prussian Legation in Florence. He was now sent to Spain by Bismarck. The last volume of his diaries deals with his Spanish tour. But it does not contain a word about his political mission. There must have been very good reasons why his son, who edited the diary, suppressed all political information. This son is the well-known General, Friedrich von Bernhardi, whose doctrines are considered in this country as the very embodiment of extreme German militarism.

What did Theodor von Bernhardi do in Spain? To some extent the question is answered by the great English historian, Lord Acton, in his essay on the Causes of the Franco-Prussian War.[1] Acton was related to the German aristocracy and had excellent connexions with German scholars. He relates that Bismarck had put at Bernhardi's disposal £50,000 out of the secret Guelph Fund. The destination of this huge sum cannot be doubted, it was used to win followers in Spain. Whom Bernhardi bribed will, of course, always be a secret. It is not likely ever to be known whether General Prim received some of this money; all that can be said is that he lived in great style and thus was often in debt.

Now, in September 1869, Salazar appeared in Germany. Werthern introduced him to the Hohenzollern Princes. He offered Leopold the Spanish crown. With the full approval of his father, Leopold refused. Salazar repeated his efforts in February 1870, this time provided with letters from Prim to the Prince, the King of Prussia, and Bismarck. Prince Anton also wrote to Bismarck. Bismarck received Salazar on 26th February, and next day made to the King, who was absolutely against the candidature, a personal report which was energetically in its favour. He explained that in

[1] *Historical Essays and Studies*, p. 204.

case of war against France a Spanish government sympathetic towards Germany would be worth two army corps, and stressed the increase of the monarchy's prestige in Prussia if the dynasty should be in a European position which "has only an analogy in the old Habsburg model". The same thought was expressed by Prince Anton in his letter to Bismarck: "History has not seen such a dynasty since Charles V". These words are especially remarkable with reference to the declaration which the French Foreign Minister, the Duke of Gramont, later gave to the French parliament.

In spite of Bismarck's warm recommendation, King William continued to be strongly opposed to the candidature. But in March 1870 Prince Charles Anton and his son Prince Leopold came to Berlin, living as his guests in the Royal Palace. Here, on 15th March, at the instigation of Bismarck, a dinner was given in honour of the Prince, to which the most important Prussian personalities were invited. Bismarck says in his *Recollections* that no ministerial council took place in the palace. From the formal point of view he is correct. It was not a formal council. There were good reasons for selecting another, more private method, and Bismarck himself had recommended this conference. But it was, nevertheless, a highly important deliberation on the question whether Prince Leopold should be advised to accept the candidature. The importance of this gathering is evident from the list of those present: besides the Crown Prince, the Hohenzollerns, and the Minister Schleinitz, there were: Bismarck; the President of the Federal Chancellery, Delbrück; the Under-Secretary of the Foreign Office, Thile; the War Minister, General Roon; and the Chief of the General Staff of the Army, General Moltke. Under Bismarck's firm leadership all Ministers and generals advocated the candidature.

But quite as important as that which was said is that which was left unsaid. Not a single Minister or general spoke a word about the question whether war with France might not result from an accession of a Hohenzollern to the throne of Spain. There can be no doubt that this question was in their minds. At the dinner Rudolf Delbrück was the neighbour of Moltke and asked the latter: "But if Napoleon takes it ill, are we ready?" Moltke nodded in a way which expressed his complete confidence in a Prussian victory. But nobody spoke a word about it in the hearing of the

King. They knew that he would be firmly opposed to the candidature if he thought that any danger of war might arise from it.

But in spite of these clever and unscrupulous tactics, King
William refused for once to follow Bismarck's lead, and Leopold
again refused the candidature. Now the affair should have been
closed with this royal decision. But Bismarck made light of it and
continued to work for the plan which the King had declined. A few
weeks later he sent Lothar Bucher to Spain. Bucher returned with
a very optimistic report. But the King considered it too *couleur de
rose* and continued in his negative attitude. Now Bismarck tried to
go the other way round and pressed Prince Anton to influence his
son to accept the candidature. As Leopold was still unwilling, Bismarck sent Bucher to Madrid again, this time with a letter to Prim.
To the King, who resented Bismarck's negotiating with Prim
behind his back, he tried to explain that this was only an act of
politeness. In fact he did, through Bucher, agree with Prim about
the tactics, the first principle of which was to make believe that Bismarck and the Prussian Foreign Office had nothing to do with the
affair. Bucher returned secretly to Germany with Salazar. Now, at
last, Leopold accepted, and on 21st June King William, "with a
heavy, very heavy heart", gave his consent, which, according to
the dynastic law, was indispensable.

So far everything had been kept secret. The plan was to make the
Cortes, who had to elect the King, suddenly acquainted with the
candidature and to have the election carried through so quickly that
Europe should learn only the accomplished fact. It failed owing
to misunderstandings. When Salazar arrived at Madrid with the
acceptance, the Cortes had been postponed, the secret became
known, and Prim was compelled, on 3rd July, to disclose the Hohenzollern candidature to the French Ambassador.

Napoleon was deeply wounded by the attitude of the House of
Hohenzollern. He had always shown them benevolence and he considered that they had now played him a shabby trick. He could not
but take the affair very seriously. Spain is the southern neighbour
of France, and a Hohenzollern on her throne meant an encirclement
and perhaps, in certain circumstances, a war on two fronts. Napoleon
knew that the French people would see the candidature in this light
and that his authority, weakened by his diplomatic defeats since

Sadowa, would suffer a definite and intolerable blow if he did not prevent it. To take it lying down could mean the end of his reign and of his dynasty. Indeed Paris was immensely excited as the news from Madrid became public.

Gramont ordered the Chargé d'Affaires in Berlin, le Sourd, to enquire at the Foreign Office if the Berlin cabinet had anything to do with this "intrigue". For at this highly critical moment all the important people were absent from Berlin. The King was taking the cure at Ems; Benedetti, the French Ambassador, was doing the same in Wildbad, and Bismarck had withdrawn into "the Pomeranian forests", to his estate at Varzin. Le Sourd had to put up with Under-Secretary Thile, one of the participants in the Hohenzollern conference of 15th March, who gave him the answer that he knew nothing of the whole affair, which did not exist for him, that is, for the Foreign Office. This answer naturally made a very bad impression on Gramont, all the more so as he had been informed from Madrid that Bismarck had corresponded with Prim directly.

What should the French government do now? They thought that they had to warn Prussia by firm language. Gramont therefore read to the Corps législatif a declaration which made an immense sensation and showed Europe that it was on the brink of a war. "We will not tolerate", he said, "a Foreign Power placing one of its princes on the throne of Charles V and thus disturbing the balance of power." We have seen that the ideas of Bismarck and of the Prince of Hohenzollern correspond rather well with this declaration. Gramont ended by declaring that in case of need the government would know how to fulfil its duty without hesitation and without weakness.

Besides making this public declaration, the French government ordered the Ambassador Benedetti to go to Ems, where King William was taking the waters, and to take up the question directly with him.

There is little doubt that up to this moment Bismarck had been the driving force behind the candidature, or that his assertion that it had nothing to do with Prussian politics was only a screen that would certainly fall before the strong gale of facts. The only doubt is whether he had carried on the affair *intending it to lead to war*. It would be a reflection on Bismarck's foresight, which surpassed by far that of all contemporary statesmen, to assume that he did not know: (1) that the French would regard the candidature all the more as a provocation as they suffered from the continuous diplomatic defeats which he had inflicted on them since Sadowa; (2) that Napoleon would be anxious for the fate of his dynasty if he put up with this provocation; (3) that the candidature of a prince belonging to a ruling dynasty was in opposition to a principle of international practice which had evolved clearly in the 19th century. Moreover, Napoleon had informed him in 1869 that he would not suffer a Hohenzollern on the Spanish throne. So Bismarck at least knew that he was *bringing war within sight*. But those who at that time had seen him at close quarters, went farther and pretended that he had *wanted* the war. Bucher, who knew more than anybody else, has called the Hohenzollern candidature a "trap" which Bismarck had laid for Napoleon, and Prince Charles Anton of Hohenzollern said to Radowitz, the future German Ambassador, on 3rd July 1871, that Bismarck had only raised the affair *with the intention and expectation of it leading to war*.

Much as Bismarck took pains to leave this in obscurity, he joyfully confessed to having, *after Gramont's speech*, been resolved on the war and having pushed it forward. Therefore he fought to the utmost against any weakening; unlike his King, who wanted to avoid a war on this issue and was working for the withdrawal of the candidature. That Benedetti called on the King and negotiated personally with him—a thing to which he was entitled according to international law—was the consequence of the negative attitude the Prussian Foreign Office had adopted. But this caused Bismarck anxiety lest the King should substitute his own policy. The contrast is clearly shown in the telegrams exchanged between Ems and Varzin, as much by what they say as by what they do not: for the King avoids informing his Chancellor of all he is doing for the maintenance of peace. He does not tell him that he is sending a letter and messengers to Prince Hohenzollern to urge him to resign, nor that he asks Benedetti to stay at Ems till the expected news from the Hohenzollerns arrives. One can understand the King's anxiety if one reads the excited remarks with which Bismarck comments on the telegrams from Ems. A telegram of 11th July contains an utterance of the King: "To Madrid, the Prince must express himself

directly". To which Bismarck adds: "Express? Why? About what?
And what?" The telegram goes on: "Benedetti said he took it upon
himself to stay 24 hours longer". Bismarck ironically comments:
"Very kind!" Telegram: "H.M. has written to Prince Hohenzollern:
attitude as before, the Prince will decide, he will consent". This last
word is underlined by Bismarck, who comments: "To what?"
When—to crown all—he gets a telegram from Ems on 12th July
saying Hohenzollern had telegraphed to the King: "Erbprinz
resigns voluntarily", Bismarck vents his anger in a double under-
lining of the word "voluntarily" and a large mark of exclamation.

When Bismarck saw from Varzin that despite all his telegrams
an amicable arrangement was developing in Ems, he resolved to go
there. But when he arrived in Berlin on 12th July and learned that
Leopold had resigned, he interrupted his journey. What his motives
were we may conclude from his words, a week later, to the French
Chargé d'Affaires who presented him with the declaration of war.
After having complained about the pressure which Benedetti had
put on the "poor sick King", he added: "Do you think I should
not, if officially interrogated, have hurried here from the depths of
the Pomeranian forests? . . . I agree that *if I had gone to Ems* I could
perhaps have *prevented the war.* . . ."

The withdrawal of the candidature was a great diplomatic success
for France and therefore a great diplomatic defeat for Bismarck.
He was resolved not to accept it and, for his part, planned energetic
steps to take the offensive, which was bound to end in war if France
did not give way. He was saved this trouble by Napoleon and
Gramont who—contrary to all political sense—were not satisfied
with their success.

Had they stopped there, the whole world would have acclaimed
them as victors, and the Hohenzollern candidature would have been
as dead as a door-nail. But now Napoleon made two fatal mistakes.
He allowed himself to be influenced by the clamour of the irresponsible Paris press and the Right-wing nationalists, who were
not satisfied with the resignation because it was represented as a
private affair of the Hohenzollern Princes with which Prussia was
not concerned. His second mistake was his relapse into the methods
of personal government by giving Gramont an order behind the
back of the other Ministers. Benedetti was sent this order, unknown

to Ollivier, who might have prevented it. Benedetti was ordered to demand from the Prussian King a declaration that he approved the resignation of the Prince and that he promised never to allow the Prince to renew his candidature in future.

By these mistakes Napoleon delivered himself into Bismarck's hands. King William could not but reject the new demands. Abeken, who represented the Prussian Foreign Office in Ems, reported these facts to Bismarck by telegram. Bismarck published this telegram in a form which was calculated to rouse national feeling in Germany as well as in France. The story of how he edited this telegram is told by Bismarck himself in his own inimitable way in his *Recollections*. It is one of his literary masterpieces, never to be forgotten. His enemies have called this "editing" a falsification, and Bismarck's own story has much to do with this. It is pointless to dispute the question whether this terminology is correct. The main point is that Bismarck gave the telegram a new meaning which was completely opposed to the King's intention, while, on the other hand, by dating it *Ems 13 July*, he made people believe that it expressed the King's policy.

What he did was this: Firstly, he connected two sentences which in the original had been separated by an important statement, and, secondly, he did not mention that the King had informed the Ambassador of having received confirmation of the resignation from Prince Anton. Thus he gave the words of the Ems text—that "the King had informed the French Ambassador through his A.D.C. that he had nothing further to tell him"—the meaning of a grave and intentional snub which was as contradictory to the facts as to the opinion of the King, which Bismarck knew very well. The same evening Bismarck had the telegram published in that offending version in a special edition of the papers, which whipped up the people to patriotic excitement. Besides—although he denied it in his official declaration on 18th July—he had all the German and foreign courts officially informed of it. In Munich, London, and St. Petersburg he even aggravated this information by the incorrect statement that "Benedetti had provocatively addressed the King against his will on the Promenade". In reality, the King had addressed Benedetti.

This communication had exactly the effect expected and intended by Bismarck. When King William read the paper he exclaimed in alarm: "That means war!" He recognized that the right of declaring war, entrusted to him by the constitution, had been usurped by his Chancellor; what remained for him to do was a mere formality. The effect of Bismarck's wording becomes apparent also in Ollivier's speech before the Corps législatif on the decisive 15th July: "*Il peut arriver qu'un roi refuse de recevoir un Ambassadeur: ce qui est blessant, c'est le refus intentionnel, divulgé dans des suppléments de journaux, dans les télégrammes adressés à toutes les cours de l'Europe*". Actually all forms of politeness had been observed towards Benedetti. "*L'offense résulte d'une publication intentionnelle.*"

Bismarck prided himself on having this "intention". Those who were opposed to it he reproached with not having wanted the result of the war, the unification of Germany.

Whether a war against France was, in fact, the only way to achieve a unification of Germany is a question open to dispute. Was it, indeed, quite impossible for the German nation, by its own free will, to form a united state? What the population of Bavaria and Wurtemberg did not want was a state in which the Prussian crown had an overwhelming ascendancy and in which Prussian militarism was the predominant force. Was it not possible to win their adherence by concessions which weakened these predominant forces? But one thing is absolutely certain: that Bismarck would not make these concessions under any circumstances. His goal was Prussian rule over the whole of Germany—as he had written quite sincerely to Roon. And we shall see that in this, too, he succeeded completely.

Looking back to the story of the Hohenzollern candidature, we can have no doubt that it was Bismarck's work, and I feel justified in saying that Bucher was right when he said it was a trap which Bismarck had set for Napoleon. I personally feel convinced that Bismarck undertook it with the intention of putting Napoleon in a formidable dilemma: either to suffer a political defeat which would in the long run cost him his throne, or to wage war—and that he foresaw that Napoleon would prefer war. Therefore, responsibility for the war rests in the first instance with Bismarck. He is, of course, not the only person responsible. The unscrupulous French journalists and politicians who frivolously cried: "*A Berlin*", the Empress Eugénie, who influenced her husband in favour of war, Napoleon himself and Gramont, who threw away a splendid chance because they did not know where to stop—they all have to bear their share of the responsibility. But they were all rather driven than driving. Bismarck alone kept the initiative by knowing beforehand how the others would react to his moves. He made them his tools, and they did what he wanted them to do. His superiority towers above them, head and shoulders. Therefore, the primary responsibility rests with him alone.

In one of his melancholy moments, Bismarck later reproached himself with these words: "Without me three great wars would not have happened and 80,000 men would not have perished". Eighty thousand! How small is their number compared with the millions whose sacrifice was the indirect consequence of that war between Germany and France, the millions who had not yet been born when the last shot in that war was fired.

Even the greatest statesman cannot foresee in their utter dreadfulness all the consequences of his fateful acts and the endless misery he brings to this earth by loosing the fury of war.

9. The Foundation of the German Empire

It is not possible to tell here the story of the war and Bismarck's part in it. I propose to deal here only with the most important results of the victory: the unification of the German people in a great Reich, the head of which—the Prussian King—became Deutscher Kaiser (German Emperor).

The idea that this war had to bear fruit in German unity was, from the outset, strong in many minds. The overwhelming majority of the population in Northern Germany was in favour of it, and the same may be said of the majority in Baden and Hesse-Darmstadt. The centre of the opposition was Wurtemberg and particularly Bavaria. The Bavarian "Patriots" had tried to keep their kingdom out of the war and to proclaim neutrality. But they were foiled in parliament by the defection of a section of their party, which, carried away by German national enthusiasm, spoke and voted for entry into the war at the side of the North German Confederation. Nevertheless, this opposition was not dead. Much depended on the attitude of the King, Louis II. In the critical days of July he had given the order for mobilization; but it is more than doubtful whether his motives had anything to do with national feeling. He was not interested in German national affairs. His royal ideal was the French King, Louis XIV, whom he tried to imitate by his luxurious and fantastic buildings. Through this unbridled passion for building he had plunged into heavy debt. This had very important consequences, as we shall see. His only political interest was the maintenance of the sovereignty and splendour of the Royal House of Wittelsbach, which he considered to be much nobler and more glorious than the House of Hohenzollern. The business of government bored him and he fled into the solitude of the mountains to escape it. His interest belonged to art and music. He was a completely pathological character. Very probably his madness had already begun to develop. In Wurtemberg the King and the Queen were decidedly anti-Prussian and many of the courtiers hoped for a French victory. Some of them expressed this hope quite openly to the French Minister when he had to leave Stuttgart.

The political group which first tried to influence popular feeling in Southern Germany in favour of unification was that of the National Liberals. The National Liberal Party was the party of German unification. Its leader in this question was Eduard Lasker, member of the Reichstag and the Prussian Chamber. He was full of national enthusiasm which swept away the reserve of his more hesitant friends. Lasker was for some years the most popular German parliamentarian. Later, when he was compelled by his conscience to oppose Bismarck, he became the first victim of the new anti-Semitic movement. On Lasker's initiative some leading National Liberal parliamentarians made a tour of Southern Germany, where they strengthened national feeling and negotiated with some success with the governments. Bismarck did not like this popular agitation. Not only because he had a personal grudge against Lasker, but still more because he did not like parliamentarians taking the initiative in a question he wished to deal with in his own personal way.

Still less did Bismarck like the activities of the German Crown Prince. Frederick William was full of the idea that the war should bring national unity to the German people, and the Imperial crown to the Hohenzollerns. His critics assert that he sought for himself alone the pomp and splendour of the Imperial purple robe. That may be so. But it is only natural that he considered himself the representative of Germany's future, the more so as he knew perfectly well that his aged and old-fashioned father did not care in the least for anything that was outside the old Prussian tradition. Bismarck was very angry at the interference of the Crown Prince, and the latter considered Bismarck lukewarm on the question he had so much at heart. Both were mistaken in their judgment of each other.

The national question began to mature when in October 1870 the representatives of the four South German states appeared in Versailles at the headquarters of the German army to negotiate on the future organization of Germany. The Bavarian Minister-President, Count Bray, the successor of Hohenlohe, who leaned more to Austria than to Prussia, wanted, if possible, to avoid Bavaria's entry into the North German Confederation and suggested instead a permanent alliance between Bavaria and the Confederation. But this idea never had the slightest chance, because the other southern States were not in the least interested in giving to Bavaria a separate and elevated position of this kind. Bismarck was able to negotiate separately with each single deputation, and here he was, of course, always more than a match for any of them. When Bray put down his objections in a memorandum, Bismarck laid this paper before the Minister for Wurtemberg, von Mittnacht, offered him some concessions should Wurtemberg enter the Confederation, and asked him whether he was ready to conclude a treaty to this effect, even without Bavaria. The Wurtemberger answered in the affirmative and with that Bismarck had won. Bavaria could not risk a possible exclusion from a unified Germany. Bray could not help offering new proposals and did so without requesting the consent of his King. For he knew that Louis would ask for conditions which were quite impossible. One was an aggrandizement of Bavaria at the expense of another German prince, the Grand Duke of Baden, and the other was a personal favour which Bray declined even to mention, and about which we shall have to speak later.

On 11th November Bismarck had so far succeeded that the three minor states, Wurtemberg, Baden, and Hesse, were ready to sign the treaties the next day. Then suddenly an unexpected incident occurred. The King of Wurtemberg ordered his delegates not to sign without Bavaria. The delegates left Versailles at once.

During these days Bismarck wrote to his son: "Unless a German thunderstorm bursts between them, nothing will go through with these old diplomats and bureaucrats". That was certainly only a diplomatic way of referring to the German princes. And the Crown Prince wrote in his diary: "I am really ashamed of the German princes who cannot and will not learn anything and whose mean character makes them unable to do their duty towards the great common fatherland". There was not much difference between the feelings of Bismarck and the Crown Prince. But, nevertheless, it was in these very days that they came into sharp conflict.

Shortly after the Wurtemberger's departure, the Crown Prince went to see Bismarck to ask him whether he wanted to settle the issue of the Imperial crown. Bismarck answered in the affirmative, but, shrugging his shoulders, emphasized the difficulties. The Prince suggested compelling the resisting Kings. Bismarck rejected this advice and told him angrily that he had no right to express an opinion of this kind. The controversy became so acute that Bismarck said that he would be ready to make room for another man more agreeable to the Prince, but that until then he would act according to his own principles. He was so enraged that, in private conversation, he called the Crown Prince the stupidest and vainest man and added that he would one day perish from "Emperor-madness" (*Kaiserwahnsinn*).

The difference of opinion about the policy to be adopted towards the opposing Kings cannot be the motive of this anger. Bismarck said that it was against his principles to employ force against an ally. This delicacy of feeling is not usual with Bismarck. Even in this case he was quite willing to use every kind of pressure against the monarchs concerned, or at least to threaten them with it. The bitterness between the two men had its source in the mutual conviction that each of them wanted to infuse the new Empire with quite a different spirit. The Prince's liberalism was anathema to the Chancellor. What separated them was not so much the end, the subjection of the recalcitrant princes, as the means of achieving it. Bismarck suspected the Crown Prince of wishing to use the Reichstag to bring pressure to bear on the princes. That was what

Bismarck wanted to avoid at all cost. If the Reichstag took the initiative in this all-important question, if the German Empire became the product of a parliamentary action, the Reichstag's political authority and power would have been raised considerably. This Bismarck would not allow. The Reichstag was to confine itself to approving the fruits of the Chancellor's own negotiations. He hastened to complete his negotiations before the Reichstag—called for the 24th November—met.

He succeeded once more! Three days after the Wurtemberg delegation had left Versailles the treaties with Baden and Hesse had been concluded, and on 23rd November—one day before the Reichstag assembled—Bavaria signed too. Bismarck had made to the Bavarian delegates some concessions which were very likely to rouse the opposition of the Reichstag. The worst was that the validity of a marriage which a Bavarian concluded in another German country depended on the permit of the King of Bavaria— quite an absurd regulation. The most sensational concession was that a committee for Foreign Affairs of the Federal Council was formed, the Permanent President of which was the Bavarian member. As a matter of fact, this concession never had any practical value. The committee for Foreign Affairs never had the slightest influence, either in Bismarck's time or under his successors. Perhaps it might have been of considerable advantage to the German people if, during the reign of William II, a committee of well-informed and sober officials of the federal states had counterbalanced some of his most dangerous eccentricities.

Bismarck knew that his concessions to Bavarian particularism were highly unpopular, and he was afraid that the Reichstag would, for that reason, either decline or amend the Bavarian treaty. He therefore quickly sent to Berlin all the parliamentarians who happened to be at the German army headquarters in Versailles, so that they might influence the National Liberal Party in favour of accepting the Bavarian treaty. The National Liberals did not like the treaty at all, but they were convinced that it had to be accepted for the sake of the great end involved. The feeling of the party was expressed by Lasker in the jesting words: "The girl is very ugly indeed, but nevertheless she must be married".

On the evening which followed the signing of the Bavarian treaty,

Bismarck invited his companions to drink champagne to the toast of "German unity is made and the German Kaiser, Emperor, too!" He was resolved upon using Bavaria to make the King of Prussia German Emperor.

Two days after the conclusion of the Bavarian treaty, a trusted agent of Louis II, Graf Holnstein, Master of the Horse, arrived at Versailles to negotiate with Bismarck. Two days later he returned to his King with the draft of a letter which Louis II was to write to William I. The letter contained an invitation to the Prussian King to become German Emperor. The draft was written by Bismarck personally. Some days later Holnstein returned to Versailles with Louis' letter. The King had copied Bismarck's draft, word for word, and added his royal signature.

Why did Louis II act in this not very majestic manner? It was well known that the Bavarian King abhorred in his innermost heart the idea that a Hohenzollern should, as German Emperor, be elevated over himself. When, at the end of November, the Grand Duke of Baden had written Louis a letter asking him to acquire "immortal glory" by inviting the Prussian King to become German Emperor, Louis had not even replied. We know that he said he would rather abdicate. Why did he now act at the instigation, nay, the dictation, of Bismarck?

Part of the answer was first given by Lord Acton in the essay mentioned earlier: after the overthrow of Bismarck, his successor, Caprivi, found that some millions out of the Guelph Funds had gone to Munich. £15,000 were paid annually to King Louis and a considerable sum to Holnstein. Now it is reasonably certain that Louis and Holnstein were bribed by Bismarck with money from the *Welfen-Fonds*, in order to induce Louis to offer the Imperial crown to William. Louis, deeply in debt, was saved from financial catastrophe by the money which belonged to his ally of 1866, King George V of Hanover, and which was put at the disposal of the Prussian government "in order to control and frustrate the subversive enterprises of King George against Prussia".

It was by means of Louis' letter that Bismarck made the world believe that the German Kaiser was a product not of the German people but of the German princes. Of course, the truth is quite the opposite. It was the German people who longed for a German

Kaiser, a *Kaiser in Freiheit und Recht* (in freedom and right), as it is expressed in the fine old student song. The German princes, with a few exceptions, such as the Grand Duke of Baden and Duke Ernest of Coburg-Gotha, did not care for a German Emperor, and some, such as the Kings of Bavaria and Wurtemberg and the Grand Duke of Hessen-Darmstadt, strongly opposed the idea. But success was again with Bismarck. The Reichstag was compelled to be satisfied with the rôle of the chorus in Greek tragedy. The way in which it was informed of the Bavarian King's letter was characteristic of its rôle. A "Free Conservative" member of the Reichstag, Friedenthal, was induced by the government to ask Bismarck's deputy, Delbrück, in the Reichstag, how the question of a German Kaiser stood. Delbrück rose to produce Louis' letter. At first he could not find it and at last he read it in the driest possible tone. With all his excellent qualities Delbrück was certainly not the man for great and solemn occasions. Somebody wrote to the Crown Prince: "It looked as if Delbrück drew the poor old Imperial crown, wrapped up in an old newspaper, from his trouser-pocket".

The Reichstag hastened to make the appropriate amendments in the constitution and substituted the words Reich and Kaiser in the place where stipulation had been made for a Bund and Bundes-Präsident. The constitution now became that of the German Empire (*Die Reichsverfassung*). The Reichstag then resolved to send a deputation of its members to King William to beg him to accept the German Imperial crown. The address was drafted by Eduard Lasker, whom the Reichstag recognized as one of its foremost leaders in the movement towards unity and Empire. When King William was told about the authorship of the address he said ironically: "Why, then I am indeed indebted to Mr. Lasker for an Imperial Crown!"

This little anecdote reveals the temper of the old King. In his heart there was only room for Prussia, and he did not care for the German Imperial crown. He did not, in any case, want to be indebted for it to the Reichstag, the representatives of the German people. True, the people had won the victories in the war against France, but he did not look at it that way. A crown which was offered by the Reichstag smacked of democracy and was, in his eyes, the same as the revolutionary crown which the National

Assembly of 1848, the Paulskirche, had offered to his brother Frederick William IV. If he had to take it, he wanted to accept it only from the German princes, as his brother said on the 3rd April 1849, even if the most important of the princes was a pathological case, like Louis II. In fact, the Reichstag did not offer him the crown but only begged that he might deign to accept it. But he was so angry that at first he declined to receive the Reichstag deputation. Bismarck had to intervene in order to avoid a public refusal. But he received the deputation only after all the princes, great and small, had joined the Bavarian King in his request.

Thus it came to pass that on the 19th December 1870 the Reichstag deputation stood in Versailles before King William. Its speaker was the President of the Reichstag, Eduard Simson, the same man who had spoken to Frederick William IV twenty-one years before as President of the Paulskirche Assembly. Nobody could overlook the symbolism of this incident. In solemn words Simson expressed the confidence of the German nation that it would find in the new Empire "Unity and power, right and law, freedom and peace". The Crown Prince wrote in his diary: "Simson's speech was a really masterly work, delivered so perfectly that this genuinely German patriotic speech moved me to tears". There was no objection then to a man of Jewish origin giving expression to the feelings of the German nation at this historical hour. Even the Prussian generals, who were assembled to hear him, were moved, and King William could not help occasionally faltering when he read the answer which Bismarck had drafted for him. In this answer William praised "with deep emotion" the Bavarian King's letter. But whoever looked at the assembly saw that among the princes one was conspicuous by his absence, the Bavarian Prince Luitpold, the representative of the Bavarian King.

This ceremony was not yet the solemn proclamation of the German Empire. King William would allow that only after the treaties with the South German states were ratified by their Chambers and governments. But the Bavarian opposition, the "Patriots", knew how to protract this procedure so long that William was at last compelled to order the proclamation without the completion of the ratification of the Bavarian treaty. The 18th January is the birthday of the Prussian kingdom, the day on which, in 1701,

Frederick III, elector of Brandenburg, assumed the crown as King of Prussia. Thus the 18th January became the day when William I, King of Prussia, was proclaimed German Emperor.

The proclamation was read by Bismarck in the Salle des Glaces (the Hall of Mirrors), in Louis XIV's palace in Versailles. It was the proudest day of his life. He could say that he had directed every step which had led to this goal.

Was it also a proud day for the King? One would have thought that he felt happy at the elevation of himself and his house to a position which made him a symbol of the realization of the finest and highest wishes of the German nation, of the fulfilment of the national dream of fifty years' duration. When he looked back on the day in September 1862 when he was ready to abdicate and Bismarck lent him his strong hand, he must have felt—one would think—that he was indebted to his Chancellor for a triumph which was almost incomparable in human history. We would presume that he drew Bismarck to his heart and assured him that he would never forget his debt to him. But the new German Emperor, descending from the dais, walked over to his generals to accept their congratulations, without shaking Bismarck's hand, without even looking at him. He was furious at his Chancellor, and he wrote to the Queen, now Empress, on the day of the proclamation that he was so "morose" that he "very nearly abdicated and handed over everything" to his son. "The most unhappy day of my life", he called the day of his proclamation.

Why was that? The reason is almost ridiculous. He wanted the title "Emperor of Germany" while Bismarck considered that the title "German Emperor" was alone permissible. It is not necessary to explain the difference between the two titles, for it is not of the slightest interest to anybody who does not happen to be a crowned head. Bismarck said to his companions that he did not care a straw for it. And to his wife he wrote: "This imperial confinement was a difficult one, and kings have in such times strange desires, like women . . . as accoucheur, I sometimes felt the urgent desire to be a bomb-shell and to explode, that the whole building would fall to pieces".

The true motive for the King's reluctance was his stubborn Prussianism. To him Prussia meant everything, Germany nothing.

He well knew his powerful position as King of Prussia, but he was afraid that as German Emperor he would be much less powerful. He did not foresee that Bismarck would be able to make the German Emperor still more powerful than the Prussian King. This tremendous position was not contemplated by anyone who had advocated a German Kaiser and Reich before Bismarck. The Liberals, who had been the advocates of the German Empire, had thought of it as a modern and liberal institution. They believed, to a certain extent, in Ludwig Uhland's words in the Paulskirche that the head that reigned over Germany should be anointed with a *drop of democratic oil*. It is the extraordinary and fateful accomplishment of Bismarck that this democratic drop was avoided completely.

From this point of view the character of the ceremony of the proclamation was significant. It was a ceremony of princes and generals. This character was impressed on the new German Reich at the outset. Princes, generals, noblemen, even Junkers became its significant classes. The Prussian Junkers, who only a few years previously had condemned the idea of nationality, the robbery of crowns, and the filth of the German Republic, became the ruling class in the new Reich and posed as its foremost champions. The situation which developed is best characterized by a passage which the third Imperial Chancellor wrote in his diary at the end of the century. This was Prince Chlovis of Hohenlohe, who considered himself a representative of South German liberalism: "When I sit among the Prussian excellencies, the contrast between Northern and Southern Germany becomes manifest to me. South German liberalism cannot prevail against the Junkers. . . . All these noblemen do not care a pin for the Empire and would give it up rather to-day than to-morrow."

This development has its origin in Bismarck's policy of 1870, when he denied to the Reichstag an active influence on the creation of the Empire. The theory of the policy he pursued at that time is expressed in the famous chapter of his *Recollections* entitled "Dynasties and Races". Here he professes his old conviction: "That the key to German politics was to be found in princes and dynasties, not in publicists, whether in parliament and the press or on the barricades". His argument is based on the following sentences: "For German patriotism, to be active and effective, needs as a rule to be dependent upon a dynasty. Independent of a dynasty, it rarely comes to a rising point. . . . The German's love of the fatherland has need of a prince on whom he can concentrate his attachment. Suppose that all the German dynasties were suddenly deposed, there would then be no likelihood of German national sentiment sufficient to hold all the Germans together amid the friction of European politics."

Now this latter situation, so improbable in Bismarck's eyes, did come true. All the German dynasties were deposed in 1918, yet the cohesion of the Reich was not loosened despite great internal and external difficulties. Nay, German nationalism was strong enough to follow the leadership of a demagogue, who was not even born within the Reich. So difficult is it, even for the greatest statesman, to foresee the developments of only half a century.

Nevertheless, in one point, and that perhaps is the most important of all, Bismarck's heritage has outlasted all the changes of the age. The militarism he impressed upon the German nation by his doctrine of "blood and iron" and its brilliant and triumphant realization remained overwhelmingly strong and proved stronger than the bitter disappointments of the first World War and the Weimar Republic, in which at least a part of the people tried to do without it.

One reason for the strength of German militarism is intimately connected with the peace which ended the war against France. As a result of this peace treaty two French provinces, Alsace and Lorraine, were torn from a defeated France and annexed to a victorious Germany. Bismarck's motive was not that historical romanticism which German historians professed, claiming that these two provinces had once, centuries ago, belonged to the Holy Roman Empire and should now return to a rejuvenated fatherland. All that he contemptuously termed a "Professor's idea". In a conversation during the war, in Vienna, Adolphe Thiers, the French statesman and historian, asked the great German historian, Leopold Ranke: "Whom are you fighting now after the downfall of the Napoleonic Empire?" Ranke answered: "Louis XIV". Bismarck would never have made a statement of this kind. As a practical statesman he knew that the historical process cannot be begun afresh after centuries during which populations have changed their feelings and interests. He knew that the population of Alsace and Lorraine felt French and would for a long time continue to be a very uncomfortable part of Germany. If he nevertheless insisted upon the annexation, it was for military reasons. He believed that the two provinces would be indispensable for the defence of Germany, especially South-western Germany, against a new French attack. Even so, he had doubts whether it would be advantageous to take Metz, the population of which was entirely French in feeling and language. But at last he gave way to the expostulations of the generals and the wishes of his King.

At this time Gladstone was Prime Minister of England. He was shocked when he heard of the German intention to annex the two provinces against the manifest wishes of their population. He deplored the relapse into "the old and cruel practice of treating the population of a civilized European country as mere chattels".

Here, he wrote to Queen Victoria, a general principle is involved whose violation "has caused much disturbance and much bloodshed in subsequent times to Europe". He wanted the neutral countries jointly to protest against the annexation, but was defeated in his cabinet. When it was apparent that the annexation would be carried out, he wrote to Granville: "I have an apprehension that this violent laceration and transfer is to lead us from bad to worse, and to the beginning of a new series of European complications".

How true Gladstone's prophecy was, everybody knows now. The annexations have made a real and lasting peace between Germany and France impossible. Bismarck's sleep at night was disturbed by the *Cauchemar des coalitions* (the nightmare of coalitions) against Germany. The whole European continent became an armed camp. Germany's first duty seemed to be to arm herself more and more strongly. Nobody seemed as important as the soldier and the officer, and militarism won a complete ascendancy.

But this criticism should not lead us to overlook Bismarck's enormous achievement, the fulfilment of the dream of the German nations, their unification in a powerful and glorious Empire. To understand what this meant for the generation which had longed for it and fought for it, we may read a letter which the historian Heinrich von Sybel wrote to his friend and colleague, Herman Baumgarten, when the Empire was proclaimed: "Tears run down my cheeks. By what have we deserved the grace of God, that we are allowed to live to see such great and mighty deeds. What for twenty years was the substance of all our wishes and efforts, is now fulfilled in such an immeasurably magnificent way." No doubt millions of the best Germans felt the same. It is not in every century that Fate allows a statesman to evoke feelings of this strength in a whole nation. And those statesmen who succeed in doing so are the heroes and the great men of history. Among these great men Bismarck will always be classed, and the critics of his methods and of his personality never can, nor will, doubt his singular greatness and his everlasting glory.

FOOTNOTE

The secret files of the Berlin Foreign Office about the Hohenzollern candidature (cf. p. 164) were published for the first time in 1957, in an English translation, in the book: "Bismarck and the Hohenzollern Candidature for the Spanish Throne", edited with an introduction by Georges Bonnin, London, Chatto & Windus. This book contains also a detailed minute of the debate at the dinner of 15th March 1870 (cf. p. 162), written by the Prince of Hohenzollern. These documents leave no doubt that Bismarck was the main German instigator of the candidature. Whether he wanted it in order to provoke a war with France remains a matter of interpretation, and the documents certainly give me no reason to change the opinion expressed in the above text.

CHAPTER IV

BISMARCK AS IMPERIAL CHANCELLOR

THE twenty years beginning with the foundation of the German Empire in January 1871 and ending with Bismarck's dismissal by William II in March 1890, are known to historians as the "Age of Bismarck", for, indeed, during these years he was the centre not only of German but of European politics. The majority of the German people looked at him as the hero of national unity, but statesmen in all other capitals of Europe considered him not only the unrivalled master of their craft, but the most important factor in every political calculation and combination. Nowhere was there a man bold enough to dispute his superiority, whether in London or St. Petersburg, let alone Paris or Vienna. Everywhere the leading statesmen, Disraeli or Gortchakoff, Andrassy or Thiers, looked to Berlin and to the Wilhelmstrasse or even to Varzin or Friedrichsruh, should the Chancellor happen to be on his estates, far from his office. In the 'seventies, in particular, Bismarck's position was comparable only to that of Napoleon I during the Congress of Erfurt in 1808, when the Czar of Russia and all the German princes gathered round to do him homage. But while Napoleon continued to plunge into fresh wars, Bismarck never drew the sword again after defeating France. A few years after Erfurt Napoleon I was driven from his throne and from France; Bismarck remained in power for almost twenty years and his overthrow was due not to a foreign enemy but to his own Emperor.

The years from 1871 to 1890 stand out in sharp contrast to the first period of Bismarck's administration from 1862 to 1870. In this initial period he waged three wars, in 1864, 1866, and 1870, but in the later period not one. This, of course, by no means implies that his views on the admissibility of war as a means of solving political problems had changed. Before and after 1870 he considered military strength the real criterion of the importance of a state. But he did not wish to jeopardize in a new war what he had won for Prussia and Germany in three previous wars. In the earlier period he had changed the map of Europe completely. He had not only enhanced Prussia enormously and united the different German states under the Prussian crown, but he had also annexed to Germany two provinces which had belonged to France for two centuries and the inhabitants of which had most unwillingly become German subjects. Bismarck believed that Germany had now got all the territory that was good for her, that she was *saturiert* (satiated). It was now in her interest to keep what she had acquired and the best way to ensure this was to preserve peace.

As a result, the situation was completely reversed. So long as Bismarck's policy aimed at changing the map, he was quite ready to join hands with such revolutionaries as the Hungarian Klapka or the Italian Mazzini. After reaching his goal, his interests assumed a conservative hue, and conservative powers were his natural allies. It is therefore hardly surprising that the first phase of Bismarck's foreign policy after the French war is characterized by the *Drei-Kaiser-Bündnis* (the alliance of the three Emperors).

1. *The League of the Three Emperors*

Czar Alexander II had done his best to help his uncle, King William I of Prussia, during the war with France. When the war broke out he let it be known in Vienna that he was ready to help his uncle with an army of 300,000 men, if the Habsburg Monarchy mobilized against Prussia. William I acknowledged this in a telegram he sent to the Czar after the defeat of France in February 1871. "Never", he wired, "will Prussia forget that it is due to you that the war has not assumed extreme dimensions." The Prussian Ambassador in Vienna, General von Schweinitz, was greatly annoyed by this telegram because it revealed to the whole world that Austria's neutrality did not spring from the feeling of the Germans in the monarchy, but only from the threat of Russia.

The Czar had not given his help for nothing. He exploited the war situation and the distress of France by striking out those clauses of the *Treaty of Paris of 1856* which forbade Russia's maintaining a *fleet in the Black Sea* (*Pontus*). After Russia's defeat in the Crimean War she had been compelled by the victors, France and Great Britain, to undertake that she would not maintain a fleet in the Black

Sea. This clause formed part of the Paris Treaty which was signed by all the European Great Powers and therefore had the force of International Law. Prussia was one of the signatories and was therefore bound to maintain the treaty. A few weeks before the outbreak of the war King William and Bismarck had met Czar Alexander and Gortchakoff at Ems. It is not known whether on this occasion the two statesmen discussed the Black Sea (Pontus) question, but it is known that Bismarck had encouraged the Russian government since 1866 to take steps in this direction. In 1866, when the war was over, General Manteuffel was sent to St. Petersburg to appease the Czar. In his instructions to Manteuffel Bismarck had ordered him to give a favourable answer if the Czar should express the wish to abrogate the Pontus clause. During the French war Bismarck had instructed the German Ambassador in St. Petersburg, Prince Reuss, to the same effect. In September 1870, three weeks after Sedan, Bismarck ordered him to inform the Czar that if he should wish to depart from the Paris Treaty, Prussia would not object. But he asked, on the other hand, that Russia should declare that she had no objection to the annexation of French territory by Germany.

The Russian government promptly seized this opportunity. In a note of 31st October 1870, Gortchakoff declared that Russia no longer felt herself bound by the Pontus clause. The only thing about this note which can have surprised Bismarck is that he had not expected such a unilateral action by Russia without a previous understanding with himself. He would have advised the Russian government to say nothing but to go ahead and build a Pontus fleet and to act as if the treaty did not exist and then wait and see if any of the other Powers raised any objections.

The only Power capable of opposing Russia's move was Great Britain. The British government did not consider the Pontus clause of the Paris Treaty politically wise. This clause represented part of Palmerston's policy, which in the days of the Crimean War had been countered by some very good arguments by John Bright, now a member of the Gladstone cabinet. Gladstone would have been quite willing to discuss amicably with the Russian government the abrogation of this clause. But what he would *not* allow was the *unilateral* abrogation of a European treaty. The British cabinet sent Odo

Russell, the Assistant Under-Secretary at the Foreign Office, to Versailles to discuss the question with Bismarck, who was considered by England as the instigator of Russia's action. Odo Russell exceeded his instructions by boldly declaring to Bismarck that *England would go to war*, with or without Allies, if Russia persisted in her unilateral action. This was a bluff, but it worked. Bismarck consented to the calling of an international conference to debate the question. The conference met in London in the spring of 1871 and abrogated the Pontus clause, but it passed unanimously a resolution that no single Power was entitled to abrogate or alter an international treaty without the consent of the other contracting Powers. Russia, too, had to subscribe to this resolution.

In this way Russia, in a particular instance, had profited by the assistance of Germany, just as Germany had profited by the benevolent neutrality of Russia. But this was only one manifestation of the collaboration with Russia at which Bismarck was aiming. He took the first step only a few days after Sedan, when he telegraphed to Prince Reuss on 9th September: "In view of the elements, not only republican but distinctly socialist, that have seized power in France, the firm closing of the ranks of the monarchist and conservative elements of Europe is all the more desirable". A few days later he instructs Reuss to draw the attention of the Czar to the solidarity of the revolutionary and republican factions in Europe. As the most certain guarantee of order and civilization he recommends the co-operation of Russia, Germany, and Austria as being the Powers which most solidly buttress the monarchical principle.

The most important characteristic of these statements is the way they combine foreign policy with ideological principles. This is in complete contrast to Bismarck's former practice. The monarchical principle which Bismarck now invoked was the ideological basis of the Holy Alliance of 1815, and the members of this alliance were the same Powers which Bismarck now wished to bring together, Russia, Prussia, and Austria.

Nevertheless, Bismarck had more realistic reasons for seeking this Alliance. The principal aim of his foreign policy during and after the war was the isolation of France. In one of his war-time notes to the German Ambassador in London, Count Bernstorff, he defends an alliance with Russia as necessary so long as Great Britain fails to realize that Germany would be her only valuable and reliable continental ally. This looks as if he would have preferred an alliance with England to one with Russia. But such a link was impossible, because the forcible annexation of Alsace and Lorraine was not at all popular in England, and because she did not wish to keep France down for ever. Unpopular as the rule of Napoleon III had been in England, feeling towards the French Republic was not hostile. On the contrary, many Englishmen had disapproved of continuing the war after the downfall of the Empire.

It is, of course, an exaggeration to call the League of the Three Emperors, which Bismarck wished to form, a new Holy Alliance. Neither Bismarck nor any of the leading statesmen of Russia or Austria aimed at a new policy of intervention. Nor were all the three Empires now absolutist Powers. But with all three there was one factor which played no part in the institutions of more liberal states, such as England, France, or even Italy. Their foreign policy was not dependent on a parliament and could not be influenced by a general election, as, for instance, British foreign policy was by the election of 1880, or France's foreign policy by the overthrow of Jules Ferry by the French parliament in 1885. In the three Empires foreign policy was in the hands of the Emperor and his Foreign Minister. In this respect it can still be called cabinet policy. Public opinion did, of course, exert a certain influence in these Empires, and later years showed that even the Russian Czar could not in the long run pursue a foreign policy which ran counter to Russian public opinion. But, as a rule, the Foreign Minister had his way, provided always that he could rely on the support of his monarch. In Germany Bismarck's authority in all questions of foreign policy was so overwhelming that the people followed his leadership most willingly. But Bismarck did all he could to prevent parliament from interfering in foreign affairs. He declined, for instance, to lay documents of foreign policy before the Reichstag in the form of Blue Books, because he was afraid that they would incite the deputies to discuss these questions. Such discussions were very infrequent indeed in the German Reichstag; as a rule, they took place only when Bismarck wished to deliver a speech and to make important declarations to the world and to foreign Powers in the course of an address. When at the climax of the Eastern crisis in 1878 the leaders of the governmental parties demanded that an explanation of Germany's policy should be given to the Reichstag, Bismarck was furious and vehemently abused these members in private conversation, although they were his firm adherents and, as a rule, his most reliable parliamentary support. Foreign policy, he said, was now difficult enough anyhow, it could only become more confused by three hundred asses, by which he meant, of course, the honourable members of the Reichstag.

In Austria-Hungary Count Beust, Bismarck's old rival, was still Minister for Foreign Affairs at the time of the foundation of the German Empire. He saw, of course, that the decision of 1866 had become definite and the line of the Main abandoned. The foreign policy of the Habsburg Monarchy had to take a fresh direction. Beust was quite willing to enter into friendly collaboration with the new German Empire. Bismarck and Beust met at Gastein in the autumn of 1871 and had highly amicable and satisfactory talks. Even a collaboration with Russia met with Beust's approval. But his days as Foreign Minister were already numbered. A few weeks after his meeting with Bismarck he was dismissed from the Foreign Office and sent as Ambassador to London.

Beust's dismissal was a consequence of certain events in Austria's domestic politics, but these events were connected with the foundation of the German Empire. In 1871 the Emperor Francis Joseph dismissed the Austrian cabinet, consisting of German Liberal parliamentarians, the so-called *Bürgerministerium.* His principal motive was that, now the German Empire had been formed, he did not consider the Germans in Austria important enough to be given ascendancy over the other nations within the monarchy. The new cabinet was led by Count Hohenwart, a clerical Conservative, who tried to go the way of federalism; that is, to favour the other nations, especially the Czechs. Beust did not belong to the Austrian cabinet. He was Minister for joint affairs; that is, for the combined affairs of Austria and Hungary. In the Habsburg Monarchy there were three ministries: (1) the Austrian cabinet; (2) the Hungarian cabinet; (3) certain Ministers for joint affairs, the foremost and most important of whom was the Foreign Minister. Beust was opposed to Hohenwart's federalistic experiments. So was Count Andrassy, the Prime Minister of Hungary. When the Germans in Austria became restive, Beust protested to the Emperor against Hohenwart's policy. The Emperor heeded what he said, and Hohenwart was dismissed in October 1871. But a few days later Beust too was dismissed. His successor was the Hungarian Prime Minister, Andrassy.

Andrassy conducted the foreign policy of the Habsburg Monarchy from 1871 to 1879. He worked, as a rule, hand in glove with Bismarck. His last act was to bring about the Austro-German alliance in 1879.

The principal factor in Hungarian policy was fear of Russia. Andrassy, as a Hungarian, was afraid that a coalition between Germany and Russia might be directed against the Habsburg Monarchy. As it was impossible to draw Bismarck away from Russia, Austria-Hungary's best policy was to join this coalition. On the other hand, Gortchakoff did not desire a combination of Germany and Austria which might be directed against Russia. When Francis Joseph went to Berlin in September 1872 as an earnest of his complete reconciliation with the victor of Sadowa, the Czar contrived to be present. Thus the three Emperors, accompanied by their Ministers, met in the capital of the new German Empire. But no alliance was concluded. The meeting was no more than a demonstration. In the following year, 1873, an agreement was reached. But it was of a very general and fluid nature. Its most interesting feature was a declaration of principle. The Emperors expressed their determination that no one should split them over those principles which they regarded as alone capable of assuring and enforcing the maintenance of the peace in Europe against all subversive activities from whatever quarter they might come. This profession of their principles and of their determination to fight subversive tendencies gives the alliance of the three Emperors its distinctive character. Where were these subversive tendencies against which the three Emperors joined forces? There was a certain amount of Socialist agitation supposedly led by the "Internationale", the head of which was Karl Marx in London. In actual fact it was much too weak to disturb the peace of Europe or the security of the Emperors. When a revolution broke out in Spain, Bismarck attached so little importance to the declaration of principle of the Imperial alliance that he recognized the Spanish Republic in

1874, without consulting his allies, who were, on principle, strongly against it. The value of the declaration of principles lay, for Bismarck, in its bearing on the isolation of France.

He hoped that the Czar and the Austrian Emperor would be prevented by these principles from entering into an alliance with France so long as she was a republic. This had the singular consequence that Bismarck did his best to maintain the republic in France against all monarchical tendencies. The republic was by no means firmly installed in the years immediately following the war. There was a strong movement for the restoration of the monarchy under a king of the ancient blood royal. Bismarck was strongly opposed to a restoration. He wanted to keep Thiers at the helm, and he was infuriated when Thiers was overthrown in May 1873 and Marshal MacMahon installed as president. The most serious reproach he levelled at Count Harry Arnim, the German Ambassador in Paris, was that he had not helped Thiers but had favoured the restoration movement.

Bismarck's attitude was, of course, dictated neither by any preference for the republic nor by the doctrine of non-intervention in the domestic affairs of other countries. His motive sprang solely from his belief that France would not be *bündnisfähig*; that is, capable of forming an alliance with a monarchical state all the while she lacked a monarch. In particular, the sharp contrast between the democratic republic in France and the autocratic régime of the Czar would, in his opinion, prevent any *rapprochement* between France and Russia, let alone an alliance—his principal nightmare. But the world was one day to see a Russian Czar saluting bare-headed while a French naval band played the "Marseillaise". This was in 1892, after Bismarck's downfall. But long before this it was evident that no constitutional difference would in the long run stand in the way of any political groupings and alliances which seemed favourable to any state from the standpoint of power politics. The French Republic was not boycotted by the monarchies, not even the most conservative ones. Bismarck himself was responsible for this, when, after the Congress of Berlin, he entered upon a policy of reconciliation towards France. How could any European statesman be prevented by scruples from joining hands with the French Republic after Bismarck himself had shown her a mark of his favour?

2. The "Liberal Era" in Germany

It goes without saying that Bismarck's authority with the German people was immense after the war. His Emperor made him a prince, Fürst, and *Se. Durchlaucht der Fürst Reichskanzler* was looked on by the great majority of the people as the real ruler of Germany. The general election to the Reichstag of March 1871 gave a majority to the various Liberal parties. The strongest of these was the National Liberal Party with about 120 out of 400 deputies. The Free Conservatives, Bismarck's staunchest adherents, had about 40 deputies, the Progressive Party about 50.

The National Liberal Party was the most important, not only by reason of the number but also the quality of their deputies. It contained most of the leading parliamentarians, men of popular authority, of wide knowledge and political wisdom. The leader of the party was the Hanoverian Rudolf von Bennigsen, the former President of the German National Union (Deutscher National-Verein). He became President of the Prussian Chamber of Deputies. Another National Liberal, Max von Forckenbeck, formerly one of the founders of the German Progressive Party in Prussia, became President of the Reichstag. Both entered into good personal relations with the Chancellor; Forckenbeck had the confidence of the Old Emperor, and, to an even greater degree, of the Crown Prince. Another Hanoverian, Johannes Miquel, a man of the highest political talents and an excellent, persuasive speaker, wielded great influence in the Reichstag, but was looked on with some distrust by the Chancellor, although he often inclined to a compromise. The leader of the Left wing, Eduard Lasker, had the greatest influence in the parliamentary party, in the Reichstag as well as in the Prussian Chamber of Deputies, because he was the most assiduous and persistent worker of them all. He was always the first to read and digest all parliamentary papers and to analyse every question coming up for parliamentary debate. As everybody knew that Lasker had no personal axe to grind, but was always concerned with the welfare of the state and the party, most members were willing to follow his lead, even if they did not belong to the inner circle of his political following. At this time he was, as one of his friends put it, the chief of staff and the sergeant-major of the parliamentary party. But this influence which Lasker enjoyed was not to Bismarck's liking. He complained in later years that he could never pass a bill without a "Lasker Amendment" which resulted in giving his bill a more liberal flavour than he liked. This is what Bismarck called "Lasker's doctrinairism", a slogan by which he tried to undermine Lasker's popularity and influence in his own party.

But those days had not yet arrived. In the years immediately following the war Bismarck gladly accepted the parliamentary assistance of the National Liberals and conceded to them a good deal of influence in the matter of legislation. A newly founded state like the German Empire needs many new laws to build up and complete its institutions. Out of the chaos of the often widely differing laws existing in the individual states, a new common code for the whole nation had to be created. Such laws were particularly needed in the field of commerce and economics. For instance, every German state had its own particular currency. One currency was valid in Hamburg, another in Prussia, yet another in Bavaria. Now a common German currency had to be created, the old coinage withdrawn and a new one, which would find acceptance in every part of the Empire, put in circulation. As a basis for this common currency a central bank had to be set up to discharge such functions as the Bank of England does in Britain. The necessary legislation was passed early in the 'seventies, and a National Liberal deputy, Ludwig Bamberger, had, as Referent of the Reichstag, the greatest influence in shaping this legislation.

Bismarck was fortunate enough to possess for this legislative task an excellent collaborator in the person of Rudolf Delbrück. He neither understood nor greatly cared for economic questions at this time and gladly left them to Delbrück, the President of the Chancellor's Office. Delbrück was a man of the widest and most accurate knowledge, an indefatigable worker, always courteous and helpful, the very best type of the Prussian *Geheimrat*, the higher civil servant whose approach was objective and not swayed by personal considerations. He was trusted by parliament, particularly by the Liberals with whom he had economic aims and ideas in common. He was an exponent of Liberal economic policy, believing in economic freedom and willing to abolish its old traditional handicaps. As this was also the aim of the Liberals, their co-operation was most fruitful and left its mark on the rich legislative work of this period.

Apart from economic questions, the most important achievement of these years was the unification of the juridical laws. As the German judge has to base his decisions on a body of written law, it was most important to create a common German written law to replace the divergent laws hitherto in force in the various individual states. The constitution of the German Empire had not provided for the unification of all these laws, and the governments of the medium-sized states, like Bavaria and Wurtemberg, were most unwilling to allow the Empire to meddle with their laws. But the national movement swept these obstacles away. The prime mover to whom success was most largely due was Lasker, who moved time and again in the Reichstag for a common code of procedure and a common civil law. Even Lasker's sharpest critics do not deny him this credit.

Bismarck was not greatly interested in these juridical questions. Once he chanced to hear the discussions of a commission dealing with questions of juridical procedure. He went away shaking his head, saying that he could not understand how intelligent men could seriously discuss such matters, and that it was of small moment whichever way they were decided. But if a question arose in which he felt the power of the state might be limited in favour of individual freedom, in connexion with the law of the press, for example, then he was most obstinate in opposing it.

To understand the position of the National Liberal Party in these years, one must refrain from drawing any analogy with the English party system. In Britain a party is either in power or in opposition. The very seating arrangements of the House of Commons show this. A member of parliament sits either on the government benches or opposite them. If a member crosses the floor of the House, he changes his political position completely. This arrangement is a quite simple but very effective means of symbolizing the political system. But in the German parliament the members sat in a semi-circle, the most conservative members on the extreme right and the most radical on the extreme left. They would not change their seats if one government were replaced by another of quite a different political complexion. The members of the government did not sit among the members of parliament, but on a rostrum facing the semi-circle of deputies. In the Reichstag this rostrum belonged to the Bundesrat, the President of which was the Chancellor. Thus Bismarck spoke from the *Bundesrats-Tisch*. The constitution provided that nobody could be at the same time a member of the Reichstag and of the Bundesrat. As the Ministers or secretaries of state became members of the Bundesrat, a deputy who was made Minister had to leave the Reichstag. In this way the constitution put up a legal barrier to the introduction of the parliamentary system of government. Indeed, not one of the parliamentary leaders of the National Liberals became Minister in the time of Bismarck. As we shall see later, Bennigsen at one moment came near to it, but failed to reach agreement with Bismarck through lack of "subordination". After Bismarck's downfall one of them, Miquel, became Prussian Minister of Finance, and nobody doubts that he overshadowed his predecessors as well as his successors. His example shows how much political and administrative capacity could have been developed in the interest of the state if Bismarck's system had not barred their way to the cabinet.

If these years are called "the Liberal Era", it must not be forgotten that Liberal influence was limited to the sphere of legislation. In the Prussian administration the Conservatives maintained their old ascendancy. As a rule, only young men of reliable conservative disposition were accepted in it and promoted to the higher posts. Many of them were sons of the old Junker families who for generations seemed almost to have vested interest in these posts. For instance, Herr von Puttkamer, later the most conservative and reactionary of all Prussian Ministers, made his "career" in this so-called "Liberal" era.

These few remarks will show that a parliamentary party in the German Empire was theoretically more independent, but less influential, than a party in this country. A party could, for example, vote against the government without being afraid of overthrowing it. On the other hand, the government could easily disregard the wish of a party which regularly voted for it. In the time of Bismarck he alone was the government. Now it was in Bismarck's nature to demand unconditional obedience from his adherents. He could not understand the independence of mind of a deputy who, although his adherent, felt compelled by his conscience to oppose him in this or that particular question, or even not to follow him the whole way. In critical cases he was capable of treating such an independent line as nothing short of desertion or disloyalty. He would assert that the voters had elected the deputy to follow his leadership; in other words, he appealed over the member's head to his constituents, and every member knew how dangerous an opponent Bismarck could be at an election.

The National Liberal Party wanted nothing better than to co-operate with Bismarck, whom they held up to their constituents as the greatest living statesman and the immortal hero of national unity. But the leaders of the party could not fail to see that in all questions of principle this great statesman was divided from them by a deep gulf. They were—more or less—Liberal, devoted to the free development of the nation and its institutions. But Bismarck was called "medieval" by a shrewd and very critical observer, the German Crown Princess Victoria, who wrote to her mother in 1875: "Bismarck's ideas about the press are very mediaeval—in fact, he is mediaeval altogether and the true theories of liberty and of government are Hebrew to him, though he adopts and admits a democratic idea or measure now and then when he thinks it will serve his purpose".

Even if the National Liberals had seen Bismarck in the same light, they would have been compelled to collaborate with him as best they could. His position was completely unassailable. He was the indispensable man for getting anything done. His authority with their own voters was so immense that they were compelled to avoid a conflict with him as long as possible. In such a position a rare combination of political adaptability and independence of mind is necessary. These qualities are found in very different proportions in different men. It is therefore hardly surprising that at times it was very difficult to hold the party together. One wing wanted to cling fast to principles, the other to compromise. The Hanoverians, Bennigsen and Miquel, were as a rule much more ready for a compromise than the old Prussians, Forckenbeck and Lasker.

An example of these difficulties is afforded by the crisis which arose in 1874 over the Army Bill. Army questions had been highly controversial since the Prussian constitutional conflicts of 1862–1866, which broke out over the reorganization of the army. The Emperor's aim was to make the army his own personal affair and not to allow parliament to meddle in army affairs. Parliament had, of course, to vote the money for the army, but Emperor and government tried to render this right of parliament illusory and ineffective by fixing the number of men to be called to the colours in peace-time (*Friedens-Präsenz-Stärke*) once and for all in relation to the size of the population. We have seen that Bismarck attempted to do this in his draft of the Constitution of the North German Confederation and that the question was temporarily shelved by the Forckenbeck compromise (p. 146). In 1871, under the compulsion of war, this compromise was prolonged till 1874. From this year onwards the annual vote for the military budget had to be approved by the Reichstag. But now the Emperor and his generals once more tried to secure a permanent vote. A bill was laid before the Reichstag fixing the number of soldiers permanently at more than 400,000 men. By adopting this bill, the Reichstag would have forfeited for ever all influence in military affairs. There arose, therefore, a strong opposition in which a great part of the National Liberal Party joined. In the committee of the House which had to consider the bill, the Left wing of the National Liberals, led by Lasker, had the casting vote. The committee rejected the proposal for a fixed figure, but the Right wing of the National Liberals made it clear that they were willing to compromise.

Only now did Bismarck take matters into his own hands. During the committee stage he had let things drift. He said confidentially to the English Ambassador, Lord Odo Russell, that the bill was not his own work, but the work of the Kaiser and his "military cabinet". It is safe to assume that Bismarck really did not desire at this time any permanent fixing of the strength of the army. He agreed, of course, to the restriction of parliamentary influence, but what he did not wish to see was the complete independence of the "military cabinet" and the generals. The "military cabinet" was subordinated neither to the Chancellor nor to the War Minister. It was considered to be a personal affair of the King and Emperor. If the generals had no further need to trouble about the Reichstag, they would not have to trouble about the help of the Chancellor either. And so it is quite likely that Bismarck was not at all sorry that the generals were now forced to realize that they were quite unable to succeed without his help. Now that their failure was manifest, Bismarck was quite ready to help them out of the impasse, and to show them that —although at the time he was on his sick-bed—he could achieve more single-handed than all of them put together. He called two deputies of the Free Conservative Party to his bedside and made them a speech which was immediately published in all the papers. It was a very angry speech which heaped reproaches on the Reichstag. He threatened either to resign or to dissolve the Reichstag. He could not, he said, sacrifice his European reputation. But the sharpest barb of his accusation was aimed at the Left wing of the National Liberal Party. He called them men elected on the strength of his name, sent to the Reichstag by the voters in order to assist him. In this way he managed to give the crisis the appearance of a Bismarck-Lasker conflict.

These words were enough to frighten the National Liberals. To fight an election against Bismarck was a thing they dared not think of. The feeling of the electorate had changed considerably since the Prussian conflict. Then the Opposition could rely on the support of the voters who returned them in spite of all governmental pressure. Now they could not be trusted to stand firm against an onslaught by Bismarck. Even among the Progressive deputies whose leader, Eugen Richter, was the most outspoken opponent of militarism, some preferred a compromise to a straight fight. The Right wing of the National Liberals hankered for a compromise. Miquel, one of its leaders, arranged it with Bismarck. It provided that the size of the army should be fixed, not permanently, but for seven years. This meant that the Reichstag would not have any say in army matters until 1881. The Reichstag, which in the normal course of events would be elected in 1877, was to be deprived of any independent decision. On the other hand, the old Emperor might well be satisfied. He was now in his seventy-seventh year. Seven years was longer than he expected his life to last.

The compromise was adopted by a majority of the Reichstag. Even Lasker voted for it, after being convinced that he would be isolated if he continued in opposition. It was a very heavy defeat for Liberalism, for it destroyed one of the constitutional postulates which until then had been considered fundamental. Moreover, the privileged constitutional position which the compromise gave to the army helped to strengthen militarist feeling, particularly among the upper-middle class, the sons of which hoped to become officers of the army or of the reserve. It became the ambition of many a young man to add the title of "Reserve Officer" to his name and to be able to don his officer's uniform on the Emperor's birthday. To serve as an officer in the army was considered a greater honour than to be a civil servant or even a judge, because the army came to be considered the personal concern of the Emperor. The ascendancy of militarism could not but weaken Liberal feeling among those classes which in former generations had been prominent in the Liberal movement.

This defeat was the more significant as Liberalism was at that time Bismarck's indispensable ally in the fight which was in the political foreground, the so-called *Kulturkampf*.

3. *The "Kulturkampf"*

The name *Kulturkampf* (cultural struggle) was given to the great campaign which Bismarck and German Liberalism fought against the Roman Catholic Church and the Catholic Party of the Centrum. In Germany this struggle dominated the minds of men for four or five years and was looked on by a great part of Europe as one of the most exciting events of the age. To-day the questions which then excited so much feeling have receded so far into the background that it is most difficult for us to understand the excitement. But there can be no doubt that in those years many of the most enlightened and highly educated men believed that the future of mankind was at stake.

If we are to try and understand this excitement, we must go back to two acts of the Roman Catholic Church, the publication of the Syllabus of 1864 and the Vatican Decree of Papal Infallibility of 1870.

The *Syllabus errorum*, or "Catalogue of the Principal Errors of our Time", was published by Pope Pius IX in his *Encyclica Quanta Cura*. It contains a list of all the modern doctrines which the Pope reproves, proscribes, and condemns. Now, in this list are to be found almost all the doctrines which Liberalism considers as fundamentals of the state and of modern civilization, and the syllabus was therefore considered a challenge to Liberalism and modern culture.

Greater still was the stir caused when the Vatican Council adopted, in June 1870, the dogma of the infallibility of the Pope. Excitement was particularly strong in Germany—which nation considered itself the birthplace of the Reformation—because the majority of the German bishops had opposed this dogma during the Council, but submitted to it according to the fundamental doctrine of the Catholic Church after it had been accepted by the Council. Only a minority of them refused to subscribe to it, and among these was Dr. Döllinger, a friend of Gladstone and Lord Acton, who was considered the leading light of Catholic theology, and the greatest of German ecclesiastical historians. One section of the opposition organized the Old-Catholic (*Alt-Katholische*) Church to which many contemporaries pinned their greatest hopes, but which, in fact, never grew strong enough to be of real importance.

We need not enter here into doctrinal controversies but only describe the impression which these events made on the contemporary world. The political importance attached to them is clearly shown—to quote but one example—in Gladstone's pamphlet: *The Vatican Decrees in their Bearing on Civil Allegiance*. If a man of such liberal and tolerant views as Gladstone feared that by these decrees the relations between Church and State were fundamentally changed and the allegiance of devout English Catholics to the state was endangered, we can understand the unrest which they provoked.

At the outset Bismarck was not greatly troubled by the dogma of Infallibility. During the Council he had adopted a rather reserved attitude, even though the Prussian Ambassador at the Holy See, Count Harry Arnim, had advised a more active policy. Bismarck rightly pointed out that Prussia, considered by the Pope as a Protestant Power, could not take the initiative in the affairs of the Catholic Church. But he was willing to follow the initiative of Catholic Powers like Austria or France. When the Council adopted the dogma of Infallibility, the French war had broken out. Bismarck's first concern was to prevent international troubles which could make his task still more difficult. But after the Pope's temporal power had vanished and the Kingdom of Italy had absorbed the Papal State (in September 1870), one of the leading Prussian bishops appeared at the German headquarters in Versailles. This was the Archbishop of Posen, Count von Ledochowsky, whom Bismarck had helped to instal in Prussia's Polish provinces and whom he favoured because he saw in him a valuable help in their Germanization, even though he was a Jesuit. Ledochowsky came to Versailles with a twofold request to Bismarck: that he would protest against the destruction of the Papal State and that he would offer the Pope asylum in Prussia, if and when he decided to leave Rome. The first plea Bismarck was bound to decline, because it was not in Germany's interest to fall out with the Kingdom of Italy. But he was quite ready to comply with the second, for he felt that, if the Pope resided in Germany, the country's influence would grow; moreover, a Pope within the Fatherland would be a valuable aid to government in home politics.

Here we are face to face with something of the utmost importance for an understanding of Bismarck's attitude. From the very beginning of his administration he had repeatedly asked the Pope to put in a word in his favour with the Prussian Catholics who sat in parliament. He was quite willing to help the Pope in international affairs provided that the Pope arranged for the Catholic deputies to vote for the government. While Ledochowsky was in Versailles, Bismarck said: "If we give asylum to the Pope, he must do something for us in return". And again in conversation with friends he said: "The opposition of the ultramontane clerical party would be checked".

This was all the more important, as a strong ultramontane party was founded just at this time. There had always been a Catholic party in the Prussian Chamber of Deputies, but it had been comparatively weak. The new party which styled itself the "Centre" was much stronger. About seventy "Centre" deputies were returned to the first German Reichstag in 1871. It was, from the outset, the second strongest party. More important perhaps than its size was the fact that it had a first-class political leader in the person of Ludwig Windthorst.

Windthorst was a Hanoverian like the National Liberal leaders Bennigsen and Miquel, but he remained loyal to his former King after he had lost his throne. Bismarck looked on him as a Guelph and particularist, and cordially detested him. There is a very characteristic saying of Bismarck: "Everyone needs somebody to love and somebody to hate. I have my wife to love and Windthorst to hate." It is very doubtful whether Windthorst returned the compliment. He was much too cool and level-headed to hate an enemy whose greatness he could not fail to appreciate. But this in no wise affected the energy of his opposition. He was not a great orator, but he nearly always knew what to say and how to say it. He kept his temper when Bismarck lost his, and was always ready with an answer. He was an admirable parliamentary tactician, perhaps the best the Reichstag has ever known. As a man he was gentle and civil in manner and of a humane disposition. Although as the foremost champion of Catholicism he was hated by the great mass of the Protestant and Liberal population, he was held in high respect by all members of parliament, however strongly they were opposed to his views and his party.

Bismarck at first tried to induce the Pope to come out against the Centre Party, and the Cardinal Secretary of State, Antonelli, did, in fact, utter a few words which could be interpreted in this sense and which Bismarck hastened to make public. But, of course, it was easier still for the leaders of the Catholic Centre to get the ear of Rome, and they induced Antonelli to make another statement which put paid to all hopes of a breach between the Papal *curia* and the Centre Party.

Bismarck now went over to the offensive. In an article (19th June 1871) in the Conservative *Kreuz-Zeitung* he declared war on the Centre, and a few weeks later he abolished the Catholic Department of the Prussian *Kultus-Ministerium*. In January 1872, when the deputies of the Centre Party questioned Bismarck in the Chamber about this step, the Chancellor replied with a vehement attack on the party. He called its formation a mobilization against the state and taxed Windthorst with not welcoming the foundation of the German Empire. He even tried to brand him as *Reichsfeind*, that is, an enemy of the Empire. Windthorst answered: "The Chancellor is not the State. Until now no minister has been so presumptuous as to call his opponents enemies of the state." This was, indeed, Bismarck's method. All the parties who opposed him were called *Reichsfeinde*. This was a new kind of proscription proclaimed by the formidable head of the government and repeated by hundreds of newspapers. It is by this means that venom and bitterness were instilled into public life in Germany.

From now on it was open warfare between Bismarck and the Centre Party as the political champion of the Catholic Church in Germany. In this struggle the great majority of the non-Catholic population, that is, about two-thirds of the country, was whole-heartedly on Bismarck's side. Many of them felt that this battle was being waged to uphold modern culture against the onslaughts of obscurantism. The term *Kulturkampf* was coined by the great pathologist, Professor Rudolf Virchow of Berlin, a Progressive member of parliament and by no means a blind devotee of Bismarckian power politics. He and his friends hoped that this struggle would free the schools from clerical influence, both Catholic and Protestant. Other more conservative politicians thought that the struggle was necessary to maintain the rights of the state. The particular bugbears of the Protestants were the members of the Society of Jesus, the Jesuits, who were looked on as extremely sly and cunning intriguers. In 1872 the Reichstag approved an anti-Jesuit measure which gave the government the right not only to dissolve all sections of the Society of Jesus, but to banish all its members from the country. This was an exceptional law of the very worst type, a negation of the fundamental liberal principle of civic equality and freedom of worship and conscience. Nevertheless, not only the Conservatives but the great majority of the Liberals voted for it. Some of the foremost Liberals were its principal sponsors. The honour of Liberalism was only saved by Lasker who, in spite of his party's vehemence, declared that his conscience compelled him to vote against so illiberal a measure.

The major battles were fought out in the Prussian Landtag. The administration of schools and churches belonged not to the Empire but to the individual states—Prussia, Bavaria, and the rest. Bismarck considered the existing Prussian laws insufficient to maintain the authority of the State against the Church militant. New legislation was necessary. For this task he required a new *Kultus-Minister*. For this post he secured Adalbert Falk, a high official in the Ministry of Justice. When he was offered the post, Falk asked the Chancellor: "What am I expected to do?" Bismarck answered: "To re-establish the rights of the State in relation to the Church, and *with as little fuss as possible*". But in this latter respect no one sinned more than Bismarck himself. The speeches with which he introduced the new legislation for Prussia caused the greatest possible stir. They are among the most vigorous and vehement he ever made. He attacked the Centre with all his tremendous strength and energy, singling out its leader, Windthorst, for particular attack and trying to loosen the ties between the man and his party. It was, of course, to no purpose whatever. One of the other leaders of the party, von Mallinckrodt, described Windthorst as a pearl to which his party had given the right setting. Windthorst himself answered Bismarck's attack on his leanings to the Hanoverian King with the dignified words: "My loyalty to the Royal family of Hanover will last until my dying day, and nothing in the world, not even the most powerful Chancellor of Germany, will be able to make me depart from it. But I remember the words of the Bible: obey them that have rule over you and submit yourselves, and I have done my duty as a subject to the best of my conscience." He closed with a sentence which Bismarck had occasion to remember many years later: "It is easy to cling to the monarchical principle in fair weather; it is harder in foul".

In other speeches Bismarck called the Centre Party "a battery against the state", and he lumped them together with the Social Democrats when he called them "two parties which opposed national development by international methods and which fought against the nation and the national state".

He made an even greater impression when he characterized his present campaign as a part of the age-old struggle between priest and king, which was older than Christendom, as the example of the conflict between Agamemnon and Calchas in Tauris showed. But what kindled the enthusiasm of the majority of the nation more than all else, was his cry to the Reichstag: "We shall not go to Canossa!" For the fact that the Emperor Henry IV had done penance before Pope Gregory VII in the winter of 1077 was considered the deepest humiliation ever suffered by the old German Empire and the greatest triumph of the Papacy. Thus Bismarck gave the nation the impression that it was involved in an eternal conflict which had brought it much misery and affliction in the past, but which this time would be fought out to a victorious conclusion.

Falk would have needed the dexterity of a conjurer to realize Bismarck's programme without fuss. We cannot go here into the details of his legislative attempts. There is no doubt that in the main he failed. Nevertheless, he is not at all a contemptible figure. He earnestly believed in his task and spared no pains to discharge it. He is, perhaps, alone among all the Ministers a personality whom history will remember, and certainly the only one who achieved popularity in his own right. In one election seven constituencies elected him to the Chamber at the same time. To this very day his name is remembered with gratitude by the elementary school teachers of Prussia, for he did more for them than any Minister before or after. Bismarck himself, who in his reminiscences tries to disclaim all responsibility for Falk's measures, cannot help acknowledging his rare gifts and his never-failing courage.

It was not Falk's fault if his measures proved abortive. Bismarck had at least as much to do with it. The trouble was that Bismarck never fully understood the Catholic Church. Odo Russell, the British Ambassador in Berlin, wrote in 1874 that Bismarck and his government were not aware of the power of passive resistance of the Roman Catholic clergy. "The Roman Church has always derived strength from persecution, but it is impotent against the power of freedom and its blessings. . . . Bismarck's anti-church policy has compelled the German bishops to rally round the Pope and to suffer martyrdom for discipline's, obedience's and example's sake."

How little Bismarck understood the nature of the resistance he provoked emerges from a well-known passage in his *Reminiscences*. "The error in the conception of the Prussian laws was made obvious to me by the picture of dexterous, light-footed priests pursued through back doors and bedrooms by honest but awkward Prussian gendarmes, with spurs and trailing sabres." He understood the moral forces which were summoned up against him in the *Kulturkampf* as little as he had understood them in the Prussian constitutional conflict.

The political effect of the *Kulturkampf* was that Bismarck was drawn closer to the Liberals and farther from the Conservatives. The Conservatives did not, as a rule, worry overmuch about the Catholics; only old Ludwig von Gerlach, who was for so many years one of the intellectual leaders of the *Kreuz-Zeitung* and who later broke away from Bismarck over his 1866 policy, now joined the Centre Party and opposed his former friend as a Centre deputy. But the majority of the Conservatives, especially those of the *Kreuz-Zeitung* school, cared very deeply about the Protestant Church and its influence in education. As Falk's law interfered with the inspection of elementary schools by the clergy of both the Catholic and Protestant Churches, they sat up in opposition and came into sharp conflict with Bismarck. One of Bismarck's oldest friends, Hans von Kleist-Retzow, attacked his policy violently in the Herrenhaus (the Prussian Upper Chamber) and was even more violently rebuked by him. Kleist had reproached Bismarck with breaking away from the Conservative Party. Bismarck answered with biting sarcasm: "The part breaks away from the whole, the mobile from the static; the King and the government have not broken loose from the Conservative party, but the Conservative party from them". At the next election in 1874 he showed the Conservatives that they were powerless without the help of the government. The number of their deputies in Reichstag and Landtag sank as low as it had in the years of the Prussian constitutional conflict. The National Liberals and the Progressives gained, but so did the Centre Party, which approached a hundred seats in both Assemblies.

But the opposition of the Conservatives had a facet to show other than the parliamentary one. The old Emperor sympathized with them in his heart of hearts. In his old age he grew very orthodox in religious matters and he feared that the Protestant Church would be weakened. He none the less appended his signature to the new laws, but with great reluctance. As early as 1874 he said: "The time has come to rule more on Conservative lines". Stronger still was the distaste which the Empress Augusta felt for the *Kulturkampf*. She strongly disapproved of the persecution of the Catholic clergy and understood the Catholic Church much better than Bismarck did. He was aware, of course, of her opposition, and his dislike of Augusta deepened. There is perhaps no person who receives such spiteful mention in his *Reflections and Recollections* as Augusta; he blames her for every set-back in his political career.

The dramatic climax of the *Kulturkampf* was the attempt which Kullmann, a young journeyman cooper, made on Bismarck's life in Kissingen in July 1874. Kullmann was a member of a Catholic working-men's club. The government tried to represent the attempt as the outcome of a Catholic conspiracy, but without success. Bismarck was wounded in the right hand, but only slightly. Nevertheless he took the attempt very seriously. In December 1874 a deputy of the Centre Party, the Bavarian Jörg, in a speech to the Reichstag made a sarcastic allusion to the excitement which the incident had occasioned in the country at large. Bismarck, in reply, made a passionate attack on the Centre Party: "You may try", he cried, "to disown this assassin, but none the less he is clinging to your coat-tails". To be thus accused of complicity in a murderous attack understandably infuriated the Centre deputies, and one of them voiced an angry "*Pfui!*" Shaking with fury, Bismarck retorted: "*Pfui* is an expression of disgust and contempt. Don't imagine these feelings are very far from me either. The only difference is that I am too polite to voice them." The member who made this notable interruption was Count von Ballestrem, twenty-five years later the highly respected President of the Reichstag. It was he of whom Bismarck said, if he had chanced to have a revolver in his pocket when the remark was made, he would have shot the man who made it.

To read of these passionate and vehement attacks by Bismarck on the Centre Party, one might think that peace between them was utterly out of the question. And, recalling his words about the undying struggle for power between kingdom and priesthood and his defiant declaration never to go to Canossa, one might imagine that Bismarck would never lay aside his sword until the enemy had surrendered unconditionally. But the amazing thing is that he not only broke off the engagement before he won a conclusive victory and annulled most of the measures for which he had so doughtily campaigned, but he also made it up with the Centre Party in order to shake off the National Liberals and undermine their parliamentary position. This will be seen when the story of Bismarck's great political change-over in 1879 is reached.

4. *The Arnim Affair*

A few days after the scene in the Reichstag described above, a most sensational trial began before the Berlin Criminal Court. The accused was no less a personage than the former Ambassador of His Imperial Majesty in Paris, His Excellency the Privy Councillor Count Harry von Arnim. Some months before, in October 1874, all Europe was startled by the news that His Excellency had been arrested and flung into prison in Berlin like a common felon. What was his crime? High treason? Conspiracy? No, nothing of the kind. He had refused to give up certain documents which the Foreign Office regarded as its own property but which he considered were his.

In the ordinary way such a difference of opinion would never have been brought before the criminal court. But this was, in fact, the culmination of a bitter political and personal feud between the Chancellor and the Ambassador.

Arnim and Bismarck had known each other from their youth. Arnim, indeed, claimed that they had been friends. When Bismarck took over the Prussian Foreign Office, he sent Arnim to Rome as Prussian envoy to the Holy See. During the Vatican Council they had not seen eye to eye about the policy to be adopted towards the Council. But in spite of this difference of opinion, Bismarck sent Arnim to France after the war to represent the Empire in the negotiations about the implementation of the armistice, and when the peace treaty was signed he made him Ambassador in Paris. This was certainly the key post in the whole German diplomatic service. One would suppose that Bismarck would entrust it only to a man in whom he had complete confidence. But it is now known that, at the same time, he wrote to the Emperor that Arnim had "an uncertain and untrustworthy character".

The political differences between the Chancellor and the Ambassador centred on the attitude towards Thiers and the republican form of the French state. After Thiers' overthrow by the monarchist majority in the French parliament in May 1873, Bismarck reproached Arnim with cutting across his policy by supporting, not Thiers but the monarchists. For, as we have already seen, Bismarck wished to keep Thiers in power and the Republic in being in order to make France *bündnisunfähig*, as he put it; that is, incapable of forming alliances. As Foreign Minister, Bismarck certainly had the right to lay down the lines of foreign policy which every Ambassador had to follow. To this extent he is right in his famous saying: "My ambassadors must fall into line like soldiers". But Arnim, although he did not share Bismarck's views, denied that he had done anything to help or promote monarchist reaction. What he complained of was that Bismarck demanded that he should accommodate to his chief's views not only his actions but also his *dispatches*. This is, indeed, a most dangerous doctrine, as was seen many years later, when the German Ambassador in London, Count Metternich, was dismissed because his pessimistic reports about the bad impression made in Britain by the expansion of the German navy displeased the Emperor William II. In Arnim's case his reports displeased Bismarck because they impressed the old Kaiser. In essence, therefore, Bismarck was blaming Arnim because his arguments, that republican developments in France would threaten the monarchic principle in Europe, found favour with William.

The tone in which Bismarck rebuked the Ambassador is sharp and insulting to a degree. Why? Because Arnim enjoyed the favour of the Emperor and, more than that, of the Empress Augusta. Bismarck knew that Arnim also criticized the *Kulturkampf,* just as Augusta did, and Arnim, as a former Minister in Rome, could speak with some authority on these questions. But the worst of it was that Arnim was spoken of in some Conservative circles as a possible chancellor, and in Bismarck's eyes, of course, that was the unforgivable sin. True, Bismarck's position was so firm and unshakable that he could have ignored rumours and rivals alike, but he was not cast in that mould. He was extremely suspicious of every rival—likely or unlikely. In the last conversation he had with Arnim, he told him bluntly: "You are plotting with the Empress and you will not stop intriguing until you sit at this very desk where I am sitting now—and then you will see—even that isn't worth a damn!"—a truly Bismarckian phrase.

To compass Arnim's downfall, Bismarck sent a spy to Paris. This was Baron Fritz von Holstein, then a Councillor of legation at the Paris Embassy, later for many years of William II's reign the most influential member of the Wilhelmstrasse. Holstein was base enough to do this dirty work. During the Arnim trial he went through what was probably the worst hour of his life, when in the witness-box, in spite of all his shufflings and evasions, he could not deny that he had spied on his chief. These revelations in open court affected the whole course of Holstein's life. They made him for some years a social pariah; they had much to do with the development of that tortuous turn to his character which was to prove so fateful for German policy. It was a sort of Nemesis that the first man to desert Bismarck in his hour of distress in 1890 was Baron von Holstein.

Arnim admittedly made some serious mistakes and so forfeited the confidence of the old Emperor, who at last allowed Bismarck to remove Arnim from Paris and ultimately to expel him from the diplomatic service altogether. But Bismarck's thirst for vengeance was unquenchable and he instituted criminal proceedings against the Ambassador which completely ruined him. The trial before the Berlin court in December 1874 was a political triumph for Bismarck, who handled matters with supreme skill. He had some of his most masterly dispatches read out, and they made an immense impression on the public, while Arnim's letters and notes appeared feeble by comparison. But the critical observer could not help feeling that Bismarck's tactics of personal attack and prosecution were as relentless and unscrupulous as they were clever. But this did not help Arnim, who had to go into exile. Some pamphlets which he wrote defending his attitude and attacking Bismarck gave rise to a fresh prosecution. In the end he was condemned *in absentia* to five years' penal servitude, a verdict which so grossly outrages justice that even Bismarck in his *Reminiscences* disclaims all responsibility for it. But even here Bismarck makes fresh insinuations against the unfortunate adversary, who had long since died in exile.

5. *The War Scare of 1875*

Bismarck's *Kulturkampf* had some very important consequences and repercussions in international affairs. Only the Kingdom of Italy was favourably impressed by his campaign against the Pope, who was, of course, the enemy of the young Kingdom of Italy as well. In England, too, many people viewed the *Kulturkampf* with approval, but Bismarck's methods were not the kind which a British government was likely to adopt. In Russia the anti-Polish bias of the *Kulturkampf* was welcome to the government, but Gortchakoff preferred to reach a peaceful understanding with the Roman Catholic clergy in Poland. In Austria the Liberal government, which had repudiated the Concordat with the Vatican, followed an anticlerical policy, but it was able to achieve its aim in a far more peaceful and effective way and to avoid any interference with the Church's internal affairs. The Emperor, Francis Joseph, a very loyal son of the Church, was, of course, averse from any kind of *Kulturkampf*. In other Catholic countries, like France and Belgium, the bishops and clergy did their best to condemn the *Kulturkampf* as sacrilegious and to encourage the German Catholics in their opposition. Bismarck was furious at this meddling by foreign clergy in German affairs, and in a couple of sharp notes to Paris and Brussels he requested the governments concerned to suppress it. But his worst fears seemed to be realized when in May 1873—that is, at the very time when Falk's so-called "May-Laws" against the Catholics were passed in Prussia—Thiers was overthrown by the French National Assembly and replaced by Marshal MacMahon. The Marshal was everywhere looked on as a Royalist, who would help in the restoration of the French Monarchy under a prince of the House of Bourbon or Orléans. Bismarck feared that a restoration of the monarchy would re-establish France in her former international position and that a new French king would find favour with the Czar and other monarchs, just as Louis XVIII's accession had been welcomed by the monarchs of Europe in the days of the Holy Alliance. But he also feared that a French king would be subject to clerical, particularly Jesuit, influence and would become a rallying point for opposition to him in his *Kulturkampf*. The régime of MacMahon, who was undoubtedly backed by the French clergy, was, in his eyes and in the eyes of many Germans, a clerical régime likely to do its best to further Catholic opposition everywhere in Europe.

As early as the spring of 1874 Bismarck had shown the French his displeasure. The German press told its readers that the Chancellor had sent a circular to the courts of Europe asserting that peace would be in danger if France identified herself with the interests of the Catholic clergy. Journalists referred to a "jet of cold water" directed by Bismarck at Paris. When the French government did its best to soothe the French bishops, the government-inspired press in Germany gloated over the tonic effect of Bismarck's "jet of cold water". French public opinion, of course, did not like this at all.

But there were other things as well to make Bismarck suspicious of France. Her recovery was rapid beyond expectation. When in the peace treaty Bismarck saddled her with reparations of no less than five milliards of francs, he hoped to prostrate her financial strength for many a year to come. But Thiers managed to pay off this enormous sum much sooner than Bismarck had expected; by September 1873 the last German soldier had left France and the liberation of the occupied territory was completed. It was an extraordinary financial achievement which showed the unbroken economical and financial vitality of the country. It followed naturally that France was proceeding to reorganize her army. Bismarck was told that the French purchased thousands of horses for their cavalry in Germany. That was sufficient for him to publish a decree in March 1875 forbidding the export of any horses from Germany. Public opinion was not slow to discover that this decree was aimed at France, and it became uneasy. The uneasiness was, of course, acutely reflected among the French people.

Bismarck was in a very dark mood in the spring of 1875. Those who worked with him, even Lothar Bucher, complained of his nervousness and irritability. His temper did at times explode, and on one occasion it was the Belgian government which felt the effect. A Catholic Belgian boiler-maker named Duchesne had written a letter to the Archbishop of Paris, in which he offered to murder Bismarck for 60,000 francs. Whether this was anything more than a hoax is not known. The Archbishop, quite correctly, passed on the letter to the German government. Bismarck demanded of the Belgian government that Duchesne should be punished, but the Belgian penal code, like, indeed, the German penal code, made no provision for punishing a crime which was neither committed nor attempted. Then Bismarck, in a very stiff note, in which he also alluded to the attack made by Belgian bishops on Prussia's anticlerical laws, requested that the Belgian government should revise the Belgian penal code. This note he not only communicated to the other Courts of Europe, but he let it appear in the German press. This incident also added to international tension.

Now, at the beginning of 1875, the French government brought before the Chamber a bill to reorganize the army. A few days after Bismarck had issued his embargo on the export of horses, this bill was adopted by the Chamber. The most important provision was the increase of the battalions in a regiment from three to four. The importance of these " fourth battalions" was much exaggerated in Germany, even by military experts like Moltke. But in any case it was a step towards greater preparedness on the part of the French army. Bismarck took it very seriously. At the same time another international event increased his anxiety. This was a meeting between the King of Italy and the Emperor of Austria-Hungary at Venice. Bismarck scented the preparation of an Austrian-Italian-French coalition, friendly to the Pope and hostile to anti-clerical Germany. Following his usual tactics, he resolved to take the offensive, not by the normal diplomatic channels, but by sounding the tocsin in the press. On 5th April the *Kölnische Zeitung* published an article which talked in grave and sombre terms of a threat to the peace of Europe and called the reorganization of the French army a preparation for war. It also commented in very critical terms on the Venice meeting. The article was dated from Vienna, but the intimate relations between the *Kölnische Zeitung* and the Wilhelm-strasse were only too well known, and, as a result, everyone suspected that it was officially inspired. And quite rightly too. It was written by Bismarck's principal press agent, Aegidi, who asked the editor to publish it without the slightest alteration, as "every word had been as carefully weighed as in an official document".

The sensation which this article created was as nothing when two days later the Berlin *Post*, which was also reputed to be very close to the Foreign Office, published an article entitled *Ist Krieg in Sicht?* (Is War in Sight?). This title alone was enough to disturb public opinion in Europe, and the answer which it supplied was hardly calculated to soothe it. Laying the blame on French rearma-ment, the writer answered: "Yes, war *is* in sight, but the threatening clouds may yet blow over". The author was a former official of the Press Bureau of the German government who asserts that he has written it independently; this, however, is greatly to be doubted.

The third shot was fired by the Chancellor's own paper, the *Norddeutsche Allgemeine Zeitung*. This reached the conclusion that there was no danger from Austria or Italy, but considerably more from France.

The stir caused by these articles was enormous. Nobody doubted that Bismarck was behind them. Odo Russell wrote from Berlin that all the diplomats came to him full of gloom and prophesying war. The stock exchanges all over Europe were completely shaken. Everywhere men spoke of the imminence of war. Among those surprised and shocked by it all was the old German Emperor, whose attention was drawn to these articles by his daughter, the Grand Duchess of Baden. He wrote Bismarck a letter in which he expressed his complete surprise, and asked to be informed what these articles really meant. Bismarck, of course, disclaimed all connexion with them and had the audacity to suggest that the article in the *Kölnische Zeitung* was a mere stock-exchange manœuvre, possibly inspired by Rothschild. William seems to have believed this, but, none the less, he put his foot down and made it clear that *he would not tolerate a fresh war*. In the middle of April he said to the French military attaché in Berlin: "Somebody wanted to poison our relations. It was all caused by the nonsense written in a couple of newspapers, but now it is over and done with."

Was it really over and done with? Let us see what Bismarck did *after* the Emperor had spoken these words.

On the very day that old William had said this, the German Foreign Office sent to the Ambassador in London a report from Moltke and commented on it in almost the same way as the sensational articles had done. All peace-loving governments were advised to make clear to the French government the consequences which French warlike preparations might have.

A few days later the French Ambassador in Berlin, Count Gontaut-Biron, who had at once returned from leave, had an interview with the Secretary of State for the Foreign Office, von Bülow, and confirmed the peaceful intentions of his government. He hoped that he had impressed von Bülow favourably. But his hopes were shattered when on 21st April, at a dinner given by Odo Russell, he met an influential member of the German Foreign Office, van Radowitz. Radowitz was reputed to possess the Chancellor's confidence to a considerable degree. Bismarck had sent him to Russia in the preceding year, and every diplomatist believed that this mission had a secret aim. Gontaut, therefore, listened with particular attention to what Radowitz had to say. He, too, declared that the crisis of recent weeks had completely blown over. But he went on to make sinister references to the future. Henceforth, he said, France, economically restored and militarily prepared, could find allies and begin a war of revenge to win back her lost provinces. "*Why should we wait so long?* Would it not be better if we anticipated it?" Such, Radowitz went on, were the arguments of some influential German party leaders. "You must admit", he concluded," that these arguments are indeed *justified on political, philosophical and even on Christian grounds.*"

On 1st May Bismarck himself told the Austrian Ambassador, Count Karolyi, that it would be the duty of Germany to take the initiative against France. Karolyi hastened to inform the English Ambassador, Odo Russell. The next day Russell was visited by the Chief of the General Staff of the German Army, Field-Marshal Count Moltke, who had some grave words to say about the political situation. He discussed the question of responsibility for a fresh war. Peace, he said, was not broken by the Power that marched first; it was the Power which provoked the necessity of defence in others which had to be held responsible. When Russell refuted this justification for a preventive war, Moltke answered: "Well, if all the great powers would come out openly on the side of Germany and prove to France how futile her dreams of revenge are, war might be avoided, possibly for ever".

Now it is quite unthinkable that Moltke would have meddled in diplomatic affairs, which were none of his business, without Bismarck's authority. Both these great men were much too jealous of each other for Moltke ever to overstep the mark.

The next day, 3rd May, the German Foreign Office sent to the Ambassador in Paris, Prince Hohenlohe, a note in much the same vein. It repeated not only the Chancellor's conviction that France was preparing to go to war against Germany, but insisted that Hohenlohe should *dispel the peaceful impression* which Gontaut's report on his conversation with Bülow had made. Hohenlohe, who was just about to go on leave, postponed his departure in order to tell the French Foreign Minister, the Duke de Decazes, that Germany felt threatened by France's measures, although he did not consider war to be imminent. Decazes had understood him quite correctly when he wrote to Gontaut that the reason behind Hohenlohe's visit was to prevent the French from considering the incident closed.

My personal impression is that all these various happenings were part of a well-weighed and concerted plan of diplomatic campaign on the part of Bismarck, which we would nowadays call a "war of nerves". He wanted to impress on the French government in every way that the reorganization of the French army brought France to the verge of war. The goal of the campaign was to intimidate France so much that she would abstain from the proposed measures.

But Decazes went the opposite way. He sent a copy of Gontaut's report on Radowitz's remarks to the courts of all the Great Powers in order to show them that *France was menaced by a German preventive war*. He endeavoured especially to impress the Czar, and with much success. Alexander II assured the French Ambassador that he would inform them if serious danger lay ahead. He made it clear that he would not allow Bismarck to attack France suddenly.

Decazes' other step was to rouse public opinion in Europe through the medium of the London *Times*, and he laid all the documents before Mr. Blowitz, the head of the Paris office of that paper. Blowitz tells the story in his memoirs in a very amusing but rather fantastic way. He sent *The Times* a well-documented dispatch which was printed on 6th May under the title "A French Scare". It caused a huge sensation and was copied by every paper of importance in Europe. Lord Derby, the British Foreign Secretary, said, after reading it: "Bismarck either is really bent on making war, or he wants us to *believe* that he is bent on it".

Just at this time Berlin was expecting a visit from the Czar and Gortchakoff. On this visit all the hopes for the maintenance of peace were centred. The British government resolved to give the Czar assistance if he would support the interests of peace while in Berlin. The Russian Ambassador in London, Count Peter Shouwaloff, who had talked to Bismarck in Berlin, told Derby that the state of *Bismarck's nerves* was a *danger to Europe*. Disraeli compared Bismarck with Napoleon I, and Queen Victoria applauded this comparison. She wrote a personal letter to the Czar, and Odo Russell was instructed to use all possible means to allay the misunderstandings which had arisen between France and Germany and to support the efforts which the Czar was expected to make to the same end.

On 10th May the Russian Emperor and Gortchakoff arrived in

Berlin. Both told Emperor William and Bismarck that Europe
would not stand quietly by if war should break out between France
and Germany. The old Emperor emphasized with complete sin-
cerity that he was far from desiring war, and Bismarck did the same.
The two Chancellors, Bismarck and Gortchakoff, had a conversation which seems to have become quite lively at some points.
Bismarck denied all connexion with Radowitz's unlucky words
to Gontaut-Biron. He asked Gortchakoff somewhat sarcastically
whether he had come to Berlin to utter a *quos ego* as Neptune did to
the raging tempests. "Those words are not to be found in my
Latin dictionary", answered the Russian. He asked Bismarck to
assure him that he was far from the thought of attacking France now
or in the future. "I do not want anything written. Your word
is good enough for me."

The next day the Czar was able to tell the French Ambassador,
Gontaut, that the peace was assured; not only had the Kaiser and
the Crown Prince told him so in the most convincing way, but
Bismarck too, he said, was quite peaceably minded. The French
breathed again. Gortchakoff advised them not to talk too loudly
about their success, although he himself affected an air of triumph
which was excessive and which, one can well imagine, was galling
to Bismarck.

But even if Gortchakoff had behaved with perfect tact, Bismarck
would still have been very angry. For the general impression was
that he, who had always emerged the winner from a political campaign, had this time been defeated. Lord Derby said: "Bismarck has
put European opinion to the test and now he has got his answer".
Never could Bismarck forget this defeat. From now on he always
asserted that he had been slandered, that he had never dreamed of
making war on France. He takes this line in his *Reminiscences*, where
he tries to make the reader believe that his intended attack on
France was a fairy-tale fabricated by two men, the French Ambassador Gontaut-Biron and the Russian Chancellor Gortchakoff,
who in his *vanité sénile* wanted to triumph as an angel of peace at
Bismarck's expense. To illustrate the attitude of the Russian
Chancellor, Bismarck relates that before leaving Berlin he had sent
out a telegraphic circular, destined for publication and dated from
Berlin, beginning with the words: "*Maintenant* [that is, under

Russian protection] *la paix est assurée*". If Gortchakoff had, in fact, sent such a telegram from Berlin, it would have been both arrogant and tactless. But we know now the true text of the telegram, which is given by both the German and the French publications from their respective archives in the following identical terms: "*L'Empereur quitte Berlin parfaitement convaincu des dispositions conciliantes qui y régnent et qui assurent le maintien de la paix*" (The Emperor quits Berlin perfectly convinced of the conciliatory disposition reigning there which ensures the maintenance of peace). I do not think that this text is open to any objection.

Bismarck had always disliked Gortchakoff, whose excessive vanity irritated him. From now on he hated him, and his subsequent policy towards Russia was more than once tainted by this personal antipathy.

The Ambassador Gontaut-Biron, too, was detested all the more by Bismarck because he was held in high esteem by both the Emperor William and the Empress Augusta. Characteristically enough, he concentrated his attacks on Augusta; in a speech to the Reichstag he even went so far as to insinuate that the war scare was due to "inexperienced diplomatists" and the "drawing-room influences of highly-placed personages". He longed to be rid of this Ambassador, but had to wait another two years before the defeat of MacMahon and the victory of the Republicans in the 1877 election ended Gontaut-Biron's diplomatic career. When he left Berlin the old Emperor William said to him: "I am sorry for you with all my heart. I will bear you in the very best remembrance and I hope that you will not forget me either." Surely a man whom William I could address in this way cannot have been the intriguer which Bismarck paints him. Odo Russell, who was well qualified to judge, calls Gontaut-Biron a perfectly honourable and intelligent gentleman.

There is still a lively controversy among historians over whether Bismarck really intended to go to war with France. In my view this question cannot be answered, because it is misleading as it stands. My impression is that Bismarck wanted to make Europe, and particularly France, believe that he was willing to go to war if France failed to revoke her measures of military reorganization, which the government had proposed and the Chamber adopted. If she complied for fear of a German attack, then there was no need for war, and Bismarck would have been quite content to continue in his policy of a conservative peace. What he would have done if France had stood firm and Europe had showed willingness to let Bismarck have his own way, we cannot say, for very likely he himself had not made up his mind. It was not Bismarck's way to commit himself irrevocably to a second step before the first had been taken. He would have examined the whole position afresh before doing anything definite. It is quite in accordance with his tactics that all his threatening and sabre-rattling found *unofficial* expression in newspaper articles which could be repudiated by an official *démenti* or by the casual remarks of a subordinate after a good dinner, or by generals, conveniently to be accused of conducting a policy of their own. It is therefore hardly surprising that to this day some historians, not only Germans, emphasize that there is no proof that Bismarck himself ever uttered one word of his intention to make war. He was much too cautious and astute to reveal his real aim before it was absolutely necessary.

Nevertheless, the war scare of 1875 left behind a very bad impression which did Bismarck's reputation no good. This current of feeling is very well summed up by an English diplomat, who was certainly a very sharp critic of Bismarck, but, nevertheless, a friend of German unity. This is Sir Robert Morier, who had lived in Germany long enough to know her political difficulties better than any other Englishman. He was a personal friend of the Crown Prince, with whom he twice had confidential talks during the crisis. At the height of the crisis he wrote to the Prince: "The malady under which Europe at present is suffering, is caused by *German chauvinism*, a new and far more formidable type of the disease, than the French, for instead of being spasmodical and undisciplined, it is *methodical, calculating, cold-blooded and self-contained* . . . the friends of Germany, and . . . myself among the number, argued and insisted, that the unity of Germany once established, Europe would have chauvinism crushed out of it. . . . But if any open and public act should take place which should officially placard this chauvinism in the face of Europe, should the doctrine of the jet of cold water such as it is openly preached in the organs of the Press Bureau, the doctrine namely, that prospective and hypothetical and abstract danger, as distinct from any immediate, palpable, real and concrete danger, is a sufficient reason for the stronger neighbour attacking the weaker, and for establishing a casus belli; should such a doctrine, I say, embody itself in any tangible and official act, such as summons to disarm addressed to France at the present moment, then I in my turn venture to prophesy that neither in Your Imperial Highness' life-time nor mine will Germany recover the stain which such a return to unalloyed *Faustrecht* will impress upon her humanity."

6. *The End of the "Liberal Era"*

After the crucial visit of the Czar, Bismarck retired to his country estates for many months. Even before the visit he had asked the Emperor to release him from office on account of his failing health. There is no doubt that he was often a tired man and a sick man too. Gortchakoff said: "Bismarck is ill because he eats too much, drinks too much and works too much". Whether this diagnosis fully met the case may be doubted. Of course the Emperor would not hear of Bismarck's retiring and a compromise was reached: The Chancellor was given indefinite leave. It is a testimony to the unique position which Bismarck occupied that the German political world quietly accepted his continued absence from the capital for many months, even though he was the sole responsible Minister of the Empire. The constitution of the Empire had not even provided for a deputy to act for the Chancellor and countersign the political acts of the Emperor during Bismarck's absence. Bismarck tried to solve this difficulty by a bold interpretation of the constitution, but a prominent Progressive member, who was at the same time a leading authority on constitutional law, Professor Hänel, protested against this infringement. The upshot of the controversy was the passing of a law in March 1878 (*Stellvertretungs-Gesetz*) providing for the representation of the Imperial Chancellor, a measure which will concern us later on (p. 235).

But apart from this technicality, it was, of course, very difficult to keep the government's business going when the head of the government was absent and only occasionally took a hand, sometimes without being adequately briefed on facts or political implications. This was not too serious while Bismarck had as his representative Rudolf Delbrück, who mastered almost every question which arose and wielded considerable authority in the Reichstag. But suddenly, in April 1876, the world was astonished by the news that Delbrück had resigned and that his resignation had been accepted. It was a complete surprise even to the best-informed politicians. What were the reasons behind Delbrück's sudden resignation? Bismarck has at different times given some very different explanations. The truth is that Delbrück recognized by small but unmistakable signs that Bismarck wanted to get rid of him. If he had been a fighter he would have held his ground, relying upon his strong position in the Reichstag. But such a thought never entered Delbrück's head. He had been happy to assist the great Chancellor, and if his master was now weary of him, he did not wish to obtrude himself upon him. He was a product not of political and parliamentary life, but of the civil service.

Delbrück's retirement was considered by many shrewd observers to be a clear indication that the Liberal era was drawing to its end and that Bismarck was casting about for the support of other parties. Nor, of course, was this the only symptom. A few months earlier Bismarck had laid before the Reichstag a bill which may be considered the forerunner of the subsequent measure against the Social Democrats. This bill sought to amend the penal law in order to lay open to prosecution certain types of agitation pursued by the Opposition. It was directed against the Socialists, although it did not say so in so many words. The terms of the bill were so elastic that nobody could foresee where prosecutions would end. The clauses in question were therefore called *Kautschuk*—that is, india-rubber paragraphs. The Liberals rightly considered this as an attempt to undermine the *Rechtsstaat* (the state ruled by law and according to law) and to replace it by administrative arbitrariness. Led by Lasker, the National Liberals rejected the bill. Although Bismarck did not appear to take this defeat too seriously, his whole method of approach left a nasty taste in the mouth. Why has he proposed such a bill without reaching any previous understanding with us, asked the Liberals, even though he must have known that we should have to reject it?

The speech which Bismarck made at the third reading of this bill contained a sensational attack on the *Kreuz-Zeitung*, the reactionary Junker newspaper, which in June 1875 had published a series of articles on the *Bleichröder-Delbrück-Camphausen-Era*. Camp-hausen was the Prussian Minister of Finance, while Bleichröder was merely Bismarck's personal banker. The notorious "Era-Articles" contained a lot of economic rubbish, but were interesting by reason of certain insinuations, made not only against Delbrück and Camp-hausen, but against Bismarck himself. Bismarck, who as a rule proceeded against every attack on himself as if it were a libel, pre-ferred on this occasion to reply by vigorously attacking the *Kreuz-Zeitung* in the Reichstag—and requesting the readers of the paper to boycott it. But the Prussian Junkers who formed the bulk of its readers answered with a very outspoken "Declaration", roundly declining to accept from the Chancellor any lesson in honourable dealing and good behaviour. The signatories of this declaration, the so-called "Deklaranten", were, of course, noted down in Bismarck's black books, and even more indelibly in his wife's. He never forgave a single one of them, until he later changed his tune and humbly asked their pardon. But he did not consider this any reason for breaking with the Conservatives. He was quite sure that they were helpless without the assistance of the government, and that sooner or later they would come to him and sue for peace. They did, in fact, found in the following year a new party, in order to eliminate those who were not looked on with favour by the Chancellor. This party was called the *deutschkonservative* (German Conservative) Party. Before they adopted their programme, one of them laid it before Bismarck in order to delete any item which might offend him.

When Delbrück retired, it was not only a large number of Liberals who felt that the Chancellor was toying with the idea of a new political alignment. A leader of the Centre Party asked the Liberals with a sneer: "Cannot you hear still the iron step of the agrarians with Prince Bismarck at their head as drum-major?" But, in fact, Bismarck himself did not yet know to which side he should incline. The Conservatives, even if they increased their poll and their seats at the next election, would never be able to secure a majority in the Reichstag and outvote the Liberals. A fresh majority was possible only with the help of the Centre Party, and the huge gap between the Centre Party and Bismarck seemed unbridgeable.

There was a practical problem which was greatly exercising the Chancellor: the reform of the Imperial finances. The ever-increasing burden of armaments could not be met out of the existing sources of revenue. The finances of the Empire were organized under the constitution in a peculiar way. Since the Reichstag was elected by universal franchise, Bismarck, ever suspicious of democracy, did not wish to entrust to it the right of direct taxation. He wanted to limit its powers to indirect taxation, in other words, mainly to levying duties on articles of mass consumption, such as beer, tobacco, spirits, sugar, and petrol. But these duties were far from sufficient to offset Imperial expenditure. To make both ends meet, the individual states had to contribute according to a scale laid down in the constitution. These contributions were called *Matrikular-Beiträge* (matriculated contributions). In order to be able to pay them, the individual states like Prussia, Bavaria, or Hamburg had to tax their subjects. Direct taxation was controlled by the individual states.

This system suited neither the Empire nor the individual states. Bismarck compared the Reich to a "troublesome sponger, who had to go begging at the door of the separate states". These, on the other hand, had to meet growing demands from the Reich and consequently to increase their own taxes. Bismarck wanted to secure to the Reich some substantial increases in its existing indirect taxation and thus make it financially independent of the states. This meant a sharp rise in the duty on such things as tobacco, beer, and spirits. Some of the Liberals, particularly the Progressives led by Eugen Richter, opposed these taxes as being a heavy burden on the man in the street; they preferred direct taxation, because it would more readily reach the rich and the well-to-do. The National Liberals were rather more friendly to Bismarck's proposal, but they raised a very important constitutional objection. In Germany indirect taxes were not voted annually in the budget, as in Britain. They were fixed permanently and remained unaltered until a new law was passed. Now a new bill passed by the Reichstag became law only when confirmed by the Bundesrat (Federal Council) made up of the delegates of the governments of the various single states. It was the same with the budget. Constitutionally the budget was classed as a law, in other words, it too required the assent of both the Reichstag and the Federal Council. In practice a vote of the Federal Council opposing Bismarck was a political impossibility. Through his influence in the Federal Council Bismarck would veto a reduction in any tax, in fact he could prevent the adoption of the budget. But even without a budget the tax revenue would continue to flow into the coffers of the Reich.

All these questions were viewed in the light of the experience which the Prussian parliament had had during the constitutional conflict a bare ten years before. At that time no budget was passed at all because of disagreement between the Chamber of Deputies on the one hand, and the Upper Chamber (Herrenhaus) and the King on the other. Nevertheless, the crown raised and spent the money on the army, because the Prussian constitution provided for existing taxes and duties to be paid so long as they were not suspended by a new law. In this way the Prussian constitution had been practically suspended for all these years, and this was Bismarck's work. Nobody now doubted that he was quite capable of repeating the same practice if ever he came into conflict with the majority of the Reichstag over the army estimates for the Reich, for example. The Reichstag would, indeed, be at the mercy of the government. The Prussian Minister of Finance, Camphausen, saw this quite clearly and told Bismarck, in January 1878, that a parliament which had no power to levy taxes and duties would be impotent.

It is therefore quite understandable that the National Liberals asked for what they termed "constitutional guarantees", if they were to vote the high indirect taxes demanded by Bismarck.

But there was one other important point. Financial problems are intimately bound up with questions of economy and trade policy. In England, for example, Gladstone's budgets, especially the great budget of 1860, were most important instruments for promoting free trade. But what economic policy did Bismarck have in mind? Until the retirement of Delbrück, Bismarck had left economic questions to him. Delbrück's dismissal suggested that Bismarck intended to take them into his own hands. Would he follow the same policy, or was he bent on a new departure?

Since the commercial treaty with France in 1862, the economic policy of the Zollverein, and later of the German Empire, might be called a policy of moderate free trade. Most of the moderate duties which the tariff contained had no protective character. One of the last protectionist duties was that on pig-iron. But under a law passed in 1873, this duty was to lapse after 1876. In these three years, however, the economic situation changed considerably. The short boom that had followed the war had spent itself, production and markets had dropped. The iron-founders, suffering from the slump, feared that the abolition of the duty would involve them in ruin. They tried to prevent this measure, and Windthorst, the leader of the Centre Party, took the initiative in the Reichstag. Windthorst's motion, however, was defeated. Led by the iron-founders and cotton-spinners, the protectionists now began to organize.

It was not yet clear what the Chancellor's attitude was. We can assume that in 1876 and 1877 he had not yet fixed on an economic policy. A landowner by origin and status, he inevitably saw things from the viewpoint of the landed interests. The agricultural interests were at this time not protectionist. Eastern Germany still exported corn. The Junkers therefore adhered to free trade. They did not want to see the price of the industrial products which they had to buy swollen by taxation. The Conservatives had voted with the Liberal Free Traders against Windthorst's motion for the maintenance of the iron duties. No one thought at this time of imposing duties on corn or other agricultural commodities.

In January 1877 a new Reichstag was elected. The Liberals lost some seats, but not so many as to change fundamentally the situation in parliament. The National Liberals held about 130 seats and were still the strongest party. Hence Bismarck had not very far to look for a majority, provided he co-operated with them. The Centre Party had about 100 deputies, the two Conservative Parties about 80. A combination of the Centre and the Conservatives was not yet sufficient to give the Chancellor a majority, even supposing he was willing to make it up with the Centre. The most important change caused by the election was that the position of Lasker and the Left wing of the National Liberal Party was much weakened. They were no longer indispensable to ensure a Liberal-cum-Conservative majority. In consequence, the position of Bennigsen, the leader of the Centre and the Right wing of the National Liberal Party, was strengthened. To Bennigsen, therefore, Bismarck turned in the winter of 1877 with a view to a fresh alignment.

Bismarck was once more on leave; from 15th April 1877 to 14th February 1878 he stayed on his country estate. This leave had come about in a curious way.

In March Bismarck had suddenly attacked in the Reichstag one of his own colleagues, the head of the Admiralty, General von Stosch. It was an extraordinary and quite unchivalrous proceeding by which he certainly hoped to compel Stosch to resign. But this time the old Kaiser, who valued Stosch highly, did not give way and declined the resignation tendered by the general. A few days later Bismarck let it be made public that he too had asked to be retired. At the same time he unleashed his pack of press-dogs and set them on his personal enemies, particularly the Empress Augusta. The articles which Busch then wrote about "Frictions" and which he later reproduced in his Bismarck book, are the most libellous attacks ever levelled at a queen. It was Bismarck himself who had given Busch the materials for these articles. Another person attacked was the Prussian Minister of Finance, Camphausen, who had hesitated to lay before the Chancellor a plan to reform Imperial finances. The general impression was that Bismarck wanted to get rid of Camphausen.

These manœuvres did not, at first, produce the effect Bismarck intended. It seems that for some days he was afraid that the Emperor really would accept his resignation. But in the end, of course, William expressed the wish never to part company with his great Chancellor. A compromise was reached by which Bismarck went on indefinite leave. This, of course, did not help to further the affairs of Prussia and the Reich. The feeling of uneasiness was general.

In the seclusion of Varzin and Friedrichsruh, Bismarck pondered over the personal problems and practical issues which the immediate future would bring. He was determined to recast the finances of the Reich so as to make it independent in this respect of the individual states. He saw that he could not do this against the wishes of the majority in the Reichstag, and so he looked about him for a man who could assist him in his task of government and could guarantee him the majority he needed. In the end he decided that Bennigsen was the right man for the job.

He invited Bennigsen, who was not only the leader of the National Liberal Party but President of the Prussian Chamber of Deputies, to visit him at Varzin. Bennigsen came to see him on several occasions. The most important of these visits was made at Christmas 1877.

At first Bismarck offered Bennigsen a seat in the Prussian cabinet as Minister of the Interior. But Bennigsen preferred the post of Minister of Finance, which in view of Bismarck's plans he considered the most important of all. Bismarck debated with himself the possibility of a more intimate connexion between the governments of Prussia and the Reich. In a letter he wrote to Bennigsen in December 1877 inviting him to Varzin, Bismarck talks about an extension of the system of personal union of the two governments. This union already existed in the persons of the King-Emperor, the Chancellor who was also the Prussian Minister-President, and the Ministers for War and Foreign Affairs. Bismarck now wanted to extend it to the Minister who acted as deputy to the Chancellor and the Prussian Minister-President. As Prussian Minister-President Bismarck was represented during his absence by the Vice-President of the Prussian Ministry, who happened to be the Minister of Finance, Camphausen. Bismarck's suggestion to Bennigsen was that Bennigsen should become his deputy in Prussia as well as in the Reich. As Minister of Finance in Prussia he would at the same time secure in the Reich government a position similar to that which Delbrück had occupied before him.

Bennigsen was willing to accept this arrangement—on one condition: he would not join the ministry alone but *only in the company of two of his political associates*. He made this clear to the Chancellor at his very first visit in July; that is, before he had consulted his friends. Now, before seeing Bismarck in December, he summoned the committee of his party and laid all his cards on the table. If he, as the leader of the party, took a step so important for the party and its future policy and standing, it was no more than his plain duty not only to keep the party fully informed but to make sure that he was acting in conformity with its views. The committee of the party agreed both to his entering the government and to his stipulating that he would only join it in the company of two of his friends. They agreed that the two most suitable candidates were Max von Forckenbeck and Baron von Stauffenberg. Forckenbeck was the President of the Reichstag, and the chief burgomaster of the second town in Prussia, Breslau. Besides, he possessed the confidence of the old Emperor, who had repeatedly consulted him, and of the Crown Prince. Baron von Stauffenberg was looked on in Bavaria as the foremost exponent there of the idea of German unity. He was a man of the highest culture and unimpeachable character. No objection could possibly be raised to these two men on personal grounds.

When Bennigsen mentioned them to Bismarck, the Chancellor replied that he very much doubted whether the old Emperor would agree to this proposal. But Bennigsen knew very well that Bismarck was fond of using the alleged opposition of the Emperor as a pretext and did not budge an inch. His impression was that Bismarck, although he did not agree to his condition, did not reject it out of hand. He was optimistic about the outcome of the talks, the more so as he was in agreement with most of Bismarck's financial ideas. We do not know for certain how far Bismarck revealed his plans, but we know one thing—that he was as silent as the grave about one of them which very soon became a focus of political controversy: this was a state monopoly of tobacco.

What were Bismarck's thoughts when Bennigsen left Varzin? No one will ever know for certain. In later years Bismarck said that he considered that the alliance he planned had miscarried owing to Bennigsen's condition that he would only come in with Forckenbeck and Stauffenberg. But such subsequent accounts from Bismarck can never be taken at their face value. The letter which Bismarck wrote to William immediately after Bennigsen's visit does not give the impression that he considered their negotiations to have foundered. But this letter crossed a very angry one from the Emperor. The old man had read and heard about Bennigsen's visit to Varzin and it had been represented to him as an attempt by Bismarck to form a Liberal ministry. Now William was more averse to Liberalism than ever, and he would have liked to get rid of every Minister who bore the smallest taint of it. Besides, he was furious that Bismarck should be negotiating behind his back. Futhermore, there was a special reason why Bennigsen should be his pet aversion. Bennigsen was a former subject of George V of Hanover, and William, although he himself had robbed George of his crown, looked on a man who had abandoned his former king to become a good Prussian and his own subject as a traitor. Kings sometimes have, it seems, a logic all their own. William's letter angered Bismarck deeply, so much so that he fell ill. Whether he took any steps to bring the Emperor round to his way of thinking is not known with any certainty. In any case, he did nothing to inform Bennigsen that he had run up against obstacles: on the contrary, he continued to bargain with Bennigsen just as if the alliance were still on the cards.

The end came at the Reichstag session on 22nd February 1878. Bismarck had returned to Berlin during this month in order to answer the interpellation which Bennigsen brought forward in the name of the government parties concerning German policy in the Balkans. We shall have more to do with this when we come to the Eastern crisis and the Congress of Berlin. In this session Bennigsen still appeared as the leader of the majority in the Reichstag which supported the government.

A few days later, on 22nd February, a finance bill, drafted by the government and proposing an increase in the duties on tobacco and other articles, came up for debate. Camphausen, as Prussian Minister of Finance, was piloting the bill. To meet the criticism levelled at new duties, he made it clear that it was not the intention of the government to ask for a *Tabak-Monopol*, that is, a government monopoly to import, manufacture, and sell tobacco. It was therefore a sensation of the first order when the Chancellor rose at once and bluntly declared: "My aim is a national tobacco monopoly and with this in view I accept the bill as a provisional measure and a stepping-stone". He went further and described the monopoly as the "ultimate ideal goal" at which he was aiming. This was a real stab in the back to a colleague, a surprise attack from an ambush, incompatible both with the loyalty between colleagues and common decency. Both the bill and Camphausen himself fell victims to this stroke. A few days later he requested and received his dismissal.

During this sensational session Bennigsen went to Forckenbeck, who presided, and said: "Do you not agree that we cannot participate in setting up this monopoly? If so, I shall now go to the Chancellor and tell him that our negotiations are at an end." Forckenbeck agreed, and Bennigsen told Bismarck that he no longer wished to be considered as a candidate for a seat in the cabinet. The tobacco monopoly was, indeed, strongly opposed by the National Liberal Party, and Bennigsen would have found himself in an utterly impossible position had he been obliged as Minister of Finance to put it through in the teeth of his own party. But there were also certainly personal reasons for his *démarche*. Bennigsen was a gentle-

man and he took offence at the far-from-gentlemanly way in which
Bismarck had treated a prominent colleague of long standing. Such
conduct, considered in conjunction with Bismarck's crafty attack
on Stosch in the previous year, showed Bennigsen how he himself
would be treated by the Chancellor, if and when he should ever
dare not to dance to his tune. And was it not true that Bismarck had
already deceived him by withholding from him at Varzin all mention
of his intention to introduce the tobacco monopoly, which he now,
only two months later, called his "supreme and final aim"?

In this way an alliance which might perhaps have given developments in Germany a completely different turn had failed. For only
a year later, Bismarck finally broke with the National Liberals and
inaugurated the Conservative, nay, the reactionary policy which
lasted until his overthrow. Can Bennigsen be held responsible for this?

Some historians criticize the National Liberal leader for not having
entered the government alone and for having insisted on the admis-
sion of two friends. But this condition was not only reasonable but
necessary if Bennigsen wanted to become an active Minister and not
a mere tool of Bismarck's grace. During the negotiations Bismarck,
in conversation with his secretary von Tiedemann, taxed the National
Liberal leaders with their lack of "subordination". Subordination is
a virtue in a soldier, but not in a statesman with convictions of his
own. Even Treitschke, who belonged to the extreme Right wing
of the National Liberal Party and was a fervent adherent of the
Chancellor, wrote: "Bismarck cannot stand independent characters
and I should not advise a friend of mine to put his head into this
noose".

Why was Bismarck so set on Bennigsen joining the government?
Simply to have a guarantee that the National Liberal deputies would
be compelled to vote for his proposals; had any of them been prevented by their political convictions from dancing to Bismarck's
tune, Bennigsen would have been obliged to expel them from the
party. In this way Bismarck hoped to get rid of Lasker and his all-
too-independent friends, and to transform the National Liberal
Party into a *Bismarck sans phrase* party. If Bennigsen had refused
to play Bismarck's game, well, he had seen from the example of
Camphausen how Bismarck dealt with a recalcitrant colleague.

Would such a prospect hold any charms for the leader of a great party? On the other hand, if he joined the cabinet in the company of two loyal and competent friends, he might hope to influence the government's policy, and, relying on these friends and the parliamentary position of his party, to upset any manœuvre which aimed at splitting his party or squeezing his party out. That would, of course, have meant that Bismarck would have to share power with the National Liberals and we can be sure that he was never willing to do that.

But there is another remarkable aspect of the scene in the Reichstag on 22nd February 1878. Why did Bismarck choose this moment to strip off the mask and to provoke the rupture with Bennigsen? What had happened since Christmas 1877?

Pius IX, the irreconcilable Pope, had died on 7th February. Some years earlier Bismarck had said that as a rule a contentious pope was followed by a pacific one. This prophecy proved correct. The Conclave of the Cardinals elected in succession to Pius the conciliatory Cardinal Pecci, who occupied the Holy See as Pope Leo XIII. This election took place on 20th February, two days before the sensational Reichstag session. On the very day of his election, Leo wrote a letter to the Emperor William expressing his hope of better relations between the Church and the Reich. We can assume that this letter was known to Bismarck when he rose in the Reichstag to attack Camphausen. This letter revived Bismarck's hopes of successfully inducing the Pope to instruct the Centre Party to vote in favour of the government. Moreover, Bismarck had seen that the protectionist movement enjoyed strong sympathy among the Centre Party. There was a way open to an understanding with this party. Not that Bismarck wanted to form an alliance with the Centre, but he now had a chance to indulge in a sport in which he was past-master, playing off one party against another. True, to attain this end, he would have to abandon the *Kulturkampf* and much of the legislation which he had passed against the Church; but having seen that there were no laurels to be gained in the *Kulturkampf*, he was quite willing to change his tactics. In the summer of the same year he had his first conversation with the Roman Catholic nuncio, Masella, in which he tried to come to terms with the Church. Although these talks were not successful, Bismarck did not drop the threads he had begun to spin. And again, in the end, he had his way.

The fiasco in which the Bennigsen negotiations ended is, in my view, one of the turning-points in the political history of the German Empire. The aged Emperor was happy to have averted a Liberal infiltration into the government. But, as things turned out, this was one of the very factors which worked towards the downfall of his dynasty. By barring the way to healthy political development, it completed the isolation of the monarchy and this isolation brought about its collapse a generation later. The National Liberal Party represented at this time the loyal and patriotic middle class of Germany more strongly and more completely than any party has ever done since then. It could have brought the monarchy and parliament into a harmonious collaboration and thereby strengthened them both. An element of stabilization would have been introduced into the political life of the Reich, and the lack of this became very clearly visible after Bismarck's downfall. While Bismarck remained in power, this was not so evident. But Bismarck was an exceptional man who could hardly be succeeded by men of quite the same calibre, and the institutions of a great state cannot be based on the unique capabilities of one man.

Bennigsen believed at first that the breakdown of negotiations was only temporary, and that Bismarck would be compelled by force of circumstances to reopen them. He even thought of exploiting the parliamentary position of his party in order to compel Bismarck to do this. But before anything could be done, chance gave Bismarck an opportunity which he turned to account with the same virtuosity as he had displayed in using the death of the Danish King Frederick VII in December 1863 to accomplish his all-important policy of setting the seal on Prussia's power. This chance was afforded him by two attempts on the life of the Emperor.

Before dealing with these attempts, I would add that in March 1878, shortly after the breach with Bennigsen, Bismarck laid a bill before the Reichstag to provide for a deputy for himself. This measure, the *Stellvertretungs-Gesetz*, appointed a general deputy to the Chancellor with the rank of Vice-Chancellor; this post, which was originally destined for Bennigsen, was now filled by a Conservative official who did not sit in parliament—the Ambassador in Vienna, Count von Stolberg-Wernigerode. In addition, the bill provided that the heads of the various Reich departments should become the Chancellor's deputies in matters falling within their own competence. Thus, the Secretary of State for the Imperial Exchequer became the Chancellor's deputy for the Reich's financial affairs, authorized to sign in his place. These heads of departments received the title of Secretary of State and not Minister, for they were not responsible Ministers. The only responsible Minister now, as hitherto, was the Chancellor. The Progressive deputy Hänel again asked for the introduction of responsible Ministers of the Reich. This had also been the demand of the National Liberals earlier on. But this time Bennigsen, in their name, dropped this demand. The whole party, even Lasker, voted for the bill. Despite this, Bismarck made an attack on Lasker during the debate, which was as sharp as it was unjustified and unprovoked. This attack reveals one of the motives behind his negotiations with Bennigsen.

The number of Secretaries of State gradually increased as the legislative and administrative business of the Reich became more and more voluminous. There were Secretaries for Foreign Affairs, the Interior, the Exchequer, the Navy, the Colonies, and so on. Their political importance increased when lesser men than Bismarck became Chancellors. Tirpitz, for example, as Secretary for the Navy, was on occasion a more important factor in Imperial policy than the Chancellor, von Bethmann Hollweg. Technically, however, he was never a responsible Minister, but only the deputy of the Chancellor who bore the ultimate responsibility for naval affairs. And until the downfall of the monarchy there was never a cabinet to deliberate and reach decisions on Reich affairs. This is one of the peculiar imprints which Bismarck left on the constitution. No Secretary of State was or could be a member of the Reichstag until 1917. Only then did the exigencies of war compel the Emperor to appoint members of the Reichstag to the office of Secretary of State, so that, for example, Payer, the leader of the Progressive Party, became Vice-Chancellor. But by then the sands were running low and the Empire's days were numbered.

7. The Law against the Social Democrats

On 11th May 1878 a plumber named Hödel fired at William I and missed. The Emperor was unhurt. Hödel was an utterly worthless scoundrel and a political weathercock. For some time he was a member of the Social-Democratic Party; later he joined Stoecker's Christian Socialist Party; Stoecker was court chaplain and an anti-Semitic demagogue. It is quite certain that there was no conspiracy and that Hödel had no accomplices. At the time of the attempt, Bismarck was at Friedrichsruh. As soon as he learned of it, he telegraphed to Bülow, his deputy at the Foreign Office, that the incident should be seized on as pretext for introducing a law against the Socialists and their press.

In the earlier years Bismarck had entered upon confidential talks and negotiations with Lassalle, the founder of the German Socialist movement. At the time of the Prussian constitutional conflict he hoped to use him as a tool against the Progressive party (p. 116). Later he changed his attitude completely. In the first years immediately following the war against France, he advocated international collaboration between monarchist and Conservative governments against the activities of the Socialists, particularly the so-called Internationale, headed by Karl Marx in London. This was one of the aims underlying his policy of allying the three Emperors. Suppression by international measures failed, notably through the opposition of Britain, which was not willing to resign her ancient custom of giving asylum to victims of political persecution. Bismarck grew steadily more determined to achieve repressive legislation in Germany. He opened his heart to Bamberger, the Liberal parliamentarian, who had written on the subject of Socialism: "If I don't want any chickens, then I must smash the eggs".

Bismarck's first step in this direction was a bill to amend the penal law, but this was thrown out by the Reichstag, led by Lasker, in the spring of 1876 (p. 224). Now, after Hödel's attempt on the Emperor a second effort at oppressive legislation was made—a government bill openly directed against the Socialists, their agitation, and their press. This bill was a very careless and clumsy piece of work. It was plain that the Ministers who sponsored it had negligently strung together a few odd paragraphs, merely in order to meet their master's wishes. They probably felt that it could not pass the Reichstag, provided that the National Liberals refused to betray their principles. For the bill was clearly discriminatory, that is to say, a measure which was not meant to be applied to every citizen alike, but only to persons of certain political convictions. Thus it grossly offended against the principle of equality before the law and against the freedom of the press and liberty of association. Indeed, the basic principle of the *Rechtsstaat* was at stake.

Some of the National Liberal deputies were none the less sufficiently scared of Socialism to support the bill. These were not the industrialists or big capitalists, but university professors such as Treitschke and Gneist. Treitschke, the prophet of power politics, was a Liberal only in name. But Gneist, the great constitutional lawyer and admirer of the English constitution, had been one of the Opposition leaders during the constitutional conflict. It was calamitous for the development of the national mentality that the German universities gradually ceased to be the strongholds of liberty which they had been in the middle of the century. But these professors had not yet gained the ascendancy in the National Liberal Party, which once more followed Lasker's lead by urging the rejection of the bill. The party voted against it almost to a man, after Bennigsen, its leader, had spoken in the name of all of them.

In this speech Bennigsen asked the government whether it was true that they had brought in the bill even though they knew full well that the Reichstag would reject it. He was all the more justified in putting this question as Bismarck had not even taken the trouble to come to Berlin to give support to his own measure. This was, of course, quite in keeping with his tactics. He wanted to sow discord between the National Liberals and those who had returned them, for these latter, he was sure, were much more scared by the Socialist bogy.

Then came a second attempt on William's life. On Sunday, 2nd June 1878, a Dr. Karl Nobiling fired at him from the window of a house in the Unter den Linden as he drove past in an open carriage. William was seriously wounded; bleeding profusely, the old man of eighty-one had to be taken back to his palace.

Nobiling's attempt was the act of a lunatic. He came from a well-to-do middle-class family, had studied economics and taken his degree at Leipzig. He certainly had no political connexions. Nobody in the Social-Democratic Party even knew his name. Whether his motive was a political one will never be known, for at the moment of his arrest he wounded himself mortally and died before a proper interrogation was possible. The most probable explanation of his crazy exploit is that he was a sort of Herostratus seeking immortality.

Bismarck was in Friedrichsruh when the attempt was made. The telegram with the news was handed to Tiedemann, his confidential assistant and secretary. Tiedemann went to meet the Chancellor, who was out walking in the woods surrounding Friedrichsruh. Here is Tiedemann's own account: "As I stepped out of the park, I saw the Chancellor walking slowly across the field in the bright sunshine, with his dogs at his heels. I went to meet him and joined him. He was in the best of tempers. After a little while I said: 'Some important telegrams have arrived'. He answered jokingly: 'Are they so urgent that we have to deal with them out here in the open country?' I replied: 'Unfortunately, they are. The Emperor has again been fired at and this time he has been hit. His Majesty is seriously wounded.' With a violent start the Prince stopped dead. Deeply agitated, he thrust his oaken stick into the ground in front of him and said, breathing heavily, as if a lightning flash of revelation had struck him: 'Now we will dissolve the Reichstag!' Only then did he enquire sympathetically after the Emperor's condition and ask for details of the attempt."

A dramatic scene of almost Shakespearean grandeur! It is, perhaps, not extravagant to recall the scene in the castle at Inverness when Lady Macbeth hears the "great news" of Duncan's arrival that night and almost in the same second resolves that he shall never depart alive. With the same uncanny speed Bismarck's resolution to use this new-found opportunity to break up the all too independent Reichstag followed hard on the news that a fresh attempt had been made on the Kaiser's life. For weeks his thoughts had revolved round this problem of the parliamentary Opposition and now there suddenly came this bolt from the blue. At once his enterprising mind had forged a link between the two and his resolution was formed and proclaimed. He himself once mentioned in a conversation about 'will' and 'thought': "I have often observed in myself that my will has decided even before my thinking is over". In the abstract one can only admire such an extraordinary strength of will and such speed of decision. But if one judges this incident from a political and moral point of view, admiration is hardly the feeling provoked. When he made this decision, what did Bismarck know about the origin of the attack, about the assailant, or his political connexions? Nothing! But despite this he had already resolved to exploit the incident in order to suppress the Social-Democratic Party, of which, for all he knew at that moment, Nobiling might have been a strong opponent. Is it not the moral and political duty of a statesman to examine the facts before taking such a far-reaching decision? Bismarck felt under no such obligation, for he was totally uninterested in the real facts of the case. All he cared about was how much political capital he could make of it in whipping up the feelings of the masses. Like all demagogues in all ages, he wanted to appeal to instinct and not to reason. He did not wish to reveal his true aim to the electorate. For the object of his manœuvre was really to break the power not so much of the Social Democrats, as of the National Liberals. This does not mean that he did not also desire the suppression of the Social Democrats, for he did. But—unlike the National Liberals—they were not a political millstone round his neck. These National Liberals, on the other hand, had voted against his bill to suppress the Socialists. Hence in the coming electoral struggle, which bade fair to be a heated contest, they could be held up as the men who had refused protection to the life and health of the dear old Kaiser. "Now I've got those fellows where I want them", said Bismarck to his intimates. "Your Highness means the Social Democrats?" somebody asked. "No, the National Liberals", was the Chancellor's reply. A popular rumour attributed to Bismarck the saying: "I shall squeeze the National Liberals against the wall until they squeal". In his *Reminiscences*, Bismarck denies using "a phrase so vulgar and in such bad taste". But, be that as it may, it sums up his feelings and intentions quite correctly.

Under the constitution the Reichstag could be dissolved only by a decision of the Federal Council with the assent of the Emperor. Neither the Prussian cabinet nor the Federal Council was unanimously in favour of dissolution. Here and there some members thought it unnecessary and dangerous: they were certain that the Reichstag would agree to a new anti-Socialist bill, as the National Liberal press was now taking this line. Nor did the Crown Prince, who now had to represent his father, favour dissolution. Bismarck had so arranged matters that the Crown Prince did not become

Regent, as he had expected to do, but was merely appointed by the Emperor to act as his deputy. The difference was that as Regent the Prince would have been entitled to conduct a policy of his own. As the Emperor's deputy he had to continue his father's policy, just as if the Emperor were in full health. Since William would certainly have dissolved the Reichstag on Bismarck's advice, the Crown Prince too had to give his consent. That Bismarck's energy overcame all other obstacles in his way goes without saying.

Thus the Reichstag was dissolved and Germany found herself amid the sound and fury of a general election. The government press did everything in its power to rouse the masses to anger against the National Liberals, who were accused of having denied protection to the Emperor's life by voting against the first anti-Socialist bill. Nobody could say, of course, how this bill, if it had been passed, could possibly have protected him against the shots fired by Dr. Nobiling. But that did not matter. Popular passion never likes cold logic.

But it is interesting to contrast with this feverish commotion the words which Bismarck uttered just at this time to the British Prime Minister, Lord Beaconsfield, who had come to Berlin to take part in the Congress there. Two days after the dissolution of the Reichstag, on 17th June, Bismarck, as President of the Congress, gave a state banquet to its members. Here is what Beaconsfield wrote to Queen Victoria about their conversation: "I sate on the right of Prince Bismarck and ... I could listen to his Rabelaisian monologues: endless revelations of things he ought not to mention. He impressed on me *never to trust Princes* or courtiers; that his illness was not, as people supposed, brought on by the French War, but by *the horrible conduct of his Sovereign,* etc. etc. In the archives of his family remain the documents, the royal letters, which accuse him after all his services of being a traitor. He went on in such a vein, that I was at last obliged to tell him that, instead of encountering 'duplicity' which he said was universal among Sovereigns, I served one, who was the soul of candour and justice, and whom all her ministers loved." The concluding words are, of course, an example of Disraeli's art of flattery. But Bismarck's remarks about his Emperor, who was still lying on his sick-bed, make strange reading beside the reports of his tirades in the open forum.

It is a symptom of the strength which the Liberal idea still possessed in Germany that the National Liberals lost only about 100,000 and the Progressives about 40,000 votes. But the loss of constituencies was larger: 30 National Liberals and 10 Progressives were deprived of their seats. The two parties could only muster about 140 deputies together, while the two Conservative Parties increased their numbers from 78 to 115 deputies; they had won almost 600,000 votes. The Social Democrats who, in the previous election, had polled half a million votes, lost no more than 60,000. The National Liberal Party still held a considerable number of seats, but most of the deputies had been returned only by promising the voters that this time they would support measures against the Socialists.

The government at once brought a fresh bill before the new Reichstag. It was called the "law against the dangerous activities of the Social Democrats" (*Gesetz gegen die gemeingefährlichen Bestrebungen der Sozialdemokratie*). This time Bismarck himself was a frequent and very energetic speaker in the debate. His speeches are to some extent of special interest to the biographer, because the attacks of the Social Democrat Bebel and the Progressive Richter compelled him to justify his earlier attitude towards the Socialists and especially his confidential interchanges with the late Lassalle. Bismarck spoke of Lassalle with the greatest respect and appreciation and paid a tribute to his conversation. "It was", he said, "so interesting, that he had always felt sorry when it stopped" (p. 116).

In the Reichstag the bill was opposed by the Social Democrats, the Centre Party, and the Progressives. The Conservative Parties backed it whole-heartedly. The National Liberal Party once more had the casting vote. The majority of its members were in favour of the bill. This time Lasker did not venture to oppose it. The current of feeling among the electorate was too strong. In any case, resistance would have been fruitless, for even without him there was an assured majority in favour of the bill. And so the best he could do was to try to tone down some of the clauses. In one important point he succeeded: he reduced the period for which the law was valid to two and a half years. The government wanted the law to be permanent, but had to give way on this point.

The consequence of this amendment by Lasker was that Bismarck had to apply to the Reichstag every second or third year for a renewal of the statute. On four occasions he got his way, but the opposition, particularly among the Liberals, was growing stronger. At last, in 1889, Bismarck tried to get a permanent law passed, but he failed. This failure was mainly due to his own queer tactics. But it had the most disastrous consequences for himself, as we shall see when the story of his downfall is told. In 1890 the *Sozialistengesetz* at last died, never to be resurrected.

The *Sozialistengesetz* had destroyed the whole Social-Democratic press and the whole Social-Democratic organization. No meetings could be held at which a Socialist wanted to speak. All the safeguards provided by the law (not that they amounted to much) were ruthlessly trampled on by the police. Socialist politicians and agitators were expelled from many cities in the most brutal way. And this inhuman persecution achieved precisely nothing. The law was quite unable to prevent an increase in the votes cast for the Social Democrats. In spite of the suppression of agitation by the spoken or written word, the votes given to Social Democrat candidates rose to 550,000 in 1884, to 763,000 in 1887, and to 1,427,000 in 1890. If we compare the aims of the law with what it did in fact achieve, it was a complete failure. Bismarck's policy of naked force miscarried as badly against the Socialists as against the Catholic clergy. The National Liberals, who supported him in this campaign, were the real losers in the end, for they had abandoned their principles, and for a political party that is the crowning sin. And in any case their sacrifice proved in vain. Only a year later they had ceased to be Bismarck's party and were to see the Chancellor turning to their bitterest rivals in order to hound them out of the position they occupied in parliament and on the political scene in general.

But before pursuing the story so far as this, we must pause to survey the state which the international situation had meanwhile reached as a result of the Eastern crisis.

8. *The Congress of Berlin, 1878*

The Eastern crisis began in the summer of 1875 with an insurrection against Turkish misrule in Bosnia. It was followed by risings in other parts of the Balkans (Bulgaria, for example) and by the outbreak of war between the Serbs and the Turks. The Balkans were ablaze from one end to the other. The European Powers most nearly concerned with these developments were Austria, Russia, and Britain. Russia looked on herself as the protectress of the Slav Christians, who belonged for the most part to the Orthodox Church, which was the Church of Russia. Austria was the next-door neighbour of insurgent Bosnia. Britain's interest was focused on Constantinople, which she was on no account prepared to allow to fall into Russian hands.

In Europe the Eastern crisis stirred up fears of a war among the Great Powers. Some attempts were made to end the bloodshed in the Balkans, such as the publication of the Berlin Memorandum of May 1875, drafted by Bismarck, Gortchakoff, and Andrassy and rejected by Disraeli, and the convening of the Constantinople Conference in December 1876, the recommendations of which were rejected by the Turks. In February 1877 Russia and Austria-Hungary concluded a secret pact by which they fixed their respective spheres of interest and reached an understanding to cover the contingency of a Russo-Turkish war which then seemed imminent. The pact forbade the Russians to set up a *grand état compact slave*, that is, a great independent Bulgarian state, and it permitted the Austrian Emperor to send troops to occupy Bosnia and Herzegovina. In April 1877 the Czar declared war on the Sultan. After some set-backs, the Russian troops had beaten down all Turkish resistance by the end of the year and stood almost at the gates of Constantinople. In March 1878 the Sultan concluded the Peace of San Stefano with the victorious Russians, and this treaty gave the victor almost everything he wanted. The most important provision was Turkey's cession of all Bulgarian territory. The *grand état compact slave* was about to be set up. This aroused the most strenuous opposition from Austria-Hungary and Britain. The British Prime Minister, Beaconsfield, who was all for a "spirited foreign policy", took the lead against the Russians and sent the British fleet to the Sea of Marmora. A clash between the two Great Powers seemed imminent. In this situation a European congress for the settlement of the whole Eastern question was proposed by Andrassy, the Foreign Minister of the Habsburg Monarchy. As the frontiers of the Turkish Empire had been drawn in 1856 by a European treaty, the Treaty of Paris, they could only be altered by the common consent of the signatory Powers. Gortchakoff was ready to lay the Treaty of San Stefano before a European congress. The Great Powers agreed to call this congress in Berlin. It was more or less a matter of course that the German Chancellor became President of this congress in the German capital. It opened on 13th June and was wound up by Bismarck on 13th July 1878.

After this brief sketch of the events leading up to the Congress of Berlin, we now have to consider the policy Bismarck followed during these years of crisis. We cannot, of course, follow in any great detail the complicated and intricate paths of his diplomacy. It will suffice if we get some idea of the principles by which he was guided.

A convenient starting-point is a passage in the diary of the German Ambassador in St. Petersburg, General von Schweinitz. In the 'sixties Schweinitz had been in St. Petersburg as Prussian military representative, in which capacity he was the personal representative of the King with the latter's Russian nephew, Czar Alexander II. In consequence, he knew the Czar intimately. After serving as Ambassador in Vienna at the time of the Franco-German war, he was again posted to St. Petersburg in February 1876, this time as Ambassador of the German Empire. He occupied this post until 1892, that is until after the downfall of Bismarck. His *Denkwürdigkeiten*, published long after his death and supplemented by a volume of correspondence, are full of the most interesting details and give a good picture of their author. Schweinitz was a typical conservative Prussian general, but his conservatism was genuine and consistent. He believed in the need for guiding principles in politics and refused to believe that expediency and force should alone govern policy. In his diary Schweinitz deplores the fact that the German government did not look on the Turkish disorders from the point of view of *humanity* "but wants to turn them to *political advantage* and bring about a constellation of the great powers, by which coalitions hostile to us shall be made impossible for a long time to come".

What Schweinitz was driving at was obviously that Turkish rule over a Christian community in Europe was an anachronism which gave rise to insurrection and bloodshed and should therefore be ended; this state of affairs was the concern of all Europe, because it must affect the conscience of everyone who was a European and a Christian. This is a point of view which transcends purely national considerations and is fully in keeping with the universalist character of the old conservative outlook. It is therefore not surprising that it bears a certain similarity to the liberal view which was at this time proclaimed by Gladstone in his unforgettable pamphlet on the Bulgarian atrocities and in his powerful and moving speeches on the subject. But Schweinitz gave the Russian government credit for also wishing to act from these motives when it asked Europe for a free hand in bringing order into Balkan affairs.

Bismarck's view of the matter was poles apart from that of Schweinitz. This is clearly shown by a marginal note made by the Chancellor on a dispatch from St. Petersburg in which Gortchakoff had said: "The problem is neither German nor Russian, but European". And Bismarck writes: "*Qui parle Europe a tort, notion géographique*". This description of Europe re-echoes the words of Metternich, who, two generations earlier, had called Italy a geographical conception in order to refute the national aspirations of the Italian people. Bismarck writes: "I have always found the word 'Europe' on the lips of those statesmen who want something from a foreign power which they would never venture to ask for in their own name". In the same way, back in those days when Prussia had bounded his political horizon, any statesman who had dared to ask something in the name of Germany was at once suspected by him of hypocrisy. Bismarck's views on the Balkan situation were shared by Beaconsfield, who considered it more important for Britain to split the League of the Three Emperors than to help the victims of Turkish misrule. This identity of outlook on the part of the leading statesmen in Germany and Britain decisively settled the manner in which the Eastern crisis was dealt with.

Germany could not look for any advantage from this crisis. She was not directly interested in Balkan affairs. Bismarck emphasized this time and again and summed it up in a speech to the Reichstag on 5th December 1876 in a particularly memorable phrase: there was at stake, he said, *no German interest worth the bones of a Pomeranian musketeer*. Bismarck's task, as he saw it, lay merely in seeing to it that Germany's international position was not affected for the worse. His main concern was to avoid having to choose between Russia and Austria as an ally. If a war broke out between these powerful neighbours of Germany, she would be compelled to make this choice.

Bismarck was faced with this problem in October 1876 when the Czar told General von Manteuffel that he hoped that, in the event of a war with Austria, the Emperor William would act as he himself had acted in 1870—in other words, would assist him. This was a very awkward question and it seems that Manteuffel's own interpretation of some of William's utterances had something to do with it. Bismarck's answer was that it would be a serious threat to Germany's interests, "if the position of the Austrian Monarchy in Europe or its independence were so threatened that one of the factors which ensured the balance of power should henceforth be eliminated". This was, no doubt, the right decision from the German point of view, but it was none the less a great disappointment to the Russians who looked on Germany as a debtor who, although well able to pay, was unwilling to help her creditor out of an embarrassment.

On the other hand, Bismarck was suspected by foreign statesmen of fomenting war between other countries. Salisbury compared him to Sir Lucius O'Trigger in Sheridan's comedy *The Rivals*, who does his best to bring about a duel between two men who are by no means anxious to fight. It made a very bad impression on the British government when Bismarck told the British Ambassador, Odo Russell, that he intended to take some military measures which would excite national feeling in France, and asked the Ambassador what Britain's attitude would be in such a case. Lord Derby, the Foreign Secretary, considered it characteristic of Bismarck's Machiavellian schemes that the Chancellor should advise Britain to annex Egypt, obviously with the idea that this would bring Britain into conflict with France.

But Bismarck's attitude towards France changed when Marshal MacMahon was defeated at the election of October 1877 by a sweeping victory of the Republicans led by Gambetta. The new Republican government hastened to improve relations with Bismarck by withdrawing the Ambassador Gontaut-Biron, whom Bismarck detested. The new Ambassador, Count de St.-Vallier, was instructed to work towards the establishment of peaceful relations, and since he was looked upon favourably by the Chancellor, he did, in fact, succeed in winning his confidence and initiating an era of *rapprochement* and conciliation.

After the Peace of San Stefano the general feeling in Europe was that only a European congress could preserve the peace. Bismarck was compelled to explain his position in the Reichstag by answering a question put to him by Bennigsen in February 1878. In his speech Bismarck coined one of his most famous phrases when he described the part Germany wanted to play at this congress as that of the "honest broker" and not that of the arbitrator who imposes his decision upon the other parties.

The preliminaries to the congress were thrashed out in secret talks between Britain and Russia, Bismarck being kept fully informed of developments. The negotiators were Lord Salisbury, who had succeeded Lord Derby as Foreign Secretary in March 1878, and the Russian Ambassador in London, Count Shouwaloff. In the protocol signed by Salisbury and Shouwaloff, Russia undertook not to set up a "Greater" Bulgaria but agreed to her partition. In this way the most thorny problem which would face the congress was largely solved before it met. The protocol was, of course, absolutely secret. But an underpaid Foreign Office clerk sold a copy to the London *Globe*, which published it just about the time that the congress opened. In another secret agreement Britain consented to Austria occupying Bosnia, and in yet another Turkey was compelled to cede Cyprus to Britain.

Beaconsfield, Salisbury, Gortchakoff, Shouwaloff, Andrassy—they all came to Berlin to deliberate under the presidency of Bismarck. The German Chancellor was certainly a most energetic President, whose authority was fully acknowledged by every statesman of every country. Each question was brought before the congress in turn and, if any controversy arose, was referred by the President to the Powers directly concerned for private negotiation. Thus it came about that the Bulgarian problem was to be settled by Anglo-Russian conversations in which Andrassy joined. At first there were some very sharp differences of opinion, particularly over the question of the frontier and the Sultan's right to fortify it. On 20th and 21st June the negotiations reached a deadlock. At this juncture Bismarck did his best to bring about an agreement by holding private conversations with Beaconsfield and Shouwaloff. To say that the settlement which followed was his work is an exaggeration, but he certainly helped a great deal. During the night of 21st June the special correspondent of *The Times*, Blowitz, was able to telegraph to his paper from Berlin that agreement had been reached. Bulgaria was split in two, the northern part becoming an autonomous principality under Turkish suzerainty, and the southern, for which the meaningless name of "Eastern Rumelia" was invented, a Turkish province with a certain degree of autonomy and a Christian governor. Beaconsfield and Salisbury considered this a great success, so much so, in fact, that on his return to England Beaconsfield felt entitled to claim that he had brought "peace with honour". But only seven years later, in 1885, the Bulgarian people put an end to this partition and reunited both parts into a single Bulgarian principality. Salisbury, who was by then Prime Minister, welcomed this act of unification against which he had worked so hard in Berlin, while the Russian government, which had championed it in Berlin, was now extremely angry about it. So much for the foresight of statesmen.

Once this stumbling-block was removed, all the other outstanding questions were very speedily resolved. Austria-Hungary was granted the right to occupy Bosnia and Herzegovina and the protest of the Turkish delegates was overridden by Bismarck in his most blunt and bullying manner. Many of Russia's Asiatic aspirations, especially the acquisition of Batum on the shores of the Black Sea, were realized. As to the Dardanelles and the Bosphorous, the provisions of the Paris Treaty were kept in force, Turkey remaining in control of them. But the agreement on this point was more ostensible than real. True, Russia and Britain agreed that the Sultan was entitled to open or to close the straits. But Salisbury declared that Britain would respect any decision taken independently by the Sultan, while Shouwaloff declared that basically any such decision must be a European one, affecting and binding on all Powers. The difference is that Britain reserved the right not to respect the Sultan's decision if it was made *under Russian pressure*. Which interpretation was accepted by the congress? The matter was passed over without comment. The question was left unanswered.

This is typical of many other questions raised at the congress. They were decided only in principle, and a number of details were left to be worked out later. But there was no time for this, nor had Bismarck the necessary patience. Besides, his health was not at its best and he was impatient to get away to Kissingen and take the waters in mid-July: so he hastened to wind up the congress. The consequence was that the courts of Europe were busy with the working out of the treaties for years after. When Gladstone returned to power in 1880, he found some of the questions still unsolved and began to tackle them in his own way, which was not at all appreciated by Bismarck.

When Bismarck closed the congress, he said in a short speech that it had "within the limits of what was possible, done Europe the service of keeping and maintaining the peace".

Can history uphold this claim? True, peace among the Great Powers was preserved, but real friendship and harmony were impossible while so many problems of the practical application of the treaty kept the chanceries of Europe a-buzz with discussions. A particularly critical controversy between Berlin and St. Petersburg, of which more will be said later, was caused by differences over the interpretation and execution of the Berlin Treaty. It is even less true to claim that the congress brought peace to the Balkans. The occupation of Bosnia and Herzegovina by the troops of the Habsburg Monarchy was a very bloody and costly business. And other peoples of the Near East struggled for years to cast off the shackles of the Berlin Treaty. This brings us to its cardinal fault. A French diplomatist, who as a young man worked on the secretariat of the congress, wrote in his memoirs: "The congress assigned or refused territory to the Serbs or the Turks without any regard to the wishes or objections of either side, which were treated with lofty indifference". It is fair to say that the congress treated the Balkan peoples like mere pawns on a chessboard. In this Bismarck was no better than the rest. He declared repeatedly that he did not care a rap for *le bonheur de ces gens là-bas*, that he was utterly indifferent to their fate, and considered as worth attention only those points which were essential for agreement between the Great Powers. He lacked the vision to see that the nationalist movement, which had already started in Italy and Germany, would also develop its full power among the Slav peoples of Eastern Europe. In this he was no more short-sighted than most of the statesmen of his day, particularly Beaconsfield, but neither was he any more foresighted. Gladstone, when he spoke of "peoples rightly struggling to be free", showed a far greater breadth of vision than Bismarck.

But there is an utterance by Bismarck which puts an even more sinister interpretation on his policy towards the peoples of the Balkans. In November 1878, four months after the congress, Bismarck wrote to the Crown Prince, then deputizing for his father: "It would be a triumph for our statesmanship if we succeeded in *keeping the Eastern ulcer open* and thus jarred the harmony of the other Great Powers in order to secure our own peace". A policy dictated by this Machiavellian maxim was, indeed, unfitted to bring lasting peace either to the Balkans or to Europe.

One of the Balkan manipulations of this period contained the seeds which later burst out so calamitously into the first World War: the occupation of Bosnia by Austria. But with this Bismarck had less to do than Russia and Britain, who made this concession to Andrassy before the congress began, but Bismarck was in full agreement with this policy; indeed, he advised Andrassy to carry out the occupation *before* the congress assembled and he scoffed at Austrian clumsiness when Andrassy declined this advice. "I have heard of people refusing to eat their pigeon unless it was shot and roasted for them," he said, "but I have never heard of anyone refusing to eat it unless his jaws were forced open and it was pushed down his throat." To this extent he shares the responsibility for this fateful step, which in the end not only destroyed the peace of Europe, but frustrated his own policy of Austro-Russian conciliation under German auspices. The French Ambassador, St.-Vallier, not a critic but an admirer of Bismarck's statesmanship, wrote in December 1881 to Gambetta, the French Minister-President and Foreign Minister at the time: "*Bismarck tient à conserver la situation d'arbitre suprême des destinées des trois Empires, et il sait que leur alliance demeure toujours exposée à un danger, celui d'une collision d'intérêts entre l'Autriche et la Russie dans la péninsule du Balkan; cette* collision *est* inévitable *dans l'avenir, et c'est* le prince lui-même qui l'a rendue telle *en poussant le Cabinet de Vienne en Bosnie et vers la Salonique*". True, Bismarck succeeded in postponing this collision, but only up to the time of his successors. That these successors should be lesser men than the great Bismarck was equally inevitable.

The occupation of Bosnia led to the overthrow of the German Liberals in Austria. Nor did they oppose the occupation only on nationalist grounds, because they feared an increase of the Slav population. One of their spokesmen, a former Minister-President, said that the occupation would be the first step towards an Eastern policy of competition with Russia. Henceforth, he went on, *Austria's honour* would be concerned while she *lacked the power to maintain it*. This prophecy was absolutely accurate. It was the Emperor Francis Joseph, who, lured from his course by the siren song of the prestige of his Empire, overestimated and overtaxed the strength of his country.

But Bismarck turned the edge of this criticism not against Francis Joseph but against the Austrian German Liberals, whom he derided in a speech in the Reichstag. He reproached them for having compelled the Emperor to seek the assistance of other parties and national elements in the interests of his dynasty. We now know that in fact Francis Joseph brought about the collapse of his dynasty by banishing his faithful German subjects to the wilderness for having opposed the occupation of Bosnia.

9. *The Change-over to Protection, and the Rift in the National Liberal Party*

The Congress of Berlin once over, Bismarck went to Kissingen to take the waters. Here he met a Papal nuncio with whom he had several conversations with a view to reaching an understanding with the Vatican about ending the *Kulturkampf*. But these negotiations came to nothing. The Vatican asked for more concessions than Bismarck was yet prepared to make. And so Falk continued in office, although he was fully alive to the uncertainty of his position. The National Liberals could not help feeling that a political change was brewing.

The air was cleared considerably in December 1878 by the publication of a letter from the Chancellor to the Federal Council in which he set forth his programme of economic and tariff reform.

He energetically inveighed against direct taxation and asked for an increase in indirect taxation by the introduction of a protectionist tariff. He not only proposed protection for certain industries which appeared to be in need of it, but a *general tariff* embracing all imports. This was a complete reversal of the trade policy which had hitherto been followed by the Zollverein and the German Reich. It had never been a policy of complete free trade, comparable with that introduced into Britain by Peel and Gladstone. But the tendency had for some decades been to diminish the number and size of protectionist duties and to put as few obstacles as possible in the way of the exchange of goods and products with the other countries of the world. Now, however, the Chancellor was officially stating that his policy aimed at precisely the reverse.

But the most startling innovation was his proposal to levy protectionist duties not only on industrial imports, but on corn and other agricultural produce. Until then nobody had thought that protection for agriculture was possible or even desirable. The majority of the farmers and landowners themselves had not asked for it. The urban population was, of course, much opposed to duties the effect of which was supposed to be higher prices and a dearer cost of living. But Bismarck grew all the more enthusiastic. He had set up a committee to work out the new tariff. This committee consisted for the most part of protectionists, and its chairman was the arch-protectionist von Varnbüler, the former anti-Prussian Minister of Wurtemberg. They proposed a duty of half a mark (sixpence) on a hundredweight of corn. Shortly afterwards a letter from Bismarck to one of the leaders of the protectionist agrarians was published, in which he not only called this duty inadequate, but *encouraged the agrarians to bestir themselves, band together and agitate* for a higher duty on corn and to press for it by motions in the Reichstag.

A protectionist tariff bill was laid before the Reichstag and Bismarck himself emerged during the debate as the foremost champion of protection. A long parliamentary struggle began. For the protectionist tariff were the two Conservative Parties and the Centre Party, and against it the Progressives—very efficiently led by Eugen Richter, and the Socialists. The National Liberal Party was split. The deputies of the western industrial constituencies were strongly in favour of industrial protection. The Left wing, led by Lasker and Bamberger, fought vigorously against it. Delbrück, who had accepted a seat in the Reichstag, joined the opponents of the movement and defended the tariff policy hitherto followed; but as a parliamentary speaker he was much less effective than he had been as Minister. The majority of the National Liberals, led by Bennigsen and Miquel, were in favour of moderate protection, but hoped to find a middle course on which a compromise with the Chancellor would be possible.

But Bennigsen was not the only party leader who wished to reach a compromise with Bismarck. There was Windthorst, quite ready to barter a protectionist tariff for governmental concessions to the Catholic Church. Windthorst's position was all the stronger as the great majority of his party was protectionist, while Bennigsen had to contend in his own party with the opposition of the free-trade minority. Moreover, there was a material difficulty facing Bennigsen. Willing as he was to support higher duties and indirect taxation, he could not but insist on so-called "constitutional guarantees". Hitherto the Reichstag had been able to influence the budget, because it had to vote the *Matrikular-Beiträge*, the sums to be contributed by the single states and without which the budget could not be balanced. In future, the new duties and the higher rates levied on tobacco, beer, and alcohol would fill the coffers of the Reich so full that it would not need any *Matrikular-Beiträge*. At the same time Prussia's coffers, too, would be overflowing, since the existing taxes would continue to be collected while nothing had to be paid to the Reich. Thus the government would become financially independent of the Reichstag as well as of the Prussian Landtag—in other words, Bismarck would have been in a position to rule without any regard to a parliament, which no longer held the purse-strings. Such a situation could not be tolerated by a Liberal leader, however moderate his Liberalism might be. Bennigsen therefore asked for constitutional guarantees by which the fiscal powers of parliament would be restored and adapted to the new financial situation. Such a guarantee could, for example, be provided by the so-called "quotization" of certain taxes, that is by voting them annually in the Reichstag, according to the actual financial situation of the year in question, as is done in Britain by the House of Commons.

Bismarck was most unwilling to agree to such constitutional

guarantees. He preferred to conclude a bargain with the Centre, which proposed a guarantee which was more apparent than real. Under this scheme only a certain proportion of the millions raised by the duties would remain in the Reich treasury and the surplus would be transferred to the treasuries of the individual states. Thus an artificial deficit in the budget would be created, which was to be met by the voting of *Matrikular-Beiträge* from the various states. In that manner the Reichstag would, it is true, have to continue to vote the *Matrikular-Beiträge*. But this would become a mere *empty formality*. Would Bismarck hesitate to spend the money raised by the taxes for military purposes, if a Reichstag should be bold enough to reject the *Matrikular-Beiträge*? Nobody doubted that he would act just as he had done during the constitutional conflict in Prussia and on the maxims he had then delivered to the Chamber of Deputies: "We shall take the money where we find it", and, "If we consider war necessary, we shall wage it with or without your consent" (p. 86).

Bismarck did, in fact, accept the proposal made by the Centre Party. Bennigsen, who had continued to negotiate with the Chancellor, was suddenly surprised by the news that Bismarck and Windthorst were at one. What only a year ago had seemed an impossibility was now a fact. The Iron Chancellor had grasped the hand of the party which a few years before he had called "a battery against the state" and "enemies of the Reich", and had joined forces with Windthorst, whom he had once attacked with the bitterest personal acrimony—and all this in order to outmanœuvre Bennigsen whom he had called his friend and to whom he had offered a post in his cabinet only eighteen months before.

This tactical *volte-face* eased Bennigsen's situation to the extent that the overwhelming majority of the party now voted with him against the new tariff. Only about a dozen of the National Liberal deputies put protection before constitution and voted with the Conservatives and the Centre for the government's bill. They broke with the party as a consequence of the vote. But the splitting of the party into protectionists and free traders was avoided—for the moment.

Of course, Bismarck was not the man to suffer in silence a party which was so bold to offer him opposition. During the first reading of the tariff bill he had concentrated his attack on Lasker, because he still hoped to separate the Left wing from the party, which would then follow him unconditionally. Bismarck's speech against Lasker is as vehement as were his most impassioned orations against the Centre and Windthorst at the height of the *Kulturkampf* and it was full of personal abuse. One can almost feel how happy he was to be able to attack this little man whose conscience was not elastic enough to let him fit into a party which supported the government unconditionally. All the help which Lasker had on earlier occasions given him was completely forgotten. Lasker was not even an out-and-out free trader like his friend Bamberger, but he was a strong opponent of the corn duty, which he considered anti-social and a tax on the bread of the common man. The objections which Bismarck hurled at Lasker are more characteristic of Bismarck than of the National Liberal parliamentarian. He reproached Lasker with conducting the financial policy of the *Besitzlose* (the have-nots). He called him one of the men of whom the Scriptures say "they neither sow nor reap" and "they toil not, neither do they spin", and he scoffed at "the gentlemen whom our sun does not warm and our rain does not moisten—unless they have forgotten their umbrellas when they go for a walk". What an impressive invective, but what an absurd doctrine! It means, in essence, that in debate on the economic policy of a great state nobody has a right to be heard who is not directly interested in its outcome. Bismarck himself had such an interest. He owned vast acres of land and forests. From these forests he sold a good deal of timber, the price of which was increased by the new duties on imported timber. He did not hesitate to attend the tariff committee when the timber duty was on the agenda, and he made a speech urging a high rate of duty. If anybody had criticized him for influencing legislation in his personal interest, he would have dismissed it as "doctrinairism". On the contrary, he would have said: "Because I am an owner of large forests, I know the economic difficulties facing the producers of timber, and therefore I am all the more entitled to speak for them". There was a certain degree of *naïveté* in this view, the same *naïveté* which allowed the Junkers to put their own personal interest before that of every other class. To have *no* personal interest was, in Bismarck's eyes, not a qualification for viewing the whole question impartially, but a distinct handicap in understanding and reaching any conclusion at all. But, strangely enough, this line of argument did not make those without economic self-interest irritable towards him. On the contrary, it was among such men—particularly students and members of academic circles—that Bismarck found his most ardent admirers.

The National Liberal Party left it to Lasker to defend himself against Bismarck's vituperation. But when Bennigsen, on the second reading of the tariff bill, proclaimed in the name of his whole party their opposition to the measure, Bismarck rounded on the party which hitherto had been his mainstay almost as angrily as he had done on Lasker. In a reference to demonstrations by a congress of great municipalities, where Forckenbeck had called for resistance to the coming reaction, Bismarck accused them of undermining the Reich in the same way as the Social Democrats did, and he talked of *destructive forces*. He confessed quite openly that his goal had been the exclusion of the "disparate" elements—that is the Left wing—from the National Liberal Party. After failing in this, he had lost confidence in the party. His own idea of the relation of parties to the government he expressed by comparing the three parties, which had hitherto supported the government, to three battalions differing only in some small details of uniform. This did, indeed, reflect his conception accurately: the government (that is Bismarck himself) was the commanding officer and the parties were troops under his command who had to obey orders. Whoever refused to do this was insubordinate and disloyal.

The situation created by Bismarck's attack on his former friends was summed up quite correctly by Windthorst, who declared triumphantly that the Liberal era had gone bankrupt and that he and his party now emerged as the best friends of the Reich and the individual states. It was, indeed, a complete political reversal.

Of course, Falk now had to go and two other Ministers went with him. Falk's successor was von Puttkamer, a representative of extreme cultural and political reaction, the very prototype of Prussian Junkerdom.

Opinions about Bismarck's tariff policy will, of course, always vary according to the economic views of the critic on the perennial question: free trade or protection? But disregarding that, we may say that the apprehension voiced at that time by the free traders was not justified in the event. Nobody doubts the enormous economic progress of Germany after 1879. How far this progress was due to protection is quite another matter. It can be said that through this protectionist policy agriculture in Germany was shielded from the competition of cheap corn from America and Russia, and was thus safeguarded in a higher degree than in free-trade Britain. But something more must be said to complete the picture.

If Bismarck and his Conservative friends hoped by this protectionist policy to conserve the predominantly agricultural character of Germany, they were completely disappointed by what actually followed. Germany became more and more industrialized with all the consequences that industrialization usually brings in its train, not the least of which are an increase of the industrial proletariat and a growth of the Labour movement. As matters stood in Germany, this movement was bound to be a Socialist one. The effect of the law against the Socialists, carried through by Bismarck in 1878, was counteracted by the effects of protection introduced in 1879.

This was all the more marked as the whole tariff was based on the corn duty. Only the *political alliance of the agrarians with the industrialists* made the victory of protectionism possible. The corn duty was considered by the working man as a taxation of his daily bread. It sharpened his antagonism to the state which at the same time destroyed his organizations.

The agricultural duties had yet another and hardly less important political consequence. The class which profited most by them was that of the great landowners. It was always a matter of controversy whether the middle-class peasants and farmers gained by them or not. But it could never be doubted that the greater part of the profits went into the pockets of the great landowners who were the principal producers of corn. Moreover, the taxation of alcohol, that is, the spirit distilled from potatoes, was organized in a way particularly profitable to the great landowners. Now these landowners who lived in Eastern Germany, or, as they were called, the *Ostelbier*, because they lived east of the Elbe, were the Prussian Junkers. Agrarian protectionism and agrarian taxation were the economic salvation of these Junkers. Without these measures many of them would have been compelled to parcel out their lands, and peasants would have been found where, in the new economic era, a great landowner's family and his hired labourers still lived. In this way protectionism conserved not only the economic existence but also the political ascendancy of the Junker class. Between them and the rising Social Democracy middle-class Liberalism was crushed. If the political structure of Germany at the beginning of the 20th century differed widely from the structure of Western Europe, protectionism, and particularly agrarian protectionism, had much to do with it.

What is more, German protectionism furthered and strengthened German nationalism. Its slogan was "protection of national labour", and free trade was combated as showing a lack of national feeling and stigmatized as international, indeed, as an English invention for the exploitation of Europe. Although, as a rule, the German free traders were not pacifists like such great English free traders as Cobden and John Bright, they none the less hoped that the free exchange of goods among the nations would lead to better mutual understanding and, in consequence, more peaceable sentiments. It is no mere chance that the nationalist and anti-Semitic movements in the German universities began after the victory of protectionism and Bismarck's break with Liberalism. Treitschke, the herald of this movement, had spoken in the Reichstag against the corn duty, but, nevertheless, voted for the whole protectionist tariff, including this very duty. He broke away from the National Liberal Party when it voted against the tariff, and in defence of Bismarck's arrangement with the Centre Party he compared the Chancellor's position to that of William III of England, who had said: "Now, while I live, they blaspheme me. But when I am dead, they will try to dig me out of the grave with their finger-nails."

Bismarck had set out on his protectionist campaign with the aim of making the Reich financially independent of the individual states by abolishing the *Matrikular-Beiträge*. This aim was not realized. On the contrary, by accepting Windthorst's conditions, he had strengthened the friends of particularism and checked the friends of Germany unity. Lasker said quite rightly that the arguments with which Bismarck justified his arrangement with the Centre Party were utterly at variance with those he had previously used.

But the most important consequence of Bismarck's swing to protectionism was the complete displacement of a policy of principle by one of *material advantage*. Parties built up on common political ideals were bound to be split by the despotism of interests. Worse still, following a political ideal was dubbed "doctrinairism", while the use of politics to further material interests was praised as *Realpolitik*. Bismarck himself had given the signal to the forces of material interest by his appeal to the agrarians to bestir themselves and band together so as to ask for more, by the general tariff which was an incitement to every group of interests to work for a higher duty for the protection of its own special commodity, and above all by his diatribe against Lasker and the men who neither sow nor reap.

The first victim to drown in this new current was the National Liberal Party. During the tariff debates Bennigsen had emphasized that free trade was not necessarily a part of the Liberal programme. In this he was right. In several countries Liberal Parties exist which are strongly protectionist. The theoretical apostle of the protectionist doctrine in Germany, Friedrich List, author of the famous *System of National Economy*, was politically a Liberal. But Bennigsen was wrong when he believed that for this reason free traders and protectionists could remain inside the same political party. At a time when tariff policy is in the centre of the political arena, a party cannot in the long run contain one wing voting against everything that the other wing professes and demands. The great stumbling-block was the corn duty. The question whether the daily bread of the common man should be taxed in favour of the grower of the corn is and always will be a question of the utmost political importance. Men such as Lasker, who was not an out-and-out free trader, none the less found it impossible to remain in a party which voted for the corn duties.

Nor were economic questions the only ones which split the National Liberal Party. Many members felt very strongly about the concessions to the Catholic Church which Bismarck wanted to put through and to which the Right wing of the party in the Prussian Chamber of Deputies consented, albeit very reluctantly. But perhaps the most important issue was the dilemma in which Bismarck himself placed the party. His latest departure made manifest the immense gulf which separated his views from every kind of liberal idea. The very basis of existence of a party which wished to combine adherence to Bismarck with liberal principles was by this departure, in fact, destroyed.

The split came in the summer of 1880. Some of the most prominent parliamentarians, such as Forckenbeck, Bamberger, Stauffenberg, and Lasker, announced their decision to leave the party. They formed a parliamentary group which was popularly called the "secession". The motives for this step were explained to the public by Bamberger in a pamphlet entitled *Die Sezession*. This is one of the few German political pamphlets which are still worth reading years after. One of its most interested readers was Bismarck. We know that his gigantic pencil filled the margin of the pamphlet with critical and angry remarks, some of which are highly characteristic of the man.

He had now reached his goal and driven the Left wing out of the National Liberal Party. But a great disappointment awaited him when the general election to the Reichstag came in 1881. The secessionists got the same number of seats as the National Liberals— about fifty—and the Progressive Party, which in his speeches Bismarck had condemned out of hand as the root of all evil, secured nearly sixty. The National Liberal Party had sunk from the level of a great party and was not even able to form a majority with the two Conservative Parties. The three battalions of which Bismarck had spoken in the tariff debate and which were to form the parliamentary army commanded by himself had dwindled to a minority of only one-third of the House.

The change in the situation of the National Liberal Party was brought out very clearly when Bennigsen, its leader, resigned his seats in the Reichstag and the Prussian Landtag in June 1883. His retirement was the result of a twofold disappointment—in the German people and in Bismarck. At last he had discovered that for a man who wanted to preserve even a small measure of independence, collaboration with Bismarck was, in the long run, impossible.

10. *The Alliance with the Habsburg Monarchy*

The Congress of Berlin had not been advantageous to Russo-German relations. The Russians felt that they had been robbed by the congress of the fruits of their victory over the Turks, and as Bismarck had been its president they held him responsible. Moreover, Gortchakoff had not been treated at all well in Berlin. Bismarck had openly favoured the second Russian delegate, Count Peter Shouwaloff, whom he hoped to see as successor to the elderly Gortchakoff. The latter therefore did his best to set Czar Alexander II against his rival, who was recalled from London a year later and had to go into retirement. Many Russians believed that Shouwaloff had been duped by Bismarck, the more so as he continued to assert that at the congress Bismarck had done his best to help Russia. In this Shouwaloff was undoubtedly right. Not Bismarck but the whole international situation was responsible for the meagre legacy which the congress left to Russia.

But the real reason for the disappointment of the Russians, and particularly of the Czar, was that since the war of 1870 they had looked to Germany in vain for help in time of trouble. Alexander felt that he had rendered his uncle William immense services during the war and he had banked on the gratitude which William had proclaimed so fulsomely and so loudly. These hopes had been disappointed and the consequent bad feeling in St. Petersburg was hardly to be wondered at.

This bad feeling increased when it became known that Bismarck had concluded a treaty with Andrassy by which Francis Joseph of Austria agreed to the annulment of Article V of the Treaty of Prague of 1866. This article had given the inhabitants of Northern Sleswig the right to decide by a free vote whether they would come under Prussia or Denmark. Although twelve years had passed since the signing of the treaty, this particular provision had never been implemented and it was now completely deleted by this new Austro-German treaty. The Russians considered this latest agreement as a recompense for the help which Bismarck had given Austria during the congress, and one Russian paper hit off the country's views in the sarcastic remark: "The honest broker acted for a big commission".

The Czar himself was still more provoked by the attitude of the German delegates to the international committees charged with carrying many clauses of the Treaty of Berlin into effect. He noted that, as a rule, the German delegates never voted with the Russians and he assumed that this attitude was dictated by Bismarck. Besides this, Bismarck seized on the outbreak of an epidemic in Russia as a pretext for taking measures against Russian imports into Germany, a step which the Russian government considered provocative and aggressive.

The Czar voiced his feelings to the German Ambassador, General von Schweinitz, a sincere adherent of friendship between the two Empires. He reproached Germany for always siding with Austria and he asked Schweinitz to alter this if he wished to preserve the friendship which had united their two countries for a century. He mentioned the language which the press was using and said: "*Cela finira d'une manière sérieuse*". Although Schweinitz tried to take some of the sting from these words by reporting that the Czar spoke them in a mild and far from menacing tone, Bismarck took them as a threat, which was to be answered by a reorientation of German policy towards Russia.

But worse was to follow. The Czar was so aggrieved by the attitude of the German delegates that he wrote a personal letter to the German Emperor on 15th August 1879 in which he set out his complaints. He was imprudent enough to refer to Bismarck's personal hostility towards Gortchakoff and to its influence on his political attitude. Such an allusion, of course, made Bismarck furious. Moreover, the Czar wrote about "*les craintes qui me préoccupent et dont les conséquences pourraient devenir désastreuses pour nos deux pays*".

Bismarck at once seized on this phrase and wrote to the Emperor from Gastein, where he received the Czar's letter, that such words would be construed as a forerunner of a declaration of war, should this letter become known to the public. He put the most sinister possible interpretation on the letter and represented it as a machination on the part of the Russian Minister of War, a Germanophobe. He warned William against any compliance with Russian wishes, and urged, on the contrary, more intimate connexions with both Russia's rivals, Austria-Hungary and Britain. But he did more than indicate this policy; he announced to his Emperor that he was expecting Andrassy to visit him in Gastein and that he himself would make his return journey via Vienna. The Emperor, who correctly guessed Bismarck's intention of negotiating a treaty of alliance with Andrassy, was utterly perplexed and wrote in the margin of Bismarck's letter: "*Under no circumstances*, because Russia would interpret this as a rupture".

William was decidedly against the new course his Chancellor was taking. Friendship with Russia was for him a sacred bequest from his parents and dated from the days of the war of liberation against Napoleon. He looked on his nephew, the Czar, as his best friend, and a break with him was unthinkable. For the first time since 1862 he tried to free himself from Bismarck's domination. In his own way he set about clearing up the misunderstanding and sent to the Czar Field-Marshal von Manteuffel, who had once before acted as his messenger of peace. Alexander invited William to meet him at Alexandrovo, the nearest station to the German frontier, and William accepted this invitation in spite of a telegram of protest from Bismarck.

Both Emperors did their best at Alexandrowo to renew their old friendship, and Alexander went so far as to express his deep regret for his letter and to assume full responsibility for it. William came back quite happy, believing that all would now be well. But the Czar's letter was not, as William had imagined, the real reason for Bismarck's new departure, but only the pretext on which he had hoped to win William's support. Even before the letter was written, Bismarck's mind had been made up, as one or two things he let fall to the French Ambassador and Schweinitz show. He now proceeded on his way as if the meeting at Alexandrovo had never taken place. He did not even take the trouble of seeing the Emperor personally and talking things over with him. On the contrary, he purposely avoided all personal contact and simply confronted the old man with *faits accomplis* in which he had perforce to acquiesce subsequently. Bismarck had talks with Andrassy at Gastein and went to Vienna to complete the negotiations.

Bismarck's proposal to Andrassy was a treaty of alliance between the German Empire and the Habsburg Monarchy, to be laid before the parliaments of both Empires and to be terminated only with their consent. By the terms of the Alliance, each ally was to be bound to assist the other against any third Power which might attack either of them. Andrassy was quite ready to conclude an alliance, but he refused to lay it before parliament, because he was afraid of the opposition of the non-German nationalities. Neither did he agree to an alliance by which the Habsburg Monarchy would be obliged to fight against France with which he had no differences. He agreed to an alliance solely against a Russian aggression. Both modifications lessened the value of the alliance to Bismarck, but he was, nevertheless, willing to accept Andrassy's proposal. For the Emperor William an alliance which left out of account a war between Germany and France was even more objectionable and abhorrent, while one which was directed solely against Russia was in his eyes hardly less than treason. He fought against it stubbornly with all the energy that was left to him. Bismarck defended it in some memoranda which are really masterpieces of argument. But the critical reader will see that these arguments are only employed to defend a decision which Bismarck had already made. It was a case in which *his will had decided*. He was resolved to conclude the treaty with Austria, and he was always capable of producing cogent reasons for a decision on which his will was bent.

In the end William gave way, not because he was convinced by Bismarck's arguments, but because Bismarck threatened to resign if the Emperor refused to sign the treaty. At first William had declared that he would sooner abdicate than sign an alliance against Russia. But what would he have gained by abdicating? The Crown Prince, who would have succeeded him, was quite willing to conclude the Austrian alliance. Thus, in the end, William bowed to the iron will of his Chancellor, and on 5th October 1879 signed the authorization for the conclusion of the treaty. But to his signature he added these words: "Those men who have compelled me to this step will be held responsible for it above"—that is, on the day of judgment. "My whole moral strength is broken", he wrote to the Secretary for Foreign Affairs, von Bülow, who was this time somewhat critical of Bismarck's policy.

As far as Austria was concerned, Bismarck had carried his point. But his initial programme had contained still another point, an *understanding with Britain*. He had, in fact, begun negotiations with the British Prime Minister, Beaconsfield, but these negotiations took a very curious course. On 16th September Bismarck instructed the German Ambassador in London, Count Münster, to find out by conversation with Lord Beaconsfield "what Britain's policy would be if Germany fell out with Russia". Münster saw Beaconsfield on 26th September at his country seat at Hughenden. We have reports on this conversation from Beaconsfield as well as from Münster.

The two accounts differ in important points, but after examining them both, I think that the one which Beaconsfield made to his Queen is more accurate. Beaconsfield writes: "Münster said that Bismarck proposed an alliance of Germany, Austria-Hungary and Great Britain". Beaconsfield replied that he was quite ready to accept this proposal. Münster's report states that the proposal came from Beaconsfield. But both reports agree that Beaconsfield expressed his *readiness to enter into an Alliance with Germany and Austria*. Immediately after this conversation the Ambassador telegraphed to the Chancellor that it would satisfy him in every respect.

But Bismarck's reception of the news was quite different from what Münster had expected. On 8th October he let Münster know that he was not satisfied because Beaconsfield had not fully answered his question: "What will Britain do if we are involved in a dispute with Russia over the Eastern question?" What was more, he *forbade Münster to continue* negotiations.

Now Bismarck's objection is inconsistent with Münster's report. By offering an alliance, Beaconsfield had answered Bismarck's question in the most satisfactory way possible, as Münster had quite correctly pointed out. Besides, if Bismarck had not been satisfied, the most logical step would have been to instruct Münster to repeat the question in an even clearer form and certainly not to break off negotiations. Bismarck's attitude would be quite incomprehensible if we were to take his objection at its face value. The only reasonable explanation is that he had *changed his policy* between 16th September, when he instructed Münster to negotiate with Beaconsfield, and 8th October, when he instructed him not to go any further. What had happened in the meantime? The answer is that the Austro-German alliance had been signed on 7th October, the day before Bismarck's counter-order was sent to London. If an understanding with Britain was for Bismarck only the means of securing a treaty with Austria, then further negotiations with Britain had become superfluous. Bismarck had not at first had this in mind. His original plan had been to make an alliance with Britain *in addition* to one with Austria-Hungary. Why did he drop it now?

In my view the deciding factor was a new approach by Russia and the Czar. On 28th September—that is, two days after Münster's conversation with Beaconsfield—Bismarck was called on by two

Russian diplomatists. One was the Russian Ambassador in Paris, Prince Orloff, the widower of Bismarck's friend Katherine Orloff of his Biarritz days. To Orloff, as an old friend, Bismarck said that not only William but also Francis Joseph eagerly desired the continuation of their old friendship with Russia.

More important still was the visit paid by Saburoff, the Russian Ambassador to Constantinople; for during the summer, before the incident of the Czar's letter, he had held long conversations with Bismarck in Kissingen, in which he had stressed his view that friendship with Germany was the best and surest foundation for Russian policy, while Bismarck spoke frankly about his complaints against the Russian court. From Kissingen Saburoff went to Russia, where he had laid his views before the Czar in a lengthy memorandum. He had now come to Berlin after seeing the Czar at his summer residence, Livadia. Alexander had approved Saburoff's sizing up of the position and instructed him to assure Bismarck of his good and peaceable intentions. Saburoff was to tell the Chancellor that the Czar's policy would in future be purely defensive and would have no other goal than the execution of the Treaty of Berlin. Bismarck's conversation with Saburoff on 28th September was so satisfactory that when it was over he wrote out in his own hand an outline of the principles of a new agreement with Russia. The first item in this draft set forth the obligation of the German Empire to remain neutral in a war between England and Russia. Such a treaty would be compatible with the German-Austrian alliance, the conclusion of which Saburoff considered certain, but quite incompatible with an Anglo-German alliance.

The impression Bismarck gained from this conversation with Saburoff can be gathered from a letter which he wrote the next day, 29th September, to Andrassy. He told him that communications received direct from the Czar's residence—he evidently refers to Saburoff's message—had shown him that the policy agreed on between Andrassy and himself was the right one; the Czar took the Austro-German alliance quite calmly as a *fait accompli* and now set his heart on the *restoration of the league of the three Emperors*. By adopting this programme, Bismarck implicitly relinquished his idea of alliance with England. This was the real reason behind his instructions to Münster on 8th October not to continue his negotiations with Beaconsfield, and the allegedly unsatisfactory reply of the British Prime Minister was only a pretext.

Hence Bismarck's diplomacy in 1879 produced two highly important results, one positive and one negative: the conclusion of an Austro-German alliance and the non-conclusion of an Anglo-German one. Both developments shaped European politics for the next generation. The alliance of the German Empire with the Habsburg Monarchy—later, in 1882, expanded but not strengthened by the accession of Italy—became the basis of German foreign policy until 1918. The refusal to negotiate a treaty of alliance with Britain, at the only juncture when such an alliance was feasible, finally separated both countries so widely that in the end the British Empire joined France and Russia against Germany. Not that this development was the logical and inevitable result of Bismarck's refusal, but it does mean that it would have been prevented if in 1879 Bismarck had taken a different course. Of course, no one can say for certain that the alliance would actually have come about if Bismarck had continued the negotiations with the Beaconsfield, for neither the Queen nor the Foreign Secretary, Lord Salisbury, greeted Beaconsfield's report very enthusiastically. But neither can anybody assert that Beaconsfield would not have had his way. That in any case the whole history of 20th-century Europe would have been changed by an Anglo-German alliance in 1879 is beyond dispute.

We know that one guiding principle of Bismarck's foreign policy was not to be compelled to choose between Germany's two eastern neighbours, Russia and Austria, or—as he himself used to say—to avoid an "option" between them. Had he now taken his "option", had he chosen between the two Empires? The general impression was that he had; actually he had not. What he had really done was to choose between Russia and Britain—and in favour of Russia. True, he had drawn Austria closer to Germany by concluding a formal treaty of alliance. But he had at the same time succeeded in keeping clear the path to St. Petersburg and, indeed, a few years later, in 1881, the new league of the three Emperors of Germany, Austria, and Russia was set up. It was renewed in 1884, but expired in 1887 on account of irreconcilable differences between the Eastern policies of Russia and Austria.

The question therefore arises: Was Bismarck's policy in 1879 a wise one? Was he right in choosing Austria-Hungary as a partner— but without Britain as third partner—in order to maintain his links with Russia? The Germany-Austria-Russia combination could be only a temporary one, because the conflicting interests of Austria and Russia made a permanent alliance impossible. On the other hand, there were in 1879 no insurmountable differences of interest between Britain and either Germany or Austria. At this time Germany had neither a fleet at all comparable with the British navy nor colonies, and Bismarck at that time was in favour neither of the one nor of the other. It is at least possible that a Germany-Austria-Hungary-Great Britain combination would have been a permanent one, and probable that such a combination would have preserved the peace of Europe.

This inherent difference between the two groupings is to-day evident to all. Are we to suppose that only Bismarck, a man of extraordinary and surpassing foresight, was blind to it? If he was not, why did he not tread this path? In order to answer this question we must read chapter 29 of his *Reflections and Recollections*, entitled "The Triple Alliance". In the opening sentences Bismarck voices his belief that sooner or later there will inevitably come a struggle between the two main tendencies in Europe: the system of order on a monarchical basis on the one hand, and the system of the Socialist republic on the other. In his view the only certain subscribers to the first system were the courts of Berlin, Vienna, and St. Petersburg, and, under certain conditions, Rome. England he leaves out of account because "the English constitution does not admit alliances of assured permanence". The practical difficulties which the conflicting interests in the East put in the way of a lasting understanding between Austria-Hungary and Russia Bismarck brushes aside with the remark that "the maintenance of order on a monarchical basis is a task which ought to weigh far more with the strong existing monarchies . . . than any rivalry over the fragments of nations which people the Balkan peninsula".

Whoever reads these sentences to-day is struck by their contrast to the real facts. What would Bismarck say if he knew that none of the countries which he considered as the pillars of the monarchical principle now has a monarch, while in England, which he dismisses with a superficial phrase, the monarchy stands as firmly as ever? It becomes evident that Bismarck's view of foreign policy was in his old age overshadowed by considerations, nay, by prejudices rooted in home affairs. This is all the more curious as Bismarck is generally considered to be the foremost practising advocate of the political system which Ranke has called *das Primat der Aussenpolitik*, the priority of a country's foreign policy over any domestic considerations.

There is yet another reason which springs directly from Bismarck's character, which influenced his decision. The great Chancellor only cared for alliances of which he himself was in reality the leader. Undoubtedly he had been the leading figure in the Prussian-Austrian alliance of 1864, which helped him to win Sleswig-Holstein for Prussia, and he had broken up this alliance when it had served *his* purpose. There was no reason to doubt that in the newly formed alliance with the Habsburg Monarchy he would once again play the leading rôle. Who among the Austro-Hungarian statesmen could compete with him? Andrassy was on the point of resigning, and his successors were even lesser men who could not be expected to snatch the reins from Bismarck's hands. In Russia the retirement of Gortchakoff, now an infirm old man of eighty-two, was only a question of time. The Czar himself was, as the events of recent months had shown, quite unable to withstand the energy of the German Chancellor in the long run. The future Foreign Minister of Russia, Giers, was an honest, conscientious, and painstaking official, but quite without personal weight, and he was looked on by his master more as a sort of glorified clerk than as a Minister. Bismarck himself spoke of him in the most contemptuous terms. And so Bismarck was quite certain to get the whip hand if Austria and Russia became his allies.

But he could never expect British policy to follow his guidance, even if Britain became Germany's ally. Bismarck knew very well that the British Empire, with its widespread interests which compassed the globe, was much too vast and too strong ever to be led by any European Power or any continental statesman, however great and respected he might be. Moreover, he knew that the ultimate deciding factor in British policy was British public opinion, which usually had its own way and was not likely to take its cue from a foreign statesman. The next year did, in fact, show that the British were able through a general election to influence the course of their country's foreign policy. At this election of 1880 they showed their dislike of Beaconsfield's "spirited" foreign policy and once more entrusted the national destinies to Gladstone, who was not at all in Bismarck's good books, representing, as he did, the spirit of liberalism and democracy which the Chancellor was resolved to repress in Germany. Although Bismarck very probably did not, in 1879, expect the downfall of Beaconsfield, the mere idea that foreign policy depended on public opinion and on elections weighed very heavily with him against concluding an alliance with England.

Such were, as far as I can see, the reasons why Bismarck did not supplement his Habsburg alliance with a British alliance, but returned to his old project, a league of the three Emperors. We may well doubt whether he himself in later years was altogether satisfied with this "option", for this would certainly be quite incompatible with what he later told the Austrian Emperor—that since 1879 his goal had been to win Britain over to the Triple Alliance. We shall subsequently see that in his closing years he made an attempt to reopen negotiations with Salisbury for an Anglo-German alliance. Then, however, he was forced to realize the truth of something he had once written in a memorandum to the old Emperor, when he pressed him to conclude the alliance with Austria: history shows that neglected opportunities do not, as a rule, return. In the meantime he had done much that was calculated to arouse unfriendly feelings in Britain, as we shall see when the story of his colonial policy is told.

But for the present, Bismarck could be well satisfied with his work in 1879. In the struggle over the tariff he had completely routed his adversaries. By forming the alliance with Austria-Hungary he had won enormous popularity for his foreign policy. His position is described by the Ambassador, General von Schweinitz, in these words: "In Berlin everyone whistles the same tune. Everything is dependent on Bismarck, and on Bismarck alone. Never was the rule of one single man so exclusive, not only from fear, but also from admiration and the voluntary subordination of men's minds to him."

11. *Bismarck's Colonial Policy*

The colonial policy of Bismarck which came into the political foreground in the years 1884 and 1885 is of particular biographical interest, because he had in former years peremptorily rejected any colonial policy for Germany, and during his final years of power he returned to this mood of aversion. In one of his last speeches to the Reichstag he cried: "I am not a colonial man" (*Kolonialmensch*), and we now know from the diary of a member of the Prussian cabinet that at a meeting of the Staatsministerium in August 1889 Bismarck thundered against the "German colonial humbug" which was clumsily upsetting his arrangements. We can therefore say that his short period of colonial enthusiasm is only an episode in his life. But it was an episode of momentous consequences, both for Germany's relations with other countries, especially with Britain, and for the whole outlook of the German people. Hence it is all the more interesting to solve the riddle of Bismarck's reasons for embarking on this policy. Many historians have tried to unravel it.

When Bismarck began to be interested in colonial problems, only two areas of the world were open to German colonization: the southern part of Africa and the South Sea Islands. In both these regions British colonies occupied the paramount position: the Cape Colony in South Africa, and Australia in the South Seas. The success of German colonial policy would therefore in a certain degree depend on the attitude of Britain and her colonies. Britain was by far the greatest sea-power and did indeed "rule the waves". But her international position had undergone a very important change by her occupation of Egypt in 1882. This occupation brought her into sharp political conflict with France, which for generations had considered Egypt as falling within her sphere of interest. We cannot doubt that Bismarck had foreseen this consequence, and that he had included it in his calculations when he repeatedly advised the British government "to take Egypt". Britain was all the more vulnerable by reason of her presence in Egypt, as many of the problems of Egyptian administration and finance were of an international character, so that to maintain their foothold the British were dependent on the goodwill and approval of other Powers, especially France.

Bismarck's relations with France had, as has been seen, undergone an important change since the Republican victory over MacMahon in October 1877 and his resignation in January 1879. This marks the beginning of Bismarck's policy of reconciliation with France, which lasted up to the overthrow of Jules Ferry by Clemenceau in the stormy session of the French Chamber on 30th March 1885. Ferry fell because he had, to quote a French historian, "too far forgotten the blue lines of the Vosges in order to become Tonkinese", that is, because he co-operated with the enemy of 1870 in order to gain for France a colonial empire in East Asia. This vote of the Chamber which defeated Ferry and which was certainly popular in France, meant the failure of Bismarck's attempt to make France forgive Sedan as she had half a century earlier forgiven Waterloo. In November 1884 Bismarck said to the French Ambassador, Courcel: *"Mon soin constant à partir de 1871 a été de me conduire de telle sorte que je pusse l'amener à pardonner Sédan comme elle en est arrivée après 1815 à pardonner Waterloo"*. Perhaps the French would have been able to overlook Sedan in time, but they could neither forget nor forgive Strasbourg and Metz.

Shortly after his policy of conciliation towards France had ended, Bismarck's colonial interest had evaporated. He was now much more interested in fostering relations with Britain.

We can therefore say that this particular alignment of circumstances—Britain's embarrassments with Egypt and the improved relations between Germany and France—gave Bismarck the opportunity for his experiment in colonial policy. But I do not believe that we have here found his motive. A much more likely motive was, in my opinion, the state of domestic politics in Germany itself.

We have seen how the election of 1881 had produced a Reichstag in which the Conservative Parties combined with the remains of the National Liberal Party were in a minority. Whenever the Centre Party joined the Secessionists and the Progressive Party, Bismarck had to face an Opposition which wielded a majority. Although the Centre voted for the government in tariff questions, there remained many political issues over which it joined the Opposition. In the summer of 1884, six months before the elections to the next Reichstag, the Secessionists and the Progressive Party amalgamated and formed a united radical Liberal Party which took the name *Deutsch-freisinnige Partei*. It began with more than a hundred deputies, among whom were some of the most prominent parliamentarians—Eugen Richter and Haenel from the Progressives, and Bamberger, Forckenbeck, and Stauffenberg from the Secessionists.

Lasker died just at this time in New York, where he had gone to see something of the New World. His death gave Bismarck an opportunity to show that he never forgave or forgot, and that not even death could assuage a personal hatred. The American House of Representatives had passed a resolution expressing its sympathy with the German Reichstag for the loss of an excellent and patriotic member. Bismarck declined to pass on this resolution to the Reichstag and sent it back to the U.S.A. When the matter was brought before the Reichstag by a friend of Lasker, Bismarck made a speech in which he condemned the political activities of the dead man, root and branch. When we compare this speech with those in which in the British parliament the leaders of all parties are accustomed to bid farewell to an opponent who has died (the speech of Lord Salisbury in which he praised his lifelong antagonist Gladstone as a "great Christian statesman" is but one example), we can see the striking difference in the political culture of the two countries.

But there was one thing about the new party which irritated Bismarck more than anything else. It was supposed to be the Crown Prince's party, *die Kronprinzenpartei*. There was a rumour that the Crown Prince had welcomed the unification of the radical Liberals in a telegram to Forckenbeck in which he expressed his congratulations on the founding of the new party. Bismarck was afraid that the Prince, when he succeeded his father, would choose the members of his cabinet from among the leaders of this party who would then supplant him. For this imaginary cabinet Bismarck coined the phrase "a German Gladstone Ministry", a name which expressed his detestation and derision. The moment when the Crown Prince would succeed to the throne could not be far off, for old William was now eighty-seven years of age. To destroy the *Deutsch-freisinnige Partei* and to kill the "Gladstone Ministry" before it was born were now the principal aims of the Chancellor. He looked for a political project likely to strengthen his own popularity and opposition to which would make his adversaries unpopular. In 1881 Bismarck had outlined a programme of social reforms, providing for social insurance covering sickness, accidents, and later, old age and infirmity. A part of this programme was realized by the law for the insurance of working men against sickness. But the programme had not been as popular as Bismarck had expected, and his hopes of tempting voters away from the Social Democrats by this means had not been fulfilled.

Now a colonial policy had a good deal of attraction for a section of the upper middle classes, particularly in certain maritime towns like Hamburg and Bremen, and it was considered by many an eminently national policy. On the other hand, Bismarck knew it would meet with vigorous opposition from the *Freisinnigen*. One of their leaders, Ludwig Bamberger, distinguished himself as an energetic opponent of a colonial policy. It would bring, he said, no practical benefit to the Reich, as all the territories worth having were already in the possession of other nations. On the other hand, it might easily bring Germany into collision with other states. Bismarck could therefore foresee that it would be possible to utilize the colonial movement at the coming election to the detriment of the *Freisinnigen*, who could be accused of lack of national feeling. Besides, he might also entertain the hope of bringing this party into conflict with the Crown Prince, who was supposed to favour the idea of German colonization.

But Bismarck seems to have had yet another motive, which is hinted at in a very curious utterance on the part of his eldest son Herbert, who at this time was his intimate collaborator. In March 1890 General von Schweinitz had a conversation with Herbert Bismarck, and asked him how Bismarck's enthusiasm for a colonial policy could be explained, as it was in striking contrast to everything the Chancellor had previously said or done. Herbert answered: "When we entered upon a colonial policy, we had to reckon with a long reign of the Crown Prince. During this reign *English influence would have been dominant*. To prevent this, we had to embark on a colonial policy, because it was popular and conveniently adapted to *bring us into conflict with England at any given moment*." While it is hard to credit a great statesmen with such a motive, we cannot doubt that Herbert had heard an argument in this vein from his father's lips.

At this time of Bismarck's colonial policy Gladstone was in power in Britain. In view of his personal hostility towards Gladstone, we may suppose that it was a particular joy to Bismarck when he succeeded in defeating the man whom German Liberals considered the foremost Liberal statesman of the age. But it was not so easy to fall out with Gladstone over colonial questions, because he was quite ready to acquiesce in German colonial expansion, and he was far from claiming that England enjoyed a privileged position in these matters or had a real interest in excluding Germany from other continents. But it was only in the later stages that Gladstone took personal cognizance of Bismarck's demands and protests; as a rule, they were dealt with by the departmental Ministers. The German notes were, of course, addressed to the Foreign Office, at the head of which was Lord Granville, the Foreign Secretary. But Granville, in making a decision, had to consult the Colonial Secretary, Lord Derby, and the Colonial Secretary had, in his turn, to consult the cabinet of the colony concerned—that of the Cape Colonies, for instance, if a demand of Bismarck's touched on an African matter. Such a complicated organization is likely to lead to procrastination if the Ministers in question do not put forth their best efforts to quicken the tempo. But that was neither Granville's nor Derby's way, and so it came about that an important question submitted by Bismarck was left unanswered for six months.

That such a delay made him furious we can well understand, and we shall not be surprised to find that he was quick to turn any mistakes made by the British government to good account. But he was certainly wrong when he put the blame on a hostile disposition on the part of Granville. Granville was far from being anti-German; Bismarck himself knew his friendly feelings, for Granville had received Herbert Bismarck, who was for some time Secretary to the German Embassy in London, with the greatest kindness.

The chief reason for the misunderstandings between Bismarck and the British government was that the British learned only too late that Bismarck was bent on a colonial policy at all. All that they knew was that Bismarck opposed German colonial expansion, and the British Ambassador Odo Russell, now Lord Ampthill, continued to report in this sense from Berlin. This was not only due to his failing health—he died in August 1884—but still more to the fact that *Bismarck purposely concealed from him his change of policy.*

In all the months that Granville could have adapted his attitude to Bismarck's wishes, not a word reached him from either the British Ambassador in Berlin or the German Ambassador in London, Count Münster, which would have enlightened him about these aspirations. Bismarck kept his intentions secret from Münster as well. When Hatzfeld, the Secretary of the German Foreign Office, suggested to Bismarck that he should inform Münster quite confidentially of his plans, he expressly forbade this in his order of 21st May 1884.

As it is impossible to give here a full survey of Bismarck's colonial policy, or to go into the details of his very shrewd and complicated manœuvres, perhaps one typical example, which had far-reaching consequences, will suffice.

On 1st January 1907 Sir Eyre Crowe drew up for the Foreign Secretary, Sir Edward Grey, his now celebrated memorandum on Germany's foreign policy, a document which Grey at the time called "most valuable". Eyre Crowe became Permanent Under-Secretary to the Foreign Office; his views were of great practical importance. In a marginal note to his memorandum, in which he defends his criticism of German colonial policy, he refers to the "famous bogey document" which Bismarck pretended to have sent to the British government but which in fact was never delivered, and he adds: "It is difficult to find a better word than 'deception' for these proceedings". This so-called "bogey document" is Bismarck's note to Münster of 5th May 1884. The details of Sir Eyre's account are inaccurate, but his remark reveals the impression which the incident left in the memory of the Foreign Office.

The facts are these: In January 1885 Bismarck had a conversation with Odo Russell's successor as Ambassador, Sir Edward Malet, on the question of why Bismarck had changed front in the Egyptian controversy. Bismarck accused the British government of having shown him malevolent opposition in colonial questions. In support of this he referred to his note of 5th May 1884 in which he had instructed Münster to tell the British government that Germany would be compelled to seek French assistance if Britain would not comply with his colonial demands. Malet immediately reported this to Granville and the Foreign Secretary ordered a search of Foreign Office records to be made to trace the dispatch in question. It was not to be found, and Münster was summoned to explain. "I had a talk with Münster", Granville wrote to Gladstone. "He was frightened out of his wits and went home to consult his archives. *He found the famous despatch, but also a telegram, not to act upon it.* He begged me to keep this secret."

The dispatch and the telegram have since been published and show that Münster told Granville the truth. The main point of the dispatch was a suggestion by Bismarck that the British government could show its goodwill towards Germany in the clearest and best possible way by surrendering to her the island of Heligoland. Münster was delighted by this suggestion which he far preferred, as he wrote to Bismarck, "to the quite unpractical and immature colonial plans". In his reply, Bismarck does not say a single word to rebut this implied criticism of German colonial policy. And once again he fails to tell his own Ambassador that he had resolved to inaugurate a colonial policy.

Münster spoke to Granville in strict confidence about Heligoland and asked him not to say anything about it to his colleagues yet. He promised to revert to the subject in the next few days. He never did. Why? Because he suddenly received a telegram from the Chancellor instructing him never to mention Heligoland again.

What was Bismarck's reason for countermanding his instructions? Certainly not the one which he himself gives in the telegram and which is quite inadequate. In my view the explanation lies in the following facts. On the very day when Bismarck sent his telegram to Münster, 25th May, he received from his Secretary of the Foreign Office, Count Hatzfeldt, a report on a conversation with the Crown Prince. The Prince had asked Hatzfeldt whether the rumour that Germany had encouraged the French to ask for the evacuation of Egypt by the British was well founded. In his reply Hatzfeldt had outlined the arguments set out in the note of 5th May, but without mentioning Heligoland. Even when the Prince asked whether the note dealt *only* with colonial questions, Hatzfeldt was still silent on the subject of Heligoland. But he now asked the Chancellor whether he should inform the Prince about Heligoland. Bismarck answered "No", and telegraphed to Münster to drop all negotiations on the subject with the British government.

In collating these facts with Herbert Bismarck's explanation to Schweinitz, mentioned above, I come to the conclusion that Bismarck stopped these negotiations not because they ran the risk of failing, but because they ran the risk of succeeding. He did not feel very strongly about Heligoland, but he did not desire relations with Britain to become too good, for this, he feared, would strengthen Britain's influence on German policy should Frederick William succeed to the throne of the Reich.

On the other hand, a few days after his order to Münster to stop the negotiations over Heligoland, he instructed him to tell Granville that Germany would not recognize the annexation of the South-west African coast by Cape Colony. Granville's consternation at this declaration shows clearly how far he was from thinking that what the Cape Colony proposed to do did not agree with the Chancellor's intentions, or—in other words—how successfully the Chancellor had hidden his intentions from those persons who would have been able and willing to comply with them, if only they had known them.

In any case, there can be no doubt that Münster was prevented by Bismarck's instructions from revealing to Granville the contents of Bismarck's note of 5th May 1884, and that Granville never heard a word about it until the Chancellor mentioned it to Malet in the interview of January 1885. Perhaps we may assume that during this interview Bismarck had forgotten that six months earlier he had countermanded the delivery of the note. But if that is so, Bismarck did nothing to rectify his mistake, even after Granville had officially stated in parliament that he had never received the note. Even then Bismarck did not say a single word to clear up the misunderstanding. But he was furious with Granville for publishing Malet's report together with his very striking answer in the form of a Blue Book which was laid before parliament. He had this Blue Book criticized very sharply and acrimoniously in a series of articles in his paper, the *Norddeutsche Allgemeine Zeitung*, which was bold enough to tax the British Foreign Secretary with a breach of confidence, but did not say a word about the fact that the note of May 1884 was never delivered. Quite the contrary: the paper wrote as if the note's delivery were an indisputable fact.

The climax of this controversy came when Bismarck, simultaneously with the publication of these polemical articles, openly attacked Granville in the Reichstag. His speech is perhaps the most vehement attack made by the Minister of one state on the Foreign

Minister of another in time of peace. True, Granville had given him an opening for this attack by an indiscreet remark in the House of Lords, where he mentioned Bismarck's advice to the British government "to take Egypt". When Bismarck asserted that he had never given this advice, he was certainly not telling the truth. But even so, Granville was in the wrong in making this suggestion public without first seeking Bismarck's permission.

Bismarck's speech caused an enormous sensation. Many people thought it the prelude to a rupture with Britain. But what did Bismarck really do? The next day he sent his son Herbert to London to bring about a settlement with the British Ministers. This settlement was, indeed, very soon reached, not because Herbert was such a skilful negotiator, but because Gladstone was resolved to come to an understanding in any case. He himself talked things over with Herbert and made it quite clear that he was willing to go to any lengths to meet Germany's just claims, but that Britain would find it more difficult to entertain them if they were presented in the form of blackmail. This word "blackmail" was without doubt plainly heard by Herbert, but he did not mention it in his very arrogant report on his negotiations. Instead, he had the impudence to write in this report to his father: "To discuss with Mr. Gladstone the essence of the foreign policy of a great state is useless, because he is quite unable to understand it". This was the tone in which the Chancellor liked to hear of a man whom his fellow-countrymen called the "Grand old Man" and whom Bismarck himself used to call "Professor Gladstone", "Professor" being an expression of his most utter contempt. Bismarck handled his controversy with Granville so cleverly as to leave the impression ultimately that the British Minister had been worsted. This had much to do with his being transferred to the Colonial Office when Gladstone formed his third cabinet in 1886.

Whether the colonies which Germany acquired in this way were worth the trouble, and especially the bad blood caused by these interchanges between Germany and Britain, may be doubted. At the end of this very disturbed year a Briton of German birth wrote a letter which to-day makes melancholy reading. This was the great orientalist, Professor Max Müller, who occupied the chair of Sanskrit at Oxford. As "Max Müller-Oxford" he was well known in Germany.

He loved both his adopted country and the country of his birth and wished nothing better than to see them good friends. He wrote the letter to his friend Schlözer, the German Minister at the Holy See in Rome and a man of considerable culture. He assured him that the British people felt no antipathy towards Germany and that the abusive language of some German papers had made no impression. But he warned the Germans not to underestimate the undeveloped might of England. "If they are driven to the wall, every Englishman will be a soldier the next day." "Only if Germany and England stand together in future will the horrible and indeed barbarous situation in which now we live, come to an end. We live like the beasts of prey in prehistoric times. What is to become of Europe if no state feels secure that has not more guns than its neighbour? For thirty years we have had almost a state of war in Europe."

Max Müller asks his friend to put these considerations before his "old chief", the Chancellor. It is extremely doubtful whether Schlözer ever did anything of the kind. He knew perfectly well that Bismarck's only answer would have been "Humanitarian rubbish!"

One episode during the colonial period must be mentioned because it throws particular light on Bismarck's methods. In the autumn of 1885 Germany came into conflict with Spain over the Caroline Islands in the South Pacific. A German captain had hoisted the German flag in these islands, which Spain looked on as her own possessions. After some haggling both Powers agreed to lay the dispute before an arbitrator. And whom did Bismarck propose as arbitrator? Pope Leo XIII! This was a well-calculated compliment which the Pope appreciated very much, but it was a sore disappointment to all the German anti-clericals who had followed Bismarck with so much enthusiasm in the struggle for power between monarchy and priesthood.

The Pope's decision went in favour of Spain, but he sent Bismarck a letter full of the most exquisite flatteries together with the Order of Christ, with which no Protestant had ever been invested. But Bismarck knew how to respond with a still greater compliment. In his reply he addressed the Pope with the word which is reserved for reigning sovereigns. He called him "Sire!" and gave him to understand that he considered the Holy Father as a temporal sovereign, even though he had lost temporal power.

12. *The Struggle for the Septennium in 1887*

In September 1886 Bismarck laid a new army bill before the Reichstag. It proposed a fresh increase in the strength of the army beginning in April 1887 and lasting for seven years, that is until March 1894. Seven years; that meant a new septennium. The last had been voted in 1880 and covered the period up to the end of March 1888. The new septennium would therefore come into force a year before the old one had expired.

Why was Bismarck in such a hurry? The official grounds for the bill pointed to the expansion of armies abroad, especially in France and Russia.

The relations between Germany and France had again deteriorated since the overthrow of Jules Ferry. True, the President of the French Republic, Jules Grévy, was undoubtedly a man of peace, and so were the Minister-President Freycinet, his successor Goblet, and the Minister for Foreign Affairs, Flourens. Even Bismarck did not doubt that. But he asserted that the Minister for War, Boulanger, who sat in the cabinets of Goblet and Freycinet, was making ready for war.

The name of Boulanger is linked with the French movement for revenge. There can, indeed, be no doubt that in the late 'eighties there was an active "revenge movement" in France led by Paul Déroulède and his *Ligue des Patriotes*, and that Boulanger was for a time the idol of this movement.

But it is remarkable that Bismarck should draw the attention of the German Reichstag to Boulanger in March 1886 when he had not yet done anything to justify any German apprehensions. Bismarck spoke of him in connexion with the Socialist ideas which would be pinned to the banners of the hostile army, recalling the French War of Revolution. Bismarck's sole support for this accusation were some reports from the German military attaché in Paris who called Boulanger a *revanche* Minister of War. But this attaché, as well as the German Ambassador, Count Münster (in the meantime transferred from London to Paris), were completely surprised by the interpretation which Bismarck and his press put on his reports. General Waldersee, Quartermaster-General—that is, deputy of the Chief of the General Staff, Marshal Moltke—called Bismarck's talk of the danger of war a comedy. No one who was really well informed of the situation in France believed in the possibility of a French attack on Germany.

But Bismarck used to emphasize that France would be lured into war if hostilities should break out between Germany and Russia. Alexander III was now reigning in Russia. He had succeeded his father Alexander II, murdered by nihilists in 1881. He was certainly not inspired by the same feeling of friendship towards Germany and her Emperor as his father had been. He had grown up in the atmosphere of the Panslavic ideas prevailing among the Russian upper classes and propagated by some influential newspapers. Nevertheless, in the first year of his reign he had concluded the new alliance with the Emperors of Germany and Austria-Hungary and had renewed it in 1884. He was at this time—in name at least—the ally not only of the German Reich but of the Habsburg Monarchy.

But in spite of this alliance events in the Balkan peninsula caused very strained relations between the two Eastern Empires. In 1885 the unification of Bulgaria under Prince Alexander of Battenberg and his war against the Serbs had revived the old antagonism. The situation was aggravated by the fact that the Prince of Battenberg, who had been looked on with favour by Alexander II, was hated by Alexander III, who was his cousin. The new Czar considered him a traitor because he tried to rule in Bulgaria not in the interests of Russia, but of Bulgaria herself. Alexander of Battenberg found much sympathy in Germany, but not with the Chancellor, who criticized him in far-from-friendly terms. He was very angry when he heard that the Prince wanted to marry the daughter of the Crown Prince, Princess Victoria, and that the Crown Princess was all in favour of the match. At his instigation the Emperor vetoed the union and the Crown Princess had to give way.

But Bulgaria was to provide a still more unpleasant surprise. During the night 20th-21st August 1886 Alexander of Battenberg was kidnapped by a gang of Bulgarian officers and taken out of the country. He was able to return and was enthusiastically received by his people. But after receiving a very harsh telegram from the Czar, which censured him for returning, the Prince resigned his crown and left Bulgaria, never to return.

His overthrow caused a great stir throughout Europe. Everyone believed that the officers who had abducted him were tools of Russia, and Lord Salisbury, the British Prime Minister, in his Guildhall speech of 9th November 1886, roundly described them as "debauched by foreign gold". In Germany, too, public opinion was aghast and furious with Russian methods, the more especially as Alexander, by reason of his victory over the Serbs, was called a "German hero". There was one man in Germany who was not only cool, but hostile—Bismarck. He ordered his press to write in such a way that one radical paper was provoked to an indignant reference to "crawling to Russia". Bismarck tried to pass this indignation off as a mere manifestation of party opposition. But, in point of fact, circles that were by no means radical or hostile to the government—a number of army officers, for instance—were also quite indignant at this attitude of the administration and its press, and a famous German general, von der Goltz, sent to Constantinople as an instructor to the Turkish army, wrote that there was nothing but bewilderment at the eagerness of the German government to kotow to Russia.

Significant light is thrown on Bismarck's reasons for disliking the Prince of Battenberg by a report about him which Bismarck made to the old Emperor a few weeks after his dethronement. He paints him in the darkest of colours as the candidate of the German Opposition parties which were hostile to the Empire and to the Emperor for his own post, that of Chancellor. He writes: "As Imperial Chancellor the Prince would be supported by the majority of the present Reichstag", by which he meant the majority made up of *Freisinnige*, Centre, and Social Democrats, who were united in their opposition to Bismarck.

The party which was hated most by Bismarck was the *Deutsch-freisinnige* Party, because he considered it as the future Emperor's following. The day when Frederick William would succeed to the throne was drawing inexorably closer. William I was almost ninety and in 1885 he had fallen seriously ill. In May 1885 Bismarck had a conversation on this subject with Baron Courcel, the French Ambassador. Bismarck was in the greatest excitement, his chin quivered convulsively, his cheeks reddened, and his eyes brimmed with tears, wrote Courcel. "*Je vis son menton s'agiter d'un tremblement convulsif, ses joues s'injecterent de rougeur, ses yeux se mouillèrent de larmes.*"

True, William had recovered, but none the less, the Chancellor had constantly before his mind the imminent change of Emperors. What turn would his own fortunes take? The much-derided and much-feared "Gladstone Ministry" would appear, composed of the able leaders of the *Freisinnigen*, with the Prince of Battenberg, the favourite of the Crown Princess, as its figurehead. This cabinet would have the enthusiastic backing of the new Emperor and the ready assistance of the majority of the Reichstag.

Nobody would expect a man like Bismarck to fold his arms and wait for this "Gladstone Ministry" to come into existence. A fighter like Bismarck attacks before the enemy is ready. The German political system that he had built up gave him the power he needed so long as he could count on the assistance either of the crown or of parliament. To change the succession to the throne was outside his compass; the point at which the master-sculptor could hammer in his chisel was the majority in the Reichstag. If Bismarck could succeed in changing the composition of the Reichstag in his own favour, the new Emperor would be powerless and the permanence of Bismarck's own régime would have been established.

To realize this aim Bismarck needed a dissolution of the Reichstag and fresh elections conducted under the slogan most favourable to the government. Bismarck knew that military questions were likely to rouse patriotic fervour on the side of the voters, especially if the people believed that a war was imminent.

This situation, therefore, explains why Bismarck would not wait until the septennium of 1880 had expired, for in the meantime the aged Emperor might well die. Bismarck was in a hurry.

The expansion of the army, which the new bill proposed, failed to afford Bismarck the opportunity of dissolving the Reichstag. Windthorst, who suspected what Bismarck was about, persuaded the majority to vote for the full armed strength which the government was demanding—*Jeden Mann und jeden Groschen* (Every man and every penny), as the popular slogan ran. But the real struggle was over the period for which the newly fixed total of men to be called to the colours (*Friedenspräsenz-Stärke*) should be applicable. The government wanted it to hold good for seven years, but had to admit that this period had never been completely utilized on former occasions. Bismarck's real reason was that he knew that the *Freisinnigen* could in no circumstances agree to seven years. When the Progressives and the former National Liberal Secessionists had amalgamated in 1884, both sides had reached a compromise by which they agreed not to vote for an army bill with a longer life than that of a single parliament, that is, three years. This was why Bismarck insisted on seven.

His tactics were the ones he usually employed when he did not want to reach agreement. Ten days before the Reichstag assembled, Bismarck retired to Friedrichsruh and stayed there during the parliamentary debate on the first reading and the highly important committee stage. From Friedrichsruh he wrote terse and angry letters to the War Minister in order to put paid to any chances of a settlement. His plan was to force the leaders of the Opposition party into taking a firm line against the septennium, so that they would be unable to drop their opposition later on.

The most interesting feature of Bismarck's tactical operation are his negotiations with the Vatican to secure a papal order to the Centre to vote for the septennium. But when the Prussian Minister to the Holy See reported that the Pope was willing to issue such an order in exchange for a declaration by the government promising the revision of the Church Laws, Bismarck declined in a very brusque telegram, in which he said that a rejection of the bill by the Centre would give the government a better operational base. Moreover, he was bold enough to say: "We shall put through the expansion of the army in any case, even without the centre, and *if necessary, without the Reichstag either*". In the meantime he spent money from the *Welfen-Fonds* in Rome in order to influence the papal *curia* in the desired direction.

Only after the committee of the Reichstag had rejected the septennium did Bismarck return to Berlin. He was now sure that the danger of his bill's being passed was over. During the second reading he made some of his most forceful and interesting speeches.

Referring to the international situation, he firmly disclaimed any intention of waging a preventive war with the celebrated argument: "I cannot see the cards which Divine Providence holds". He did not deny that the French government and the majority of the French people were peacefully disposed. But he asserted that in France the decisions were taken by energetic minorities, and he mentioned the name of General Boulanger as a man who might attack Germany if ever he became the head of the French government. "We have to fear", he said, "a war started by a French attack; whether in ten days or in ten years, I cannot say." The character which such a war would assume he depicted in the most horrifying terms. It would be waged *bis zum Weissbluten*, that is, until at least one country had been bled white. Before Bismarck made this speech, he got possession of a report to the Emperor from the German Ambassador in Paris, Graf Münster, which pointed out that there was no sign at all of a coming French attack on Germany. Bismarck compelled Münster to withdraw his report, using the argument that if the Emperor accepted the Ambassador's view the government would be unable to maintain the army bill before the Reichstag. This shows how Bismarck exploited foreign policy in the interests of his home policy. The arguments in Bismarck's speech about the danger of a French attack, whether they were true or not, had no bearing on the question of whether the Army Law should be made valid for seven years or only three, as the *Freisinnigen* proposed. Windthorst hit the nail on the head when he asked: "Why all these long deductions by the Chancellor to prove the necessity for expanding the army? The great majority of the house is ready to vote every man and every penny." Bismarck knew that well enough. But he was making his speech with an eye to the coming election. It was, in fact, a platform speech.

The Reichstag voted the army bill for three years. The moment the president announced this result, Bismarck rose from his seat, took from his portfolio the Imperial order dissolving the Reichstag and read it to the House. Not a moment was to be lost which might be used by Windthorst to propose fresh concessions to the government with a view to compromise.

Bismarck ran the election campaign with all his extraordinary skill, energy, and unscrupulousness. He conducted it on the lines indicated by his Reichstag speeches, dangling before the voters the bogy of a French war of aggression. He used every possible manœuvre to create the impression that a French attack was imminent, that Boulanger was preparing for war, and that there was only one thing to prevent it—the acceptance of the septennium. The same paper which in 1875 had startled the world by its article "Is war imminent?" published an article entitled "On the Razor's

Edge" (*Auf des Messers Schneide*), which proclaimed that Boulanger was the dominant figure in France and that he would not be able to return to peaceful ways. Of the Berlin correspondents of the English papers many were under Bismarck's influence and helped to influence public opinion in the way he wanted. To secure a victory at the polls, Bismarck induced the three government parties, Conservatives, Free Conservatives, and National Liberals, to form an alliance, the so-called *Kartell*, by which, in order to secure all the government votes at the first ballot, only *one* candidate out of these three parties should stand in each constituency. Under the German electoral law only the two candidates who head the poll qualify for the second ballot (*Stichwahl*). By means of the *Kartell* a government candidate had the best chance of getting into the second ballot. Moreover, Bismarck succeeded in inducing Bennigsen to emerge from his retirement and to stand for the Reichstag. Miquel, too, who was then Chief Burgomaster of Frankfurt, put up for the Reichstag.

The result of the elections was a sweeping victory for Bismarck and a heavy defeat for the *Freisinnigen*. Although they did not lose very many votes, they lost half of their seats. On the other hand, the Centre kept all its hundred seats, although Bismarck had succeeded in extracting a letter from the Papal Cardinal Secretary of State, expressing the Pope's disapproval of the vote by the Centre against the septennium. It is one of Windthorst's greatest and most skilful achievements to have averted any evil consequences from this letter and to have brought his ship safely into harbour once more. All the same, he took a very gloomy view of the future. After these elections he said to a friend: "I begin to despair of the future of a people which allows its best friends to be so defamed as the German people does".

The National Liberals achieved a victory the like of which they had never expected since the secession of the Left wing. But their triumph was nothing like a resurrection of Liberalism. On the contrary! Bamberger characterized them in these words: "The spirit of National Liberalism is *pompous submissiveness*, and this expresses the feeling of the middle classes". "German parliamentarism was an episode", he adds sadly. And, indeed, how far down the hill had National Liberalism gone since 1866! In Bamberger there still lived something of the spirit of 1848, and he could not but be a dis-illusioned man when he saw how low the Liberal flame was now guttering in the great German Empire under Bismarck. During these years he once more met his old friend of revolutionary days, Karl Schurz, who, like himself, had had to go into exile after the defeat of the revolution. But whereas Bamberger had returned to the old country after 1866 to help in building the new Empire, Schurz had stayed in the U.S.A. and become one of its leading citizens. Comparing his lot with that of Schurz, Bamberger wrote: "We too could have become men of that calibre, if we had not been condemned *to live in a dog-kennel*!"

But Bamberger was shrewd enough to see what Bismarck's real aim had been in dissolving the Reichstag and destroying its majority. "The Crown Prince", he wrote, "is now compelled to do what Bismarck wants." Indeed, the spectre of the Crown Prince's party and of the "Gladstone Ministry" was laid. If William died the next day, the new Kaiser would have been dependent on Bismarck.

But now followed one of the greatest ironies of world history: a few months after the electoral struggle which Bismarck had fought and won against his future Kaiser, it became obvious that this future Kaiser was dangerously ill, so ill that there was scarcely a hope that he would ever ascend the throne. It was a shadow, a tragic shadow, over which Bismarck had won his last great triumph.

13. *The Reinsurance Treaty with Russia, 1887*

The war scare by which Bismarck had won the elections of 1887 made a deep impression in France, where everyone feared that the attack would come from the other side. Naturally enough this impression was not dispelled even after the electoral struggle was over. The feeling which prevailed in France was clearly shown a few weeks later when an incident occurred which in normal times would have been considered as trivial. In April 1887 a French official of the frontier police, named Schnaebele, was arrested by the German police as a spy on one side or the other of the Franco-German border. The odd thing about this arrest was that a German official had lured Schnaebele across the frontier on the pretext of settling some minor routine matter. The French took the view that the arrest was a trap laid by Bismarck, who wanted to wound French national feeling and provoke a war. But this suspicion was unfounded. Bismarck soon realized that the German position was untenable and ordered the release of Schnaebele. The excitement which for a few days had seemed to endanger the peace of Europe died down. But, nevertheless, the incident had thrown into sharp relief the feeling existing between the two countries. Even Boulanger's dismissal from the French War Ministry did not restore a peaceful atmosphere.

Bismarck was all the more bent on completing the diplomatic and political isolation of France. In a series of negotiations with Austria, Italy, and Britain he forged quite a chain of treaties, all calculated to secure Germany's position. His activity during this year, 1887, was quite extraordinary for a man of seventy-two. One can only marvel at his energy and versatility.

The most interesting link in this chain of treaties is the secret pact which Bismarck concluded with Russia on 18th June 1887 which became famous as the "Reinsurance Treaty". So well kept was the secret that the first Germany—or, indeed, Europe—heard of it was from Bismarck himself and in very peculiar circumstances. In the autumn of 1896 the Czar paid a visit to Paris which was thought to be the solemn affirmation of the Franco-Russian Alliance and which evoked enormous enthusiasm in France. Bismarck, by this time a Chancellor dismissed from office and burning with resentment against his successors and the Emperor William II, accused the successors and the Emperor—through the medium of one of his favourite papers—of being responsible for the Franco-Russian Alliance, by failing to renew the secret treaty which he had concluded with Russia and which would have prevented any Russian-French *rapprochement*. This almost incredible disclosure of a state secret of the first magnitude has right to this day kept alive the impression that the Reinsurance Treaty offered a means of preventing a development which would never have come about if only Bismarck had remained at the helm.

What are the facts?

In 1887 the Three Emperors' Pact still existed and not only the Austrian government, but also the Russian Minister for Foreign Affairs, Giers, hoped for its renewal before the pact expired in June

1887. But the Czar was opposed to it, and Bismarck did nothing to dispel this opposition.

In January 1887 Count Peter Shouwaloff, the former Russian Ambassador in London and Bismarck's favourite Russian delegate to the Congress of Berlin, came to the German capital and proposed a treaty between Germany and Russia alone—that is, leaving out the third ally, Austria. The suggestion was very favourably received by Bismarck, and he grew very angry when the Russian government hesitated to take up Peter Shouwaloff's proposal officially. But the influence which Peter Shouwaloff and his brother Paul Shouwaloff, Russian Ambassador in Berlin, enjoyed with the Czar helped to stiffen the Czar's opposition to a renewal of the Three Emperor's League. Both brothers persuaded the Czar to decide in favour of concluding a treaty with Germany alone. In May 1887 Paul Shouwaloff returned to Berlin with the treaty in draft form.

In his first conversation with Paul Shouwaloff Bismarck committed an indiscretion which in itself was a breach of faith with his Austrian ally. *He read to the astonished Russian the text of the secret treaty of alliance with Austria-Hungary.* He wanted to show him how far he could go in an understanding with Russia and to make it clear that he could never assist Russia in a war of aggression against Austria. Everything else he was ready to concede. He evidently hoped to get in exchange Russia's benevolent neutrality in a German war against France. He was consequently a very disappointed man when Shouwaloff told him in a second interview that Russia would not feel obliged to remain neutral if Germany attacked France. The Czar himself had instructed him on this point. The result was that under the terms of the new treaty each party promised the other to remain neutral in the event of war with a third Great Power. But this undertaking was qualified by a twofold proviso: it would not obtain if Russia attacked Austria or if Germany attacked France. In addition to this principal clause, Germany acknowledged Russia's predominant interest in Bulgaria and she promised not only her benevolent neutrality but also her moral and diplomatic support, if the Czar should desire to defend the entrance to the Black Sea, and to take measures *pour garder la clef de son Empire.* This key to the Russian Empire was, of course, a reference to the Bosphorus and the Dardanelles, the straits giving access from the Mediterranean to the Black Sea.

Such was the treaty which was signed in Berlin on 18th June 1887 —the very day, that is, when the treaty of alliance of the three Emperors expired.

Two questions here present themselves: (1) Was this Reinsurance Treaty compatible with the other existing German treaties? (2) Did it, in fact, realize the ends for which it was concluded? Did it insure Germany against a war with Russia or against Russia's assisting France in the event of a fresh Franco-German war?

The first question is one which concerns the law of nations and political morality, and the second is one of political effectiveness. In considering the first we must pay particular attention to the Austro-German treaty of alliance. This not only remained in existence, it was officially the permanent basis of German foreign policy. Under its terms, Germany promised her assistance to the Habsburg Monarchy if it was attacked by Russia. Under the new treaty Germany promised Russia to stay neutral if she was attacked by the Habsburg Monarchy. Those who defend the new treaty maintain that therefore both treaties are compatible with each other. But the difference depends solely on the question: Who is the aggressor? And this is really the most complex and most disputable question known to politics. It has been the experience of all of us that during and after every war this question is discussed *ad nauseam*. Enough books to fill a library have been written on the theme of who was the real aggressor in the Seven Years' War, in the Franco-Prussian War, or in the first World War.

But to return to the matter in hand, suppose a war did break out between Russia and Austria. Both countries would apply to Germany to fulfil her treaty obligations. Then the problem would have to be decided not by a leisurely and lengthy investigation in which the historian twenty or a hundred years later can indulge, but on the spur of the moment, in twenty-four hours. And who was to decide it? The German Emperor! Or—as long as Bismarck was in power— the German Chancellor. That meant that the question "who is the aggressor?" was to be decided by the very same man who had to put this decision into effect either by going to war or remaining neutral. True, by the treaty of alliance with Austria the German Emperor also had to decide this question. He was entitled to say: "In this war Austria is the aggressor, and therefore I shall now draw the sword". But the difference in the situation before and after the conclusion of the Reinsurance Treaty is this: As long as Germany was bound by her treaty to Austria alone, the Austrian Emperor could rely on the German Emperor's deciding this question in the spirit of an ally. From the moment that Bismarck concluded the secret Reinsurance Treaty, he could *not*. For now Germany had an interest in weighing the benefits which would come to her from the fulfilment of the one treaty against those she would receive by fulfilling the other. Germany's attitude depended solely on the view she took of her *own* interests and not on the treaty. In other words, Austria's alliance with Germany was robbed of any real value by the conclusion of the Reinsurance Treaty.

This treaty was a secret one, but what if it had by some chance become public knowledge in Austria? The government and the peoples of Austria-Hungary would have felt themselves betrayed by their ally, and nobody could have blamed them. Can any treaty which one ally concludes behind the back of his other ally with the very power against which the alliance is directed, be defended? In private life nobody would answer such a question in the affirmative. Nor, in my view, is any other answer admissible in public life.

All these speculations are by no means theoretical. The published documents show how delicate the practical problems became in the months immediately following the new treaty.

There were other points as well which clashed with German treaty obligations, such as the recognition of Russia's predominant interest in Bulgaria and, to an even greater extent, the concession of Russia's right to seize the straits. But enough has probably been said to show that, judged by the law of nations and political morality, the Reinsurance Treaty cannot be defended.

And now, turning to the second question, what about the effectiveness of the treaty?

The supporters of *Realpolitik*, that is pure power politics, will perhaps say that these legal and moral objections are outweighed by the fact that the treaty effectively prevented, for a time at least, a Franco-Russian alliance. They may say that such an alliance was concluded only after Bismarck's successors had been foolish enough to renounce the Reinsurance Treaty. As a matter of fact, the treaty was terminated by Caprivi in 1890, the *entente cordiale* between Russia and France began in August 1891, and the military convention which breathed life into it was concluded in August 1892. But this is not the whole story.

I will here deal only shortly with the argument that just as Germany had been able to conclude the Reinsurance Treaty with the Czar in spite of her alliance with Austria, so also the Czar could equally well have made a defensive alliance with France in spite of his Reinsurance Treaty with Germany. He had expressedly retained his liberty of action in the event of Germany's attacking France. But this is not the real point. The crucial question is whether the Reinsurance Treaty did bring about a *rapprochement* between Germany and Russia and whether the feeling, at least between the two governments let alone the peoples, really did grow more friendly in consequence of it. The answer is most certainly "No".

Only a few days after the conclusion of the treaty, the German press very sharply attacked the worth of the Russian state bonds which the Berlin stock exchange dealt in. Russia's national finances and her whole economic situation stood very much in need of foreign loans. The principal market for these loans was the Berlin stock exchange. The German press now argued that these bonds were unsafe, because in May 1887—that is, during the negotiations for the Reinsurance Treaty—the Czar had issued a ukase prohibiting the tenure of land property in Russia by any foreigners. That was a heavy blow to many Germans who owned estates in Russia. The Czar's ukase was a reprisal for the expulsion in 1885 of thousands of Russia's Polish subjects by an order of Bismarck (p. 70).

Bismarck did nothing to call off the press attacks on the Russian bonds. On the contrary, he gave them his official blessing. At his instigation the German Imperial Bank (Deutsche Reichsbank) and the Prussian State Bank officially announced in November 1887 that they would not in future grant loans against Russian bonds as security (*Lombard-Verbot*). As all German banks had at one time or another to borrow from these two central banks, they too were compelled to refuse Russian bonds as security. The consequence was that the Russian bonds were driven from the Berlin stock exchange and out of the hands of German investors. Russia could not exist without foreign loans. Where was she to raise them? The only market of sufficient financial strength to which Russia could get access was Paris, and the French bankers were ready to fill the gap. As early as the spring of 1888 they were in St. Petersburg negotiating a loan to the Russian Empire, and in the autumn it was fully subscribed on the Paris Bourse. Other loans followed with increasing success. The French public eagerly invested in Russian bonds, and in a short time Paris had replaced Berlin as the principal market for these bonds.

This was a development of the utmost political importance. The financial ties drew the two countries together. Russia became highly interested in the welfare of France and even the Czar could not in the long run keep up his attitude of contempt—or even indifference —towards the French Republic, the citizens of which were subscribing millions upon millions for his army, his railways, and the economic development of his Empire. Finances smoothed the way to a Franco-Russian alliance. Bismarck believed that political relations were independent of commercial, financial, or economic relations. It was now demonstrated how wrong this theory was.

Did the treaty have the effect of making Czar Alexander III personally more friendly to Germany and to Bismarck himself? Once again the answer is "No". This became evident when he very reluctantly paid a visit to Berlin in November 1887. Bismarck came up from his country seat for an audience. He was nervous, fearing that the Czar would not receive him. Why? The Czar suspected him of playing a double game in the Bulgarian question. Bismarck was able to produce some documents which disproved Alexander's suspicion. To this extent he might count the meeting a success. But is it not strange that the Czar could suspect Bismarck of such manœuvres only a few months after concluding with him a treaty that was supposed to cement the friendship between the two countries? Even Paul Shouwaloff, who had negotiated and signed the treaty, said in December 1887 to the French Ambassador: "You need not worry. We shall not allow Germany to dominate us. The era of illusions is past. We know full well the value of our *freedom of action*."

How slender was Bismarck's own confidence in good relations with Russia is proved by the new army bill which he laid before the Reichstag in December 1887. This bill provided for a huge increase in the number of Germans to be put under arms in the event of war. It incorporated the Landsturm—a kind of militia—into the army. This marks the beginning of the process by which, in time of war, armies were increased to millions of men. It was, perhaps, the first step towards that conception which we now term "totalitarian" war.

Bismarck's speech in defence of the bill was clearly aimed at Russia. A few days earlier Bismarck had published the Austro-German treaty to show the world where he stood. Now, in his speech, he expressed himself even more clearly. *"We no longer sue for love either in France or in Russia. We do not run after anybody."* That could not be misunderstood in St. Petersburg. Perhaps the Czar was driven to reflect on the Reinsurance Treaty when Bismarck said: "No great power *can in the long run be guided by a treaty* which conflicts with the *real interests* of the country". The bill was voted unanimously by the Reichstag, not because all opposition to militarism had ceased, but because the House believed in the danger of a Russian war.

In spite of the Reinsurance Treaty, the Czar continued to be suspicious of Bismarck. His own brother, Vladimir, said as much to Herbert Bismarck in April 1888. "He [the Czar] is always afraid of being deceived by him", he said. The German Chancellor was far too clever and skilful for Alexander's limited vision. He knew how Bismarck had duped the Austrian Emperor, and possibly this made him all the more afraid of being treated in the same way. What would happen if by some ruse of Bismarck the Russian people came to learn of the treaty? For this was how things stood: *the Czar knew that his people expected him to be anti-German.* As Schweinitz said, he considered secrecy about the treaty absolutely necessary in the interests not only of his popularity, but of his personal safety.

What practical benefits were to be expected of a treaty which the one partner had to keep secret from his ally and the other from his people? A treaty of this kind was never able to give either of the partners the security for which it was concluded. It was artificial and meaningless, far too weak to be of any real importance. It would not have stood the test of a real crisis, and the esteem in which it is held by some historians can only be explained by the fact that this crisis never came. But it is utterly remote from a true *Realpolitik* to exaggerate the value of a few paragraphs which were, indeed, no more than a scrap of paper.

Bismarck had, of course, too much insight into the real facts to be under any illusions about the value of his own treaty. True, after his downfall in 1896, he exaggerated its worth. But that does not prove that he thought the same in 1887. It merely shows that the dismissed Chancellor hit out recklessly with any weapon which he thought capable of dealing a blow to the Emperor. What he really thought in 1887 is shown by his alacrity in trying to improve relations with Britain. In November 1887, four days after the Czar's visit to Berlin and less than six months from the conclusion of the Reinsurance Treaty, the Chancellor wrote to Lord Salisbury the celebrated personal letter which must be numbered among the most interesting documents he ever penned. In this letter he outlines his views on the European situation by classing Germany and Austria with Britain among the saturated states, while he speaks of the permanent danger to the peace of Europe from France and Russia. Then he says: "The goal of our policy must necessarily be to secure ourselves alliances which are open to us in view of the eventuality of Germany's being compelled to fight two powerful neighbours at the same time!" I will not here discuss whether this was a veiled offer of alliance to Britain. It is certainly not the language of a statesman who feels that he has secured the frontiers of his country by his system of treaties.

Only fourteen months later, in January 1889, Bismarck took one step further. In the meantime the two Emperors William I and Frederick III had died and William II had become Emperor. The Reinsurance Treaty existed, but so small was Bismarck's confidence in it that he tried to arrange an alliance with Britain. This time he took the step from which he had recoiled in 1879. On that occasion he had withdrawn his instructions to the German Ambassador and stopped the negotiations with Beaconsfield because a return to the old friendship with Russia seemed possible and it held more charms for him than one with Britain. For ten years Bismarck had done his best to manage without Britain, and his expedients for preserving peace had become more and more artificial. But now, with his complicated system of treaties complete, his anxieties still preyed on him. True, he tried to silence the German generals who were talking of the inevitable war with Russia and wanted to hasten it forward. But his hopes for the maintenance of peace were not much stronger. Now he turned his eyes to London and ordered his Ambassador Hatzfeldt to propose to the British Prime Minister an Anglo-German treaty against French aggression. But this time Bismarck was too late. Salisbury did not favour such an alliance. He had been sceptical in 1879, when he was Foreign Secretary in Beaconsfield's cabinet. What he had seen in the meantime of Bismarck's policy and of his conception of the word "ally" had only strengthened his disinclination. He told Herbert Bismarck that the time for such an alliance had not yet come. "Meanwhile we leave it on the table, without saying yes or no. That is unfortunately all I can do at present." In reality this was a "No!" and the time for saying "Yes" never came.

This offer of an alliance to Britain was the last important initiative Bismarck took in Foreign Affairs. A year later his rule was over. And so it is on a note of failure that Bismarck's long and triumphant career as the leader of German foreign policy ends.

14. *The Tragedy of Frederick III*

In 1888 the long reign of Emperor William I came to an end. On 9th March of that year Bismarck stood before the assembled Reichstag to tell them that their old master had just died. It was an enormously impressive scene. The Iron Chancellor was deeply moved. Tears were in his eyes.

This was one of the most important moments in Bismarck's life. He knew that in the old Emperor he had lost his mainstay. Whoever now sat on the Imperial throne would not be willing in the same degree to give his name and authority to everything his Chancellor did. The new Emperor Frederick III came to the throne a dangerously sick man, whose reign would be measured in months, if not weeks. He suffered from cancer of the throat, and, following an operation, had already lost the use of his voice. Only ninety-nine days were, in fact, left to him.

No one will ever be able to say how Frederick would have ruled the German Empire if fate had given him good health and the normal span of life. But one thing is certain: he was a man of liberal and humane ideas, which he would not have forgotten on becoming King and Emperor. He would have bridged a gap in the development of the Reich, which, as things turned out, proved a crucial one and has made itself felt right up to the present day. A whole generation, the one which was young in 1848 and in its prime at the time of the Prussian constitutional conflict and the movement towards national unity, a generation grown up under the influence of liberal ideas, was passed over, and a new generation came to the fore, which exalted national splendour and military glory above all else. A new Emperor appeared, too, a green youth, who was stupid enough to rant to his soldiers that, at a mere word from their Emperor, they would have, if need be, to shoot their fathers and mothers. How different the course of German history would have been if in his stead there had arisen a man who knew the true worth of liberty and who spoke words of humanity!"

Frederick III was not popular among influential circles at court and in the army. Even more than the Kaiser himself they disliked his wife, the Empress Victoria, daughter of the British Queen. The harshest reproach which they laid at his door was that he let himself be influenced by his wife, who, they said, far excelled him in energy and intelligence. That may be an exaggeration, but there is no doubt that Victoria was, indeed, a very intelligent woman. Her father, Prince Albert, had early recognized this and had taken special care with her education.

The Empress had very decided political views, and these were quite the opposite of Bismarck's. In a letter written to a friend after the death of her husband she says: "Why were we, so to speak, in opposition? Because our patriotism wanted to see the greatness of our fatherland connected with the noble sense for right, morality, for freedom and culture, for individual independence, for the improvement of the single person as man and as German, as European and as cosmopolitan. Improvement, progress, ennoblement—that was our motto. Peace, tolerance, charity—these most precious possessions of mankind, we had to see them trampled upon, laughed at. . . . *Blood and iron* alone had made Germany great and unified—all national vices were called patriotism!"

Words like these are clearly a criticism of Bismarck's iron system, but also of her son, William II. The relations between mother and son were very strained. Victoria resented his arrogance, but she also considered him as an embodiment of political views which would be calamitous for Germany. Bismarck and, to an even greater degree, his son Herbert, added fuel to the flames. William posed as an unconditional admirer of the Chancellor and revealed this preference in some very tactless speeches. Bismarck tried to use him as a tool against his father and more especially against his mother. Perhaps Victoria, too, lacked the tact necessary in her difficult position. But she felt isolated, surrounded by enemies and spies and cut off from every disinterested and experienced adviser.

The new Emperor had, of course, to confirm Bismarck in his office and to collaborate with him as best as he could. Suddenly, on 5th April 1888, the nation was startled by the news, published in a paper intimately connected with the Foreign Office, that the Chancellor was on the verge of resigning because of a private quarrel with the Imperial pair. The dispute, the readers learned, centred round Prince Alexander of Battenberg, the former ruler of Bulgaria, to whom the Empress and her mother, Queen Victoria, wanted to marry Princess Victoria, the Empress's daughter.

The facts are these. Bismarck had heard that the Emperor had invited Prince Alexander to Berlin and that he intended to bestow a high order on him and to reinstate him in a post in the German army. The Chancellor had at once protested in the strongest possible way, asserting that good relations between Germany and Russia would be in danger if the Empress's wishes should be fulfilled. He had threatened to resign if the Emperor refused to follow his advice. The Emperor had given way and had sent Alexander a telegram cancelling his invitation. All this took place *before* the news of the impending resignation was made known to the public. Thus Bismarck had already won his point before he whipped up popular indignation with this sensational news. Bismarck certainly foresaw the inevitable consequence: an outcry against the Imperial pair, particularly against the Empress, *die Engländerin* as the national Germans called her, who, it was said, wanted to sacrifice Germany's greatest statesman to a feminine caprice.

A vivid description of the uproar is given in a letter written by the British Minister in Dresden, Sir George Strachey, to Sir Henry Ponsonby, Queen Victoria's private secretary: 'Leipzig which is hyper-Bismarckian (specifically National-Liberal) and Dresden, which is ultra-conservative, have shewn a maximum of hatred of the Empress and the Queen. The Leipzig *Grenzboten*, which has often been utilized by Bismarck, published the other day a long tirade against the two royal ladies, in which the insolence and venom of the Prussian 'reptiles' were almost surpassed. The folly and vulgarity of similar lucubrations pass belief. The *Freisinnige* party in Saxony is weak, so that their voice cries in the desert; but they have defended the Emperor, the Empress and the Queen, with great courage and pertinacity and their Dresden organ exhausts the superlative of eulogy every day in praise of all three. As in Berlin, the radicals (who after all, are only on the political level of our Tories) are admirably loyal, while the Bismarckites are behaving like Anarchists.

"For the moment, it would seem as if the 'reptile' press had received a hint, to prepare for a change of front. One of the Bismarck gang has the audacity to dilate on 'the Reichskanzler's touching, devoted love for his all-highest master', which may indicate that Bismarck thinks that the Emperor's recovery is possible.

"At the great official dinner on the King of Saxony's birthday, I found that all the political summits agreed that Bismarck was the moral, perhaps the material author of the whole '*Hetze*' and although the majority present were 'grave-diggers', no one much dissented from the very undiplomatic language in which I relieved my feelings at his expense."

But what is most interesting about the whole story, is the way Russia was brought into it. Bismarck made the assertion which thoroughly roused national fury, that the Czar would lose confidence in the German government if the Prince of Battenberg, whom he hated so fiercely, became the son-in-law of the Emperor. This too was untrue and Bismarck had to suffer one of his greatest disappointments when he tried—and failed—to get a declaration from the Russian government supporting his assertion.

Czar Alexander III had been very favourably impressed by the proclamation with which the new Emperor had inaugurated his reign. Schweinitz was able to report to Berlin that the Czar had never expressed himself so satisfied with his relations with Germany as he had since the accession of Frederick. Giers, who had tried hard to remain on good terms with Bismarck, could not help saying that nothing would be changed in Berlin *excepté le ton, et ce sera déjà beaucoup*. Schweinitz now approached him on Bismarck's instructions to elicit the declaration that a visit by the Battenberg Prince to Berlin would be considered in Russia as an anti-Russian demonstration. But the gist of Giers' answer, which he formulated very carefully, was: "Although we would regret it, we would be convinced that neither the Emperor Frederick nor the Chancellor would change their policy of friendship towards Russia". In other words, the Czar would not draw any political conclusions from the visit, which Bismarck had represented to his people as an insufferable affront to the Czar. The Russian reply was exactly the opposite of what Bismarck had expected and wished. In spite of this correction, Bismarck talked to his newspaper henchman, Busch, of the danger of a Russian war which a marriage with the Battenberg Prince would provoke and which could only turn out to Britain's advantage.

That Bismarck talked to Busch in this way about Britain's advantage was part and parcel of his attempt to whip up feeling against Queen Victoria, who, it was announced, was about to visit her daughter and her son-in-law, now seriously ill. He even tried to influence the British Ambassador to persuade the British government to advise the Queen to cancel the visit. But Salisbury wrote in reply to Malet's letter:

"I am very sorry not to be able to comply with Prince Bismarck's wishes, but he is asking me *to assist him in thwarting the wishes of his Emperor and my Queen to gratify the malignant feelings of the Russian Emperor*. This would certainly be inconsistent with my duty and, if German co-operation can only be held at this price, *we must do without it*."

The Queen herself called Bismarck's conduct "really disloyal, wicked and really unwise in the extreme". When she came to Berlin her enthusiastic reception by the people of the German capital showed that anti-British feeling was prevalent only in the sparse ranks of courtiers, officials, and generals, whose connexion with diplomatists and newspapers gave them the chance to pose as representatives of German opinion.

Why did Bismarck incite the violent agitation against the Imperial pair, even though the question of the Battenberg visit was settled *before* he unleashed his press-hounds? I can only explain it by referring to his report of 1886 to the old Emperor, in which he spoke of Alexander as a possible Chancellor, backed by the opposition in the Reichstag. This opposition had in the meantime been smashed by Bismarck in the elections of 1887. But the pendulum was already swinging the other way. A number of by-elections showed that the voters had shaken off the intoxication of the war scare. I consider it quite possible that Bismarck's somewhat perverted imagination conjured up a plan laid by the Empress to make the Prince of Battenberg Chancellor, to dissolve the Reichstag and to bring back by means of a new election the old majority of *Freisinnige*, Centre, and Socialists, who would support him against Bismarck. True, neither the Prince nor the Empress harboured any such ideas. But whenever his personal power was in question, Bismarck was often inclined to see ghosts.

The Emperor and Empress were almost completely powerless against this outburst of national fanaticism. They had no independent and competent adviser, because nobody could come near them without rousing the Chancellor's suspicion. It is characteristic of the situation in Germany at this time that they finally got helpful advice only by underground means. The Empress Victoria had a friend, the Baroness von Stockmar, widow of Ernest von Stockmar, who some years before had been private secretary to the Crown Prince. Ernest von Stockmar was the son of the famous Dr. Stockmar who had been the confidential adviser to Albert, the British Prince Consort, and a man of outstanding intelligence and sagacity, much respected by Queen Victoria. The Baroness von Stockmar knew the Liberal Radical deputy, Dr. Ludwig Bamberger, who lived near her, very well. She went to see Bamberger and laid before him the problems which disturbed the Empress. Bamberger gave her his advice. This had to be done in utter secrecy, so that no word should reach Bismarck's ears. The Empress would write a letter to the Baroness von Stockmar, who would take it to Bamberger, and he would write one in reply to the Baroness who, in turn, would deliver it to the Empress. In this way the Emperor and the Empress got the benefit of the advice and help of a most cultured, intelligent, and experienced parliamentarian who knew Bismarck and his ways better than anyone else, and could warn them whenever they were in danger of being deceived by his artful manœuvres. The only political act of importance taken by Frederick during his brief reign was based on Bamberger's advice, and that was the dismissal of the most reactionary of the Prussian Ministers, von Puttkamer, who had offended the Emperor's sense of fair play by his brazen attempts to influence the elections. Puttkamer was dismissed on 8th June. Exactly a week later Frederick died.

When Frederick felt his end to be near, he called Bismarck and laid the Empress's hands in the Chancellor's. He could not utter a word, but his gestures showed that he wanted to entrust to him the protection of his wife, whom, he was certain, he was leaving surrounded by enemies. He knew his son, William, now to become Emperor, and he was convinced that this son would do the very opposite of all he himself had wished to do, and that he would treat his own mother without consideration or tact. But his hope that Bismarck would assist her was completely vain.

On the contrary, the heaviest blow dealt to the memory of the dead Emperor was delivered by Bismarck. This was the affair of the Emperor's diary.

In September 1888, a few months after Frederick's death, a well-known and highly respected German review, *Die Deutsche Rundschau*, published anonymously an extract from the diary which Frederick had kept during the Franco-Prussian War. It related something of the struggle which had gone on in the German headquarters at Versailles over the creation of Emperor and Empire. It revealed the Crown Prince as an ardent supporter and advocate of the national idea and a believer in the Liberal organization of the Reich. Here and there the Crown Prince criticized Bismarck's attitude as too hesitant. But no one who read it impartially could possibly think that it detracted in the least from Bismarck's real and incontestable merits. The historian would consider it a highly valuable document for correcting certain wrong impressions and for gaining a balanced view of a great moment in German history.

But when Bismarck's eyes fell on these pages he was completely infuriated, the more especially as the hated Radical Liberal press printed copious extracts from the diary with highly laudatory comments. He had criminal proceedings taken against the person who had sent these extracts to the *Deutsche Rundschau*. This unfortunate man, Professor Geffcken, a personal friend of the dead Emperor, was arrested on a charge of having falsified the diary. Bismarck knew perfectly well that the diary was completely genuine. He said so himself to his press-agent, Busch. But his rage so far blinded him that he completely forgot the ninth commandment.

Bismarck embodied all his complaints about the diary in a report to William II. Reports to the Emperor were called *Immediat-Berichte* (immediate reports), and this *Immediat-Bericht* was published on Bismarck's instigation with young William's consent. It created an enormous and very painful impression, for it showed quite clearly that Bismarck would stop at nothing and spare no one if his wrath was provoked. The report contained unprecedented slanders on the Emperor who was barely in his grave. One of the first sentences of this lamentable document runs: "I was not allowed by King William to discuss the more confidential aspects of our policy with the Crown Prince, because His Majesty feared indiscretions leaking out to the English Court, which was full of French sympathisers". That the greatest statesman of the century could not only write but publish such a defamatory sentence is hardly credible. One of his admirers hitherto, a Conservative politician, wrote indignantly: "Even if it is true, it should not have been said, for not only does the memory of the dead Emperor suffer by it but the confidence of the nation in the dynasty must be shaken by it". He hints that this slander is really aimed at the Empress Victoria. Doubtless this was Bismarck's intention, although he knew from a letter written by Victoria's aide-de-camp that she had nothing whatever to do with the publication. This, then, was the way in which Bismarck fulfilled his Emperor's dying wish.

From a legal point of view Bismarck's campaign against Emperor Frederick's diary ended in defeat. The supreme court of the Empire, the Reichsgericht, decided that the indictment against Geffcken was untenable. He had to be released after a detention lasting more than three months. The political consequences were perhaps worse, for the affair gave the young Emperor perhaps the first hint that Bismarck's advice was not always as wise and disinterested as he had supposed. True, he had allowed himself to be guided by Bismarck's advice in this matter, particularly over the publication of the

Immediat-Bericht. But what reply could he make if someone told him that this publication was detrimental to the authority of the Hohenzollerns? And there were many men around him who were eager to attack the Chancellor's all-powerful position.

15. *Bismarck's Fall*

William II was not yet thirty years old when he ascended the throne of Germany and Prussia. This is hardly a ripe age to become the ruler of a great Empire. But unfortunately William was even less ripe than his years. His father had seen this quite plainly, and he had for that reason protested against the attempts by the old Emperor and Bismarck to occupy young William prematurely with Foreign Affairs. "In view of the immaturity and inexperience of my eldest son, as shown by his tendency to overestimate himself," he wrote to the Chancellor in 1886, "I cannot but call it dangerous to introduce him thus early to foreign questions." He ought, continued his father, to familiarize himself with conditions at home before exercising his rash and over-hasty judgment in politics. But the father's advice fell on deaf ears and only subsequent events showed how right he was.

During the few years after this letter was written the Prince had not learned much. Professor Gneist, who was charged with introducing him to the constitution and administration of his country, complained to the French Ambassador that the Prince imagined he knew everything—without having learned anything. His father's critical illness had given him the chance to thrust himself into the foreground and to pose as the champion of national sentiment. His vanity was inflated by the applause of his military entourage, the officers of the Potsdam guard whose company he preferred to any other. They praised him as the embodiment of all military virtues, and even Bismarck asserted that he was the hope of Germany for the very reason that he possessed the qualities of an officer of the Prussian Guards.

But there were deeper and stronger reasons for his tendency to over-estimate himself and his position. Bismarck's whole political endeavour tended to exalt the position of the King of Prussia and to make him the real ruler of Germany. His whole system was based on the pretence that the power of political decision lay in the hands of the King of Prussia and the Emperor of Germany alone. Once he went so far as to say in parliament that the real Minister-President of Prussia was His Majesty the King. Any political step which Bismarck wished to take was labelled "the policy of the Emperor", and whoever opposed him was branded as the enemy of the Emperor. Every experienced politician knew, of course, that this was only a manner of speaking, but can we wonder that a young and ambitious emperor, tasting power for the first time, should take it as the literal truth and seriously believe that "the Emperor's policy" must in actual fact be his own policy.

Moreover, worship of the Imperial family of Hohenzollern had become part and parcel of the patriotic creed. It was taught in thousands of schools and proclaimed from hundreds of university chairs. Not only was the old Emperor himself glorified, but almost every Hohenzollern who had ever occupied the throne. Treitschke, who may be regarded as the high priest of this Hohenzollern cult, even went so far as to hold up the mediocre and wooden Frederick William III as a great statesman, and the sharp protest of another historian, Baumgarten, against the whole tendency of Treitschke's German History, was considered by many of his colleagues as hardly short of an unpatriotic act.

Such an atmosphere explains much of the young Emperor's arrogance. Only a strong and seasoned character can withstand the insidious effects of perpetual applause and adulation. William II was not blessed with such a character, but he did possess some qualities which impressed most of those who knew him closely. He was undeniably a man who was quick to see the point and he also had a certain talent for expressing himself. But these qualities were more dangerous than useful or helpful, because he recoiled from serious and sustained work. General Waldersee, who had enthusiastically greeted William's accession, soon writes in this diary that the Emperor ignored oral reports by his Ministers or generals because they bored him. Bismarck himself complained to the Ministers as early as February 1889, that His Majesty would rather drive out to Potsdam for a regimental dinner than follow his advice and hold a council of Ministers every week in order to get acquainted with his new task.

It was not to be expected that a man like this would acquiesce in the rôle his grandfather had played by the side of Bismarck. True, he had praised the Chancellor to the skies when he was at odds with his mother and father. During that time the Chancellor had used the Prince for his own ends, and he and his son had endeavoured, not to compose but to sharpen the conflict in the Imperial family. Herbert Bismarck, in particular, meddled in this conflict with the most unfortunate results. He had been made Secretary for Foreign Affairs at the age of thirty-six, and was evidently marked out by his father to be his heir and successor. But the son possessed none of his father's outstanding capacities, either in statesmanship or in the art of handling men. He was arrogant and tactless. The intervention of the father and son in the Imperial family quarrel did much to inflate William's self-conceit.

And now those people around William whispered in his ear that he would never become a great ruler while he was only the tool of his formidable Chancellor. Frederick the Great, they said, would never have become the great monarch he did, if he had been directed by a Bismarck. The Chancellor was not unaware of all this, and in particular he suspected General Count von Waldersee of working against him. The general was a very ambitious man and Bismarck believed that he coveted the Chancellorship for himself. An instance of the tactics which were used to drive a wedge between William and Bismarck is furnished by the notorious *Scheiterhaufen-Brief* (stake letter) written by Stöcker, the court chaplain. Stöcker was a Conservative member of parliament and a vehement agitator, and the man who introduced anti-Semitism as a party slogan into German political life. He belonged to the extreme Right wing of his party, the organ of which was the *Kreuz-Zeitung*. The editor of the *Kreuz-Zeitung*, Baron von Hammerstein, a gifted but dissolute man, who ended up in penal servitude, was also a member of the Reichstag. This extreme Right wing, led by Stöcker and Hammerstein, hated Liberalism even in the mild form of National Liberalism and sought the destruction of the *Kartell*, which at Bismarck's wish allied the Conservative and National Liberal Parties. Stöcker had been a favourite of William and his wife in their earlier days and he hoped to dominate the Emperor once Bismarck was out of the way. As early as August 1888 Stöcker wrote a letter to Hammerstein giving him advice on how to separate the Emperor and the Chancellor in such a way that William should not be conscious of the manœuvre. In this letter occurs the famous sentence: "We must kindle faggots around the *Kartell* and make them blaze up". "If the Kaiser perceives", writes the pious chaplain, "that we want to sow discord between him and Bismarck, he would be offended. But if we nourish his discontent in matters in which he instinctively takes our side, we shall strengthen him on principle without irritating him personally." And then he quotes William as saying: "I shall give the old man six months to recover his breath. But then I shall reign myself." Hammerstein put his plan into practice in the *Kreuz-Zeitung* by—to quote one example—criticizing the Chancellor of having offended monarchical feeling by publishing the *Immediat-Bericht*.

At this time Bismarck's influence was still strong enough to frustrate such intrigues. At his instigation the Kaiser confronted Stöcker with the choice of either resigning his office at court or of putting a stop to the agitation. Stöcker preferred to keep his post and gave up his press campaign. The Kaiser went further; he publicly repudiated the *Kreuz-Zeitung* and declared in favour of the *Kartell*. He made the leader of the National Liberal Party, Bennigsen, Chief President of the Province of Hanover, and he offered a similar post to Miquel, who greatly impressed him by his fascinating conversation. But Miquel, who knew that Bismarck neither liked nor trusted him, declined the offer. He expected that his moment would come when Bismarck had gone.

Bismarck could not fail to see that many influences around the Kaiser were working against him. To maintain his own ascendancy he should have taken the trouble to stay in Berlin as much as possible to see the King and advise him out of his fund of seasoned political wisdom. But he did the very opposite, retiring to Varzin or Friedrichsruh for months at a stretch. He probably imagined that his son Herbert could influence the Kaiser in his interest. But Herbert was by no means equal to this task, and Bismarck, usually the most acute judge of men, utterly failed to see the shortcomings of his own son.

But it was not merely personal questions which led to Bismarck's downfall. There were political difficulties and differences which separated the young Kaiser from the old Chancellor.

The first serious difference occurred in May 1889 when a big strike broke out among the Westphalian miners. Bismarck had not the slightest sympathy with their grievances. As a Junker he was at heart on the side of the employers. But the Kaiser had heard from unofficial sources something of the living conditions of the miners, and he had been greatly affected by their plight. No one to-day will blame William for his sympathy with the working man; unfortunately he had a very clumsy and tactless way of voicing it. He suddenly appeared at the Council of his Ministers, presided over by the Chancellor, and delivered them a vehement speech against the employers, treating the whole dispute as if it were something of which he could dispose by royal decree. When he left the Council, Bismarck remarked sarcastically that the young monarch had the outlook of Frederick William I, the despotic father of Frederick the Great, and he added that it would be necessary to protect him from his own impetuosity.

Bismarck could see from this incident that the Emperor looked at social questions in quite another way than he did himself. But there were worse troubles to come, and these centred on the law against the Socialists.

The Reichstag elected in consequence of the septennium struggle of 1887, and known as the *Kartell* Reichstag, was the most favourable Bismarck had had since 1881. The *Kartell*, which followed him through thick and thin, had an absolute majority. The opposition was impotent.

The Chancellor was anxious to profit by this exceptionally strong position to make the law against the Socialists permanent. He did not like having to approach the Reichstag every second or third year to secure its prolongation. He had never considered it as a temporary measure, to be used only in time of emergency. Nor, on the other hand, could he bring himself to draw the moral from the marked ineffectiveness of the measure. It had not prevented an increase in the Socialist vote even though it had now been in force for over ten years. Bismarck reached the conclusion that it should be made permanent. The *Kartell* majority was quite willing to back this policy, and the bill brought in by the government in the autumn of 1889 had every chance of being passed. Even the National Liberals had no qualms. They asked for only one modification. The law gave the police power to expel Socialist agitators from their domiciles, and this power had been used excessively and sometimes brutally. This had caused indignation even among many people who were far from sympathizing with the Socialists. The National Liberals now objected to making this power of expulsion permanent and they voted against the clause in the committee of the Reichstag which considered it in December 1889. The Conservatives who had fought most ardently for the clause, declared that the law was useless if the clause were not restored. The committee read the bill a second time and once again the clause was rejected by the votes of the National Liberals and the Opposition members. The Conservatives now voted against the whole bill, and thus it might well have been thrown out in the committee stage. But Windthorst saw how valuable this discord between two *Kartell* parties was for the opposition, particularly in view of the coming elections, and in order to compel them to fight it out in the presence of the plenary session of the Reichstag and, indeed, of the whole German people, he and his friends voted for the mutilated bill, which in consequence had to be referred to and discussed by the whole Reichstag. The plenary sessions of the Reichstag were to be held in January 1890, and in the February of that year a new Reichstag was to be elected. The elections would therefore be powerfully influenced by the battle over the anti-Socialist law.

During the committee stage the leader of the Conservative Party, von Helldorf, went to Friedrichsruh to discuss the attitude of his party with the Chancellor. He knew that the bill was doomed if the government insisted on the power of expulsion, and he was willing to vote for it without this provision, if only the government made it clear that it would accept it in this form. But the Chancellor gave him no such undertaking. In later years Bismarck asserted that Helldorf had misunderstood him and he even hinted that he was in league with his enemies. But the question was quite a plain one, and Bismarck could, if he had wished, have given quite a plain answer. But he did not, and he himself knew why.

While the fate of the anti-Socialist law was still in the balance, another problem arose which was bound to separate Kaiser and Chancellor even more effectively. William became increasingly interested in social problems. Unofficial advisers told him about the need for protecting working people, particularly women and children, against overwork and other forms of exploitation. This, of course, was nothing new, even in Germany. For years the parties in the Reichstag had been demanding measures for the safeguarding of labour and the Reichstag had passed resolutions on these lines. There was only one stumbling-block: the Chancellor himself. Bismarck had the most obsolete ideas on such questions, ideas which the Manchester school of economics had had perhaps half a century earlier, but which it had long outgrown. To Bismarck such measures were *Humanitätsdusel* (humanitarian rubbish). The truth is that he opposed reform in every direction in his old age. There were many reforms which were long overdue, and the Ministers themselves knew it. For instance, income tax in Prussia cried aloud for adjustment. The Prussian Minister of Finance, an unconditional admirer of Bismarck, had drafted a reform bill. The King had given it his assent and his signature. But, before it could be debated in parliament, Bismarck wound up the session of the Landtag and the bill went into the wastepaper-basket.

Now, when William II began to be interested in social legislation, it was manifest to any impartial observer that sooner or later it was bound to come. The Reichstag on the one hand and the Kaiser on the other would inevitably overcome the Chancellor's opposition. Bismarck's deputy in the government of the Reich and of Prussia, von Boetticher, the Reich Secretary of State for the Interior, saw clearly that the Chancellor would fight a losing battle if he did not come round in time. He went to Friedrichsruh to give the Chancellor advice. But Bismarck was adamant. The only effect of his visit was that he began to suspect Boetticher of being a secret adversary, of turning his face towards the rising sun of the young Emperor, and of coveting the mantle of Chancellor. This last, of course, was the worst possible sin in Bismarck's eyes. Such a suspicion was at any time capable of poisoning his mind. On this occasion it had a double sting; to him the appearance of a rival meant not merely a threat to his own position but a danger to his son Herbert, whom he already regarded as his successor. That Boetticher should attempt to go his own way or even to make proposals of his own, Bismarck considered not only presumptuous but ungrateful. He had helped Boetticher out of financial difficulties which had befallen him through no fault of his own, by a gift from the *Welfen-Fonds*, pretending to Boetticher that it was a private gift from the old Emperor (p. 150). He considered that by virtue of this gift Boetticher ought to be grateful to him personally and that he had, so to speak, bought Boetticher with the money he had taken from the pocket of the dethroned King of Hanover.

Boetticher visited Friedrichsruh on 9th January 1890. On the same day the Reichstag had reassembled. The second reading of the anti-Socialist law was on the order of the day for the 23rd January. Bismarck's obvious course was to return to Berlin at once. Not only Boetticher, but the Chief of the Chancellor's Office, von Rottenburg, Bismarck's most intimate collaborator, suggested it. But Bismarck turned down their advice and listened instead to that of Herbert, who was all for remaining in Friedrichsruh.

Only on 24th January did Bismarck return to Berlin in compliance with the wish of the Kaiser, who had summoned a Kronrat for the afternoon of that day. A Kronrat was the official designation of a session of the Prussian Ministry of State under the personal presidency of the King.

The Kronrat was fixed for 6 P.M. Before it met, the Kaiser desired to see Bismarck privately. Bismarck called a meeting of the Ministers in his office at 3 P.M.

When the Ministers met the Chancellor, he spoke to them about the proposal for labour protection which the Kaiser would presumably lay before the Crown Council. He advised them neither to accept nor to oppose these proposals, but to ask for time to think them over. Every Minister agreed. Then Bismarck turned to the anti-Socialist law. It had been given a second reading in the Reichstag the day before. All its clauses, except the one providing for the expulsion of Socialists by order of the police, had been accepted by the majority. The National Liberals had voted against this clause together with the opposition parties. In the debate, von Helldorf had declared in the name of his party that if this clause was not restored they would vote against the whole bill, unless the government officially declared that it would accept the bill in its truncated form. This decision by the Conservative Party represented a compromise between its two wings, one of which wanted to smash and the other to preserve the *Kartell*, and it had an eye to the coming elections. The Conservatives wanted to have some explanation to give the electorate if they should finally vote for the mutilated bill in spite of all their vigorous speeches against it, and it was for this reason that they needed the public declaration by the government for which they asked.

Bismarck now told the Ministers that it was unwise to facilitate the passing of the mutilated bill through the Reichstag by a government declaration, because this would absolve the parliament of its responsibility. Boetticher pointed out that without the government declaration the bill was lost, and he produced a number of arguments against such a course. Other Ministers took his side. But once again Bismarck stood firm. His arguments were based on a subtle theory which served the same purpose as some other similar casuistry in which he had indulged—to conceal his true motives.

At six o'clock the Ministers assembled for the Kronrat. When they entered the Council chamber they met the Kaiser and the Chancellor, who had talked matters over but had not reached agreement.

The Emperor opened the proceedings with a speech setting out his social reforms. There was nothing extravagant in these proposals: prohibition of Sunday work in factories and restriction of the labour of women and children, all of them things to which nobody would nowadays give a second thought. But the speech in which William set forth these proposals was, indeed, couched in curious terms. He said, for example, that German employers squeezed their workers like lemons and let the old people rot on the dunghill, and he finally declared that he wanted to be a *roi des gueux* (king of the beggars) —the self-same slogan Bismarck had used twenty-five years earlier when he wished to infuriate the Progressive Party. He was far from pleased to hear the phrase fall now from the lips of his young Kaiser in support of a social policy which he abhorred.

The Kaiser mentioned his wish to make a proclamation to his people on that very day, which happened to be Frederick the Great's birthday—an instance of his flair for the dramatic. But when the Ministers, following the instructions they had received, replied, they said that they wanted time to think the matter over, and William gave way.

But the real storm broke when William turned to the anti-Socialist law. He pleaded for the acceptance of the bill, even without the power of expulsion. But this time Bismarck opposed him. Seeing that his theoretical arguments did not impress the Kaiser, he grew more and more excited, and at last exclaimed that if the law fell through, they would have to do without it and let the waves mount higher and higher until a clash occurred.

Here was Bismarck's real motive. He hoped that the Socialists, freed from the fetters of the law, would go to extremes, and he would then be ready to suppress them with armed force. William understood him quite correctly. Bismarck meant to steer towards a bloody conflict, and so he replied that he did not wish to stain the first years of his reign with the blood of his subjects. He appealed to the other Ministers and asked them to give their opinion. He had reason to believe that they agreed with him. But he was greatly disappointed. Not one of them dared, in the Chancellor's presence, to side with the Kaiser. William was compelled to back down. Bismarck had his way and the anti-Socialist law was lost.

The Kaiser left the Kronrat in high dudgeon. He felt that he had been deserted by the Ministers. "They are not my ministers", he said, "but Bismarck's." What had become of Bismarck's theory, so often proclaimed, of the "Emperor's policy"? It was wrecked on the first occasion that he and his Emperor did not see eye to eye.

The next day the anti-Socialist law was read in the Reichstag for the third time. When the general vote was taken, the Conservatives voted against the whole bill, as no government declaration of the kind they wanted was made, and the measure was rejected by these votes combined with the votes of the *Freisinnige*, Centre, and Social Democrats. It was, in fact, the end of this exceptional law. The old law did not expire until 30th September 1890, and the elections in February still had to be held under the shadow of its restrictions. But what then? Would any future Reichstag be prepared to pass a law which even the *Kartell* Reichstag had declined? Nobody who knew the feelings of the German people could believe that. On the contrary, most observers were sure of a heavy defeat of the *Kartell* parties at the next election, and the mismanagement of the anti-Socialist law by the government, the manifest lack of leadership and the conflict between Conservatives and National Liberals made their defeat a certainty. Never again, in fact, was a resurrection of the dead anti-Socialist law attempted.

We cannot doubt that Bismarck saw as clearly as anyone how impossible it was to get a more favourably disposed Reichstag. His attitude can only be explained by the supposition that he really wanted a conflict. But what a mistake to blurt it out in the Crown Council! How differently he had managed these things in the Crown Councils of his heyday, from 1864 to 1866, when he led William I along his own path without telling him more than was good for him. Bismarck's second son, a cool observer and a bit of a cynic, said: "My father lacks the old hammer-stroke". Bismarck himself felt that he had blundered in the Kronrat. The next morning his Chief of Chancery found him lying on the sofa with tears in his eyes. He could not remain in office, he said, the Kaiser being completely estranged from him. But this mood passed. He was not the man to relinquish power of his own free will.

He tried to compromise. At the next meeting of the ministry he urged support for the Kaiser's idea of protection for the working man. William was happy. The next day, 27th January, which was the Emperor's birthday, had all appearance of a festival of reconciliation. But a few days later he learned that Bismarck was making fresh difficulties. The Kaiser had suggested to the King of Saxony that he should bring proposals embodying his wishes before the Bundesrat. But Bismarck threatened the Saxon Minister that he would resign if he dared to do this. William was suspicious when he heard that the ministry was deliberating over his drafts of a proclamation in which he intended to announce his social programme to his people and to the world. Bismarck divided the draft into two proclamations, one containing the proposed alterations of the law, the other containing an invitation to the other governments for an international conference on social problems to be held in Berlin. In the midst of the meeting of the Ministers, the Kaiser arrived unannounced, jingling his spurs. This was not the manner in which Bismarck was accustomed to be treated by his King. But when Bismarck told William what the Ministers had resolved, he was satisfied and withdrew.

A few days later the proclamations were ready. Bismarck himself had helped in editing the texts, but when the Kaiser had signed them and asked for the counter-signature of the Chancellor, as prescribed by the constitution governing state acts of the Emperor, Bismarck declined. This was a very serious matter. But William was so pleased at being allowed to make his proclamations, that he published them without Bismarck's counter-signature in the *Reichsanzeiger*, the official gazette, on 4th February 1890.

At this time the elections were in full swing. The general excitement was increased still more by the sensation which the proclamations caused, not least by the missing counter-signature of the Chancellor. The opposition members were now certain not only that the anti-Socialist law was dead and buried, but that the Kaiser's policy was in open conflict with Bismarck's. Bamberger was shown the proclamation just as he was setting out for his constituency. Half seriously, half in jest, he said to a friend: "Perhaps Bismarck will celebrate his birthday on April 1st in Friedrichsruh as a private citizen".

Bismarck felt that things could not stay as they were. At the next meeting he told the Ministers that he would resign his office as Prussian Minister-President and retain only his post as Reichskanzler, and that the Kaiser had agreed to this. But if he had hoped that the Ministers would protest against his partial retirement, he was greatly disappointed. They all agreed to the arrangement, and Boetticher made an eloquent farewell speech. Bismarck's anger towards him was all the greater.

On the same day that this ministerial meeting was held, Bismarck took a step which surpassed all his former intrigues. The French Ambassador was completely taken aback when Bismarck, who never called on a foreign diplomatist, suddenly appeared in his embassy. But he was still more surprised when the Chancellor proposed quite bluntly that he should induce the French government to wreck the international labour conference to which the German Emperor had issued invitations. "The Chancellor has unambiguously taken sides against his sovereign", writes the French Ambassador. But the most astonishing feature of the whole incredible story is that Bismarck felt no whit embarrassed in his more than questionable situation. He was in high feather and talked amusingly and sarcastically to the Ambassador about one of the German princes, the Grand Duke of Baden, who was the Emperor's uncle. Finally, he chatted with the

Ambassador about the pictures in his room which represented the story of Jason and Medea. The Ambassador mentioned a legend that Medea had in the end returned to Jason. Bismarck laughed and hummed the couplet: "*On revient toujours à ses premiers amours*". And he left with the words: "Perhaps that will happen to me as well!"

This was not the only manœuvre that Bismarck undertook to wreck the international labour conference on which the Kaiser had set his heart. As a matter of course the Kaiser heard of these stratagems and he was now convinced that he might expect any underhand trick from the Chancellor. He was offended in his sense of sovereignty. "I owed it to the Crown", he said later, "to get rid of such a man."

Bismarck now tried the same method that he had so effectively used against the Emperor Frederick. He let it be known through a foreign newspaper that differences of opinion between himself and the Kaiser compelled him to ask for his retirement from the Prussian government. But once again he was disappointed. The papers which had wept and wailed in 1888 took the news quietly, or, worse still, were quite content. A National Liberal paper coolly wrote that this would be in the best interests of the Prussian Ministers, whose initiative was suppressed by Bismarck.

And then, on 20th February, came the elections for the new Reichstag. The *Kartell* parties were heavily defeated, the *Freisinnige* doubled their seats, and the Social Democrats their votes. They polled almost one and a half million votes, in spite of all the irksome restrictions imposed by the existing anti-Socialist law.

This was the heaviest blow ever dealt to Bismarck's system. Thousands of voters felt they had been duped by Bismarck and his war scare at the previous election in 1887. Many felt that his old mastery had gone. The leading Centre paper had come out with an article entitled *Es gelingt nichts mehr!* (He no longer has any success), and this slogan was repeated time and again, because it perfectly expressed the feelings of a large section of the people.

In a parliamentary state such an unmistakable defeat at the polls would have been followed by the resignation of the leading Minister. But Germany was not a parliamentary state, and the very last thing Bismarck would do was to yield in the face of the people's vote.

Quite the contrary. He now gave up his idea of partial retirement. He resolved to keep all his offices, and, moreover, to rule his Ministers still more completely. On the other hand, he set to work on a fresh combination of parties. The *Kartell* was gone. Why not try an alliance of the Conservatives and the Centre? True, this combination would have a majority in the Reichstag only if the Poles and Guelphs joined it. Poles and Guelphs had, in Bismarck's eyes, always been the *Reichsfeinde*—enemies of the Empire *par excellence*. But now he was nevertheless ready to include them in the new combination.

But far more important was another project which Bismarck was nursing. He remembered perfectly well the situation in which he had first come to office in 1862. At that time William I had not liked him at all, but he was compelled to cling to him, because nobody else could steer him through the constitutional conflict with the Chamber of Deputies. A fresh conflict would put William II in the same situation. Bismarck had laid his plans for stirring up such strife. There were two ways of setting about it: an enormous increase in the military budget and an anti-Socialist bill even more severe and repressive than the one which had fallen through. Such measures would be rejected by the new Reichstag. Then it would have to be dissolved and fresh elections would follow. But was it equally certain that the voters would elect a more docile Reichstag? Bismarck knew that this was more than doubtful. But for this eventuality, too, he was prepared. He had thought out a new theory, which would serve him equally as well as the famous *Lückentheorie* (the theory of the constitutional gap) had served him in the 'sixties (p. 55).

His new theory was quite a simple one. The Reich, he argued, was a federation of the German princes, *not* of the German states. If the princes were not satisfied, they could give notice and dissolve the Reich, just as partners wind up a company when they are not satisfied with its results. The German people would not be consulted and would have no say in the matter; they would have to wait until the German princes resolved to form a new Reich with a new constitution, which, no doubt, would diminish the authority of parliament and abolish universal suffrage.

This theory was, of course, a complete negation of German

nationalism, indeed, of German national sentiment. It meant the destruction of all that had endeared Bismarck to his people. The hero of German unity seeking to compass its ruin—truly, a most pitiable spectacle.

Fortunately for the German people—and fortunately for Bismarck—these plans were never realized or even attempted. The Emperor declined to take the first steps proposed by Bismarck even without knowing to what extreme lengths the Chancellor was willing to go. He also withheld his assent to the introduction of a new and severer anti-Socialist bill.

Meanwhile two other incidents brought the crisis to its head. In a session of the Ministers Bismarck drew their attention to an old royal decree (*Kabinettsorder*) of 1852, which enjoined the Ministers to report personally to the King only in presence of the Minister-President. This decree had been obsolete for twenty years or more. Nobody had paid any heed to it, and nobody could say how it could be observed when the Minister-President was away from the capital in Varzin or Friedrichsruh for six months or even longer. William saw in this attempt to revive a dead letter only an attempt to deny him free intercourse with his Ministers and to put him under the control of Bismarck.

The other news that roused him was that Bismarck had been visited by Windthorst, the leader of the Centre Party. Windthorst knew that Bismarck was toying with the idea of a fresh combination in which his own party would be of the highest importance. On the other hand, he had suspected since the struggle over the septennium that Bismarck was ready to destroy the German constitution. He had said to Bamberger: "If I see a locomotive travelling straight towards me, I do not stand still, but jump on it and ride along with it". He was now quite willing to hear what Bismarck had to say, and Bleichroeder ushered him into the Chancellor's office. The conversation lasted an hour and a half. But when Windthorst went away, he said to a friend: "*I am just leaving the deathbed of a great man*". As a matter of fact, it was Windthorst's visit which dealt Bismarck the *coup de grâce*.

William was beside himself with rage when he heard of Windthorst's visit. In a parliamentary state, the head of the government who depends on the confidence of a majority in parliament certainly has the right to form party combinations in such a way as to ensure himself a majority. But in Germany, where the Chancellor always proclaimed that he depended on the Emperor's confidence alone and that he himself fulfilled the Emperor's policy, the Emperor's right to be informed before his Minister tries to arrange a new combination cannot be disputed. To this extent William cannot be blamed for calling his Chancellor to account. But the way in which he set about it was completely wrong and demonstrated those characteristics his father had deplored in him—his arrogance and his immaturity.

The last heated conversation between William and Bismarck took place on the morning of 15th March at the house of Herbert Bismarck. The Chancellor told the Emperor what the latter already knew—that Windthorst had visited him. William gave the worst possible answer: "I hope you had him thrown out of the door". After this unfortunate start the interview became stormier and stormier. Bismarck grew so furious that William, as he afterwards told a friend, feared that Bismarck would throw the inkstand at him. He himself reproached the old statesman with having dealings with "Jews and Jesuits".

Then he demanded the abolition of the old royal decree of 1852. Bismarck refused and became angrier still. He began to speak of the Kaiser's intention of paying a visit to the Czar. He advised him against it, because he had received reports which proved that the Czar's feelings were unfriendly. These reports he held in his hands, but, he declared, he could not show them to the Emperor because they would offend him. These are the same tactics that Mark Antony used when he wanted the Romans to compel him to read Caesar's will.

William, of course, was eager to read these intriguing documents. Bismarck handed them to him and now the Emperor had to read, under Bismarck's gaze, that the Czar had called him *un garçon mal élevé et de mauvaise foi* (an ill-bred youngster of bad faith). The King, who had tried to prescribe to his Chancellor whom he might see, himself received a lesson like a schoolboy.

This was the end. William went off, after again having ordered the abolition of the royal decree.

After this scene both men knew that they had, finally and inevitably, reached the parting of the ways.

But Bismarck made no move. He neither issued a cancellation of the decree nor tendered his resignation, although William sent a general to request once more the abolition of the decree.

William, quite unnerved, made another foolish blunder. From the Chancellor's office he had received reports by a consul in Kiev on the warlike preparations of the Russians. Still smarting under the Czar's offensive remarks, William exaggerated the importance of these reports in his own peculiar way. In an unsealed letter he reproved Bismarck for not having drawn his attention to this "terrible danger" earlier. "It is high time to warn the Austrians and to take counter-measures", he said.

Bismarck now had exactly what he wanted: the Emperor meddling in Foreign Affairs. He let his pressmen know that he was compelled to resign because the Emperor demanded military measures against Russia. Now he was ready to send in his letter of resignation.

The letter was written for publication, but the Emperor forbade this. On the day of Bismarck's death, Busch published the letter in a Berlin newspaper, where it appeared as the dead Chancellor's indictment of the living Emperor. It was written with consummate skill. Only those points of difference were emphasized on which Bismarck was sure to have public opinion on his side. The strongest terms were reserved for William's interference in foreign policy. Bismarck declared himself unable to execute his orders and wrote: "By doing so I would jeopardise all the success, so important for Germany, which our foreign policy in agreement with the views of Your Majesty's two predecessors has achieved and in spite of unfavourable conditions in our relations with Russia, results that have attained a significance great beyond all expectation for the present and for the future, a circumstance which Count Shouwaloff has just confirmed to me." In these words the retiring statesman accuses the Emperor of being willing to destroy his life's work. In weighty sentences, turned with masterly skill, he makes the young man who had dethroned him responsible for every misfortune that will be visited upon the German Reich. There is one sentence in this letter which no one can read without the deepest emotion. "Attached as I am to the service of the Royal House and of Your Majesty, and accustomed for many years to conditions which I have hitherto regarded as permanent, it is very painful to me to sever my wonted relations with Your Majesty, and to break off my connection with the entire policy of the Reich and of Prussia." Here speaks the born ruler who is suddenly robbed of everything that had made life worth living. This is a human tragedy no less sombre than those conjured up by the great poets.

But this cannot blind us to the fact that Bismarck's resignation was as necessary as it was tragic. Great and incomparable as Bismarck was, he was nevertheless now at his wit's end. He saw no way out of his dilemma but that of strife and of the *coup d'état*. If we consider the plans he turned over in his mind for dissolving the Reich, we can only be thankful to the fate that prevented his destroying what he had created. He left his work in the hands of a man who was quite unable to develop it or, indeed, to preserve it. That was Germany's misfortune. But it was Bismarck's fault that this man possessed power far too great for a mediocre mortal. And it was, too, Bismarck's fault that there was no parliament capable of bridling this extravagant ruler, and that there was far from enough independence of mind in the German people.

Under Bismarck's leadership the German nation had become united, strong, and powerful. But the sense of freedom and individual independence, of justice and humanity, had been lamentably weakened by *Realpolitik* and *Interessenpolitik*—the politics of power and of material interest—and by the personal régime which the Iron Chancellor had imposed upon his countrymen. It is therefore no mere chance that his work did not last, and that the Prussian crown and the Hohenzollern dynasty, which he had exalted to heights never before known, ceased to exist twenty years after his death.

INDEX OF NAMES